SCALABLE SHARED-MEMORY MULTIPROCESSING

Scalable Shared-Memory Multiprocessing

Daniel E. Lenoski
Wolf-Dietrich Weber

Morgan Kaufmann Publishers
San Francisco, California

Executive Editor   Bruce Spatz
Production Manager   Yonie Overton
Assistant Production Editor   Julie Pabst
Cover Design   Feroza Unvala
Text Design   Jim Love/Studio Arno
Composition   Ed Sznyter
Copyeditor   Ken DellaPenta
Proofreader   Liz Sizensky
Printer   Quebecor Printing

Morgan Kaufmann Publishers, Inc.
Editorial and Sales Office
340 Pine Street, Sixth Floor
San Francisco, CA 94104–3205
USA
Telephone   415/392-2665
Facsimile   415/982-2665
Internet   mkp@mkp.com

Library of Congress Cataloging-in-Publication Data

Lenoski, Daniel E.
   Scalable shared-memory multiprocessing / Daniel E. Lenoski, Wolf-Dietrich Weber.
            p.   cm.
   Includes bibliographical references and index.
   ISBN 1-55860-315-8
   1. Multiprocessors.   2. Memory management (Computer science)
I. Weber, Wolf-Dietrich.   II. Title.
QA76.5.L457   1995
004'.35--dc20

95-19615
CIP

*To Karen and Véronique
and Veronica, Steven, and Nicole, too*

Foreword

by
John L. Hennessy

The idea of multiprocessors dates back to the first electronic computers. As early as the 1950s, MPs were advanced as a technique both to increase reliability and to improve performance. Early efforts concentrated on building small-scale machines, which avoided a number of problems. Two exceptions were the C.mmp and Cm* machines built at Carnegie-Mellon University in the 1970s. These systems included many of the features found in more recent large-scale machines. However, simpler structures, adequate for the smaller systems being built at the time, became more popular.

In the early 1980s, the first commercially successful multiprocessors became available. Almost all of these designs were bus-based, shared-memory machines. Their development was enabled by two key factors: the incredible price-performance advantages of microprocessors and the extensive use of caches in microprocessor-based systems. These technological factors made it possible to put multiple processors on a bus with a single memory, relying on caching to reduce the memory bandwidth demands of the processors to an acceptable level. Coherency among the caches was maintained through a snoopy protocol, which, while simple, employed broadcast, making these systems fundamentally unscalable.

In the mid 1980s, the interest in scalable multiprocessors grew quickly. The bus-based, cache-coherent, shared-memory machines were clearly not scalable, so designers focused on two other approaches. One approach gave up on coherence but maintained shared memory. Three important designs of this genre were the BBN Butterfly, the IBM RP3, and the NYU Ultracomputer. As in earlier experiments, the absence of caching significantly increased the cost of shared access—each shared access had to traverse the network—and made it hard to obtain good performance on such machines. The Cray T3D is the major machine in this camp at the present. In practice, it appears that such machines are most effectively used as message-passing machines, with the shared address space providing a convenient naming mechanism.

The second approach to scalability relied on message passing rather than shared memory. The problem of memory latency on the non-coherent shared-memory machines, together with the impossibility of scaling the snoopy approach, led some designers to conclude that message passing was the only viable approach for scalable multiprocessors. However, message-passing machines have proved very difficult to program.

This book explores a new class of machines supporting both cache-coherent shared memory and scalability to a large number of processors. The first part of the book looks at the general concepts involved in building scalable multiprocessors, especially scalable shared-memory machines. The authors begin with a description of the challenges in designing scalable architectures. They then discuss the trade-offs between shared memory and message passing, as well as the challenges of scalable cache coherency. In considering the scalability of performance of any particular scheme for shared memory, the results are substantially affected by the communication and sharing characteristics in the applications. Chapter 2 presents extensive data on this important topic. Designing a large-scale, shared-memory machine requires attention to minimizing memory latency and hiding that latency whenever possible. These two topics provide the key focus of Chapter 3. Chapter 4 examines a variety of design alternatives that arise in the actual implementation of such systems. These first four chapters are valuable to both designers and programmers of scalable machines who wish to understand the performance of various architectures, as well as the variety of design alternatives. Finally, Chapter 5 surveys historical and proposed scalable shared-memory machines, including the Stanford DASH multiprocessor.

The DASH project began in 1987 to explore whether it was possible to build scalable shared-memory multiprocessors that efficiently support cache coherence. By using a distributed-memory model, explored in both the Cm* and RP3 projects, DASH allows memory bandwidth to be scaled, unlike that in a bus-based system. To implement scalable cache coherence, DASH uses a distributed directory protocol. In 1991, DASH became the first operational shared-memory multiprocessor with a scalable hardware cache coherence mechanism. Kendall Square Research and Convex became the first companies to market scalable shared-memory multiprocessors commercially. Such machines have become known as Distributed Shared Memory (DSM). The interest in DSM architectures is growing quickly, both because of the scalability advantages and because of the increasing difficulty of building bus-based multiprocessors as processors increase in speed.

The second part of this book is a retrospective examination of the design of the DASH multiprocessor. It provides not only a detailed description of the design, but also a rationale for the design and an exposition of the challenges arising in any such machine. For people interested in scalable machines, this portion of the book is a must-read. Unlike the documentation of industrial projects, which rarely criticizes their products, this book supplies many frank assessments of the strengths and weaknesses of the DASH design, providing readers with extensive input on how the design might be improved upon in the future.

Although the largest multiprocessors seem to be moving toward shared memory and away from message passing, it remains a point of debate whether cache coherency will play a major role in very large machines. The final section of the book explains how a cache-coherent design like DASH could be extended to the range of thousands of processors and TERAOps of performance. In addition to examining the structure of such a design, this section estimates the performance that might be achievable. The analysis shows that building large-scale parallel machines does not mean abandoning the efficient and easy-to-use shared-memory programming model.

I found this book extremely interesting. The first portion of the book lays a solid foundation, showing why it is possible to build a shared-memory scalable machine. Then, in the second portion, the description of the landmark DASH machine by one of its original designers is both fascinating and informative. Finally, the third portion gives a glimpse at the not-so-distant future of scalable shared-memory multiprocessors. Such scalable, cache-coherent machines appear to be major candidates for next-generation multiprocessors. Anyone involved in the design of such machines, in software development for them, or even in using such machines will find this book useful and enlightening.

Contents

Foreword   **vii**
Preface   **xvii**

PART   1
GENERAL CONCEPTS

CHAPTER 1   Multiprocessing and Scalability   **3**

1.1   Multiprocessor Architecture   **6**

     1.1.1 Single versus Multiple Instruction Streams   **7**

     1.1.2 Message-Passing versus Shared-Memory Architectures   **8**

1.2   Cache Coherence   **13**

     1.2.1 Uniprocessor Caches   **14**

     1.2.2 Multiprocessor Caches   **16**

1.3   Scalability   **20**

     1.3.1 Scalable Interconnection Networks   **24**

     1.3.2 Scalable Cache Coherence   **31**

     1.3.3 Scalable I/O   **33**

     1.3.4 Summary of Hardware Architecture Scalability   **34**

     1.3.5 Scalability of Parallel Software   **35**

1.4   Scaling and Processor Grain Size   **37**

1.5   Chapter Conclusions   **39**

CHAPTER 2   Shared-Memory Parallel Programs   **41**

2.1   Basic Concepts   **41**

2.2   Parallel Application Set   **46**

     2.2.1 MP3D   **48**

     2.2.2 Water   **48**

     2.2.3 PTHOR   **49**

     2.2.4 LocusRoute   **49**

     2.2.5 Cholesky   **49**

2.2.6 Barnes-Hut **50**

2.3   Simulation Environment **50**

2.3.1 Basic Program Characteristics **51**

2.4   Parallel Application Execution Model **52**

2.5   Parallel Execution under a PRAM Memory Model **53**

2.6   Parallel Execution with Shared Data Uncached **55**

2.7   Parallel Execution with Shared Data Cached **56**

2.8   Summary of Results with Different Memory System Models **58**

2.9   Communication Behavior of Parallel Applications **59**

2.10   Communication-to-Computation Ratios **59**

2.11   Invalidation Patterns **62**

2.11.1 Classification of Data Objects **62**

2.11.2 Average Invalidation Characteristics **64**

2.11.3 Basic Invalidation Patterns for Each Application **65**

2.11.4 MP3D **67**

2.11.5 Water **67**

2.11.6 PTHOR **69**

2.11.7 LocusRoute **71**

2.11.8 Cholesky **73**

2.11.9 Barnes-Hut **73**

2.11.10 Summary of Individual Invalidation Distributions **76**

2.11.11 Effect of Problem Size **76**

2.11.12 Effect of Number of Processors **76**

2.11.13 Effect of Finite Caches and Replacement Hints **78**

2.11.14 Effect of Cache Line Size **80**

2.11.15 Invalidation Patterns Summary **83**

2.12   Chapter Conclusions **84**

CHAPTER 3   System Performance Issues **87**

3.1   Memory Latency **88**

3.2   Memory Latency Reduction **89**

3.2.1 Nonuniform Memory Access (NUMA) **90**

3.2.2 Cache-Only Memory Architecture (COMA) **91**

3.2.3 Direct Interconnect Networks **93**

3.2.4 Hierarchical Access **93**

3.2.5 Protocol Optimizations **94**

3.2.6 Latency Reduction Summary **95**

3.3   Latency Hiding **95**

3.3.1 Weak Consistency Models **96**

3.3.2 Prefetch **100**

3.3.3 Multiple-Context Processors **103**

3.3.4 Producer-Initiated Communication **108**

3.3.5 Latency Hiding Summary **110**

3.4 Memory Bandwidth **111**
3.4.1 Hot Spots **112**
3.4.2 Synchronization Support **113**

3.5 Chapter Conclusions **116**

CHAPTER 4 System Implementation **117**

4.1 Scalability of System Costs **117**
4.1.1 Directory Storage Overhead **119**
4.1.2 Sparse Directories **127**
4.1.3 Hierarchical Directories **132**
4.1.4 Summary of Directory Storage Overhead **133**

4.2 Implementation Issues and Design Correctness **134**
4.2.1 Unbounded Number of Requests **134**
4.2.2 Distributed Memory Operations **136**
4.2.3 Request Starvation **139**
4.2.4 Error Detection and Fault Tolerance **139**
4.2.5 Design Verification **141**

4.3 Chapter Conclusions **142**

CHAPTER 5 Scalable Shared-Memory Systems **143**

5.1 Directory-Based Systems **143**
5.1.1 DASH **144**
5.1.2 Alewife **144**
5.1.3 S3.mp **146**
5.1.4 IEEE Scalable Coherent Interface **147**
5.1.5 Convex Exemplar **149**

5.2 Hierarchical Systems **150**
5.2.1 Encore GigaMax **151**
5.2.2 ParaDiGM **152**
5.2.3 Data Diffusion Machine **154**
5.2.4 Kendall Square Research KSR-1 and KSR-2 **155**

5.3 Reflective Memory Systems **157**
5.3.1 Plus **157**
5.3.2 Merlin and Sesame **158**

5.4 Non–Cache-Coherent Systems **159**
5.4.1 NYU Ultracomputer **159**
5.4.2 IBM RP3 and BBN TC2000 **160**
5.4.3 Cray Research T3D **161**

5.5 Vector Supercomputer Systems **162**
5.5.1 Cray Research Y-MP C90 **163**
5.5.2 Tera Computer MTA **164**

5.6 Virtual Shared-Memory Systems **166**

5.6.1 Ivy and Munin/Treadmarks **166**

5.6.2 J-Machine **167**

5.6.3 MIT/Motorola *T and *T-NG **169**

5.7 Chapter Conclusions **170**

P A R T   2

EXPERIENCE WITH DASH

CHAPTER 6 DASH Prototype System **173**

6.1 System Organization **174**

6.1.1 Cluster Organization **175**

6.1.2 Directory Logic **177**

6.1.3 Interconnection Network **180**

6.2 Programmer's Model **181**

6.3 Coherence Protocol **184**

6.3.1 Nomenclature **185**

6.3.2 Basic Memory Operations **187**

6.3.3 Prefetch Operations **192**

6.3.4 DMA/Uncached Operations **193**

6.4 Synchronization Protocol **198**

6.4.1 Granting Locks **198**

6.4.2 Fetch&Op Variables **200**

6.4.3 Fence Operations **200**

6.5 Protocol General Exceptions **201**

6.6 Chapter Conclusions **202**

CHAPTER 7 Prototype Hardware Structures **205**

7.1 Base Cluster Hardware **206**

7.1.1 SGI Multiprocessor Bus (MPBUS) **206**

7.1.2 SGI CPU Board **207**

7.1.3 SGI Memory Board **210**

7.1.4 SGI I/O Board **211**

7.2 Directory Controller **211**

7.3 Reply Controller **218**

7.4 Pseudo-CPU **224**

7.5 Network and Network Interface **226**

7.6 Performance Monitor **229**

7.7 Logic Overhead of Directory-Based Coherence **232**

7.8 Chapter Conclusions **236**

CHAPTER 8 Prototype Performance Analysis   **237**

  8.1 Base Memory Performance   **237**

  8.1.1 Overall Memory System Bandwidth   **238**

  8.1.2 Other Memory Bandwidth Limits   **240**

  8.1.3 Processor Issue Bandwidth and Latency   **241**

  8.1.4 Interprocessor Latency   **244**

  8.1.5 Summary of Memory System Bandwidth and Latency   **244**

  8.2 Parallel Application Performance   **246**

  8.2.1 Application Run-Time Environment   **246**

  8.2.2 Application Speedups   **247**

  8.2.3 Detailed Case Studies   **250**

  8.2.4 Application Speedup Summary   **257**

  8.3 Protocol Effectiveness   **260**

  8.3.1 Base Protocol Features   **260**

  8.3.2 Alternative Memory Operations   **264**

  8.4 Chapter Conclusions   **271**

PART 3
FUTURE TRENDS

CHAPTER 9 TeraDASH   **277**

  9.1 TeraDASH System Organization   **277**

  9.1.1 TeraDASH Cluster Structure   **278**

  9.1.2 Intracluster Operations   **280**

  9.1.3 TeraDASH Mesh Network   **283**

  9.1.4 TeraDASH Directory Structure   **284**

  9.2 TeraDASH Coherence Protocol   **286**

  9.2.1 Required Changes for the Scalable Directory Structure   **286**

  9.2.2 Enhancements for Increased Protocol Robustness   **288**

  9.2.3 Enhancements for Increased Performance   **294**

  9.3 TeraDASH Performance   **296**

  9.3.1 Access Latencies   **297**

  9.3.2 Potential Application Speedup   **298**

  9.4 Chapter Conclusions   **303**

CHAPTER 10 Conclusions and Future Directions   **305**

  10.1 SSMP Design Conclusions   **306**

  10.2 Current Trends   **307**

  10.3 Future Trends   **308**

APPENDIX Multiprocessor Systems   **311**
References   **317**
Index   **333**

Preface

Scalable shared-memory multiprocessing (SSMP) systems provide the power of hundreds to thousands of high-performance microprocessors all sharing a common address space. SSMP is appealing because it addresses a number of problems with existing parallel systems. Relative to large-scale message-passing machines, SSMP provides a much simpler programming model, which makes the system easier to use. The shared-memory paradigm also reduces communication overhead, making finer-grained work sharing possible. Compared with traditional bus-based shared-memory machines, SSMP does not have the bus bandwidth problem, which limits the number of processors that can be combined in a single system.

SSMP has been a popular research topic since the development of the IBM RP3 and NYU Ultracomputer in the early 1980s. The problem with these early SSMP machines was that the performance of individual processing nodes was limited by memory latency and by the modest performance of the highly integrated processors (i.e., microprocessors) available at the time. The performance of the latest microprocessors has eliminated the internal performance limits, but the challenge of keeping memory latency low enough so that performance scales when the processors are combined remains.

This book describes the architecture and hardware design of SSMP systems that combine high-performance processors with a scalable cache coherence mechanism. Caching helps to keep the effective memory latency low and processor utilization high. The material from the book is drawn from experience with the DASH project at Stanford University. In early 1991, this work resulted in the first operational SSMP machine with a scalable cache coherence mechanism. The prototype machine combines up to 64 RISC processors, with an aggregate performance of 1.6 GIPS and 600 MFLOPS, all sharing a hardware-supported cache-coherent memory address space.

We wrote this book with three audiences in mind: (1) designers and users of commercial SSMP machines (the first generation of SSMP systems such as the Kendall Square Research KSR-1 and Convex Exemplar are already in the market), (2) researchers of parallel machine architecture, and (3) anyone studying advanced computer architecture and parallel processing.

The book is broken into three major parts. Part I introduces general SSMP concepts and the design issues that all SSMP systems face. Part II is a detailed study of the DASH prototype machine and its performance. Part III concludes with an outline of a very large-scale machine based on the DASH design that could be built with today's state-of-the-art technology. It combines up to 2,000 processors to deliver a peak performance of over one trillion instructions per second and 400 GFLOPS.

The general SSMP concepts presented in Part I are broken into five chapters. Chapter 1 relates the base SSMP design to other major classes of parallel machines. Chapter 2 analyzes the characteristics of a number of parallel applications and their implications for system design. Chapter 3 discusses the important performance issues that every SSMP system must address. Chapter 4 covers design issues related to scalability of the system. Chapter 5 surveys the major SSMP systems that have been proposed and highlights their unique features.

Part II of the book details the design and performance of the DASH prototype machine. Chapter 6 gives an overview of the DASH architecture and a description of the coherence protocol. Chapter 7 describes the detailed hardware design of the system and calculates the overhead of the scalable coherence mechanism quantitatively. Chapter 8 summarizes performance measurements taken from full applications run on the prototype. It also uses stress tests to demonstrate the effectiveness of extensions made to the standard memory protocol.

Part III addresses the future of SSMP systems. Chapter 9 outlines the design of a very large-scale system based on the DASH prototype. It gives solutions to the major problems not addressed in the smaller DASH prototype and an estimate of the performance of the system. Chapter 10 concludes the book with an overview of the trends in SSMP systems and an outlook for this class of system.

The DASH project at Stanford was an exciting research project to which many individuals contributed. We are proud to have been part of such an inspiring group. In particular, we would like to acknowledge the guidance of our advisors, Anoop Gupta and John Hennessy, and the hard work of our DASH hard-core teammates (Jim Laudon, Dave Nakahira, Truman Joe, and Luis Stevens) that made DASH a reality. The project also received contributions from a much wider audience of Stanford faculty (especially Mark Horowitz and Monica Lam) and students (too many to mention). We would also like to acknowledge the generous support from DARPA and Silicon Graphics, without which DASH would not have been possible.

For help with this book, we would first like to thank those who reviewed the manuscript: Rick Bahr (Silicon Graphics), Andreas Nowatzyk (Sun), J. P. Singh (Princeton), Jim Smith (University of Wisconsin), Len Widra (Silicon Graphics), and others. Their input greatly improved the presentation and accuracy of the book. We would especially like to thank Jim Smith, whose careful reading and insightful comments led to a major restructuring of the material. The leaders of the projects surveyed in this book also reviewed the manuscript to verify that their projects were discussed accurately. We'd like to thank the following for their input: Anant Agarwal (MIT), Mike Beckerle (Motorola), David Cheriton (Stanford), Bill Dally (MIT), Allan Gottlieb (NYU), Erik Hagersten (Sun), Dave James (Apple), Kai Li (Princeton), Burton Smith (Tera Computer), and Steve Wallach (Convex). We would also like to thank the folks at Morgan Kaufmann for making the book a reality. In addition, we are grateful to our employers for their patience during the project. Finally, a large undertaking such as writing this book has a certain impact on the home life of the participants. We thank our families, and in particular our wives, Karen and Véronique, for their loving support in this effort.

Daniel E. Lenoski
Wolf-Dietrich Weber

PART 1

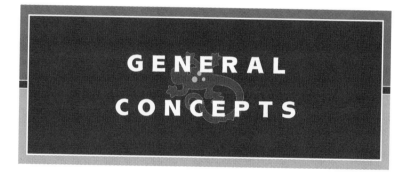

GENERAL CONCEPTS

C H A P T E R

1

Multiprocessing and Scalability

Large-scale multiprocessor systems have long held the promise of substantially higher performance than traditional uniprocessor systems. Because of a number of difficult problems, however, the potential of these machines has been difficult to realize. One of the primary problems is that the absolute performance of many early parallel machines was not significantly better than available, or soon-to-be-available, uniprocessors—both because of the tremendous rate of increase in the performance of uniprocessors and also because multiprocessor architectures are more complex and take longer to develop. Another problem is that programming a parallel machine is more difficult than a sequential one, and it takes much more effort to port an existing sequential program to a parallel architecture than to a new uniprocessor architecture. This problem has been aggravated by the lack of good parallel programming environments and standard parallel languages.

Recently, there has been increased interest in large-scale or massively parallel processing systems incorporating hundreds or even thousands of processors [Thi93, FRB93, Cra93a]. This interest stems from the very high aggregate performance of these machines and other developments that make such systems more tenable, such as the advent of high-performance microprocessors and the widespread use of small-scale multiprocessors.[1]

Improvements in integrated circuit technology now allow microprocessors to approach the performance of the fastest supercomputers [Sit93, Shi93, Hsu94]. This development has implications for both uniprocessor and multiprocessor systems. For uniprocessors, the pace of performance gains because of further integration is likely to slow. In the past, microprocessor designs had to sacrifice performance in order to fit on a single die. Today, virtually all the performance features found in the most complex processors can be implemented on a single chip, and additional functionality has diminishing returns. RISC technology has

---

[1] In this text, "small-scale" refers to machines using 2–16 processors, while "large-scale" refers to systems with 64 or more processors. As discussed in more depth later in this chapter, this breakdown is based on when mechanisms that rely on broadcast communication are applicable and when they begin to become untenable.

reduced the number of clocks per instruction to approximately one, and many studies indicate that more advanced superscalar designs may not offer more than a factor of two to four in improvement for general applications [Joh89, SJH89, Wal91]. Thus, the performance growth of uniprocessors is likely to slow to something closer to the 30% annual improvement seen in the speed of silicon technology itself, as opposed to the 60% rate demonstrated recently by processors overall [HeJ91]. On-chip multiprocessing, with two to four CPUs per die, may be the most effective way to utilize the increased silicon area available in next-generation technology [GGP+89, NHN+92, NaO94].

High-speed microprocessors have also had direct benefits for parallel machines. First, these chips can be easily combined to build small-scale multiprocessors with good cost-performance, which has led to the increased use of parallel processing. Second, microprocessors can be used to form large-scale machines that do not compromise the performance of the individual processing elements. In the past, a parallel machine might have processors that are only 1/100 to 1/20 the power of the fastest uniprocessor. For example, consider the Cray X-MP (first available in 1983) and Intel iPSC/2 (first available in 1987). The Cray X-MP processor had a peak MFLOPS rate of 235 [Don94], while the nodes in an Intel iPSC/2, even with attached vector units, had a peak performance of only 10 MFLOPS [AtS88]. Thus, a 256-processor iPSC/2 would offer less than 11 times the peak performance of a single Cray X-MP. Today, a 256-processor system might offer 100 times the peak performance of the fastest uniprocessor. For example, the Cray C90 has a peak MFLOPS rate of 952, while a 256-processor system using the MIPS R8000 would have a peak of 76,800 MFLOPS [Hsu94]. This large performance potential offers much more justification for the extra effort in programming the parallel machine.

The final, and possibly most important, impact of high-performance microprocessors on high-performance computing is economic. While the highest performance uniprocessor may always be found in supercomputers such as the Cray C90 or Convex C4, which exploit exotic IC and packaging technology, such machines are certainly less than a factor of ten more powerful than their microprocessor peers. The number of ICs together with the small sales volume of these machines push the price of each processor to over $1 million. In contrast, the integration and use of microprocessors in high-volume workstations and personal computers implies a price in 1994 of approximately $5,000–50,000 per processor. By using a small number of microprocessors, equal performance can be achieved at a cost-performance advantage of at least 4:1. With a larger number of processors, higher aggregate performance can be obtained while maintaining the cost-performance benefits of high integration and higher volumes.[2]

The widespread use of small-scale multiprocessors [BJS88, LoT88, Cro90] has also contributed to improved parallel processing technology. Multiprocessing has even come to the desktop in the form of multiprocessor workstations [Sun94b] and high-end multiprocessor PCs [Com94], which has led to improvements in parallel processing hardware and software. On the hardware side, almost all high-end microprocessors [Als90, BlK92, MIP91b,

---

[2] See Section 1.4 for a more detailed analysis of this comparison.

AlB93] directly support small-scale multiprocessing. Likewise, modern bus standards include mechanisms for keeping the processor caches consistent with one another and with main memory [SwS86]. Because standard components can be used, both the cost and development time of parallel machines have been reduced.

On the software side, improvements have been made in the usability of parallel machines. Standard multiprocessor operating systems such as Mach, UNIX V.4, and Windows NT are widely available. These operating systems provide the basis for the management of multiprocessor resources and create standard parallel processing environments. Parallel languages and tools have also greatly improved. Parallelizing compilers and performance debugging tools that help automate porting sequential code to parallel machines have become commercially available [Sil94, Zos93]. Likewise, parallel language extensions, such as Linda [ACG86], the Argonne National Laboratory's parallel macro package (ANL macros) [LOB+87], and the Parallel Virtual Machine (PVM) package [Sun90], make it possible to write portable parallel programs.

Of course, many challenges must still be overcome to achieve the potential of large-scale multiprocessors. Two of the most difficult problems are system scalability and ease of programming. *Scalability* refers to maintaining the cost-performance of a uniprocessor while linearly increasing overall performance as processors are added. Programming a parallel machine is inherently more difficult than a uniprocessor, where there is a single thread of control. An important way to alleviate this problem is to provide a single shared address space to the programmer. A shared-memory architecture allows all memory locations to be accessed by every processor. Shared-memory helps ease the burden of programming a parallel machine because there is no need to distribute data or explicitly communicate data between the processors in software. Direct access to all data also makes it easier to balance the computational load between processors by dynamically partitioning the work. Finally, shared-memory is the model provided on small-scale multiprocessors, so it is easier to move programs that have been parallelized for a small system to a larger shared-memory system.

Scalable shared-memory multiprocessors (SSMP) represent a new class of computer systems that provide the shared-memory programming model while removing the bottlenecks of today's small-scale systems. SSMP systems have become the focus of academic and industry research and development in high-performance computing. This chapter establishes the background and motivation for SSMP systems. We begin with an outline of the high-level architecture options for parallel machines. We then introduce caches and multiprocessor cache coherence. Caches have been vital to the tremendous growth in processor performance and are the key to modern SSMP design. We then turn to system scalability, defined in terms of system performance, cost, and the range of system sizes. A review of the interconnection networks that support scalability follows. We then return to caching and discuss directory-based cache coherence because directories provide cache coherence without sacrificing the scalability of the interconnection network. Software scalability is then discussed since it is often the practical limit on the useful scalability of a system. Finally, we conclude with an analysis of multiprocessor price-performance points that can be reached with state-of-the-art microprocessors to illustrate the potential of scalable systems.

TABLE 1-1

Examples of Parallel Systems and Characteristics

	SINGLE INSTRUCTION, MULTIPLE DATA (SIMD)	MULTIPLE INSTRUCTION, MULTIPLE DATA (MIMD)
Message-Passing	Illiac IV TMC CM-1 MasPar MP-1 and MP-2	Intel iPSC and Paragon nCUBE 2, TMC CM-5 Meiko CS-2 IBM SP1 and SP2
Shared-Memory	TMC CM-2	IBM RP3, IBM ES/9000 Cray X-MP, Y-MP, C90 Sequent Symmetry BBN Butterfly

1.1 Multiprocessor Architecture

The architecture of a multiprocessor defines the relationship between the processors, memory, and I/O devices within the system. There are two major dimensions to multiprocessor architectures. The first dimension is based on whether all processors execute a single instruction stream in parallel (SIMD), or whether each processor executes instructions independently (MIMD). The second dimension is based on the mechanism by which the processors communicate. Communication can either be through explicit messages sent directly from one processor to another, or through access to a shared-memory address space. Some example systems that illustrate these variations are given in Table 1-1.[3]

The choice of architecture affects many of the important attributes of the system. First, and most importantly, it affects the usability of the system by all levels of software (i.e., operating system, compiler, run-time support, and applications), which can directly impact the acceptance of the architecture. Second, the architecture also affects the performance and utilization of the individual processors when performing independent tasks. Third, it affects interprocessor communication performance, and thus the ability of the processors to work on the same task. Fourth, it implies the type and amount of hardware needed to tie the processors together, especially as the performance metrics are optimized. Note that the usability of the machine can also indirectly impact the performance of the machine, if there is a fixed amount of programming time that must be split between both coding an algorithm and tuning its performance. The next sections discuss the two major dimensions of multiprocessor architecture in more detail and their impact on performance, cost, and ease of use of the system.

---

[3] Note that throughout this chapter and the rest of the book, references to various multiprocessor systems are given. The appendix lists all of the systems mentioned in the text and gives references for each system.

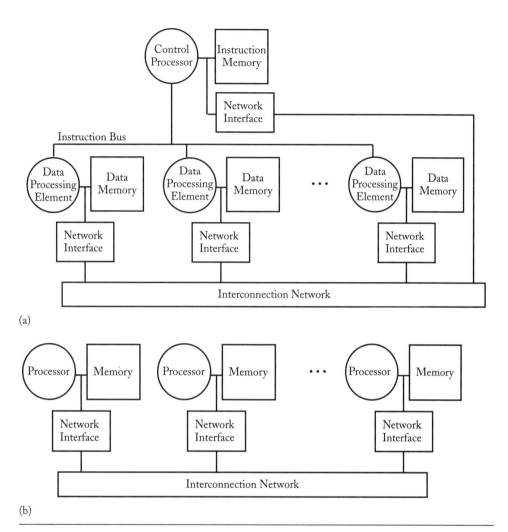

FIGURE 1-1 *(a) SIMD and (b) MIMD Multiprocessor Architectures.*

1.1.1 Single versus Multiple Instruction Streams

As originally defined by Flynn [Fly72], SIMD refers to an architecture with a single instruction stream that is capable of operating on multiple data items concurrently. In an SIMD machine, all processors do the same work on separate data elements. The only variance between processor execution is based on local condition codes, which can temporarily enable or disable individual processing steps. For example, both sides of every "if" statement are executed: some processors execute the "then" clause, while other processors execute no-ops, and then vice versa for the "else" clause. Conversely, in an MIMD architecture, each processor executes its own instruction stream independently.

Simplified block diagrams of each of these system types are shown in Figure 1-1. The SIMD structure consists of multiple data processing elements that operate on data in the local registers and memory. Each data processing element receives instructions over a common instruction bus from a central control processor. The control processor is a complete computer that runs the main thread of the program. It is responsible for invoking parallel execution on the individual data processing elements when possible. All of the data processing elements and the control processor communicate via an interconnection network. The MIMD structure consists of a set of independent processors with local memory, in which each processor executes its own instruction stream. Like the SIMD machine, the processor-memory pairs are connected by an interconnection network. While each MIMD processor may execute the same program (i.e., a single-program, multiple-data (SPMD) model), each processor executes only the instructions relevant to its data items and can make progress independently.

An SIMD machine has two primary advantages over an MIMD machine. First, each SIMD data processing element is simpler than its MIMD counterpart, since it only has a datapath and shares its instruction sequencer with the other processing elements. Many of the early large-scale parallel machines (e.g., Illiac IV, BSP and MPP, CM-1 [HwB84, Hwa93]) were SIMD machines because of this reduced hardware requirement. For a given fixed amount of hardware, an SIMD machine can have more processors, and thus a higher peak performance rate, than an MIMD machine. The second advantage of an SIMD architecture is that there is no performance penalty for synchronizing processors since all processors operate in lockstep, which reduces the overhead of coordinating the processors.

Conversely, there are significant advantages of MIMD over SIMD. First, since each processor executes its own instruction steam, only instructions useful to each data item need to be executed. In contrast, all processors in an SIMD machine execute both paths of all branches. Thus, while an SIMD machine may have more processors, the utilization of these processors is lower than in an MIMD machine. Independent processors also make MIMD machines more flexible to program than their SIMD counterparts. For example, wholly different tasks can be assigned to different processors, or sets of processors, on an MIMD machine. This is not possible in an SIMD machine. Another important practical advantage of MIMD machines is that they can utilize commodity microprocessors while SIMD machines are based on custom parts whose performance lags behind that of the latest microprocessors.

Overall, the trend has been away from SIMD and toward MIMD architectures. For example, Thinking Machines has moved from the SIMD architecture of the Connection Machine CM-2 to the MIMD CM-5 architecture [Thi93]. Increasing levels of integration are likely to continue the trend from the simpler SIMD architectures to the more flexible MIMD machines. The only remaining niche for SIMD is likely to be for applications that are "embarrassingly parallel" where the SIMD machine can effectively use its larger number of processors to deliver a higher performance at a given cost point.

1.1.2 Message-Passing versus Shared-Memory Architectures

Message-passing and shared-memory architectures are distinguished by the way processors communicate with one another and with memory. In message-passing systems, also called *distributed-memory systems*, the programmer sees a collection of separate computers that communicate only by sending explicit messages to one another. In a shared-memory system,

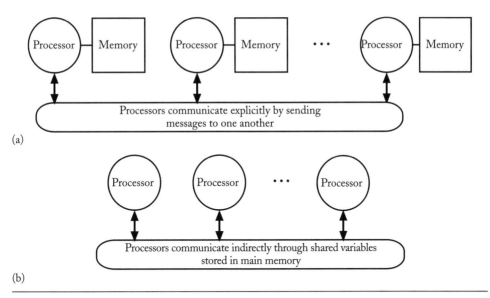

FIGURE 1-2 *Programmer's View of (a) Message-Passing and (b) Shared-Memory Architectures.*

the processors are more tightly coupled. Memory is accessible to all processors, and communication is through shared variables or messages deposited in shared memory buffers. This logical difference is illustrated in Figure 1-2 and has profound effects on the ease of programming these systems. In a shared-memory machine, processes can distinguish communication destinations, type, and values through shared-memory addresses. There is no requirement for the programmer to manage the movement of data. In contrast, on a message-passing machine, the user must explicitly communicate all information passed between processors. Unless communication patterns are very regular, the management of this data movement is difficult.

Interprocessor communication is also critical in comparing the performance of message-passing and shared-memory machines. Communication in a message-passing system benefits from its directness and its initiation by the producer of the data. In shared-memory systems, communication is indirect, and the producer typically moves the data no farther than memory. The consumer must then fetch the data from memory, which can decrease the efficiency of the receiving processor. However, in a shared-memory system, communication requires no intervention on the part of a run-time library or operating system. In a message-passing system, access to the network port is typically managed by system software. This overhead at the sending and receiving processors makes the start-up costs of communication much higher on a message-passing machine (typically tens to hundreds of microseconds). The effect is to reduce performance, or to force the programmer to use coarser-grain parallelism, which may limit the available parallelism. In a shared-memory architecture, the start-up overhead of communication is much less (typically on the order of microseconds). Since communication in a shared-memory machine is usually demand-driven by the consuming processor, the problem here is overlapping communication with computation. This is not a problem for small data items, but it can degrade performance if there is frequent communication or a large amount of data is exchanged.

To illustrate this performance difference between message-passing and shared-memory systems, consider the case where a producer process wants to send 10 words of data to a consumer process. In a typical message-passing system with a blocking send and receive protocol, this would be coded simply as

Producer Process   *Consumer Process*

```
send(Proc_i, Process_i, @sbuffer,
        num_bytes);
```

```
                                  receive(@rbuffer,max_bytes);
```

Since the operating system is multiplexing the network resources between users, this code would usually be broken into the following steps:

1. The operating system checks protections and then programs the network DMA controller to move the message from the sender's buffer to the network interface.

2. A DMA channel on the consumer processor has been programmed to move all messages to a common system buffer. When the message arrives, it is moved from the network interface to this system buffer, and an interrupt is posted to the processor.

3. The receiving processor services the interrupt and determines which process the message is intended for. It then copies the message to the specified receive buffer and reschedules the user process on the processor's ready queue.

4. The user process is dispatched on the processor and reads the message from the user's receive buffer.

On a shared-memory machine, there is no operating system involvement, and the processors can transfer the data using a shared data area. Assuming this data is protected by a flag indicating its availability and the size of the data transferred, the code would be

Producer Process   *Consumer Process*

```
for(i:=0; i<num_bytes; i++)
    buffer[i] := source[i];
flag := num_bytes;
```

```
                                  while (flag == 0) ;
                                  for (i:=0; i<flag; i++)
                                      dest[i] := buffer[i];
```

A comparison of the timing of these operations is given in Figure 1-3. For the message-passing case, the dominant costs are fixed and determined by the operating system overhead, programming the DMA, and the interrupt processing. For the shared-memory system, the overhead is primarily on the consumer reading the data since it is then that data moves from the global memory to the consuming processor. Thus, for a short message the shared-

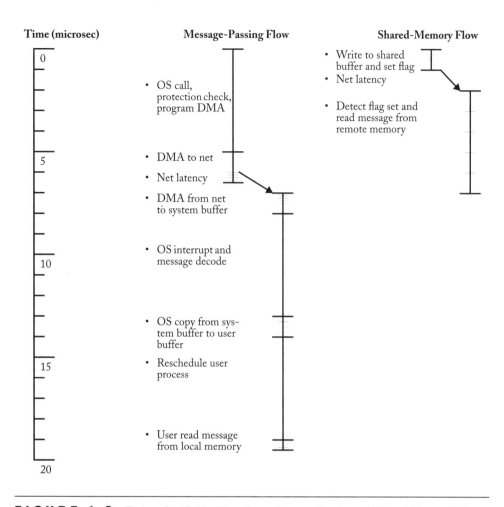

FIGURE 1-3 *Timing of a 10-Word Transfer on Message-Passing and Shared-Memory Systems.*

memory system is much more efficient. For longer messages, the message-passing system has similar or possibly higher performance, depending on the operating system overheads in the message-passing system and the efficiency of the shared-memory consumer reading the message.

Block diagrams of typical distributed-memory and shared-memory machines are given in Figure 1-4. The structure of the message-passing MIMD machine is the same as given in Figure 1-1(a). The network interface in the message-passing machine provides the DMA controllers and other hardware to send and receive messages from different processors. A simple MIMD shared-memory machine is shown in Figure 1-4(b). In most shared-memory machines the processors and memory are separated by an interconnection network. For small-scale shared-memory machines the interconnection network is a simple bus, while larger machines use multistage networks similar to the message-passing machines. Section 1.3.1 discusses the structure of the interconnection networks in more detail.

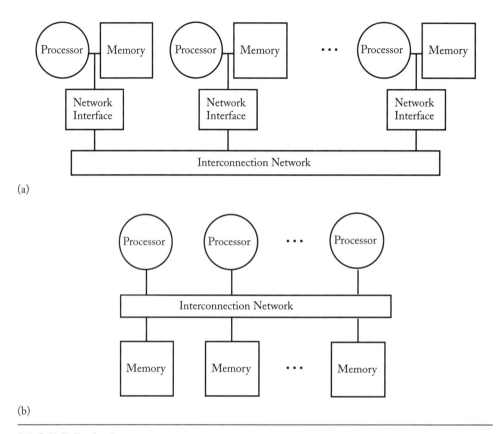

(a)

(b)

F I G U R E   1 - 4   *(a) Distributed-Memory and (b) Shared-Memory Multiprocessor Architectures.*

It is also possible to build a shared-memory machine with a distributed-memory architecture. Such a machine has the same structure as the message-passing system shown in Figure 1-4(a), but instead of sending messages to other processors, every processor can directly address both its local memory and remote memories of every other processor. This architecture is referred to as *distributed shared-memory* (DSM) or *nonuniform memory access* (NUMA) architecture. The latter term is in contrast to the *uniform memory access* (UMA) structure shown in Figure 1-4(b). The UMA architecture is easier to program because there is no need to worry about where to allocate memory—all memory is equally close to all processors. Since most shared-memory machines only support a small number of processors, where there is minimal benefit from the local memory of the NUMA structure, UMA is more popular for those machines. As detailed in Chapters 3 and 5, most large-scale shared-memory machines utilize a NUMA structure. Since the delay through a large interconnection network can be significant compared with memory access time, there are significant performance advantages to be gained from trying to keep memory accesses local in these large machines.

There are many trade-offs between message-passing and the two forms of shared-memory architectures. One of the biggest advantages of message-passing systems is that they minimize the hardware overhead relative to a collection of uniprocessor systems. Even a group of workstations can be treated as a single message-passing system with appropriate cluster software. The HP 735CL and IBM SP1 and SP2 are examples of this type of cluster machine. Both of these designs are actually separate workstations packaged in a single cabinet. More traditional message-passing systems, such as the Intel Paragon and nCUBE 2 machine, use a more integrated design and a higher-performance interconnection network, but still basically add a network interface to a fairly standard uniprocessor node. Another benefit of a distributed-memory system (whether message-passing or NUMA-based) is that single-thread performance is as high as in a uniprocessor, since memory can be tightly coupled to a single processor.

The primary advantage of a shared-memory over a message-passing system is its simple programming model, which is the same as a small-scale multiprocessor and an extension of the uniprocessor model. In this model, all data is directly accessible to every processor, and explicit communication code is only needed to coordinate access to shared variables. In a message-passing system, the user is responsible for explicitly partitioning all shared data and managing communication of any updates to that data.

Overall, the shared-memory paradigm is preferred since it is simpler to use and more flexible. In addition, a shared-memory system can efficiently emulate a message-passing system, while the converse is not possible without a significant performance degradation. Unfortunately, a shared-memory system has two major disadvantages relative to a message-passing system. First, processor performance can suffer if communication is frequent and not overlapped with computation. Second, the interconnection network between the processors and memory usually requires higher bandwidth and more sophistication than the network in a message-passing system, which can increase overhead costs to the point that the system does not scale well.

Solving the latency problem through memory caching and hardware cache coherence is the key to a shared-memory multiprocessor that provides both high processor utilization and high communication performance. While the coherence mechanism adds costs to the shared-memory machine, careful design can limit this overhead. Furthermore, the growing complexity of microprocessors allows for a more sophisticated memory system without drastically altering the cost-performance of the overall system.

The next section introduces the principle of caching and cache coherence. Following this, we outline the scaling issues for the system as a whole and the cache coherence mechanism in particular. The subsequent chapters cover these issues in detail, and validate the assertion that scalable cost-performance can be achieved in an SSMP system that provides cache-coherent shared-memory.

1.2 Cache Coherence

Caching of memory has become a key element in achieving high performance. In the last 10 years, microprocessor cycle times have shrunk from 100–200 ns to less than 4 ns, a factor of more than 25 times. In this same time frame, DRAM access times have only improved from 150–180 ns to 60–80 ns, a factor of about three [HeP90]. This gap has been bridged only with a memory hierarchy consisting of varying levels of high-speed cache memories that reduce average memory latency and provide the additional bandwidth required by today's processors. In the next section, we review the principles of caching in uniprocessor systems. We then discuss the complications of extending caches to shared-memory multiprocessors.[4]

1.2.1 Uniprocessor Caches

Caches consist of high-speed memory components that hold portions of the memory space addressable by the processor. Access to cache memory is much faster than main memory because the cache consists of a small number of very fast memory parts located close to the processor (often on the processor chip). In a cache-based system, the average memory access time (T_{avg}) is given by

$$T_{avg} = T_{cache} + F_{miss} T_{mem} \qquad \text{(1.1)}$$

F_{miss} is the fraction of references that are not found in the cache and T_{cache} and T_{mem} are the access times to the cache and memory, respectively. Cache access time is typically one or two processor cycles, while main memory access times range from 30 to 60, or more, processor clocks. Thus, if a high percentage of accesses are satisfied by the cache, average memory latency can be drastically reduced.

Caching memory is effective (i.e., most programs exhibit high hit rates—F_{miss} is small) because programs exhibit temporal and spatial locality in their memory access patterns. *Temporal locality* is the propensity of a program to access a location that it has just accessed. Access to loop indices and the stack are examples of data that exhibit a high degree of temporal locality. A cache can exploit temporal locality by allocating locations in the cache whenever an access misses the cache. *Spatial locality* is the tendency of a program to access variables at locations near those that have just been accessed. Examples of spatial locality include accessing a one-dimensional array in different loop iterations and the sequential fetching of instructions. A cache captures spatial locality by fetching locations surrounding the one that actually caused the cache miss.

The general structure of a cache is shown in Figure 1-5. It consists of a set of data and tag memory arrays. Each of these arrays are broken into individual entries called *cache lines*. Each line consists of a single tag and its corresponding data block. The data block holds the values of a block of main memory. The tag stores the address of the memory location corresponding to the data block. The tag also keeps state information on the cache line, which might include a bit indicating whether this line is valid or not. When the cache is accessed, a set of the tags and data items are accessed in parallel (in this case four). If one of the tags matches and its valid bit is set, then the corresponding data is forwarded to the processor. If there is no match, then the data must be fetched from main memory. The size of the data block is a compromise between decreasing the cache miss rate (F_{miss}) by capturing more spatial locality, and increasing the penalty for a cache miss (T_{mem}) as more data is fetched from memory. Block sizes vary from 16 to 128 bytes, with most systems using 32 or 64 bytes.

---

[4] This section provides background and definitions of the terms relating to caching used in this text. It can be skipped by those familiar with caching on uniprocessors and small-scale multiprocessors without a loss in continuity.

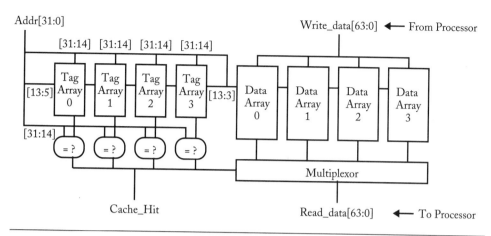

FIGURE 1-5 *A Four-Way Set-Associative 64-KByte Cache with a 64-bit Datapath.*

Cache misses can be classified as compulsory, capacity, conflict, and coherence misses [Hil87a]. *Coherence misses* are primarily an issue in multiprocessor systems, so we will defer them to the next section. *Compulsory misses*, also referred to as *cold misses*, refer to those cache misses caused by the first access to a particular data item. Compulsory misses are usually a small fraction of all misses. *Capacity misses* are caused by the limited size of the cache versus main memory. Capacity misses occur when the number of unique locations accessed between successive accesses to a given location is greater than the size of the cache. Reducing capacity misses is usually limited by technology (i.e., how much cache can fit on chip) or system cost goals.

Conflict misses occur when restrictions are placed on where a particular memory location can be placed in the cache. The organization of the cache has the largest effect on conflict misses. Figure 1-5 illustrates a four-way set-associative cache. In this structure, a particular memory location can be placed into one of four "ways" in the cache. A small degree of associativity removes most conflict misses, so set-associative caches usually have only two or four ways. A *direct-mapped cache* is a set-associative cache with only one way. In this structure, a given memory location can be placed in only one specific cache location. If more than one active location map to the same cache location, they contend over that location and conflict misses result. Obviously, a direct-mapped cache has more conflict misses than a set-associative cache. However, the direct-mapped cache is simpler and has the advantage of a reduced access time T_{cache}. In particular, with a direct-mapped structure the data can be returned to the processor before the cache hit is determined. Since hit rates are typically over 90%, useful work can be done speculatively with this data while hit is being determined. In contrast, in the four-way set-associative cache, hit must be determined and data multiplexed before it is forwarded to the processor. If not, the odds that useful work is being done are less than 25%. In general, set-associative caches are most applicable for on-chip caches where cache size is small (< 16 KByte) and the cost of interfacing to the multiple ways is low. Off-chip caches are larger (> 64 KByte) and are typically direct-mapped because their size makes conflict misses less of an issue.

Another important cache design issue is write policy. A *write-through* policy sends all writes to memory regardless of cache hit or miss. This is the simplest strategy since memory and the cache are always up-to-date. However, the strategy can limit performance because of the limited bandwidth of main memory and the delays in servicing read misses while write-throughs complete. A *write-back* policy updates only the cache on write hits. Cache lines that have been written are not synchronized with memory and are called *dirty*. A write-back policy can reduce memory bandwidth since memory writes only occur when dirty cache lines are displaced. In addition, these write-backs can be scheduled to occur after the memory read for the data that caused the write-back. The disadvantage of write-back caches is that they complicate the hardware design, especially in multiprocessor systems.

While there are other subtleties in the design of uniprocessor caches (e.g., the use of multiple levels of caches, hardware prefetch, and critical word restart), they are beyond the scope of this book. For a more in-depth study of uniprocessor cache design issues and options see [HeP90, Prz90].

1.2.2 Multiprocessor Caches

Just as in uniprocessor systems, caching is also vital to reducing memory latency in multiprocessor systems. In fact, caching offers even more benefit in a multiprocessor because memory latencies are usually higher. Unfortunately, multiprocessor caches are more complex because they introduce coherence problems between the independent processor caches.[5]

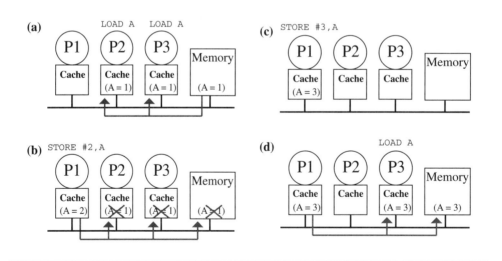

FIGURE 1-6 *Multiprocessor Cache Coherence.*

---

[5] Even in uniprocessors, coherence issues exist if the system supports DMA I/O devices. DMA writes can cause processor cache contents to become invalid. Likewise, with a write-back cache, DMA reads can return stale data from memory.

Figure 1-6 illustrates the two major coherence problems that caches introduce. First, when multiple processors read the same location they create *shared* copies of memory in their respective caches (Figure 1-6(a)). By itself, this is not a problem. However, if the location is written, some action must be taken to insure that the other processor caches do not supply stale data. These cached copies can either be updated or simply eliminated through invalidations (Figure 1-6(b)). Invalidation is more commonly used and assumed in the following discussion. At the end of this section, the trade-offs between update and invalidate coherence are examined. After completing its write, the writing processor has an exclusive copy of the cache line (i.e., it holds the line *dirty* in its cache). This allows it to subsequently write the location by updating its cached copy only; further accesses to main memory or the other processor caches are not needed (Figure 1-6(c)). After a write invalidation, other processors that reread the location get an updated copy from memory or the writing processor's cache. The misses caused in invalidations are referred to as coherence misses.

The second coherence problem arises when a processor holds an item dirty in its cache. When lines are dirty, simply reading a location may return a stale value from memory. To eliminate this problem, reads also require interaction with the other processor caches. If a cache holds the requested line dirty, it must override memory's response with its copy of the cache line (Figure 1-6(d)). If memory is updated when the dirty copy is provided, then both the dirty and requesting caches enter a shared state (as in Figure 1-6(d)). This state is equivalent to the initial state after multiple processors have read the location (Figure 1-6(a)). Thus, three cache states—invalid (after a write by another processor), shared (after a read), and dirty (after a write by this processor)—provide the basis for a simple multiprocessor cache coherence scheme.

Most small-scale multiprocessors maintain cache coherence with snoopy caches [BJS88, LoT88, Cro90]. The structure of a typical snoopy cache-coherent system is shown in Figure 1-7. Snoopy coherence protocols rely on every processor monitoring all requests to memory. This monitoring, or snooping, allows each cache to independently determine whether accesses made by another processor require it to update its caching state. Because snooping relies on broadcasting every memory reference to each processor cache, snoopy systems are usually built around a central bus. Figure 1-7 also shows that each processor maintains a duplicate set of of snoop tags. The primary tags are used for local processor accesses while the snoop tags are dedicated to monitoring the bus. The duplicate snoop tags filter memory traffic that does not affect this processor cache, thus reducing contention for the processors' caches.

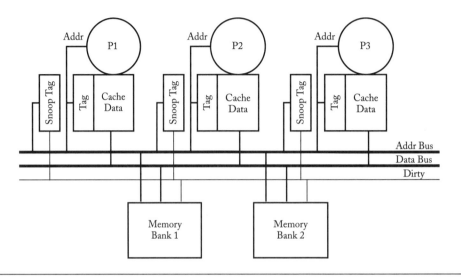

FIGURE 1-7 *Bus-Based Multiprocessor with a Simple Snoopy Cache Structure.*

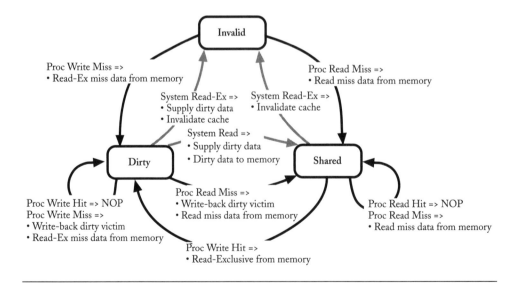

FIGURE 1-8 *Simple Snoopy Protocol State Transition Diagram.*

Let us look at how the operations given in Figure 1-6 would be executed on a snoopy bus. First, as processors 2 and 3 read location A from memory, all processors perform snoops, but since no one has a copy of the data, they do not interact with these reads. Second, processor 1 issues the store to A, which is translated into a read-exclusive bus operation to retrieve an exclusive copy of the cache line. When processors 2 and 3 see this read-exclusive that matches their snoop tags, they invalidate their cached copies of A. Third, processor 1 performs multiple writes to A and, because it holds the block dirty, completes these operations locally in its cache. Finally, processor 3 rereads the block. Processor 1 snoops the line and sees that it has the line dirty. Processor 1 flags this using the dirty signal on the bus, which disables memory and enables it to drive the data. Processor 1 then transitions to a shared state (along with processor 3, which reads the data). The memory controller also triggers a memory write in order to update main memory. This action is required because both processors are now in the shared state and expect memory to supply an up-to-date copy of the line on the next read access. Figure 1-8 illustrates the state machine for maintaining the snoopy cache tags and responding to processor and snoop operations.

Snoopy coherence schemes are very popular. Dozens of commercial machines rely on variations of the scheme outlined above. These variations include allowing a processor to have an exclusive copy of a cache line if it is the only one to read a location, and eliminating the write-back to memory when a dirty copy is read from another processor. Archibald and Baer [ArB86a] provide a good survey of these techniques. One reason for the popularity of snoopy schemes is that they put most of the burden for cache coherence on the caches themselves. The only requirement on other portions of the memory system is that the processor be able to override responses from memory in order to respond with dirty data. This property has allowed existing buses to be upgraded to support cache coherence, and for coherence protocols to be improved as new processors are introduced. Unfortunately, the broadcast nature of snoopy buses make them unsuitable for scalable systems. These systems have a fixed amount of bandwidth that usually limits them to less than 32 processors.

1.2.2.1 Invalidate versus Update Coherence

The last major issue with multiprocessor cache coherence is whether coherence should be maintained via updates or invalidates. A simple update scheme propagates every write to memory. In a snoopy update scheme, any snooping processor that hits on this write updates its cached copy. More sophisticated update protocols use a SHARED line to indicate whether any snoop found a hit. If SHARED is driven, the writing processor continues to write-through to main memory and update other caches. If SHARED is not driven, the writing processor can go to an exclusive state, and subsequently just write its cached copy without a bus cycle.

Let us examine the benefits of update. First, invalidations force the processor that reads the updated data to read it from the writing processor's cache or memory. If this data is read soon after it is written, then having the cache updated is more efficient for the consuming processor. Of course, if the producing processor writes the data multiple times before it is consumed, less system bandwidth is used if the item is invalidated after the first write and subsequently reread. Second, invalidations can lead to problems with *false sharing* [EgK89a, EgK89b, TLH90]. In this situation, different processors write to different locations that happen to be in the same cache line, forcing the cache line to ping-pong back and forth as each processor performs its writes. In an update scheme, there are write-throughs for each write, but all reads can still be satisfied by the processors' caches.

The largest drawback of update coherence is its write-through nature. It can use substantially more bus and memory bandwidth than an invalidation scheme. Furthermore, since the updates are usually single data items, not full cache blocks, the memory system and bus handle them less efficiently. The most troublesome issue with update protocols is their potential for excessive, useless updates. This situation can occur when an update is issued that has a snoop hit, but not to an actively shared data item. If an item that was previously accessed by another processor just happens not to be displaced from that processor's cache, then each write is written through to memory and uselessly updates that cache. In an invalidate scheme, the first write eliminates all shared copies, and subsequent writes only need to go to the bus if some processor has read the cache line in the interim.

In short, update coherence uses system bandwidth to improve interprocessor communication overhead, while invalidate coherence is optimized for noninterprocessor traffic. The performance trade-off is between the extra bandwidth used by fine-grain updates versus the communication overhead when the processor is stalled due to coherence misses. Systems have been built with both schemes, but analysis has not shown either to be conclusively better than the other [ArB86a, EgK88]. Hybrid schemes [KMR+86, EgK89b] that incorporate both features have been proposed as well, but have not been shown to improve performance enough to justify their extra complexity. Overall, invalidation schemes have become more popular because of their better uniprocessor performance, less pathological behavior, and greater simplicity. In the remainder of this book, we focus on invalidation-based coherence protocols.

1.3 Scalability

Having established the basis of MIMD shared-memory multiprocessing and cache coherence, we now turn to the issue of extending the SSMP model to a large number of processors. This scaling requires a more sophisticated interconnect and coherence mechanism than the bus and snoopy schemes outlined in the previous section. In this section, we also discuss the practical limits of scalability imposed by software algorithms, but we defer the detailed discussion of software issues to Chapter 2.

Intuitively, a *scalable system* is a system whose performance varies linearly with the cost of the system. Alternatively, a scalable system can be defined as a system supporting a constant cost-performance ratio while allowing absolute performance to be varied. Although these definitions can be made more precise, we will see that it is very difficult (and maybe irrelevant) to classify a system as scalable or not [Hil90, Sco91, NuA91]. What is more meaningful is the degree to which a system scales. Scalability can be measured on three dimensions:

1. How does performance vary with added processors? That is, what is the speedup ($S(N)$) over a uniprocessor when N processors are used to solve a problem in parallel?

2. How does the cost of the system ($C(N)$) vary with the number of processors in the system?

3. What range of processors (N) does the system support, or provide useful speedup over?

While parallel speedup is usually the most limiting factor to scalability, it is also the most

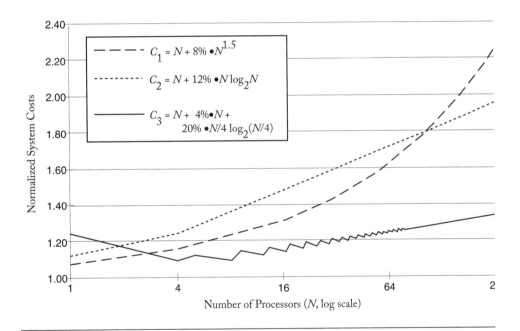

FIGURE 1-9 *Scalability of System Costs.*

complex to analyze, so we first address the issues of scalability range and cost. A system that supports one to two processors is scalable, but only minimally so. Conversely, a system that scales from 1 to 1,000 processors is not infinitely scalable, but is very close to the practical limit of scalability in current technology because of two issues: the absolute cost of such a system (i.e., there are very few buyers for systems costing more than $10 million) and, more importantly, the small number of applications that can exploit thousand-way parallelism.[6] Thus, even those that could justify very large systems are unlikely to have applications that

---

[6] Although SIMD systems with tens of thousands of processors have been built, each processor is more than an order of magnitude less powerful than that of a comparable MIMD machine (e.g., Thinking Machines CM-2 versus CM-5).

achieve significantly more than 1,000-times speedups. Sections 1.3.5 and 1.4 explore this issue in more detail.

The scalability of system costs involves two issues. The first is the marginal cost of adding processors. Since additional processors yield linear performance at best, it is important that $C(N)$ be close to linear. The majority of system cost is in processors and memory (assuming memory is added in proportion to the number of CPUs), but if overhead items (such as the interconnection network or coherence hardware) grow by something like N^2, then they can become very significant when N is greater than 100. The second issue is the absolute cost of adding any expandability to a uniprocessor system. The fixed overhead of a general interconnection port and other multiprocessor features increases the costs of a multiprocessor node compared with those of a uniprocessor system. Any amount of overhead implies nonideal scalability, but a small percentage of overhead (e.g., less than 25%) is likely to be acceptable, while a doubling in costs is unlikely to be justified.

In most cases, the system designer must chose to trade off the initial cost of providing the ability to scale with the marginal costs of adding processors. For example, each processing node can have one or more physical processors per node. The single-processor node adds less overhead to the base nonscalable system, but a multiprocessor node can amortize the network connection over multiple processors. Likewise, some mechanisms are cost-efficient for a fixed range of processors, but can be asymptotically less efficient. For example, consider three systems with different cost functions as shown in Figure 1-9. C_1 is a system that has an 8% overhead that grows as $N^{1.5}$ as processors are added. C_2 is a system with a 12% overhead per processor that grows as $N \log_2 N$. In comparing C_1 and C_2, note that C_1 has a much worse asymptotic cost, but for systems up to 100 processors it is less expensive than C_2, and for 256 processors, it is only 12% more expensive. Finally, C_3 is a system with multiprocessor nodes. It has a 20% overhead per node and up to four processors per node, which each have a 4% overhead. This system is more expensive if only one or two processors are used, but becomes more cost-effective than either C_1 or C_2 when more processors are desired, since the costs are amortized over larger units of expansion.

The most complex issue with scaling is how performance scales as processors are added. If speedup is defined as the ratio of the execution time of a program on one processor versus N processors, then speedup can be expressed as

$$S(N) = \frac{T_{EXEC}(1)}{T_{EXEC}(N)}$$

(1.2)

Ideally, speedup would be linear with N such that $S(N) = N$. If $T_{EXEC}(N)$ is broken down into the time that the application spends computing and the time spent communicating, then $S(N)$ is given as

$$S(N) = \frac{T_{comp}(1) + T_{comm}(1)}{T_{comp}(N) + T_{comm}(N)} \tag{1.3}$$

where $T_{comm}(1)$ represents the time that the uniprocessor accesses global memory, while $T_{comm}(N)$ represents the time for N processors to access global memory, synchronize, and communicate with one another through global memory. If one assumes that the total amount of communication is independent of N, then perfect speedup will only be achieved if

$$T_{comp}(N) = T_{comp}(1)/N \tag{1.4}$$

$$T_{comm}(N) = T_{comm}(1)/N \tag{1.5}$$

From a hardware architecture perspective, the requirement of scaling T_{comp} is easily met with N processors working independently. Unfortunately, this requires the software algorithm to be perfectly split between the N processors. Although software usually sets the limit on scalability, we first discuss the limits imposed by the hardware architecture. We return to discuss the software limits on scaling T_{comp} in Section 1.3.5.

Unlike T_{comp}, scaling T_{comm} is dependent on both software and the hardware architecture. With the assumption that the total amount of communication is independent of N, scaling T_{comm} requires that each processor communicates with an average latency that is constant and independent of N. Unfortunately, this requirement is not realizable. First, if one assumes that the uniprocessor is not artificially slowed down (i.e., the NUMA and not the UMA structure given in Figure 1-4(a) is used), then average communication latency for any multiprocessor with more than one processor node is larger than the uniprocessor because of the need for some of the communication to cross the interconnection network. Furthermore, as the size of N increases, the delays through the interconnection network go up, as a result of either the 3-D volume of the system and speed of light limitations (i.e., $T_{comp}(N) = kN^{1/3}$) or, more commonly, the limited fan-in of the logic gates in the interconnection system (i.e., $T_{comp}(N) = k \log N$). Another constraint on the interconnection system is that if T_{comm} is reduced by $1/N$ and the total amount of data communicated is held constant, then the bandwidth of the interconnection system must grow linearly with N. Although this requirement can be realized by practical hardware, doing so can have an adverse effect on system costs as N grows. In the next section, we examine a number of interconnection networks that, while not ideally scalable, approach the goals listed above.

Overall, we see that no system can be ideally scalable since the cost of communication can not be ideally scaled because of increases in the latency of individual communication. Thus, linear performance growth cannot be maintained for large systems. Furthermore, as we will discuss in more depth in the following section, communication bandwidth cannot grow linearly with system size unless costs grow more than linearly, which further hurts cost-performance. Although these architecture limits are important to understand, practical considerations make the goal of ideal scalability itself dubious. In particular, ideal scalability requires software algorithms that are perfectly parallel and have a constant amount of communication independent of the number of processors. All algorithms break these rules to some degree, and thus limit useful system sizes. Likewise, hardware implementations must optimize the cost-performance for a given range of system sizes, thus compromising the cost-performance of systems outside of that range. Taken together with the limitations of software, having the best asymptotic scalability is not necessarily ideal. Nevertheless, SSMP systems that can scale from a few to a few thousands of processors are highly desirable since they enable extremely high performance to be achieved using the same programming paradigm and at the same cost-performance ratios as small systems. In the next two sections we discuss scalable networks and scalable cache coherence techniques that can be used to achieve this goal.

1.3.1 Scalable Interconnection Networks

As shown in the previous section, the interconnection network is a key element of system scalability. In this section, we outline the common interconnection networks that balance the trade-offs between scaling costs, latency, and bandwidth. An in-depth study of this topic is beyond the scope of this text (in fact, full texts have been dedicated to this subject [Ree87, VaR94]). This section gives an overview of the networks applicable to large-scale systems.

To summarize the goals derived in the previous section, an ideal scalable network should have

1. a low cost that grows linearly with the number of processors N,
2. minimal latency independent of N, (given logic fan-in limitations, the best that can be achieved is to limit latency growth to $\log N$), and
3. bandwidth that grows linearly with N.

With respect to bandwidth, if we assume that communication is uniformly distributed, then half of all traffic passes any partition of the interconnect network that separates the system into two equal halves. The minimum bandwidth across any of these partitions is referred to as the *bisection bandwidth* [Dal90b]. Under the uniform traffic assumption, bisection bandwidth must grow linearly with the number of processors in the system. Stated another way, bisection bandwidth per processor must be constant as the system grows. A related bandwidth issue is that many algorithms are dominated by neighbor-to-neighbor communication. Most networks have a better local communication bandwidth than bisection bandwidth, but some networks further optimize this form of communication by supporting lower latency to neighboring nodes.

Other characteristics that are orthogonal to the network topology, but important to the design of such networks include the following:

- Direct or indirect networks [Pea77]. Direct networks have routing switches that are distributed with the processing nodes, while indirect networks connect nodes only to the edge of the network and concentrate the switches centrally. Direct networks tend to have better support for nearest neighbor communication, while indirect networks attempt to optimize uniform traffic.

- Packet-switched or circuit-switched routing [Tan81]. Circuit-switched communication first establishes a connection between nodes and then uses the pre-established connection to provide lower latency for subsequent messages. Packet-switched routing establishes a route for each message sent. It provides less start-up overhead per communication. Packet switching is much more applicable to shared-memory machines where messages are short and communication patterns are very dynamic.

- Store-and-forward versus wormhole routing [Dal90b]. Wormhole routing allows a message to be routed through a switch before the entire message has been received. Store-and-forward networks fully buffer each message within each routing switch. Wormhole routing is more complicated, but has become more popular due to its reduced latency. Virtual cut-through [KeK79] is a combination of these two: Packets are forwarded before being fully received, but are never blocked across more than one channel, as can happen in a wormhole scheme.

- Adaptive routing versus fixed routing, also referred to as dynamic versus static routing. Adaptive routing makes better use of routing resources by switching traffic away from congested areas. It can also provide fault tolerance, since a broken link or router appears as an infinitely congested portion of the network. Of course, adaptive routing adds more complexity. It also implies that messages sent between two points can be received out of order.

- Error checking, message acknowledgment, message retry, and other features to support data integrity and fault tolerance within the network.

While the above features are important in determining the realized performance of any interconnection network, the fundamental scalability of the network is determined by its topology. In the next sections we examine the most popular interconnection schemes, ranging from the full crossbar to the simple bus topology.

1.3.1.1 Full Crossbar

The structure of a crossbar is given in Figure 1-10(a). In a crossbar, every node is directly connected to every other node through one level of switches. The primary features of a crossbar are linear bisection bandwidth growth and a constant, low latency since each node is only one switch away from every other node. Unfortunately, the cost of the crossbar structure scales as N^2, so this structure is only applicable to systems with a small number of nodes. Small systems such as the C.mmp, which supported no more than 16 processors, utilize a crossbar interconnection network.

1.3.1.2 Multistage Interconnection Networks

Multistage interconnection networks (MINs) represent a class of interconnection networks that include the Omega, Benes, Baseline, Banyan, and Butterfly networks [VaR94]. An example Omega network is shown in Figure 1-10(b). The common feature of these networks is that they consist of $\log_f N$ levels of switches that provide at least one path between each input and output. Each switch is a crossbar between its f inputs and f outputs. MIN networks provide linear scaling of bisection bandwidth and minimal growth in the latency ($\log_f N$). The rate of increase in the network cost is small with respect to N ($N \log_f N$). The

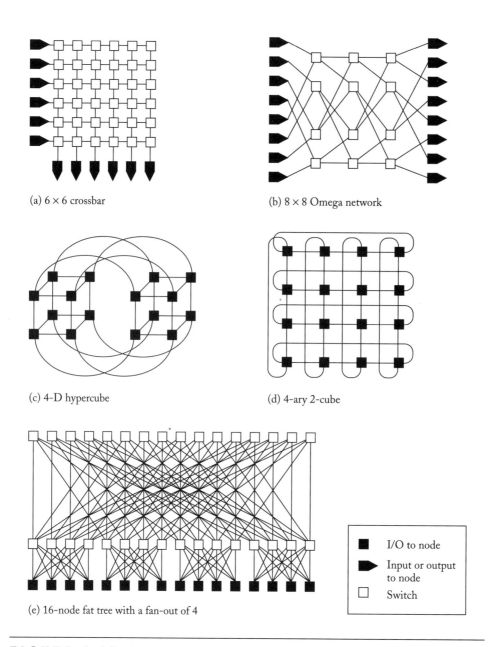

(a) 6 × 6 crossbar

(b) 8 × 8 Omega network

(c) 4-D hypercube

(d) 4-ary 2-cube

(e) 16-node fat tree with a fan-out of 4

■ I/O to node

▶ Input or output to node

□ Switch

FIGURE 1-10 *Scalable Interconnection Networks.*

main disadvantage of the MIN network is that it does not support any optimizations for local communication, all end-points are equally far away. Another drawback can be the requirement for varying lengths of communication wires, which can slow down the network. MIN networks have been used in many systems. Most large-scale systems that support a UMA style of shared memory architecture use MIN networks. These include the IBM RP3, University of Illinois Cedar, Cray Y-MP and C90, and IBM SP1 and SP2.

1.3.1.3 Hypercube

The structure of a hypercube is shown in Figure 1-10(c). An n-dimensional hypercube, or more specifically an n-dimensional binary hypercube, connects 2^n nodes. Each switch supports n external connections and one connection to the local node. Each node is connected to every other node whose address differs from this node in one binary bit position. Like MIN networks, hypercubes support a linear growth in bisection bandwidth and minimal growth in latency ($\log_2 N$). As with MIN networks, the cost grows as $N \log_2 N$, but in the hypercube this growth is due to increasing the number of links exiting each switch. This feature of the hypercube is awkward because it requires that the maximum system size be set when the system is initially built, or that all switches be changed if the hypercube grows beyond its originally intended size. In a MIN network, one only needs to add more layers of switches to grow the system to an arbitrary size. Hypercubes have the advantage over MIN networks, however, in optimizing support for nearest neighbor communication. Hypercube networks have been used in a variety of systems including the Caltech Cosmic Cube, Intel's line of iPSC computers, the TMC CM-2, and nCUBE 1 and nCUBE 2.

1.3.1.4 *k*-ary *n*-cubes

k-ary n-cubes are a generalization of the hypercube structure in which each of the n dimensions contains more than two nodes. Thus, if a hypercube contains 2^n nodes, its corresponding k-ary n-cube would have k^n. An example 4-ary 2-cube is shown in Figure 1-10(d). While the binary hypercube is a subset of a k-ary n-cube, in practice, most k-ary n-cube sys-

---

TABLE 1-2

Comparison of 2-D and 3-D Torus Versus Binary Hypercube

TOPOLOGY	AVERAGE LATENCY	BISECTION BANDWIDTH	WIRE COST
8 × 16 torus	6	16 BW_L	256 W_L
Binary 7-cube	3.5	64 BW_L	448 W_L
8 × 8 × 8 torus	6	128 BW_L	1536 W_L
Binary 9-cube	4.5	256 BW_L	2304 W_L

---

tems have fixed n at either 2 or 3. These smaller dimension systems are also referred to as 2-D or 3-D meshes or tori. The distinction between a torus and a mesh is whether the edges are connected in a wraparound fashion or not. The wraparound connections in a torus reduce the average latency by a factor of 2 and make the configuration symmetric. However, a torus has a more complex routing algorithm, and supporting the wraparound connections can make wiring more difficult. Once the dimension is chosen, the cost of the k-ary n-cube grows linearly with the size of the system. Unfortunately, this is at the expense of nonideal bisection bandwidth growth (only by $N^{1/2}$ or $N^{2/3}$ for the 2-D and 3-D meshes, respectively). These networks also have greater than minimal latency growth, $N^{1/2}$ and $N^{1/3}$.

Depending upon system size, the degradations in performance can be small compared with a MIN network or hypercube. The absolute differences for a 128-node 2-D torus and a 512-node 3-D torus compared with the equivalent binary hypercube are given in Table 1-2. In this table, latency is measured by the number of switches traversed, BW_L is the bandwidth per link, and W_L is the width of each link. Table 1-2 shows that the torus and the hypercube have similar latencies and are within a factor of 2–4 in bandwidth. Furthermore, for equal wire cost, the links of the torus can be 50–75% wider than the hypercube, which reduces the latency to receive a complete message in the k-ary n-cube. Dally demonstrates that for equal wire cost and a switch delay equal to network cycle time,[7] average message latency is lower in a torus than a hypercube under both uniform and nonuniform traffic assumptions [Dal90b].

Torus and mesh networks are very popular, owing in part to the existence of the Caltech Mesh Routing Chip (MRC). Variants of this chip are used in the Intel Delta, Stanford DASH, MIT Alewife, and CMU Plus systems. Torus topologies have also been used in the MIT J-Machine and Cray T3D.

1.3.1.5 Fat Tree

The structure of a 16-node, fan-out of four, fat tree is given in Figure 1-10(e). A fat tree has a tree structure with a constant number of links at each level of the hierarchy. Thought of in another way, the logical bandwidth of the links gets fatter as one moves up the tree so that the root of the tree is not a bottleneck. Fat trees support a linear growth in bisection bandwidth and a log N latency increase as processors are added. The structure of a fat tree amounts to two Omega networks, in which the first and last layer of switches are replaced with nodes on one side and the tree roots on the other. The two Omega networks are then folded back on one another to allow messages that stay within a particular branch of the tree to be routed within that subtree. The fat tree also offers higher network bandwidth than an Omega network because each node and tree root have multiple inputs into the fat tree.[8] The disadvantage of the fat tree is that messages without a common subtree incur twice the latency they otherwise would have if the nodes were directly connected in a simple Omega network. Some of this increased latency is recovered because of the fat tree's ability to adaptively route messages to any of the tree roots and avoid congestion.

As with MIN networks and hypercubes, the costs in a fat tree increase as $N \log N$ (i.e., more levels for a larger system). The advantage of fat trees over hypercubes is that they can be grown by adding layers of switches instead of having to increase the fan-out of each node switch. Fat trees were first introduced by Leiserson [Lei85] and have been used in the TMC CM-5 and the Meiko CS-2.

---

[7] Network cycle time is the inverse of the rate that individual words of width W_L are sent through the network. This assumption does not hold for many networks (e.g., those based on the Caltech MRC), but does hold for some networks including the one used in the Cray T3D.

[8] Of course, this added bandwidth is at the cost of proportionally higher wire and switch costs.

1.3.1.6 Bus and Hierarchical Bus and Rings

The most widespread interconnection network used in multiprocessors is a simple bus in which the processors and memory are connected by a common set of wires. The advantages of this structure are that it has constant latency between all nodes and a linear cost with the number of processors. The big disadvantage, however, is that the amount of bandwidth is fixed and does not grow with the number of processors, which puts an obvious limit on the scalability of bus-based systems. It also forces a difficult trade-off to be made as to the width and speed of the bus. Increasing both of these permits a larger maximum system size. Unfortunately, increasing width increases costs, especially for small systems that may not need all the bandwidth. Increasing speed can limit the scalability due to degradation in the electrical performance as system size increases (i.e., as the bus speed increases, the bus must be shorter and have fewer loads attached to it). Some bus-based systems get around the fixed bandwidth problem by supporting multiple buses and interleaving them on low-order address bits. For example, the Sun SparcCenter 1000 uses one 64-bit bus to support 8 processors, the SparcCenter 2000 replicates this bus to support up to 20 processors, and the Cray Super-Server 6400 utilizes four copies of this same bus to support up to 64 processors. Electrical constraints on the bus put a limit on how well this technique can be scaled, and also imply increased cost with system size.

Ring topologies are similar to buses in that they have a fixed bisection bandwidth. They have better electrical properties than buses, and they often run at a much faster clock rate than buses, which can allow the ring to use narrower links and reduce costs. The drawback of rings in comparison to buses is that they have a linear increase in latency as nodes are added. For small systems, a ring can have very comparable performance to a bus. For example, the IEEE 1596-1992 SCI standard (see Section 5.1.4) can be implemented as a simple ring and provides performance that is comparable or better than the IEEE 896.1-1991 Futurebus+ [IEE91].

Both buses and rings can be extended into hierarchical structures. However, if they are not extended in a fat tree manner, then bisection bandwidth remains constant and scalability is limited unless communication patterns match the hierarchy. The Encore GigaMax and SICS DDM system use hierarchical buses, while the KSR-1 and KSR-2 employ hierarchical rings.

1.3.1.7 Summary of Interconnection Networks

Table 1-3 summarizes the characteristics of the networks discussed in the preceding sections. In this table, "switch cost" is the number of switching elements or bus/ring interfaces. "Wire cost" is the total number of individual links in the system. "Average latency" is measured for a uniform load without contention. "Neighbor optimized" indicates whether network delay between all pairs of nodes is equal, or whether communication to neighboring nodes has reduced latency and increased system bandwidth.

For the hierarchical bus, the number of switches or bus interfaces is equal to the number of nodes in a tree with fan-out f that has N leaves. If $n = \lceil \log_f(N) \rceil$, then this sum is approximately given by

TABLE 1-3

Scalable Interconnection Network Summary for Systems With N Nodes

TOPOLOGY	TYPE	SWITCH COST	WIRE COST	AVERAGE LATENCY	BISECTION BANDWIDTH	NEIGHBOR OPTIMIZED
Crossbar	Indirect	N^2	N	const. [a]	N	No
MIN[b]	Indirect	$N/f\log_f N$	$N\log_f N$	$\log_f N$	N	No
Hypercube	Direct	$N\log_2 N$	$N/2\log_2 N$	$1/2 \log_2 N/2$	$N/2$	Yes
2-D torus	Direct	N	$2N$	$N^{1/2}/2$	$2N^{1/2}$	Yes
3-D torus	Direct	N	$3N$	$3N^{1/3}/4$	$2N^{2/3}$	Yes
Fat tree[b]	Indirect	$N\log_f N$	$fN\log_f N$	$2(\log_f N - 1) < L < 2\log_f N$	fN	Yes
Bus	Direct	N	const.	const.	const.	No
Unidirectional ring	Direct	N	N	$N/2$	2 const.	No[c]
Hierarchical bus[d]	Indirect	$Switch(N)$	$Switch(N)/N$	$2(\log_f N - 1) < L < 2\log_f N$	const.	Yes
Hierarchical ring[d]	Indirect	$Switch(N)$	$Switch(N)$	$2N(\log_f N - 1) < L < 2N\log_f N$	2 const.	Yes

[a] This parameter is constant—independent of the number of processors in the system (N).
[b] MIN or fat tree with fan-out of f (i.e., network I/O ports have f connections and internal switches with f inputs and f outputs) at each stage.
[c] A unidirectional ring is not optimized for neighbor communication. A bidirectional ring is.
[d] Hierarchical bus or rings with f nodes per bus and ring, respectively.

$$Switch(N) \approx N\frac{f^{n+1}-1}{f^{n+1}-f^n} - 1 \qquad (1.6)$$

One important thing to note about Table 1-3 is that none of the networks support both ideal switch cost (i.e., no worse than linear with N) and an ideal bisection bandwidth (i.e., linear with N). Unfortunately, such a network is not possible due to fan-in limitations of real logic. As with the inevitable increase in latency, this fact means that no architecture can be ideally scalable.

While all of the networks listed in Table 1-3 have been employed in one system or another, the trend has been towards networks that provide low latency, neighbor-to-neighbor communication optimizations, and a reasonably scalable bisection bandwidth. Two- and three-dimensional meshes have become very popular (e.g., Stanford DASH, MIT Alewife, Cray T3D, Tera Computer MTA, and Intel Paragon); some systems have employed hypercubes (e.g., Intel iPSC and nCUBE 1 and 2); and others, fat trees (e.g., TMC CM-5 and Meiko CS-2).

1.3.2 Scalable Cache Coherence

As shown in Section 1.2, caching is vital to providing high performance. To retain the performance of a small-scale system, a large-scale system should support cache coherence. However, an assumption made in the preceding section is that memory traffic is proportional to the number of processors in the system. Although this is what might be expected in a system without caches, once caches are added the overhead of maintaining cache coherence must be considered. If one uses a snoopy scheme, then all processors must snoop all requests to memory. This situation generates traffic that is proportional to the number of processors squared (N^2), which, in turn, implies that even networks that scale bandwidth linearly with N see memory bandwidth drop off as $1/N$. Thus, while snoopy cache coherence works well on bus- and ring-based systems that can naturally broadcast memory requests, it restricts scalability considerably when a general interconnection network is used.

Directory-based coherence [CeF78] removes the bandwidth scalability problem of snoopy schemes by eliminating the need for broadcast messages. The structure of a directory is illustrated in Figure 1-11. Directory-based coherence relies on caching state maintained

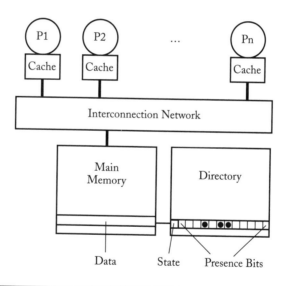

FIGURE 1-11 *Directory-Based Cache Coherence.*

with each memory block and each cache line. A memory block is a portion of main memory that corresponds to the size of a processor cache line. In a simple directory scheme, each directory entry consists of state information and a set of pointers to the processor caches. The pointers are implemented as *presence bits*, where each bit position corresponds to a processor cache. For a directory scheme that supports write-back caches and an invalidation-based coherence protocol, the required states are *uncached*, *shared*, and *dirty*. The uncached state implies that this memory block is not cached in any processor cache. The shared state implies that this memory block is cached by one or more processors as indicated by the presence bits. The dirty state implies that the single processor with its presence bit set holds this line in an exclusive state. The directory entries allow the system to avoid broadcasts since only caches whose presence bits are set can be involved in coherence operations.

Operation of the directory can be illustrated by the same example given in Figure 1-6. First, as processors read a memory block (Figure 1-6(a)), their corresponding presence bits are set and the directory state becomes shared. Upon a write to a block that the directory indicates is shared (Figure 1-6(b)), invalidation messages are sent to those processors caching the location (i.e., whose presence bits are set). The write also updates the state bit in the directory to indicate that memory is not up-to-date, and sets the presence bit of the writing processor. As before, once a processor has an exclusive copy of a memory block, it can retire writes within its cache without interacting with the directory (Figure 1-6(c)). Upon a subsequent read by another processor, the directory relays the requests directly to the dirty processor. The dirty cache supplies the data to memory, which then passes it on to the requesting processor (Figure 1-6(d)). This updates the directory presence bits to show the additional sharing and resets the state bit back to the shared state.

The state transitions for the directory are summarized in Figure 1-12. The transitions

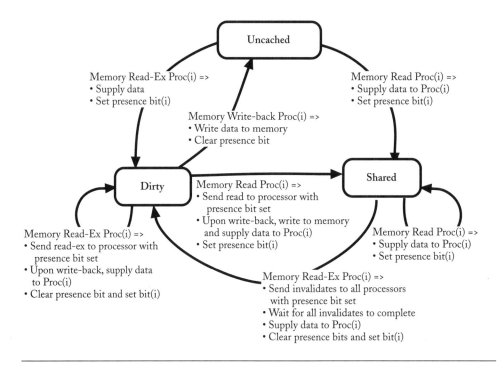

FIGURE 1-12 *Directory Protocol State Transition Diagram.*

for the processor caches are the same as for the snoopy case given in Figure 1-8. The only difference is that the caches only see the memory references issued by other processors if they have cached that particular memory block. The caches are not required to monitor all memory requests, only the requests for blocks they have cached. Since there is no need for broadcasts, coherence does not limit memory bandwidth. Furthermore, the connection between the processors and memory can be any general interconnection network since there is no reliance on the broadcast nature of the bus.

The first published work on directories was by Tang [Tan76] in 1976, and similar structures have been used in IBM mainframes to the current day [Tuc86]. Tang's directories were implemented at memory, but stored duplicate tags for each processor cache in what amounted to a snoopy cache structure with the duplicate tags centralized. The directory structure explained above (with presence bits and state associated with memory blocks) was originally proposed by Censier and Feautrier in 1978 [CeF78]. Subsequently, Archibald and Baer [ArB86b] and Yen, Yen, and Fu [YYF85] discussed minor variations of this original proposal. The S-1 project at Lawrence Livermore National Laboratory even began to build a directory-based system, but the multiprocessor portion of this work was never completed [WiC80]. Over the last decade, snoopy caches have become the dominant cache coherence mechanism because they mesh well with the bus structure of small-scale multiprocessors and require less memory overhead, especially when caches are small. The original directory schemes envisioned a centralized directory that did not offer any scalability advantages.

As researchers have begun to investigate large-scale cache-coherent architectures, there has been much interest in directory-based systems with distributed directories [ASH+88, CFK+90, LLG+90, Ste90]. By partitioning memory and the directories into independent modules, each memory/directory access is independent and memory bandwidth can be scaled with processor count. Furthermore, since only the processors that have cached a particular location will see coherence traffic for a block, total memory and network bandwidth demand grows no worse than if memory was uncached. In contrast, it is difficult to scale snoopy-based schemes because the caching information for a particular memory block can only be obtained by querying all the processor caches.

Even when distributed into independent modules, there are still potential scalability problems in directory systems. First, the overhead of the presence bits in the directory grows as processors are added. Since the overhead of the coherence mechanism must be kept small, this growth limits system size as the directory entry becomes a sizable fraction of a memory block (i.e., on the order of 15%). Alternative directory organizations that solve this problem will be outlined in Chapter 4. Second, there are still communication costs in a directory-based system in the form of cache misses. As detailed in Chapter 3, achieving scalable performance in directory-based systems relies on minimizing the latency within the memory system and from mechanisms that allow the overlap of communication and computation.

1.3.3 Scalable I/O

A scalable architecture must have scalable computation, memory, and I/O subsystems. As with computational power, scalable I/O performance can only be achieved by a highly parallel I/O system. Given the distributed shared-memory (NUMA) structure of Figure 1-4, I/O interfaces can be scaled naturally by adding I/O ports to each or a subset of the processor-memory nodes. Alternatively, I/O interfaces can be added as peers on the interconnection network. As with the trade-offs between UMA and NUMA structures, distributing I/O among the processors allows for optimizations of I/O accesses to a given processor or memory, while I/O peers provide more efficient global I/O access.

Assuming a parallel I/O subsystem, achieving scalable I/O performance is similar to achieving scalable processor performance. As a slave device, I/O interfaces need to be accessed with relatively low latency and with scalable interconnect bandwidth. As a master (DMA) device, I/O interfaces need reasonable latency and scalable bandwidth to memory. Because individual I/O devices are primarily block oriented and usually operate at a slower rate than processors, aggregate bandwidth is usually more important than latency for I/O devices.

From a hardware perspective, scaling I/O connectivity is easier than scaling processor performance. The more difficult problems for I/O are the performance of the devices themselves and the software management of these devices. A thorough treatment of these issues is beyond the scope of this text (see [Pat94a, JWB94] for more detailed discussions of high-performance I/O), but to summarize some of the important issues:

- Mechanical I/O devices such as disk and tape drives are increasing in performance more slowly than processors. Techniques to help address this growing gap include using a large main memory as a disk cache to reduce latency, and using highly parallel *redundant array of inexpensive disks* (RAID) [PGK88, CLG+94] configurations to deliver higher bandwidth.

- Network interfaces have been increasing in speed dramatically (e.g., 155- and 622-Mbit ATM, 100-Mbit Ethernet, and 1-Gbit Fibre-Channel). However, software protocol processing for these interfaces can limit achieved throughput. Intelligent network interfaces [Ste94] can help reduce this problem.

- Balancing the load for I/O devices can be very difficult. Typically, a subset of the disks or network ports see a high percentage of the traffic. Thus, the hardware and management software for these devices can be a bottleneck in overall I/O throughput.

1.3.4 Summary of Hardware Architecture Scalability

Unfortunately, no real system can be ideally scalable. However, there are structures that provide good approximations of the ideal. In particular, MIN networks, hypercubes, and fat trees provide ideal bandwidth scaling with only a $\log N$ increase in latency, and at a cost that is only a $\log N$ factor over linear. The increase in costs is mitigated by the fact that the interconnection network is only a fraction of the total system cost. Alternatively, costs can be kept constant by using a 3-D mesh or torus, but these topologies have less than ideal bandwidth scaling ($N^{2/3}$ instead of N) and latency growth $N^{1/3}$. For systems on the order of 1,000 processors or less, though, these limitations can be very acceptable.

Providing a scalable coherence mechanism such as directories allows for shared data to be cached. As with caching in smaller systems, the benefit of caching is increased processor performance through reduced memory latency, which gives the multiprocessor the potential to deliver N times the computational power of a uniprocessor. Directories also allow coherence to be maintained without compromising the scalable bandwidth of the interconnection network. Unfortunately, a simple directory structure has an N^2 increase in costs as the system grows, which can be unacceptable for large systems. Luckily, alternative directory structures can mitigate this problem (discussed in Chapter 4).

1.3.5 Scalability of Parallel Software

As shown in the previous sections, a multiprocessor with a scalable interconnection network and directory-based cache coherence can be built to be highly scalable. Realizing the potential of this hardware is dependent upon two key assumptions concerning the software using the machine—first, that the software is partitioned so that the computation is evenly divided among the processors and, second, that the amount of communication is independent of the number of processors employed. In practice, given a scalable architecture, the degree to which the software does not adhere to these assumptions often limits the scalability more so than any nonideality of the hardware.

To illustrate the problem with software scalability, consider the simple problem of forming the sum of M numbers where M is much larger than the number of processors N. In this case, N partial sums can be formed in parallel by breaking the list up into N lists, each with M/N numbers in it. Combining the N partial sums, however, can not utilize all of the processors. At best, the sum can be formed in log N steps using $N/(2i)$ processors at the ith step. For 100 processors to sum 10,000 numbers, it would take on the order of 100 time steps to form the partial sums, and then at least another 7 steps to add the partial sums. Thus, for this size input the speedup is 10,000 / 107 or 93.4 times. The amount of communication also grows with the number of processors since the number of partial sums is equal to the number of processors. Further, when adding the partial sums, communication delays dominate. In many cases, using a single processor to add the partial sums may be just as fast as using a tree of processors. If a single processor is used in the final phase, then speedup is limited to 10,000 / 200 = 50.

The execution pattern of the above example is typical of many parallel programs (see Chapter 2 for more examples). Parallel programs typically exhibit alternating phases of limited and full parallelism: limited parallelism while the computation is initialized or the results are summarized, and full parallelism while the primary computation is done across the data by all of the processors. If we approximate the phases of execution as a strictly serial portion followed by a fully parallel section, then the time to do a computation on N processors ($T_{comp}(N)$ given in Equation 1.4) can be written in terms of the percentage of serial code (s) as

$$T_{comp}(N) = T_{comp}(1)\,(s + (1 - s)\,/N) \qquad\qquad \textbf{(1.7)}$$

Likewise, if we ignore the log N factor in parallel communication time from increased hardware latency, and assume that the total amount of communication does not increase, then communication, $T_{comm}(N)$, is given by

$$T_{comm}(N) = T_{comm}(1)\,(s + (1 - s)\,/N) \qquad\qquad \textbf{(1.8)}$$

resulting in an overall speedup equation of

$$S(N) = \frac{T_{comp}(1) + T_{comm}(1)}{(T_{comp}(1) + T_{comm}(1))\,(s + (1-s)/N)} = \frac{1}{s + (1-s)/N} \tag{1.9}$$

This last formula was originally derived by Gene Amdahl in 1967 [Amd67] and is known as Amdahl's Law. An important implication of Amdahl's Law is that the maximum speedup of an application (on an infinite number of processors) is given by

$$S(N) \leq \frac{1}{s} \tag{1.10}$$

For the simple summation example, the final partial sum takes either 7 or 100 cycles compared with the approximately 10,000 cycles that can be parallelized to form the partial sums. Thus, $s = 7 / 10,000 = 0.07\%$ for the parallel partial sum addition and $s = 100 / 10,000 = 1\%$ for the serial addition, and the resulting maximum speedup given by Amdahl's Law is 1,429 and 100 respectively.

In many cases, Amdahl's Law can be the limiting factor for realizing the scalability of a parallel machine. However, if we are interested in solving a limited size problem in less time by utilizing parallel processors, Amdahl's Law is a fact of life. Amdahl's Law implies that we are not likely to succeed in attempting to reduce a two-minute execution time down to one second by using 120 processors in parallel because there is typically too much serial overhead to achieve this goal. Likewise, even for a more typical supercomputer job that may take two hours to run, reducing the execution time to less than two minutes on a 100-processor system requires a highly parallel algorithm. Of course, solving the same problem faster is not the only use of a more powerful computer. We can also try to solve larger problems. In other words, we can scale a problem to fit the machine. Exactly how to scale a problem is a tricky issue [SHG93].

Scaled speedup as introduced by Gustafson et al. [GMB88] suggests solving a problem that is N times larger on an N-processor machine. Scaled speedup attempts to keep the ratio of serial code the same on the larger machine with the larger problem as it is on the smaller machine with the smaller problem. Although scaled speedup does result in good speedups, it has the unfortunate side effect of increasing the absolute run time of many algorithms on the larger machine. For example, if a parallel machine is used to compute a matrix multiply, then the input matrix would be N times larger on an N-processor machine. A matrix multiply takes $N^{3/2}$ computations for a given size matrix, and the parallel machine achieves no better than N times speedup. Thus, execution time for the scaled problem is $N^{1/2}$ larger than the original problem. On a 100-processor machine, the implied 10-times increase in execution time may not be acceptable.

Fixed execution time scale-up is usually more appropriate for most applications. In fixed execution time scale-up, the larger machine is used to solve the largest problem it can in the same time that the smaller machine solved the smaller problem [Gus88]. Thus, for the matrix multiply example, the data set size would only be increased by $N^{2/3}$. Although this increase results in a better speedup than if the problem size was fixed, note that since the data set size increases less than linearly, then as the machine increases in size each processor gets a smaller amount of data. Ultimately, this limits the scalability of the problem, and generally leads to nonideal speedup due to additional interprocessor communication.

Others [SuN90, SHG93] have proposed more sophisticated application scaling models. Unfortunately, there is no universal problem scaling rule. If a problem is scaled to achieve higher accuracy, many application-dependent factors may need to be scaled along with problem size [SHG93], which tends to make the run time of scaled jobs increase even more dramatically, and can limit the scaling for fixed execution time jobs. In practice, if a fixed-size problem must be sped up, Amdahl's Law often limits speedup to 10–30 times or less, and even if a problem is scaled, rarely can more than a few hundred processors be used without an inordinate increase in run time.

1.4 Scaling and Processor Grain Size

Although a scalable machine can be built from any type of processor, at a fixed total system cost, one must choose the performance level and cost of the individual processor. In the introduction to this chapter, we asserted that a state-of-the-art microprocessor would have the best price-performance ratio. In this section we take a closer look at this issue in terms of current processor price and performance points. Table 1-4 gives three processors that represent the range of processors that could form the basis for a scalable multiprocessor.

TABLE 1-4

Potential Processors for Use in a Scalable Shared-Memory Machine

PROCESSOR	COST	MFLOPS	$/MFLOP	SPECINT92	$/SPECINT
Supercomputer	$1M	902	$1,109	< 200	$5,000
Supermicro	$50K	260	$192	120	$417
PC micro	$4K	25	$160	100	$40

In Table 1-4, the supercomputer processor is modeled after a Cray C90. The supermicro is equivalent to an IBM Power2 or SGI R8000 processor. The PC micro is based on a 100 MHz, Intel Pentium-class design. The cost numbers are based on system costs per processor and include overheads such as memory, buses, enclosures, and power supplies. The MFLOPS ratings are based on "Towards Peak Performance" rating on 1000 × 1000 LIN-PACK [Don94].[9] The SpecInt92 numbers are a measure of integer performance [Spe94a, Spe94b] and are estimated for the supercomputer since there are no published C90 SpecInt92 results.

---

[9] The PC micro numbers are optimistic extrapolations based on the standard LINPACK rating of a 60 MHz Pentium system of 5.4. A TPP rating of 25 would be based on clock scaling of 1.67 and a standard to TPP ratio of 2.78. Other microprocessors have reported a standard to TPP of 1.87 (MIPS R4400), 2.3 (Sun Supersparc), and 3.46 (DEC Alpha).

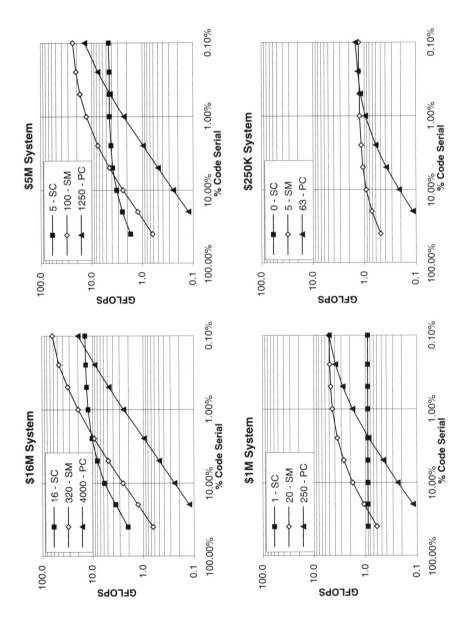

FIGURE 1-13 *MFLOPS Achieved by a Supercomputer (SC), a Supermicro (SM), or a PC Micro (PC)*

Figure 1-13 shows the performance of the three options at four price points with varying degrees of serial code. Performance is estimated given Amdahl's Law and the number of processors that a particular budget would allow. Note that although we are using Amdahl's Law, the problems could be scaled using any of the methods listed in Section 1.3.5, assuming that the serial percentage is taken as that of the problem run on the larger machine.

There are a number of points to note from Figure 1-13. The first is that for the range of system prices, a supercomputer-based system always has a small number of processors. Even a PC micro–based system with a $16 million price has only 4,000 processors. The second feature of the curves is that, at most price and serial percentage points, the supermicro-based system provides higher performance than the supercomputer because of the relatively small difference in uniprocessor performance (less than a factor of 4) between these two solutions, and the huge advantage in price (a factor of 20) for the supermicro. Thus, even when there is limited parallelism with a percentage of serial code as high as 2.5–10%, the supermicro solution outperforms the supercomputer. In most cases the supermicro delivers 2–4 times the performance. In contrast, the much larger performance degradation for the PC micro relative to the supercomputer (a factor of 36), makes it harder for it to achieve better performance unless there is a very high degree of parallelism (i.e., a serial fraction less than 0.5%). Finally, since the supermicro has much higher uniprocessor performance than the PC micro and has a similar $/MFLOPS rating, the PC micro rarely outperforms the supermicro.

The graphs for integer performance are similar, with a much larger bias toward microprocessor-based systems, especially the PC micro, because of the relative closeness of the SpecInt ratings for all of these machines and the clear advantage in $/SpecInt offered by the microprocessor solutions. Overall, Figure 1-13 confirms our initial conjecture that highly parallel systems based on state-of-the-art microprocessors represent the future of large-scale computing.

1.5   Chapter Conclusions

Microprocessor-based multiprocessors are becoming an increasingly viable way to achieve high performance because of the narrowing gap between microprocessors and the fastest supercomputers, and the tremendous cost-performance advantage of microprocessor-based systems. Programming a parallel machine remains a challenge, however. Of the alternative parallel architectures, a multiple instruction, multiple data (MIMD) architecture supporting global shared-memory is preferred because of its flexibility and ease of programming.

The biggest problems with shared-memory multiprocessors are keeping their performance per processor high, allowing scalability to large processor counts, and dealing with their hardware complexity. Scalable shared-memory multiprocessors (SSMPs) address both the performance and scalability problems of earlier shared-memory designs. Although SSMPs employ complex memory subsystems, such systems have been built and demonstrate the feasibility and cost-effectiveness of this approach.

High performance in an SSMP system is achieved by hardware cache coherence that allows the caching of both shared and private data. Scalability of an SSMP results from two factors. First, an SSMP utilizes a general interconnect (as opposed to a bus), which provides near ideal bandwidth and cost growth as system size is varied. Examples of these interconnects include MIN networks, hypercubes, meshes, and fat trees. The second basis of scalability in an SSMP is a coherence protocol that does not rely on broadcast coherence messages. Directory-based cache coherence supports coherence by maintaining pointers to the cached copies of each memory block. Thus, all coherence actions are point-to-point messages to the processors that have already cached the memory location. Thus, directory-based coherence supports caching without compromising the bandwidth characteristics of the general interconnect.

Ideally, a scalable system would also be infinitely extensible and maintain a constant cost-performance over this entire range. Unfortunately, it is impossible to build hardware that does not have performance degradations or nonlinear cost increases. More importantly, software algorithms do not exhibit ideal scalability. In particular, if there is any section of an algorithm that is not completely parallel, Amdahl's Law dictates that there will be a limit to the speedup of the code. In most cases, the software limit allows, at most, a few hundred to a few thousand processors. Over this range, SSMP systems can be designed that support the shared-memory paradigm and exhibit near-ideal scalability. Thus, the cost-performance, scalability, and ease of programming of microprocessor-based SSMP systems is likely to make them the dominant architecture for future high-performance computers.

C H A P 2 T E R

Shared-Memory
Parallel Programs

In this chapter, we take a detailed look at the factors that affect the performance of parallel programs. We start with a brief overview of parallel programming for shared-memory machines. In keeping with the book's main thrust, the remainder of the chapter focuses on the architectural factors, such as memory latency and caching, rather than the algorithmic reasons for nonideal performance of parallel applications. There are three major sections. First, we introduce a set of parallel applications and explain their execution behavior. Next, we introduce a parallel application execution model and give data for our applications with different memory system organizations. We show that the memory system has a strong effect on the performance of applications and is thus a key element of any scalable shared-memory multiprocessor. Finally, we delve more deeply into the communication behavior of shared data in parallel applications. We look at computation-to-communication ratios for the applications and study the behavior of shared data.

2.1 Basic Concepts

While the intricacies of programming a shared-memory multiprocessor are beyond the scope of this book, in this section we provide a quick overview of the basic concepts. It can be skipped by the more experienced reader without any loss of continuity. The key concepts covered are access to shared data, the problem of dividing work and data, synchronization, static versus dynamic scheduling, and performance improvements. Code examples are shown in C, using the Argonne National Labs (ANL) macros [LOB+87] for constructs related to parallelism.

In a shared-memory multiprocessor, access to shared data is as straightforward as access to private data: it is done simply by address. This simplicity is one of the major advantages of the shared-memory programming style. A slight inconvenience is that it is often necessary to declare up-front whether a given data structure might be accessed by more than one processor during the run (i.e., whether it is to be placed in a shared data area). For example, with the ANL macros, shared data is allocated using the *G_MALLOC* macro, which behaves similarly to a UNIX *malloc* system call. It returns a pointer to a shared data area of the requested size.

```
shared_struct *shared;
shared = (shared_struct *) G_MALLOC (sizeof (shared_struct));
```

The division of a problem into independent tasks that will be executed in parallel on different processors is the most challenging aspect of parallel programming. Sections of work that can be done independently and in parallel have to be identified. It is desirable to make the tasks as large-grained as possible to amortize any overhead that might be incurred in distributing the tasks to the processors. While dividing the work into independent tasks, it is important to keep in mind the data set that each task will be accessing. If different tasks are going to be accessing the same piece of data, the accesses often have to be protected from simultaneous access by some mutual exclusion mechanism such as locks. It is therefore desirable to have the tasks access data sets that are disjoint from one another. Work and data division normally are interdependent and must be considered together to achieve good parallel performance.

Let us illustrate the ideas of work and data division using the simple example of a matrix multiplication program. A straightforward way to program the problem of multiplying a matrix A by another matrix B to yield a result matrix C is as follows.

```
double sum;
int i, j, k;

for (i = 0; i < rows_of_A; i++) {
  for (j = 0; j < cols_of_B; j++) {
    sum = 0;
    for (k = 0; k < cols_of_A; k++) {
      sum += A[i][k] * B[k][j];
    }
    C[i][j] = sum;
  }
}
```

The program proceeds by taking a row vector of matrix A and a column vector of matrix B, and then performing a dot product to yield one value of matrix C. The dot product of row vector V_r of matrix A with column vector V_c of matrix B yields element E_{rc} of matrix C.

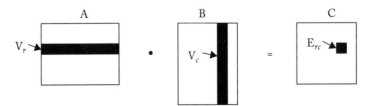

To parallelize this program, we first have to identify independent tasks (also called processes). For matrix multiplication, it is readily apparent that the computation of each element E_{rc} of the result matrix C is independent of the computation of any other element of C. We have thus identified $r \bullet c$ independent tasks that could be performed in parallel on different processors. Let us assume that we want to run this application on a multiprocessor with four processors. While a total of $r \bullet c$ tasks is available, it is better to collect the tasks together into four much larger grain-sized tasks, in order to minimize the task distribution overhead. We are thus left with the following assignment of work and data to the processors:

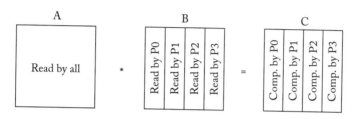

Each of the processors is assigned a vertical strip of matrix C to produce. Each processor will be reading all of matrix A and a vertical strip of matrix B, and each will be writing a vertical strip of matrix C.

Task creation is handled by the ANL macros using the *CREATE* macro, which spawns a new process running the given procedure name. In the parallel version of our matrix multiplication program, we spawn four processes that each execute the procedure *Task()*.

The following code fragment assumes that the three matrices have been allocated in shared space using *G_MALLOC*. Similarly, all the global scalar variables (*rows_of_A*, *cols_of_B*, and *cols_of_A*) have been allocated as one shared structure pointed to by the pointer *shared*. Note that all variables not declared as shared are process-private variables that are not visible by any other process.

```
#define PROCS 4
int i;
for (i = 0; i < PROCS; i++) {
  CREATE (Task);
}

Task ()
{
  int proc_num;
  int i, j, k;
  double sum;

  GET_PID(proc_num);
  for (i = 0; i < shared->rows_of_A; i++) {
    for (j = proc_num * shared->cols_of_B / PROCS;
       j < (proc_num+1) * shared->cols_of_B / PROCS; j++) {
      sum = 0;
```

```
        for (k = 0; k < shared->cols_of_A; k++) {
          sum += A[i][k] * B[k][j];
        }
        C[i][j] = sum;
      }
    }
  }
```

Each task starts by finding its own process number using the macro *GET_PID*. It then uses this number to select the columns of matrix C assigned to that process. In this manner the computation of result matrix C proceeds in parallel.

Next, we will discuss the concept of synchronization between tasks. Although it is desirable to have each task perform as much work as possible independently of all other tasks, there are always some points in the program where the control flow requires the tasks to interact with one another. This control interaction between tasks is called *synchronization*.

In our matrix multiplication program, we have parallelized the computation of the result matrix C. Next, we might like to find the product of the elements in each row. We do not wish to start the row element multiplication section of the code before all tasks have completed the calculation of matrix C. This is an example of a *barrier synchronization*.

A barrier works as follows. Upon reaching a barrier, all but the last task simply wait. The last task to reach the barrier releases all the waiting tasks and continues itself. In this manner it is guaranteed that no task will continue to the section of code following the barrier until all tasks have completed the code before the barrier. In our matrix multiplication program, a barrier can be used to make sure that all tasks have completed their computation of the result matrix C before they start into the row element multiplication. We use the *BARRIER* macro from the ANL macro set. This macro takes as arguments a barrier name and the total number of processors to expect at this barrier.

```
  Task ()
  {

    /* compute matrix C in parallel */

    BARRIER (shared->barrier, PROCS); /* wait for computation to be
                                          complete */

    /* compute product of each row in parallel */
  }
```

Task scheduling is an important concept of parallel programming. There are two major varieties of task scheduling: static and dynamic. Static scheduling is done at compile time; dynamic scheduling must be delayed until run time because it is data dependent. Our matrix multiplication program so far is an example of a statically scheduled parallel application. The amount of computation required to complete each task is known exactly at compile time. Furthermore, the amount of work done by each task is identical to the amount of work done by all the other tasks. We are thus able to simply assign one task to each processor statically and start them all on their way. All of the tasks will finish their work at roughly the same time, i.e., the application shows good load-balancing.

Let us now move on to the next section of our example program: the calculation of the product of the elements of each row of matrix C. The run time of each product task is data dependent, because it can be cut off as soon as a zero element is encountered. Simply assigning product tasks to processors statically at compile time might lead to very poor load-balancing. A processor that has a very short task is done very quickly and spends most of its time sitting idle while other processors are still working on longer tasks. One way to avoid load-balancing problems is to break the work into small tasks and then schedule the tasks dynamically at run time, as shown below.

```
/* shared->next_row is initialized to 0 before entering this code */

while (!done) {
  LOCK (shared->row_lock); /* enter critical region */
  my_row = shared->next_row;
  if (shared->next_row == shared->rows_of_C) {
    done = TRUE;
  }
  else {
    shared->next_row++;
  }
  UNLOCK (shared->row_lock); /* leave critical region */

  if (!done) {
    product[my_row] = 1;
    col_index = 0;
    while ((col_index < shared->cols_of_C)
        && (product[my_row] != 0)) {
      product[my_row] *= C[my_row][col_index];
      col_index++;
    }
  }

}
```

With this code fragment, we also introduce a new synchronization primitive: the lock. Locks are used to assure mutual exclusion among tasks. Before one task enters a critical region, it must acquire a lock protecting that critical region. While the lock is held by that task, the lock cannot be acquired by any other task. Other tasks are thus excluded from entering the critical region protected by the lock. When the task holding the lock has completed the critical region, it releases the lock, thus allowing another task to acquire the lock and enter the critical region.

In the above code, the lock named *row_lock* is used to serialize access to the critical region that is used by the processes to obtain the index of the next row to be worked on. A task first has to obtain the lock using the LOCK macro. Once inside the critical region, it obtains the index of the next row (*next_row*). If the last row of the matrix has been reached, the task remembers that it is done. Otherwise, the *next_row* variable is incremented to make sure that the next task in the critical region will get the next row. The process in the critical region gives up the lock using the UNLOCK macro. The second section of code simply calculates the product of the row elements, stopping if a zero element is encountered.

This code is an example of dynamic scheduling, since the tasks are assigned to processors at run time. Each processor picks up new rows to work on until all row products have been calculated. No processor sits idle until the very last stages of the computation, when there are no more row products to calculate. Dynamic scheduling is thus used to obtain a good load balance between the processors.

By now we have a working parallel matrix multiplication and row product calculation program. As we have seen, it is relatively simple to get a parallel application up and running on a shared-memory machine. This simplicity is one of the major advantages of the shared-memory programming model. However, we may not have obtained optimal performance of this application on our machine yet. On a shared-memory machine, improved performance can be obtained after program correctness has been achieved. For example, if we are running on a NUMA machine, it might be important to distribute matrix B into memory in such a manner that the data used by a given processor is placed into memory close to that processor, in order to minimize access latency.

2.2 Parallel Application Set

A consistent set of parallel applications is used in this chapter, and most of this set is used throughout the book. The problem of choosing such a set is very difficult. On one hand, we would like the set to be representative of *all* parallel applications that we might wish to run on a scalable shared-memory multiprocessor. On the other hand, there are very few real applications available, and it is not clear whether the existing applications are always the best parallel implementations in terms of algorithms or coding. Many existing applications are not portable across parallel machines with different architectures. Finally, many parallel applications were written for small-scale multiprocessors (4 to 16 processors) and do not necessarily scale to machines with a large number of processors (64+ processors).

In addition to the limitations of the applications themselves, our use of the applications to study different aspects of parallel program behavior introduces further limitations. Because the execution of the applications is simulated, and the execution time of each simulation run has to be limited, the runs have to use much smaller data sets and total run lengths than might be expected from runs on a real machine. The results are still meaningful because of the hierarchy of working set sizes that many scientific parallel applications exhibit. Rothberg et al. found the smallest (and most important) working set size to be either small enough to fit in very small caches, or too large to fit in even the largest caches [RSG93]. Moreover, if the important working set is small, its size is only a weak function of the overall data set size; that is, even with much larger data sets the smallest working set size remains largely unchanged. In our experience, scaling down the data set sizes retains the important characteristics of the parallel applications. Scaling down the run times is also acceptable,

TABLE 2-1

Application characteristics

APPLICATION	SOURCE LINES	SCHEDULING	MAJOR DATA TYPE
MP3D	1,500	Static	Single-precision floating point
Water	1,500	Static	Double-precision floating point
PTHOR	9,200	Dynamic	Integer
LocusRoute	6,400	Dynamic	Integer
Cholesky	2,000	Dynamic	Double-precision floating point
Barnes-Hut	2,700	Dynamic	Double-precision floating point

because we only do it for applications that would normally run through a large number of repetitive iterations or time steps. For these applications, we can reduce the number of iterations to a handful while still retaining the important application behavior, because the program behavior is very similar from one iteration to the next.

Although it is very difficult to satisfy the goal of representing all parallel programs, we have chosen a set of applications that represents a variety of scientific and engineering codes in use today: the SPLASH parallel application set, developed at Stanford University. More detailed information on the SPLASH applications can be found in the SPLASH report [SWG92].

Here is a list of the applications:

- MP3D: simulates rarified hypersonic flow using a particle-in-cell method
- Water: simulates water molecule interaction
- PTHOR: simulates digital logic
- LocusRoute: routes wires for VLSI standard cell designs
- Cholesky: performs a Cholesky factorization of a sparse matrix
- Barnes-Hut: performs a hierarchical *N*-body gravitation simulation

The applications are all written in C and use the ANL macros discussed in the previous section for constructs related to parallelism.

Table 2-1 presents the basic characteristics of the chosen application set, including the source code size, primary method of scheduling work, and major data type used. We show the number of source lines to give an idea of the complexity of the applications. They are not simple kernels or inner loops, but fully functional programs. The scheduling column gives the scheduling method (dynamic or static) employed to distribute parallel tasks. In addition to the synchronization required for the task scheduling, many of the applications use locks for mutual exclusion on access to individual data items. The last column of Table 2-1 gives the major data type used in each of the applications. Two applications are integer applications (PTHOR and LocusRoute), and four are floating-point applications. Of the four floating-point applications, all but MP3D use double-precision floating-point variables.

In the following sections we describe the applications. For each application we give a brief summary of the computational behavior of the application, the most important data structures, and the synchronization behavior.

2.2.1 MP3D

MP3D [McB88] simulates a three-dimensional wind tunnel using particle-based techniques. It is used to study the shock waves created as an object flies at high speed through the upper atmosphere. MP3D is written without data locality in mind and is thus considered a communications stress test for most parallel architectures. A more advanced version of MP3D (PSIM4)—it has a more sophisticated molecule interaction model and is more conscious of data locality—is used at NASA for aerospace research. Nonetheless, we use MP3D here because it raises many interesting program behavior and architecture issues.

MP3D evaluates the positions and velocities of molecules over a sequence of time steps and gathers relevant statistics. During each time step, molecules are picked up and moved according to their velocity vectors, taking into account collisions with the boundaries, objects in the wind tunnel, and other molecules. The main data structures are a particle array and a space array. The *particle array* holds the molecules and records their positions, velocities, and other attributes. The *space array* corresponds to a fine grid imposed on the three-dimensional space being modeled. Attributes of the space array cells specify the boundaries of the tunnel and the locations of physical objects in it. The space array is also used to determine collision partners for molecules (a molecule can only collide with other molecules in its space cell) and to keep track of statistics (e.g., density and energy of molecules) on the physical space it models.

The particle simulator can be easily parallelized because each molecule can be treated independently at each time step. In our program, the molecules are assigned statically to the processors. No locking is employed while accessing cells in the space array. Contention is expected to be rare, and occasional errors can be tolerated because of the statistical nature of the computation. A single lock protects the global number of collisions counter. The only other synchronization used is a barrier, which is invoked between the different phases of the program. There are six barrier invocations per time step.

2.2.2 Water

Water is adapted from the Perfect Club MDG benchmark [Ber89] and performs a molecular dynamics simulation of the forces and potentials in a system of water molecules. It is used to predict some of the physical properties of water in the liquid state.

The main data structure in Water is a large array of records that stores the state of each molecule. As in MP3D, the molecules are statically split among the processors. During each time step, the processors calculate the interaction of the atoms within each molecule and the interaction of the molecules with one another. For each molecule, the owning processor calculates the interactions with only half of the molecules ahead of it in the array. Since the forces between the molecules are symmetric, each pair-wise interaction between molecules is thus considered only once. The state associated with the molecules is then updated. Although some portions of the molecule state are modified at each interaction, others are changed only between time steps. As will be explained in detail later, this arrangement leads to interesting data-sharing patterns. There are also several variables holding global properties that are updated periodically.

2.2.3 PTHOR

PTHOR [SoG91] is a parallel logic simulator developed at Stanford University. It uses a distributed-time simulation algorithm, which is a modified version of the Chandy-Misra algorithm [ChM81].

The primary data structures associated with the simulator are the logic elements (e.g., AND gates, flip-flops), the nets (the wires linking the elements), and the task queues, which contain activated elements. Each element has a preferred task queue to increase data locality. PTHOR alternates between two distinct phases: element evaluation and deadlock resolution. During element evaluation, each processor executes the following loop: It removes an activated element from its task queue (activation list) and determines the changes on the element's outputs. It then looks up the net data structure to determine elements that are affected by the output changes and potentially schedules those elements onto other processors' task queues. When a processor's task queue is empty, it takes elements from other processors' task queues. When all activation lists are empty, a simulation deadlock has been reached and is resolved in a separate phase. This deadlock resolution phase activates new elements and allows the computation to proceed.

2.2.4 LocusRoute

LocusRoute [Ros88] is a global router for VLSI standard cells. It has been used to design real integrated circuits and results in a high-quality routing. The LocusRoute program exploits parallelism by routing multiple wires in a circuit concurrently. Each processor executes the following loop: It picks a wire to route from the task queue, explores alternative routes for the wire, and finally chooses the best route and places the wire there. The central data structure used in LocusRoute is a grid of cells called the *cost array*. Each row of the cost array corresponds to a routing channel. LocusRoute uses the cost array to record the presence of wires at each point, and the congestion of a route is used as a cost function for guiding the placement of new wires. Although the cost array is accessed and updated simultaneously by several processors, no locking is needed because the effect of the occasional loss of an update is tolerable. Each routing task is of a fairly large grain size, which prevents the task queue from becoming a bottleneck.

2.2.5 Cholesky

Cholesky performs a parallel Cholesky factorization of a sparse matrix. It uses a dynamically scheduled version of the supernodal fan-out method [RoG90]. The matrix is divided into supernodes, each of which is a set of columns with identical nonzero structure in the factor. Supernodes are further divided into conveniently sized chunks of columns called *panels*. A panel receives updates from other panels to its left in the matrix. Once it has received all of its updates, it is placed on the task queue. A free processor pulls the panel off the queue and performs all the modifications done by this panel. These modifications in turn yield other ready panels that are placed on the task queue.

The principal data structure of Cholesky is the structure used to hold the matrix itself. Since the matrix is sparse, it is stored in a compressed manner similar to the method used in SPARSPAK [GLN80]. The primary operation that needs to be performed repeatedly is the addition of a multiple of one column of the matrix to another column. Contention occurs for the task queue and for column modifications. Both of these cases are protected by locks.

2.2.6 Barnes-Hut

Barnes-Hut [SHT+92] is a hierarchical *N*-body gravitational simulation. Each body is modeled as a point mass and exerts forces on all other bodies in the system. To speed up the interbody force calculations, groups of bodies that are sufficiently far away are abstracted as point masses. In order to facilitate this clustering, physical space is divided recursively (forming an octree) until each cell contains at most one body. The tree representation of space has to be traversed once for each body and rebuilt after each time step to account for the movement of bodies.

The principal data structure of Barnes-Hut is the tree itself, which is implemented as an array of bodies and an array of space cells that are linked together. Bodies are assigned to processors at the beginning of each time step in a partitioning phase. Each processor calculates the forces exerted on its own subset of bodies. The bodies are then moved under the influence of those forces. Finally, the tree is regenerated for the next time step. There are several barriers for separating different phases of the computation and successive time steps. Some phases require exclusive access to tree cells, and a set of distributed locks is used for this purpose.

2.3 Simulation Environment

We use a simulated multiprocessor environment to study the execution behavior of our applications. The simulation environment consists of two parts: a reference generator that executes the parallel applications and an architectural simulator that models the memory system of the multiprocessor. We use Tango-Lite [Gol93] as our reference generator. Tango-Lite works by augmenting the assembly code at places of interest—in our case, memory references and synchronization events. The application is run in native mode on a uniprocessor, but different processes (threads) of the parallel application are interleaved so as to preserve the proper ordering between global events. Instruction execution time (in cycles) loosely follows that of the MIPS R3000 processor. The memory system simulator models caches, memories, and an interconnection network. It feeds back timing information to the reference simulator to facilitate the correct interleaving of global events (i.e., execution-driven simulation as opposed to trace-driven simulation).

Caches are kept coherent using a directory-based invalidating cache coherence protocol similar to the DASH protocol (see Chapter 6). Architectural parameters such as cache sizes and memory latencies can be varied for different studies. Many of our studies use infinite caches, in which case the cache line size is not important. For studies with finite caches, the default cache line size is 64 bytes unless otherwise noted.

When running the applications, we generally only measure application behavior for some portion of the parallel execution section of the code. We do this because the effect of serial start-up and finish code in simulation runs with reduced data sets and run lengths is much larger than in real runs, where the parallel section dominates. For the applications with multiple repetitive steps (MP3D, Water, PTHOR, Barnes-Hut), we measure only a few steps, and we start with the second step to allow the caches to warm up. For the other two applications (LocusRoute and Cholesky), only the parallel section of the code is measured.

2.3.1 Basic Program Characteristics

Table 2-2 gives an overview of the characteristics of the six applications when run with 64 processors. For each application, the input data set used for the runs is shown. Next, the table gives the total number of cycles run by all processors, the number of data references, and the breakdown into reads and writes. The numbers of shared reads and shared writes are also shown. In addition to absolute numbers, the shaded columns list the number of references in each category as a fraction of all data references.

The total cycles executed is roughly equivalent to the total instructions executed. There are two reasons for differences between the two numbers: multicycle instructions and wait cycles during synchronization operations. *Multicycle instructions* are instructions that cannot be executed in a single cycle, such as floating-point arithmetic instructions. *Wait cycles* are introduced during synchronization operations; they advance the cycle count but cannot be counted as useful instructions.

In our studies, private and shared references are distinguished as follows. By default, all data except stack references are in "shared space" and are potentially shared. However, our applications use the ANL *G_MALLOC* macro to allocate data that can be accessed by more than one process. Only this special data space is considered shared here; all other data are private. We define *shared blocks* to be those that are in the shared data space. We define *shared references* to be reads and writes to shared blocks. Note that depending on the task distribution strategy used and the dynamics of a particular run, it is possible that some shared blocks are referenced by only one process during the entire run. Thus our definition of *shared* is aggressive, not conservative.

From Table 2-2, we see that the proportion of shared references varies considerably from application to application. For example, the fraction of shared references is only 9.1% for Barnes-Hut, but 63% for MP3D. In Barnes-Hut, each update of the position of a particle requires a sizeable amount of local calculation. Thus updates to the states of the particles are relatively infrequent, and the fraction of shared references is very low. In MP3D, on the other hand, most of the data manipulation occurs directly on the shared data, and hence the proportion of shared references is large. Although these variations are not unexpected, since they depend closely on the nature of the application and the way in which it is parallelized, they are indicative of the variety in the applications being evaluated. The ratio between shared reads and writes varies from 1.5:1 for MP3D to about 30:1 for Barnes-Hut. Overall, read/write ratios for shared data tend to be larger than typical uniprocessor read/write ratios.

TABLE 2-2

Basic Application Characteristics (64 Processors)

APPLI-CATION	INPUT DATA SET	TOTAL CYCLES (mill.)	DATA REFER-ENCES (mill.)	READS	WRITES	SHARED READS		SHARED WRITES	
				(mill.) %	(mill.) %	(mill.)	%	(mill.)	%
MP3D	50 K molecules, test.geom (2352 cells), 5 steps	49.5	13.5	8.6 64	4.9 36	5.1	38	3.4	25
Water	256 mols, 3 steps	323	54.0	37.4 69	16.6 31	5.7	11	0.84	1.6
PTHOR	RISC (5 K elements), 5 steps	82.7	16.0	13.3 83	2.8 17	6.9	43	1.1	6.7
LocusRoute	Primary1 (8.7 K cells, 0.9 K wires)	199	16.2	12.4 76	3.8 24	6.8	42	1.1	6.7
Cholesky	grid63	90.4	9.2	6.5 70	2.7 30	4.2	46	0.86	9.3
Barnes-Hut	1024 bodies, 3 steps	150	28.6	17.2 60	11.4 40	2.5	8.8	0.081	0.3

2.4 Parallel Application Execution Model

We now introduce a model for parallel application execution. In order to help explain parallel application behavior, we divide total application run time into several components:

1. Busy time doing useful work
2. Busy time doing redundant work
3. Idle time waiting for synchronization
4. Idle time due to memory latency
5. Idle time due to the latency of synchronization

When the processor is executing instructions, it is said to be busy. Busy time is divided into time spent on useful work and time spent on redundant work. Useful work is the work that is performed to accomplish the task of the program and is the same as what would be required in a uniprocessor application. Redundant work is due to parallelization. It typically encompasses the work required to do the parallelization itself and redundant calculations performed by more than one processor in order to avoid interprocessor communication.

When the processor is not executing instructions, it is said to be idle. It is either waiting for synchronization or is encountering a long-latency memory or synchronization operation. When the processor is waiting on synchronization, it is typically waiting for another process to reach that synchronization point in the program. For example, if there is a critical section that is becoming a bottleneck in the application, many processors could be waiting to obtain the lock protecting the critical section while a given processor is in the critical section. The remaining idle time results from the long latency of completing memory references, such as a cache misses, or synchronization operations, such as barriers. In our studies we do not

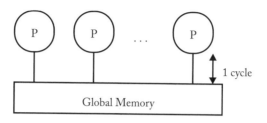

FIGURE 2-1 *PRAM Memory Model.*

distinguish between latency resulting from memory accesses and latency resulting from synchronization accesses. Since memory references are much more frequent, they will generally dominate this category.

It is important to recognize that synchronization operations cause two different kinds of idle time in this model: (1) there is the latency to complete the sync operation even when there is no interprocessor synchronization to accomplish (e.g., the latency to obtain an unlocked lock), and (2) there is the time to accomplish the synchronization (e.g., time spent waiting on another processor to free up a lock).

The experimental results of the following sections use a processor model of a simple pipelined RISC processor. Instructions are issued one per cycle and complete in order. Floating-point latencies are on the order of a few cycles and cannot be overlapped (floating point unit is not pipelined).

2.5 Parallel Execution under a PRAM Memory Model

We start the study of the execution behavior of our applications using a very simple parallel random access memory (PRAM) memory model [FoW78]. A PRAM is an ideal parallel memory that can satisfy a request from every processor in every cycle, even if multiple references are to the same location. Under this model, all memory and synchronization references complete in a single cycle (see Figure 2-1). Since memory latency is nonexistent, components 4 (idle time due to memory latency) and 5 (idle time due to synchronization latency) of our execution model disappear completely. A uniprocessor application would have only component 1 (busy time doing useful work). A parallel application adds component 2 (busy time doing redundant work) and component 3 (idle time waiting for synchronization).

Figure 2-2 shows the magnitude of the different execution time components for our applications on 64 processors. The lowest black bar is the useful work component. The larger this component, the greater the speedup obtained under this ideal memory system model. MP3D, Water, and Barnes-Hut all show useful work fractions in the 80–95% range. These are fairly regular scientific codes that allow for good speedups. PTHOR and Locus-Route are much less regular, and much more redundant work is done to manage the parallelism, limiting useful work to the 30% range. Cholesky is a different case again. The problem with Cholesky is that the amount of available parallelism decreases as the matrix factorization proceeds, leading to load-balancing problems and a large idle fraction due to synchronization wait.

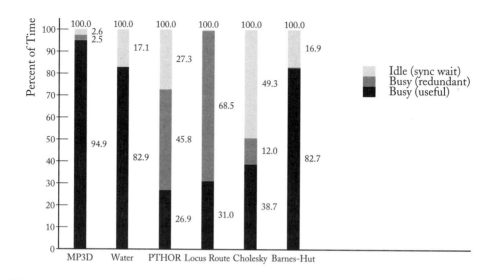

FIGURE 2-2 *Execution Time Breakdown with PRAM Memory Model (64 Processors).*

Table 2-3 summarizes the speedups obtained using the PRAM memory model. The speedups follow directly from the busy fractions seen in Figure 2-2. MP3D, Water, and Barnes-Hut all show very good speedups, while the speedups obtained with PTHOR, Locus-Route, and Cholesky are less spectacular. The speedups of Cholesky and LocusRoute are limited by the relatively small problem sizes we are able to simulate. With larger problems, they would both obtain better speedups, but simulation time would be unreasonably long. PTHOR, on the other hand, is not expected to achieve much better speedups even with a much larger input circuit because the circuit connectivity and topology limit the amount of available parallelism.

TABLE 2-3

PRAM Model Speedups

APPLICATION	SPEEDUP
MP3D	61/64
Water	53/64
PTHOR	17/64
LocusRoute	20/64
Cholesky	25/64
Barnes-Hut	53/64

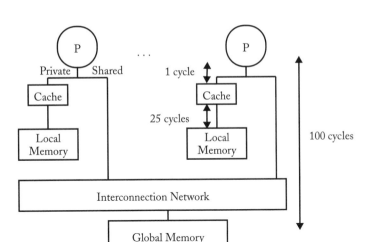

FIGURE 2-3   *Uncached Memory Model.*

2.6   Parallel Execution with Shared Data Uncached

The PRAM model demonstrates the speedup inherent in the parallel application, what might be called the *algorithmic speedup.* It does not, however, account for communication costs and their impact on load-balancing. In any real machine, communication is not free and is often the determining factor for application performance. In this section we examine application behavior using a more realistic memory system model. We treat all shared data as uncached with a latency of 100 cycles. Private data are still cached (using 256-KByte direct-mapped caches, with 64-byte lines), with a miss penalty of 25 cycles. These parameters are chosen to represent a memory system that allows local data to be cached and refilled from local memory, while all shared data is uncached and located on the far side of the interconnection network (see Figure 2-3). Instruction caches are assumed to be perfect (always hit).

Figure 2-4 shows the resulting breakdown of execution time. This graph is similar to the previous one, except that each bar now includes an additional category, idle time due to latency (both memory and synchronization). From the graph we see that latency-induced idle time dominates the execution time for all applications. Only the applications with a low fraction of shared references (Water and Barnes-Hut) still have sizeable portions of busy time. Although the absolute amount of busy time is the same as in the PRAM model, the relative fraction of busy time is much smaller. In other words, the applications are running much more slowly because of the increased memory latency. Any architectural improvement of execution time of these applications has to address memory latency as the first-order effect.

As an aside, we note that although the latency-induced idle time is due to both cache misses on private data and uncached shared-data accesses, private data cache miss rates are extremely low. Thus by far the largest component of memory latency results from shared references in this model.

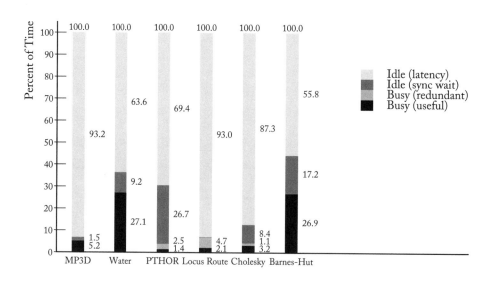

FIGURE 2-4 *Execution Time Breakdown with Shared Data Uncached.*

2.7 Parallel Execution with Shared Data Cached

Shared-data latency can be cut dramatically by allowing shared data to be cached. However, caching of shared data raises the cache coherence problem, which must be solved to retain correct memory semantics. The cache coherence protocol should match common sharing patterns, in order to minimize coherence overhead in the form of memory system traffic and system activity at the processor caches. We have chosen to use an invalidating cache coherence protocol for the reasons presented in Chapter 1 (Section 1.2.2.1).

Choosing an appropriate cache size for this study is a difficult problem. The data sets we are using have been scaled down to make simulation runs possible in a limited amount of time. If we were to use data caches of the magnitude employed in real shared-memory multiprocessors today—256 KBytes and up—the caches would look essentially infinitely large compared to the scaled-down data sets. The problem of scaling down caches in architectural studies is a complex one and has been addressed in some detail by Weber [Web93]. For these studies, we have chosen to use two different sets of cache sizes: infinite and scaled caches. Using infinite caches limits all misses to coherence misses (i.e., misses induced by actual sharing and invalidation by another processor). For the second set of results, the caches are scaled to obtain the miss rates that might be expected from a run with a large data set on a machine with large caches. The resulting scaled cache sizes are shown in Table 2-4. Compared with using infinite caches, using scaled caches increases the miss rates because some replacement misses are now included as well. We expect the actual miss rates of full-sized applications on a real machine to be roughly equal to the results obtained with scaled caches, but definitely higher than the results obtained with infinite caches.

The memory system model being used for this study is shown in Figure 2-5. All data are now allowed to be cached. The cache line size is 64 bytes. Cache hits still only take a sin-

TABLE 2-4

Scaled Cache Sizes

APPLICATION	CACHE SIZE
MP3D	4 K
Water	32 K
PTHOR	4 K
LocusRoute	64 K
Cholesky	32 K
Barnes-Hut	4 K

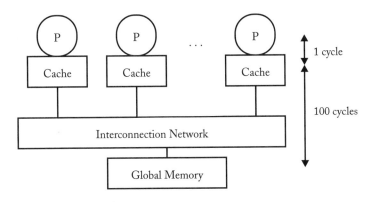

FIGURE 2-5 *Cached Memory Model.*

gle cycle, while cache misses are satisfied from global memory on the other side of the interconnection network. Cache miss latency is set at 100 cycles.

Let us start by looking at the results obtained with infinite caches (Figure 2-6). Compared with the uncached shared-data case shown previously, there is a marked reduction in idle time due to memory latency. Useful busy time is correspondingly larger. All applications see an execution time reduction by a factor of 2.5, and some almost by a factor of 10. Clearly, caching of shared data is a big help in reducing the idle time due to memory latency.

Let us now look at the results obtained with scaled caches. In Figure 2-7 we see that although the increased miss rates over infinite caches have reduced the proportion of useful busy time, we still get a respectable reduction in latency-induced idle time compared with that of the uncached model. This translates to reductions in execution time. Most applications show execution time reductions by factors of 2–4 over the uncached model; LocusRoute execution time is reduced by a factor of 8. Clearly, allowing shared data to be cached is a very important technique for decreasing processor idle time and improving parallel application performance.

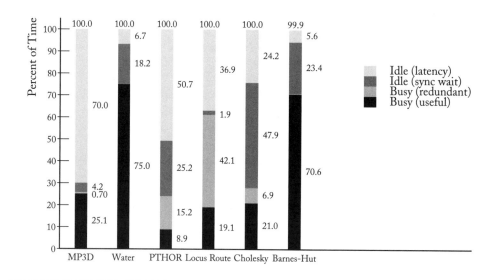

F I G U R E   2 - 6 *Execution Time Breakdown with Shared Data Cached (Infinite Caches).*

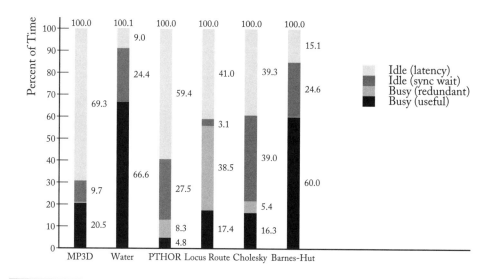

F I G U R E   2 - 7 *Execution Time Breakdown with Shared Data Cached (Scaled Caches).*

2.8 Summary of Results with Different Memory System Models

In Section 2.4 we introduced a model for studying the execution of parallel applications. Total execution time is broken down into two components: processor busy and processor idle time. Each component is further broken down according to the cause of the busy or idle state of the processor. We then analyzed the behavior of our applications under different memory models. When using an ideal PRAM memory model, only synchronization and redundant work produce nonuseful cycles, and the processor busy fraction due to useful work was generally quite high. When we introduced a more realistic memory system model with real latencies and shared data uncached, the idle time due to memory and synchronization latency dominated execution time. Finally, we allowed shared data to be cached. Under this memory system model, idle time due to memory latency was reduced significantly, resulting in reductions of total execution times by factors of 2–8 depending on the application. Thus, reducing the average memory latency is an extremely important factor in obtaining good performance from parallel applications.

2.9   Communication Behavior of Parallel Applications

We have seen that reducing average memory latency due to shared data is crucial in obtaining good performance from parallel applications. We now study the communication behavior of shared data in parallel applications in order to better understand what can be done to reduce processor idle time caused by memory and synchronization latency. We start by looking at the communication-to-computation ratios of the applications, and then we look at the sharing behavior of the applications in detail, using invalidation patterns as the vehicle of study. *Invalidation patterns* are the patterns of cache line invalidations observed when a shared-memory application is run under an invalidating cache coherence protocol.

2.10   Communication-to-Computation Ratios

The PRAM memory model can be simulated by using caches that have no miss penalty—all accesses take a single cycle. This model also allows us to make a convenient measurement of the communication-to-computation ratios of the applications. The computation effort is simply estimated to be the total number of busy cycles. The communication traffic is found using cache misses. If we use infinite caches and an invalidating cache coherence scheme, only coherence invalidations can cause cache misses. The line size is kept equal to the dominant data type size. Thus, the total number of misses multiplied by the size (in bytes) of each access is the ideal data traffic. It is definitely a lower limit for communication traffic because only the data traffic itself has been counted, while coherence traffic and communication overhead has been ignored completely.

   The first column of Table 2-5 shows the communication-to-computation ratios of our applications using this simple method. Overall, MP3D has by far the largest communication-to-computation ratio (0.224 bytes per cycle per processor). This is because, for each particle moved, the particle's effect on the space array has to be communicated to all other processors that have particles in that portion of space. Cholesky and PTHOR have much lower communication-to-computation ratios than MP3D, but their ratios are higher than those of the remaining applications. In Cholesky, the major communication is the broadcasting of the pivot column to the other processors. In PTHOR, the communication results from elements sharing nets and elements moving from one processor to another for load-balancing. In LocusRoute, communication is down to 0.027 bytes/cycle/proc. Communica-

TABLE 2-5

Communication-to-Computation Ratios

APPLICATION	IDEAL TRAFFIC		UNCACHED TRAFFIC		CACHED TRAFFIC	
	Data bytes/cycle/proc	Data MBytes	Data MBytes	Total MBytes	Data MBytes	Total MBytes
MP3D	0.224	11.1	34.0	122.3	148.5	193.1
Water	0.016	5.3	52.1	126.8	31.9	41.6
PTHOR	0.062	5.1	32.9	127.2	155.6	198.6
LocusRoute	0.027	5.3	30.2	116.8	64.6	87.4
Cholesky	0.075	6.8	34.0	91.8	62.5	77.4
Barnes-Hut	0.011	1.6	15.1	46.0	20.7	26.8

tion is required whenever wires are placed by two different processors in the same area of the cost array. Since the program is optimized to enhance geographic locality in the assignment of wires to processors, communication is reduced. Finally, both Water and Barnes-Hut have very small communication-to-computation ratios. Both of these applications have large sections of code where each processor is doing a lot of computation while requiring only very limited communication with other processors.

The second column of Table 2-5 gives the data traffic over the entire run of the application, assuming the same ideal PRAM model. This column is included to allow comparison with the remaining columns of the table. Again, the ideal data traffic shown in the second column is the minimum data traffic that is required by the communication patterns of the application and ignores both communication overhead and coherence traffic.

The rest of Table 2-5 shows the traffic volume for the uncached and cached memory system models. The third column shows data traffic generated when shared data is not allowed to be cached. Data traffic is made up of the data only, 4 or 8 bytes for every shared read or write, depending on access size. Data traffic is many times larger than ideal data traffic when shared data is not cached. Uncached data traffic is between 3 times larger (MP3D) and almost 10 times larger (Water) than ideal data traffic. The fourth column adds overhead traffic to data traffic, yielding total traffic for the uncached model. Overhead traffic is made up of the address and routing information required to access memory and return the data to the requesting processor. For writes, we assume 4 bytes of address and 4 bytes of routing/command information. For reads, there is a request packet, consisting of 4 bytes of address and 4 bytes for routing/command, and a reply packet, which again has 4 bytes for routing/command in addition to the data being returned. Overhead traffic is a factor of 1.5–3 times larger than data traffic. Thus, we see that when shared data cannot be cached, the required traffic volume is dramatically larger than the ideal traffic.

Finally, the rightmost two columns of Table 2-5 show the amount of traffic generated when caches are used, and an invalidation-based protocol is used to keep the caches coherent. We again assume scaled caches and a 64-byte line size here. Comparing the amount of data traffic required when caches are used with the uncached case described previously, we see that there is only one application for which caches reduce the amount of data traffic (Water). In Water the data objects (molecules) are large, and a large proportion of each cache line moved is actually used. In all other applications the data traffic has gone up in comparison with the uncached case. Data traffic now includes write-backs and transfers between caches; in the uncached case, data traffic included only the data required to be transferred by the read or write operation. In addition, only a small fraction of each cache line fetched may actually be used. For some applications, where the underlying data objects are smaller than the 64-byte cache lines (MP3D, PTHOR), the cached data traffic is about 5 times as large as the uncached data traffic. If we add overhead traffic, we get the total traffic shown in the rightmost column of Table 2-5. For the cached case, the overhead traffic includes address and routing/command information for all messages as well as overhead messages required for the coherence protocol, such as invalidation messages and acknowledgments. Although the coherence protocol requires additional messages, the overhead is seen to be only about one-third of the data traffic. This situation stands in sharp contrast with the uncached case, where the overhead was a factor of up to 3 times larger than the data traffic. Overhead traffic is less important for the cached case because overhead is amortized over larger units of data transfer: the 64-byte cache lines.

To summarize, we have seen that realistic memory system traffic (including message overhead, processors communicating with memory rather than with each other, and added messages required for a coherence protocol) is much larger than the ideal traffic volume that needs to be communicated in these parallel applications. When shared data is uncached, the data traffic is between 3 and 10 times larger than the ideal traffic. This scheme incurs an additional factor of 1.5 to 3 in overhead for address and routing information. When shared data is cached, we generally do not get a savings in data traffic. Only one application has a reduced data traffic volume when caches are introduced. All others have a rise in data traffic by up to a factor of 5. Looking at overhead of the caching scheme, we find that it is generally only about a third of the data traffic. Thus, the total traffic of the cached scheme is less than that of the uncached scheme for four of the applications. In the remaining two applications (MP3D and PTHOR), the cached scheme generates about 1.5 times as much traffic as the uncached scheme. So, although the caching of shared data improves the run-time performance of the applications dramatically, it generally does not reduce the data traffic dramatically.

Although there may be a reduction in total traffic, bear in mind that the bandwidth requirements of the cached scheme are larger than those of the uncached scheme because there is such a dramatic reduction in run time. Table 2-6 compares the bandwidth requirements of the three memory system models presented. The first column repeats the ideal data traffic column from Table 2-5 using the PRAM model. The second column shows bandwidth requirements using the uncached model. Although total traffic has gone up substantially, bandwidth requirements have not increased correspondingly because of the large increase in execution time. Finally, the rightmost column shows bandwidth requirements for the cached model. For all but one application (Water) the bandwidth requirements have gone up when moving from the uncached to the cached model. For one application (MP3D)

TABLE 2-6

Bandwidth Requirements

APPLICATION	PRAM MODEL	UNCACHED MODEL	CACHED MODEL
	Data bytes/cycle/proc	Total bytes/cycle/proc	Total bytes/cycle/proc
MP3D	0.224	0.136	0.840
Water	0.016	0.129	0.103
PTHOR	0.062	0.083	0.434
LocusRoute	0.027	0.040	0.247
Cholesky	0.075	0.086	0.365
Barnes-Hut	0.011	0.100	0.130

bandwidth requirements have gone up by a factor of 6 because execution times have been reduced substantially. Caching shared data does not always decrease the total traffic and usually increases the bandwidth requirements, sometimes dramatically.

The overall magnitude of required memory system bandwidth is shown in bytes/cycle/proc and derived from a system modeling the equivalent of a 33 MHz MIPS processor. For a more modern processor running at 100 MHz, we might expect an increase of throughput by a factor of 10–20, which makes 1 byte/cycle/proc equivalent to 330 to 660 MBytes/sec/proc. Thus, the bandwidth magnitudes shown in Table 2-6 are not necessarily small.

2.11 Invalidation Patterns

In the previous section, we looked at the volume of communication traffic generated by our parallel applications. In this section, we take a deeper look at the underlying causes and characteristics of the communication. We use invalidation patterns as the vehicle of study of the communication behavior of the applications. As each application is run using infinite caches with a small line size (4 or 8 bytes, depending on the most common data type) and an invalidating cache coherence protocol, we can tell how many processors are sharing a given cache line by the number of invalidations that are generated by a write. We then relate each write and corresponding invalidation count back to the high-level data object that resides at the address of the write. We have identified several recurring sharing patterns and have introduced a classification of data objects in parallel applications [WeG89a]. We will be discussing the invalidation patterns in terms of this classification.

2.11.1 Classification of Data Objects

Data objects of parallel applications are classified according to their invalidation and thus sharing behavior. This classification allows us to explain a given application's invalidation patterns in terms of the underlying high-level data structures of that application. More importantly, it represents a model that enables us to predict an application's invalidation behavior for much larger number of processors and much larger problem size than is feasible for us to simulate.

We distinguish the following classes of objects:

1. Code and read-only data objects
2. Migratory objects
3. Mostly-read objects
4. Frequently read/written objects
5. Synchronization objects, both low- and high-contention

2.11.1.1 Code and Read-Only Data Objects

These objects cause very infrequent invalidations because they are written only once, at the time when the relevant page is first brought into memory, or when the data are initialized. A fixed database is a good example of read-only data.

2.11.1.2 Migratory Data Objects

These objects are manipulated by only one processor at any given time and written during each manipulation. Shared objects protected by locks often exhibit this property. While such an object is being manipulated by a processor, the object's data reside in the associated cache. When the object is later manipulated by some other processor, the corresponding cache entry in the previous processor is invalidated. Migratory objects occur frequently in parallel programs. The space cells in MP3D are a good example of migratory data. Each space cell is looked at by many processors over the complete run, but there is typically only one processor manipulating a given space cell at any one time. Migratory data usually cause a high proportion of single invalidations, irrespective of the number of processors working on a problem.

2.11.1.3 Mostly-Read Data Objects

Most references to these objects are reads with only occasional writes. An example is the cost array of LocusRoute. It is read frequently, but written only when the best route for a wire is decided. It is a candidate for many invalidations per write, because many reads by different processors occur before each write. However, since writes are infrequent, the overall number of invalidations is expected to be small.

2.11.1.4 Frequently Read/Written Objects

These objects are both read and written frequently. Although each write causes only a small number of invalidations, writes occur frequently, and so the total number of invalidations can be large. There are no examples of frequently read/written objects in our application set. However, we have encountered frequently read/written data objects in other applications. They are often caused by the misuse of a normal data object for synchronization purposes.

TABLE 2-7

Average Invalidation Characteristics

APPLICATION	AVERAGE INVALIDATIONS PER INVALIDATING WRITE	INVALIDATING WRITES PER 1,000 DATA REFERENCES	AVERAGE INVALIDATIONS PER 1,000 DATA REFERENCES
MP3D	1.0	190	190
Water	1.4	8.8	12
PTHOR	3.4	16	54
LocusRoute	1.8	36	66
Cholesky	1.0	75	75
Barnes-Hut	7.7	0.91	7.0

2.11.1.5 Synchronization Objects

These objects correspond to the synchronization primitives used in parallel programs; the most frequent examples in our applications are locks and barriers. We assume no special hardware support for synchronization; that is, synchronization objects are handled through the standard cache coherence protocol. Special synchronization support in hardware may well be required as the number of processors is scaled. We divide synchronization objects into two categories, low-contention and high-contention objects, since these two exhibit different invalidation behavior. Low-contention synchronization objects, such as distributed locks that protect access to a collection of shared data objects, usually have very few or no processes waiting on them. As a result, most often they cause zero or a very small number of invalidations. High-contention synchronization objects, on the other hand, usually cause frequent invalidations, and the invalidations may be large if there are many contending processes. A lock protecting a highly contended task queue is an example of such an object.

2.11.2 Average Invalidation Characteristics

Table 2-7 gives the average invalidation characteristics of the applications. We define an *invalidating write* to be a write to shared data that can cause invalidations (i.e., it is either a write miss or a write hit to clean data in the cache). This definition of invalidating writes also includes writes that cause no invalidations, simply because no other processor had the line cached at the time. Table 2-7 shows the average invalidations per invalidating write, the number of invalidating writes per 1,000 data references, and the number of invalidations per 1,000 data references, which is the product of the first two columns.

The number of invalidations per invalidating write is an important metric for cache coherence schemes because a large value indicates that a large amount of coherence traffic is incurred on each invalidating write. In addition, this number indicates the suitability of directory cache coherence schemes, which rely on the fact that not every cache in the system needs to be invalidated on every write. This number is two or less for all applications except PTHOR and Barnes-Hut, even though all runs are with 64 processors. Barnes-Hut has 7.7 invalidations per invalidating write. However, note that the frequency of invalidating writes is very low for Barnes-Hut (0.91 invalidating writes per 1,000 data references). In general, we see that either the invalidation size or the invalidation frequency is low. The product of average invalidations per invalidating write and number of invalidating writes per 1,000 data references gives the number of invalidations per 1,000 data references, shown in the right-most column of Table 2-7. This product is a good indicator of the amount of invalidation traffic that an application is expected to generate. We only give average numbers here, but we provide detailed information on the invalidation distributions in the next section.

2.11.3 Basic Invalidation Patterns for Each Application

In this section we present the results of the detailed analysis of the invalidations produced by each of the applications. This information is crucial to the design of cache coherence directories because the behavior of the directory depends in a large part on the application sharing patterns observed. For each application, we discuss the overall invalidation patterns, the high-level objects causing the invalidations, and the synchronization behavior. When discussing invalidations, we distinguish between *large* invalidations and *frequent* invalidations. A large invalidation is caused by a write to a line that is cached by many processors. Frequent invalidations are caused by frequent writes and need not necessarily be large invalidations.

We present the invalidation behavior of the applications with a series of graphs (see Figure 2-8, for example). Most importantly, there is the invalidation distribution graph, labelled (a) in the figures. This graph shows what proportion of invalidating writes causes 0, 1, 2, etc., up to 63 invalidations. Toward the right edge of the graph, invalidation sizes are grouped together in fours to make the graphs narrower. Invalidation distributions that contain a large proportion of small invalidations are desirable because they indicate that each write does not cause a large amount of invalidation traffic. This is an important factor for directory-based cache coherence schemes. The graph labelled (c) shows the composition of each of the bars of the invalidation distribution graph. Each bar of this graph is normalized to 100 and broken down into its data object components. With the help of this graph, we can tell which data objects cause the various features of the invalidation distribution graph. The graph labelled (d) gives a key to which shading pattern represents which data object and also shows the proportion of invalidating writes and invalidations that each object group is responsible for. The graph labelled (b) shows a breakdown of all data references by private/shared and read/write. Finally, we present a lock waiter distribution graph, labelled (e), which shows the distribution of waiting processes at all unlock operations. It is very similar to the invalidation distribution graph, but is specialized to locks instead of the shared data shown in the invalidation distribution graph. We indicate the number of barriers encountered in the text of the lock waiter distribution graph.

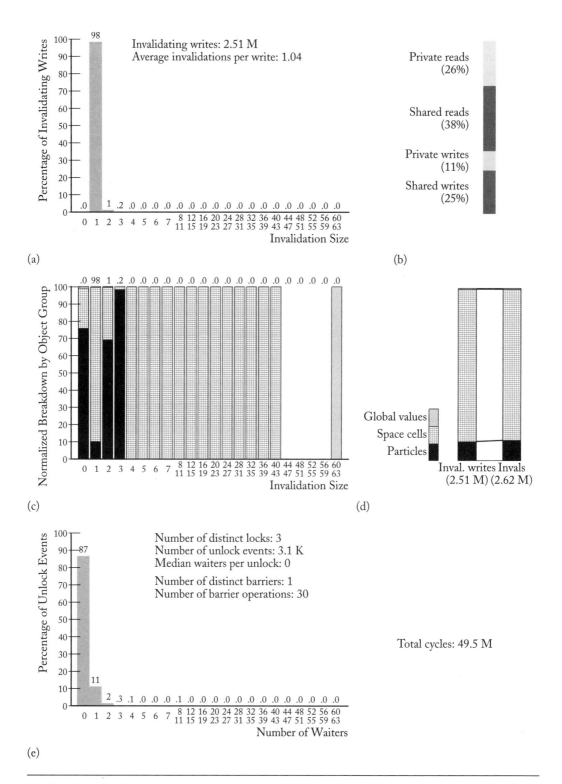

FIGURE 2-8 *MP3D Invalidation and Synchronization Behavior.*

2.11.4 MP3D

Figure 2-8(a) shows the invalidation distribution for MP3D, the three-dimensional particle simulator. The distribution is very much dominated by single invalidations. In fact, less than 2% of all invalidating writes cause two or more invalidations.

We can tell what data objects cause these invalidations with the aid of Figure 2-8(c) and (d). Most accesses to shared data by MP3D consist of updating the properties of a given particle or space cell. This results in a sequence of reads, closely followed by writes to the same locations. Depending on whether the data object was previously accessed by the same processor or not, either a single invalidation or no invalidation results. These data behave in a migratory fashion, with each interval of active use being very short.

For the particles, most of the time the same processor accesses the same set of particles and very few invalidating writes result. The exceptions are collisions between particles and the special set of reservoir particles that are used to keep track of the overall dynamic properties of the fluid. Most of these still produce single invalidations, but occasional double and triple invalidations result. The reservoir particles are almost exclusively responsible for the triple invalidations.

The space cells are not assigned to processors and are typically touched by many processors in one time step. However, most of the accesses are of the read-modify-write type, which again results in migratory behavior with single invalidations. The one exception is a value that keeps track of the collision probability within each cell. It is read by all processors with particles in that cell, but is updated only at the end of each time step. It is thus mostly-read and is responsible for the tiny number of large invalidations in MP3D (too small to be visible in Figure 2-8(a)).

Finally, there is a set of global variables that keeps track of such properties as the number of molecules in the stream. They are accessed very infrequently and do not have a large impact on the invalidation distribution.

Figure 2-8(e) shows the synchronization behavior of MP3D. Work is distributed statically in MP3D, and there is very little synchronization overhead. There are three locks that protect access to global counters, and there is very little contention for those locks. The number of waiters at unlock time is typically zero, with only 13% of all unlocks seeing one or more waiters.

2.11.5 Water

Figure 2-9(a) shows the invalidation distribution for the Water code. The distribution is made up almost entirely of single invalidations, with a small number of large invalidations near the halfway mark in the number of processors.

The main data structure in the Water code is a large array of records, one for each water molecule. Most of the time is spent calculating the pair-wise interaction of molecules. At the end of each interaction, a portion of the state of the two molecules is updated. This portion of the molecule data is migratory and causes only single invalidations. There is another portion of the molecule record that is also read while computing the pair-wise interactions, but it is updated only between time steps. Since the molecules allocated to a processor interact with only half of all the other molecules, at the end of each time step half of the processors

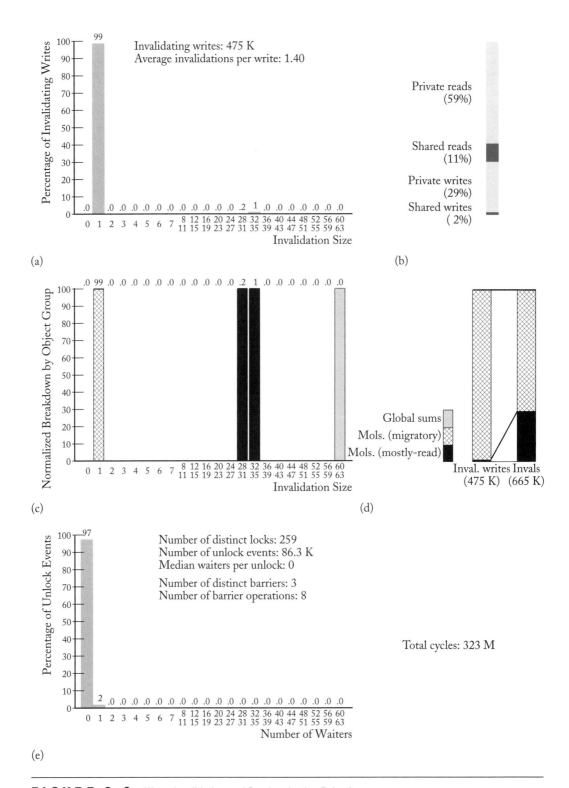

FIGURE 2-9 *Water Invalidation and Synchronization Behavior.*

have cached this mostly-read data. Consequently the update causes invalidations to be sent to half the total number of processors. Figure 2-9(c) illustrates this clearly.

There are also a small number of variables that hold global properties of the water molecule system. These again fall into the mostly-read category. They are read by all processors throughout and updated between time steps. At each update, invalidations are sent to all processors.

There is very little synchronization in Water, since the work is partitioned statically. There is a set of distributed locks, one for each molecule, and a small number of individual locks to protect the updates of global values. There is very little contention for the distributed locks. They are excellent examples of low-contention synchronization objects. Although there is some contention for the update of the global values, contention is low enough that it is not a significant factor in the overall lock-waiter distribution (Figure 2-9(e)).

2.11.6   PTHOR

Figure 2-10(a) shows the invalidation distribution for PTHOR. We again find that very few of the shared writes cause large invalidations. The basic data objects of PTHOR are the logic elements and net data structures. Besides these, there are activation lists for elements, free lists, and a set of global arrays ("per-process values") and global scalars ("global values"). The global arrays hold data on the progress of each process, while the global scalars are values such as the count of processors that has reached the deadlock phase of the algorithm. Refer to Figure 2-10(c) as we discuss each of the data object groups.

During the program run, the logic elements behave like migratory objects and produce mostly single invalidations. Some portions of the element data structure, however, are not modified by every processor that references them. These longer-lived values, such as the minimum valid time of an element, fit into the mostly-read category and result in larger invalidations when they are updated.

In PTHOR, sharing of net data is determined by the connectivity of the circuit. Some nets, such as the clock net, are attached to many elements. They are thus cached by many processors and cause large invalidations when written. Typically though, most nets connect only a few elements and writes to them cause a small number of invalidations.

The head pointers of the free lists for data structures are usually migratory. However, the head pointer is checked before taking an item off a given free list. If the list is empty, many processors could cache the head pointer and it becomes mostly-read for a short phase.

The largest proportion of invalidations in PTHOR result from the element activation lists, which act as task queues. The lists are typically traversed by many processes, thus fitting in the mostly-read category. They are also responsible for the bulk of the large invalidations.

The per-process values generally cause only small invalidations, except for the case of the per-process minimum-time value. This value is looked at by all processors when trying to determine whether a deadlock has been reached. During the deadlock resolution, the value is then written, causing invalidations in all processors.

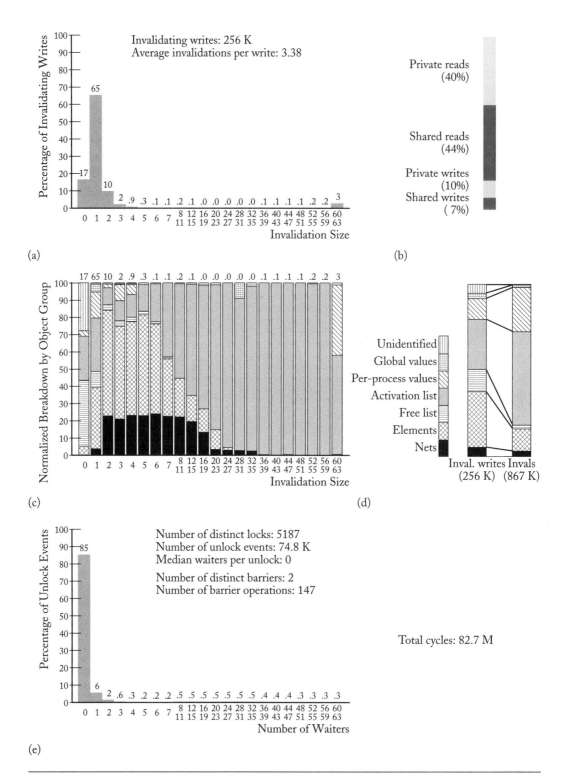

FIGURE 2-10 *PTHOR Invalidation and Synchronization Behavior.*

One single variable dominates the invalidations of the "global values" category—the count of the number of processors that have reached deadlock. This variable fits into the mostly-read category and causes some very large invalidations.

The zero invalidations seen in Figure 2-10(a) are caused by initialization of data structures after they are pulled off a free list.

The synchronization behavior shown in Figure 2-10(e) is dominated by element locks. These distributed locks show very little contention. Most of the time there are no waiters when an unlock occurs. The larger number of waiters at unlock operations are almost all due to a single lock that is used to protect the count of processors that have reached the deadlock phase of the Chandy-Misra simulation algorithm.

2.11.7 LocusRoute

Figure 2-11(a) shows the invalidation distribution for LocusRoute. There is a noticeable "tail" of invalidating writes with up to 15 invalidations, usually the sign of mostly-read data. By far the largest source of invalidations in LocusRoute is the global cost array—a good example of mostly-read data. It is frequently read while testing different routes for a wire, but is written only when a given wire route is decided. The average number of invalidations per invalidating write of the cost array is about three, but some writes can cause up to 20 invalidations. (These writes are too infrequent to show up in the invalidation distribution graph.) Small invalidations are much more common, because in LocusRoute there is enough locality to keep the number of processors actively sharing a region of the cost array small.

The object group labeled "density array" in Figure 2-11(c) and (d) is used in a read-modify-write fashion and thus causes only single invalidations.

The third large source of invalidating writes is a collection of variables, labeled "misc. data" in Figure 2-11(c) and (d), that are mostly migratory. The most frequently used variables of this set are the RouteRecords, which are used by the processors as they route a wire. They are reused by other processors for routing other wires, and cause only zero and single invalidations. A similar situation exists for the data structures related to the wire tasks, which are also migratory.

The group labeled "global values" represents a small number of global variables. These fall into one of two categories: global counts that are updated using read-modify-write operations and act as migratory objects, and global flags that are read by many processors, but modified infrequently and act as mostly-read objects.

The "implicit sync." group represents flags that are used for synchronization of the processes. They indicate, for example, when a task queue is full or empty. This kind of data object is usually mostly-read and can cause large invalidations, but it is accessed very infrequently, so it does not have a large impact on the overall invalidation distribution.

Figure 2-11(e) shows the synchronization behavior of LocusRoute. There are a total of 131 locks, 128 of which are distributed locks with very little contention. Of the remaining three, only two locks that control the task queues from which processors obtain their wire tasks have any noticeable contention. However, they are used infrequently, and thus do not cause a problem.

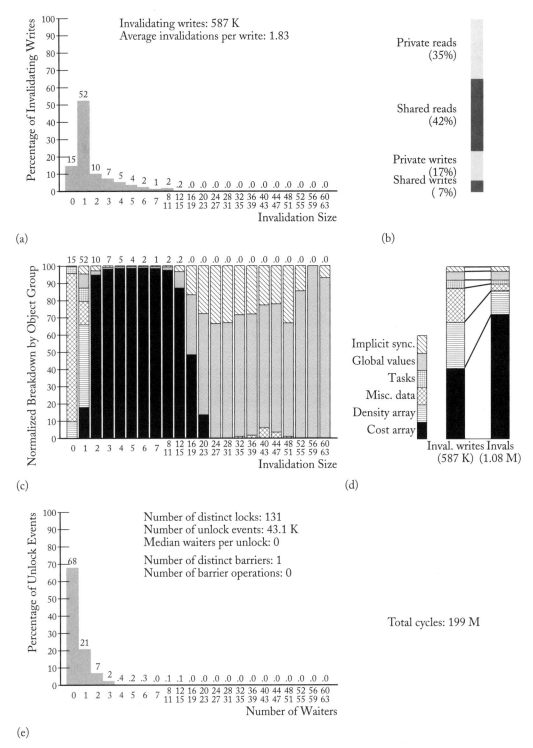

FIGURE 2-11 *LocusRoute Invalidation and Synchronization Behavior.*

2.11.8 Cholesky

Figure 2-12(a) shows that there are almost no invalidations larger than size 1 in Cholesky because during the calculation, a panel of the matrix being factored undergoes read-modify-write operations at each update. Once all updates are complete, the panel is read by the processor that uses it for further updates, but the panel is never written again. From Figure 2-12(d) we see that most of the invalidations are due to panel updates of the matrix being factored.

The second source of invalidations is the array of incoming counts, which is used to determine when a supernode is completely updated. This data is updated by processors as they modify the panels, and again causes almost exclusively single invalidations. The data labelled "done flag" and "task queue" produce almost no invalidations.

The synchronization behavior of Cholesky is shown in Figure 2-12(e). There are 256 distributed column locks, which show very little contention. Occasionally, there are one or two waiters when several processors want to update a column. The remaining lock controls access to the task queue and is responsible for all of the unlocks with a large number of waiters. There are a significant number of unlocks with around 40–55 waiters—an indication that the problem being solved is too small for 64 processors and that there is a load imbalance.

2.11.9 Barnes-Hut

The Barnes-Hut application is unique in that it has comparatively little migratory data. Most of the calculations are performed by the processors on their portion of the data set, which is mostly-read. Between time steps, the data are written, resulting in large invalidations (Figure 2-13(a)). The main data structure of Barnes-Hut is the cell-and-particle tree. We divide this structure into the particle and cell data (labelled "node data"), the links (labelled "tree"), and the root, which is part of the "global" data group.

The largest number of invalidations is caused by the node data, which are mostly-read. The second largest group of invalidations is caused by the link structures that make up the cell-and-particle tree. These structures are also mostly-read, with the result of relatively infrequent and large invalidations.

Finally, there is a set of global data. This set can be divided into two groups: a set of counters and the root of the cell-and-particle tree structure. The counters are always read and modified, so they only cause single invalidations. The root of the tree is mostly-read and is responsible for many of the very large invalidations. However, this structure is also accessed infrequently, and the overall number of invalidations is small.

Figure 2-13(e) shows the synchronization behavior of Barnes-Hut. Out of the 532 locks found in the application, 529 are distributed locks protecting the particle and cell structures. Each lock is used for several particle and cell structures. Further down in the tree these locks show almost no contention, but the higher nodes and especially the root node lock show some degree of contention. The remaining three locks protect global structures. Out of these, only the lock protecting the global counters has any contention.

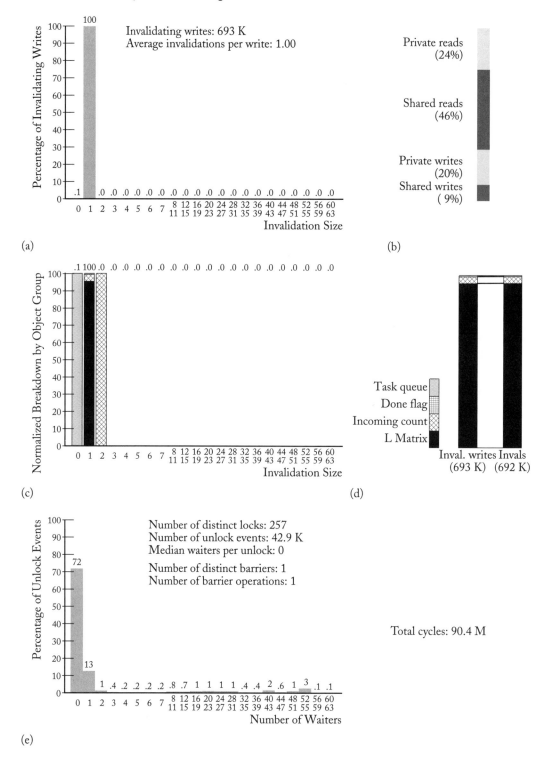

FIGURE 2-12 *Cholesky Invalidation and Synchronization Behavior.*

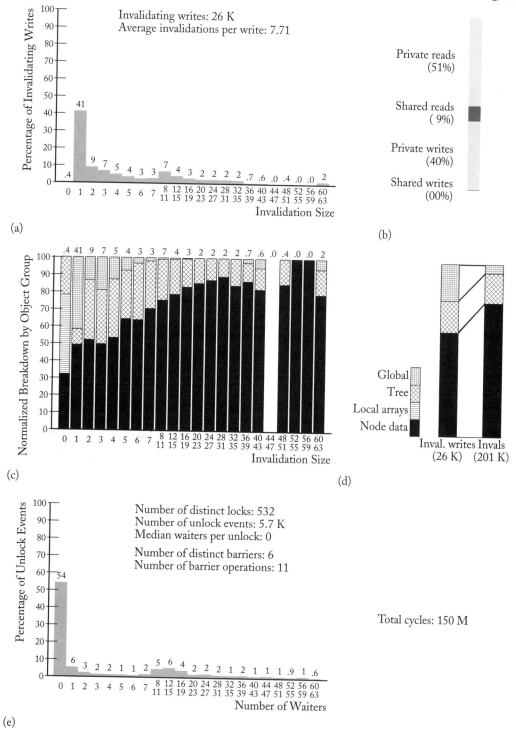

FIGURE 2-13 *Barnes-Hut Invalidation and Synchronization Behavior.*

2.11.10 Summary of Individual Invalidation Distributions

Most of the invalidation distributions of our applications were dominated by small invalidations, typically the result of migratory data, which cause single invalidations as the data object migrates from one cache to the next. Larger invalidations were caused by mostly-read data objects. By their very nature, these objects are written relatively infrequently. So we see that data objects are either not widely shared or not written frequently. This is a strong endorsement of invalidating cache coherence protocols and directory-based cache coherence. Synchronization objects have behavior that can be quite different from data objects. Low-contention synchronization objects cause few invalidations because the number of waiters is typically zero or small. High-contention objects can result in large invalidations and can also be accessed relatively frequently. These objects are the most likely target for hardware support.

In the remaining sections of this chapter we look at how the invalidation patterns observed in the applications change as we vary such parameters as the number of processors, the problem size, or the cache line size.

2.11.11 Effect of Problem Size

Since our studies rely on relatively slow simulations, we are forced to use relatively small data sets. To study the effect of problem size on invalidation distribution, we run the applications under the same conditions as before, with the same number of processors. The only change we make is that we vary the size of the problem being solved. We use three different data sets: one is the same data set used so far, and the other two are a data set twice the size and one half the size.

The general trend in invalidation distributions is to have the same or fewer invalidations per invalidating write when the problem size is increased. As the problem size increases, fewer objects are shared and shared data objects tend to be less widely shared. The sole exception is LocusRoute, where the size of invalidations is more a factor of circuit density rather than circuit size. The second important trend is a constant or decreasing frequency of invalidating writes as the problem size is increased. This trend can be attributed to a more favorable communication-to-computation ratio for the larger problem sizes. The amount of work that needs to get done generally scales at least as fast as the problem size, leading to equal or better communication-to-computation ratios when the problem size is increased.

2.11.12 Effect of Number of Processors

To study the effect of number of processors, we run the applications with 16 and 32 processors and contrast the resulting invalidation distributions with those previously obtained using 64 processors. We use the same simulation problem size for each of the runs with different number of processors.

Changing the number of processors affects two important areas of the invalidation distribution: number of invalidating writes and shape of the invalidation distribution. For our applications, generally the number of invalidating writes stay constant or increase slightly when the number of processors is increased because of the higher probability of a data item being shared when there are more processors. This behavior is illustrated nicely by Cholesky

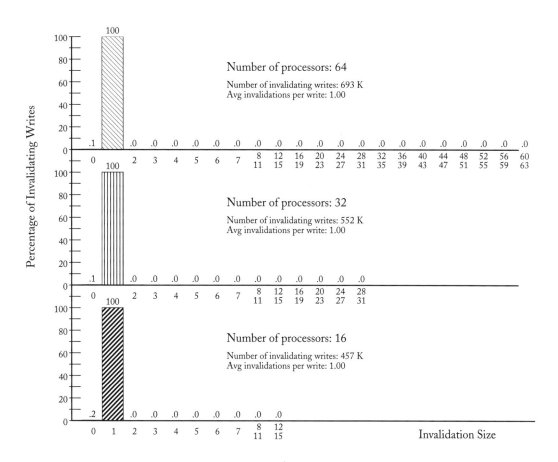

FIGURE 2-14 *Cholesky Invalidation Distribution with Different Numbers of Processors.*

(Figure 2-14). Here the average number of invalidating writes increases from 457 K to 693 K as we increase the number of processors from 16 to 64.

The trend in the number of invalidations per invalidating write is also flat or shows a slight increase with a larger number of processors. The major cause of larger invalidations is the mostly-read data in the applications. With more processors, a mostly-read data item has a greater chance of being accessed by a larger number of processors before each write, thus causing larger invalidations. The invalidation distributions of LocusRoute with different numbers of processors exhibit this trend (Figure 2-15).

The dominance of small invalidations in the invalidation distribution persists even for much larger numbers of processors. For applications dominated by migratory data, the single-invalidation peak does not shift as the number of processors increases. For applications with mostly-read data, there is a growth in invalidation size, but this growth is small even for large increases in the number of processors.

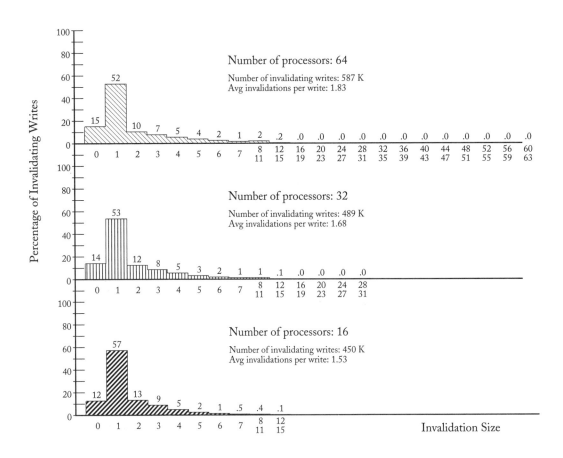

FIGURE 2-15 *LocusRoute Invalidation Distribution with Different Numbers of Processors.*

2.11.13 Effect of Finite Caches and Replacement Hints

So far all invalidation distribution results have been obtained with infinite caches. This arrangement has allowed us to study the true sharing patterns because a data item remains in a given cache from when it is first referenced until it is invalidated by another processor. In real machines, however, finite caches are used, and we can expect some changes in the invalidation distributions. In particular, finite caches increase the number of invalidating writes and decrease the size of invalidations. We discuss each of these effects in turn and then investigate their impact in our applications.

Invalidating writes increase with finite caches because a string of writes by a single processor to a given data item can cause multiple invalidating writes if that data item is replaced several times in between the writes. With infinite caches, only the very first write is an invalidating write because all further writes hit dirty data in the cache. The additional invalidating writes seen in the finite cache case never cause any invalidations, though. They are thus easily identified in the invalidation distributions and do not affect coherence traffic or machine performance.

Invalidation sizes decrease with finite caches because write-backs of dirty lines tell the directory that the line no longer resides in that cache. Invalidation sizes are always reduced by at most one. If a line that is dirty in a cache is written back and then becomes shared, a subsequent write causes one fewer invalidation than if the line had not been written back. The proportion of invalidations that are reduced by one depends on the amount of capacity and conflict misses, and on the fraction of lines that are typically dirty in the caches.

While write-backs tell the directory about replacements of dirty lines from the caches, we can take advantage of the replacement of clean lines as well, if we let the directory know about such replacements. This can be achieved with the aid of explicit messages that notify the directory that a given cache line has been replaced out of a particular cache. We call such messages *replacement hints*, indicating that they are a performance aid and do not need to be reliably sent or acknowledged. While write-backs of dirty lines reduce the number of invalidations caused by a particular invalidating write by at most one, replacement hints can potentially achieve much larger reductions in invalidation size. For example, if cache lines were always replaced before they were invalidated, invalidations would be completely eliminated.

To study the effect of finite caches on invalidation patterns, we use scaled caches. Unlike the cache scaling applied in Section 2.7 to preserve miss rates, here the caches are scaled in a way that preserves the probability of replacement-before-invalidation [Web93]. The probability of replacement-before-invalidation is the probability that a given cache line will be replaced before it is invalidated from the cache. If the line is replaced, it can affect the invalidation distribution through write-back or replacement hint messages. The resulting cache sizes are 32 KByte for Water, 4 KByte for PTHOR, and 2 KByte for Barnes-Hut.

Finite caches affect invalidation distributions because dirty write-backs inform the directory about cache line replacements. This effect is most pronounced for applications where the data size is large relative to the caches, and replaced data tends to be dirty. In PTHOR, the average number of invalidations per invalidating writes drops from 3.4 to 2.2 when going from infinite to finite caches (see Figure 2-16). Note that the invalidation distributions for the finite cache distributions (top two graphs) have been normalized to the infinite cache distribution to ease comparison between the graphs.

Migratory data, frequently read/written data, and mostly-read data that is only touched by a small number of processors have the highest chance of being found dirty in the caches. Hence the largest reductions in invalidation sizes are seen for single and other small invalidations.

Whereas dirty write-backs tell the directory about replaced lines that were dirty in the cache, replacement hints send information about clean lines that are replaced out of the caches. Their effect is thus greatest for mostly-read data, which tend to be clean in the caches. When the invalidation distribution is dominated by mostly-read data, such as with Barnes-Hut, the effect of replacement hints is significant. For Barnes-Hut the use of replacement hints decreases the average number of invalidations per invalidating write from 3.9 to 0.4 (see Figure 2-17). However, in the more common case, mostly-read data causes

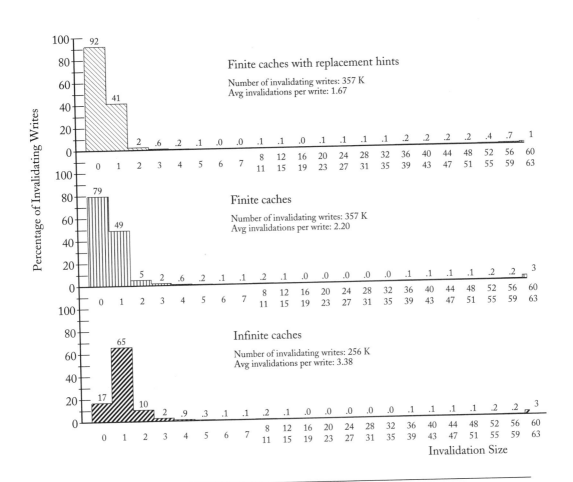

FIGURE 2-16   *PTHOR Normalized Invalidation Distribution with Finite (4-KByte) Caches.*

only a small fraction of invalidations and the effect of replacement hints is small (for example, Water in Figure 2-18).

Another factor to consider when evaluating replacement hints is memory traffic. While each replacement hint message can potentially save an invalidation/acknowledgment message pair, any replacement hint that does not save an invalidation adds to the overall memory traffic. From our simulations we have found that replacement hints result in a net increase in traffic by up to 25% [Web93]. Thus, replacement hints are not a traffic-saving measure. As we will see in Chapter 4, replacement hints may be desirable for some scalable directory organizations, though.

2.11.14   Effect of Cache Line Size

In the invalidation patterns presented in this chapter so far we have used a cache line size of 4 or 8 bytes, depending on the size of the most common data type. We will now look at invalidation distributions for three different cache line sizes—the default line size of 4 or 8

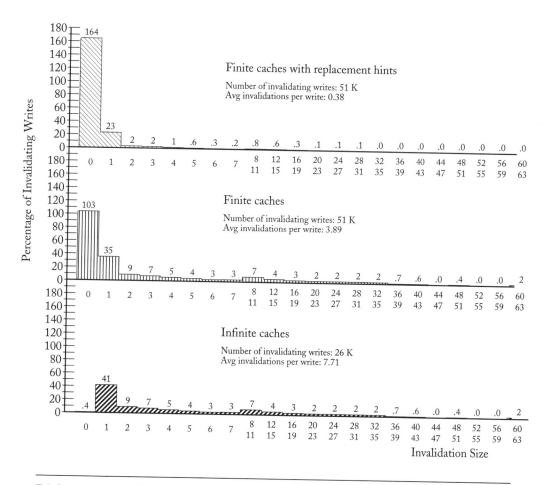

FIGURE 2-17 *Barnes-Hut Normalized Invalidation Distribution with Finite (2-KByte) Caches.*

bytes, a large line size of 256 bytes, and an intermediate size of 32 bytes—with infinite caches, so the 4- or 8-byte distribution corresponds to the base case studied in the previous sections.

The effect of cache line size on the number of invalidating writes depends on the size of the data objects in the program relative to the size of the cache lines. If the typical data objects are larger than the line size, we see a decrease in the number of invalidating writes as we increase the cache line size. This effect can be seen in all applications when the line size is increased from 4 bytes to 32 bytes. It is especially obvious when data objects are large, as is the case for MP3D, Water, and Barnes-Hut (see Figure 2-19), or when there is good reference locality that effectively creates larger objects, as is the case for LocusRoute (see Figure 2-20) and Cholesky. On the other hand, when the line size gets larger than the typical objects, several objects fit into each cache line, and additional invalidating writes are generated due to false sharing [EgK89a, TLH90]. MP3D, PTHOR, and Barnes-Hut (Figure 2-19) exhibit this trend when going from 32- to 256-byte lines.

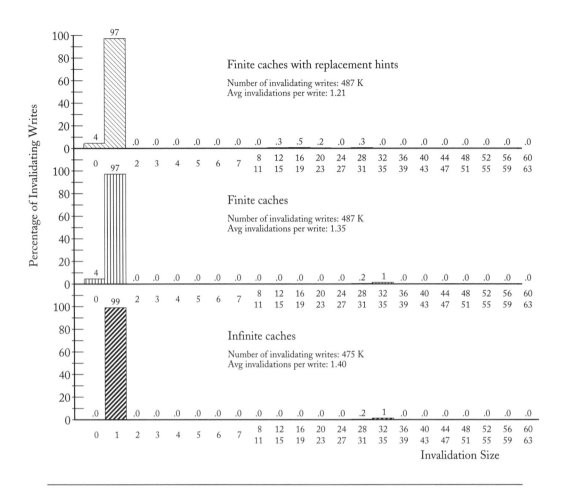

FIGURE 2-18 *Water Normalized Invalidation Distribution with Finite (32-KByte) Caches.*

Considering the effect of line size on the average size of invalidations, there are again several distinct effects that come into play. First, a larger line size is expected to increase the number of processors sharing a cache line (due to false sharing), thus increasing the size of invalidations. Second, depending on the spatial locality exhibited by different classes of objects (e.g., migratory versus mostly-read objects) in the program, an increased line size may reduce the number of invalidating writes in any section of the invalidation distribution. Third, additional invalidating writes caused by false sharing may add invalidations anywhere in the distribution. In the case of Barnes-Hut, when increasing the line size from 32 bytes to 256 bytes, for example, most of the additional invalidating writes cause small invalidations, thus skewing the distribution towards smaller invalidations (see Figure 2-19). Last, false sharing can also change the invalidation behavior of an object class. Often a single data object in a program contains a mix of migratory and mostly-read portions—for example, the molecule structures in Water. When the line size is small, these portions fall in distinct lines and exhibit their characteristic invalidation behavior. However, when the line size becomes

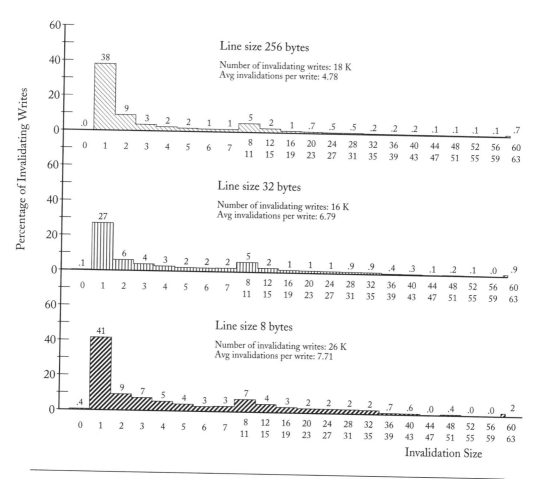

FIGURE 2-19 *Barnes-Hut Normalized Invalidation Distribution for Different Cache Line Sizes.*

large, false sharing causes all of the data structure to become migratory, thus reducing the number of large invalidations seen.

The effect of line size on invalidation distribution is complex and not easily predicted. In general though, we see a reduction in invalidations per invalidating write when going from 4- or 8-byte lines to 32-byte lines. At the same time there is a significant reduction in invalidating writes.

2.11.15 Invalidation Patterns Summary

In this section, we have looked at the behavior of shared data using invalidation patterns as our vehicle of study. Looking at each application in detail, we were able to relate the invalidation behavior to the underlying data objects in the applications and to identify several common classes of data objects.

After explaining the detailed invalidation behavior of the applications, we looked at the change in invalidation behavior while varying different parameters. Changing the problem

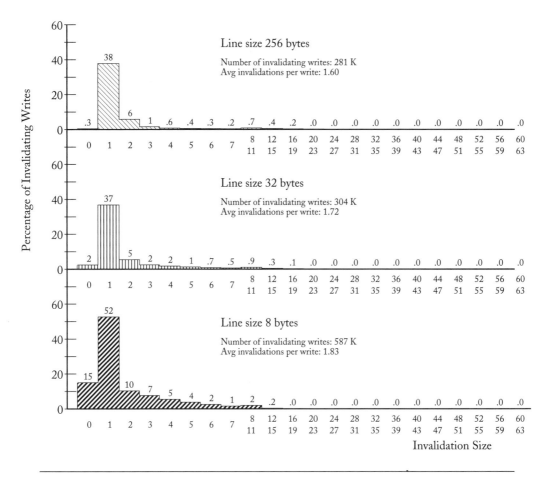

FIGURE 2-20 *LocusRoute Normalized Invalidation Distribution for Different Cache Line Sizes.*

size kept the invalidations per invalidating write the same, or decreased them slightly. The effect on frequency of invalidating writes was similar. Increasing the number of processors had the opposite effect. Both number of invalidations per invalidating write and frequency of invalidating writes remained the same or increased slightly. Using finite caches enables write-backs to decrease the number of invalidations per invalidating write by one. If replacement hints are used, much larger reductions in invalidation size are seen, especially for applications that are dominated by mostly-read data. The effect of changing the cache line size is more complex, and no simple trend is obvious.

2.12 Chapter Conclusions

In this chapter we looked at the execution behavior of a set of scientific/engineering applications. We started by presenting a model of execution time, breaking it down into the categories of processor busy and processor idle time, and then breaking each of these into subcategories, depending on the cause of the busy or idle state of the processor.

Next, we looked at application behavior under different memory models. In a simple PRAM memory model, only synchronization wait times produce any processor idle time, and the processor utilization is generally quite high. However, when more realistic memory system models are introduced, a significant portion of total time is spent on idle time due to memory latency. Allowing shared data to be cached significantly reduces this idle time and thus improves application performance.

Finally, we studied the sharing behavior of parallel applications, by looking at communication-to-computation ratios and invalidation patterns of these applications. Although ideal communication traffic was quite low for all applications (0.01 to 0.2 bytes/cycle/proc), introducing a real memory system model increases traffic by an order of magnitude or larger. For the uncached case, most of this traffic is due to address/command overhead. In contrast, for the cached case with 64-byte cache lines, most of the additional traffic is due to write-backs, transfers, and inefficient use of the data transferred. Because of the significantly reduced run time when shared data is cached, the bandwidth requirements are generally much higher than for the uncached case—as high as 0.4 to 0.8 bytes/cycle/proc for some applications.

Looking at the invalidation patterns generated when the applications were run under an invalidating cache coherence protocol, we found that data objects in parallel applications are generally either shared between very few processors or written infrequently. Most invalidating writes cause only a single invalidation, even for a wide range of problem sizes, numbers of processors, and cache line sizes. Thus, directory-based cache coherence using an invalidating protocol matches well with application behavior. The large fraction of migratory data is ideally suited to invalidation-based protocols, and the small average invalidations per invalidating write indicate that directories will not generate an excessive amount of coherence traffic.

CHAPTER

3

System Performance Issues

Realizing scalable performance depends upon both the hardware architecture and application software. The previous chapter touched on the software aspects of system performance. In this chapter, the focus is on the hardware aspects of attaining scalable performance while maintaining a shared-memory paradigm.

Scalable shared-memory performance relies on a scalable memory system. The fundamental performance of a memory system is given by its bandwidth and latency. The ideal memory system (i.e., a PRAM) provides unit time latency access to all memory, and it does so without any contention between processors. Clearly, an actual memory system has finite latency and cannot provide infinite bandwidth to all of memory. Techniques to deal with the problems of long latency and limited bandwidth in scalable shared-memory multiprocessors are the two major topics of this chapter.

Even in today's uniprocessor systems, unit access time to memory can only be sustained for the small fraction of memory that is cached. Although multiprocessor systems can match the cache performance of uniprocessors, latency to main memory in a shared-memory multiprocessor is inevitably longer than in a uniprocessor. This is because the memory is accessible to all processors and cannot be close to all of them given physical and logic fan-in limits. In a large-scale machine, latency becomes a bigger problem because the majority of memory must be accessed through an interconnection network.

A real memory system can only support a finite memory bandwidth. In particular, although it is possible to add memory banks when processors are added, the interconnect system between the processors and memory cannot provide linearly increasing bandwidth to all memory (e.g., provide a crossbar) without adding costs that grow larger than linearly (e.g., N^2 for a crossbar). Thus, although crossbars are implemented in small-scale machines (e.g., Cray X-MP), scalable systems must trade off a reduction in bandwidth per processor for cost per processor. Suitable network topologies, introduced in Chapter 1, include the hypercube [AtS88], 2-D and 3-D meshes, and multistage interconnection networks, such as Omega, Banyan, or Butterfly networks [Fen81]. As will be discussed further in

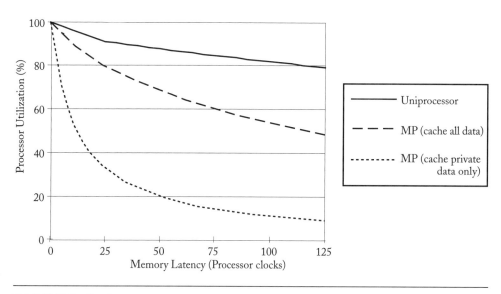

FIGURE 3-1 *Processor Utilization as a Function of Memory Latency.*

Section 3.4.1, additional bandwidth problems result from nonuniform reference patterns that underutilize some of the system's resources.

3.1 Memory Latency

Memory latency is the most critical performance issue in the design of a scalable shared-memory system because of the processor's essential dependence on memory access time. In a cache-coherent shared-memory multiprocessor, not only are memory access latencies higher than in a uniprocessor, but cache miss rates are higher, too. This is because data sharing causes invalidations and extra misses because of coherence. The effect on processor utilization can be dramatic. For example, assume a 100-MHz processor executes 20% load instructions, has a miss rate of 2%, and sees a 25-processor-cycle (250 ns) cache miss penalty, yielding a processor utilization of 91%. The solid line in Figure 3-1 gives processor utilizations for other memory latencies. In the multiprocessor case, if we assume 40% of memory references are to shared variables and 10% of these miss (representative of the miss rates seen for the parallel scientific applications of Chapter 2), processor utilization is much lower (79%), even assuming the same memory latency. For the larger latencies expected in typical multiprocessor systems, especially large-scale multiprocessors, processor utilization is lower still. The dashed line in Figure 3-1 shows processor utilization for different shared miss latencies, with private miss latency capped at 25 cycles. At a shared miss penalty of 100 processor cycles, processor utilization is down to 54%. Thus, even for a cache-coherent multiprocessor, it is not difficult to lose a factor of two in processor performance relative to the uniprocessor due to memory latency. Of course, if caching of shared data is not allowed, processor utilization falls even more dramatically with memory latency (down to 11% at 100-clock latency), as shown by the dotted line in Figure 3-1.

There are two fundamentally different ways to attack memory latency. The first set of techniques attempt to *reduce* memory latency. These techniques reduce the average time between when the processor issues a reference and when memory responds with the requested data. The best example of a latency reduction technique is caching. The second set of techniques to address memory latency attempt to *hide* it. These techniques overlap memory accesses with useful computation by the processor or with other communication. One latency hiding technique is prefetching data. Prefetching attempts to anticipate memory requests and brings the requested data closer to the processor before it is actually accessed. Thus, the delay for accessing the next location is overlapped with computation on the current data. Another technique to hide latency is multiple-context processors. In a multiple-context processor such as the Denelcor HEP [Smi81], the processor switches from task to task on a per clock basis, and memory operations can appear to occur in unit time if the latency to memory (in processor clock cycles) is equal to the number of tasks active at one time.

Fundamentally, all latency hiding techniques rely on parallelism within a single process or between processes to mitigate the delays of memory. In the case of the multiple-context processor, this parallelism is explicit. In the case of prefetch, the manipulation of the current data item must be independent from the value of the next data item in order that the computation can be executed before the return of the prefetched data. In both cases, if there were additional processors, each could manipulate the data in parallel. Thus, latency reduction is generally preferred to latency hiding, because the application parallelism utilized by the hiding techniques could be used instead to run the application faster over a larger number of processors if latency was lower. Furthermore, many applications have only limited parallelism, which impairs the effectiveness of the latency hiding techniques. Of course, memory latency can only be reduced so far, and latency hiding techniques are important in maximizing performance, especially in cases where large data sets or frequent interprocess communication lead to high cache miss rates. In this chapter, we consider latency reduction techniques first and then latency hiding techniques.

3.2   Memory Latency Reduction

As discussed in Chapter 2, caching of shared data significantly improves processor utilization because it reduces the effective latency of memory when cache hit rates are high. Because of the small latency of a cache, maximizing cache hit rates is the most important aspect of keeping overall memory latency low. The second most important aspect is to minimize the cache miss penalty.

As with uniprocessors, optimizing the cache's organization (i.e., size, associativity, and line size) can improve hit rates. Unlike uniprocessors, however, maintaining coherence between the processor caches can be a dominant factor in multiprocessor hit rates. These coherence misses are independent of the cache size and associativity. Cache line size can affect coherence misses (because of false sharing), as discussed in Section 2.11.14. In an attempt to limit excessive misses caused by false sharing, the line size used by most cache-coherent multiprocessors is relatively short (32 or 64 bytes).

Assuming false sharing is minimized, coherence misses are affected primarily by the actual cache coherence protocol. For example, support of a *clean-exclusive* state (this state is entered on a cache read miss when the block is uncached at the time of the cache fill) in the protocol [PaP84] reduces cache misses in the common case of a processor updating a location through a read-modify-write sequence. When there is actual processor-to-processor communication through shared-memory locations, however, an invalidation-based coherence protocol must cause cache misses. Some techniques attempt to delay or combine the implied invalidations [DBW+91], but maintaining coherence with invalidations will inevitably cause coherence misses. Update protocols can be used to eliminate these misses, but at the cost of substantial interconnect bandwidth to propagate updates [GDF94]. Unfortunately, these updates may not even represent real communication if the updated processor does not reread the updated location.

After minimizing cache misses, the next important task is to reduce the penalty of cache misses (see Section 1.2.1). Reducing the latency of these cache miss requests requires reducing the latency of the lower levels of the memory hierarchy. Generally, the levels of hierarchy below the cache include the following:

1. Additional levels of caches close to the processor, including structures such as cluster caches or snooping on the caches of neighboring processors

2. The main memory array that holds the requested location

3. A remote processor cache that holds the most up-to-date (i.e., dirty) copy of the location

The latency in accessing these levels, especially levels 2 and 3, is highly dependent on the latency of the interconnect network. The most obvious way to reduce latency is to use aggressive technology and implementation techniques to reduce the absolute time of accessing each level and traversing the network between the levels. While this technique is always desirable, it is not likely to be sufficient because the processor usually uses the same implementation technology as the memory system. Thus, the speed of memory in CPU clock cycles is likely to be large if the system is large. Even worse, given the significant investment in a given system and interconnect implementation, many systems eventually use next-generation processors with the previous-generation memory system. Thus, technology alone is insufficient, and architectural techniques must be used as well. In the next sections, we outline a number of the architectural techniques to reduce memory latency.

3.2.1 Nonuniform Memory Access (NUMA)

NUMA architectures attempt to reduce the average latency of memory by partitioning system memory and allocating a portion of memory to each processor node. While the most general definition of a NUMA architecture is simply a system with varying delays to different portions of memory, NUMA usually refers to systems in which nodes of the system include both processors and memory, as shown in Figure 3-2. The NUMA structure has been used on a number of systems (e.g., BBN Butterfly, Stanford DASH, and Cray T3D). For small systems, the NUMA structure reduces latency even if random locations are

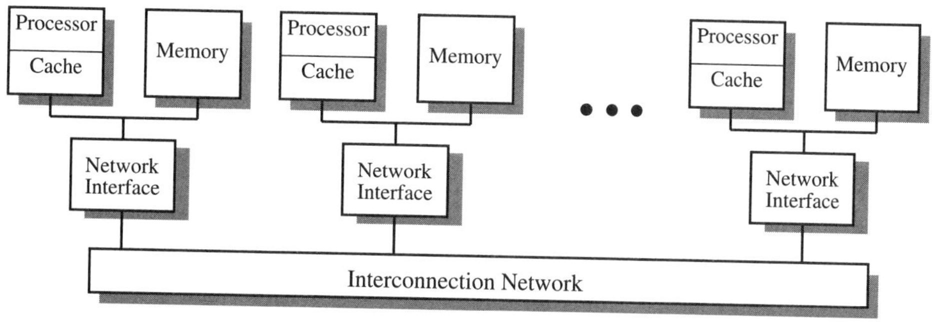

FIGURE 3-2 *Nonuniform Memory Access (NUMA) Architecture.*

accessed because it will significantly reduce memory latency on the fraction of locations that are in the *local* memory (i.e., memory in the same node as the processor). For example, if there is a 3:1 ratio of remote to local memory delay, a NUMA architecture will reduce the average memory latency by 16% in a four-processor system, when compared with an architecture where all memory is remote.

On larger systems where local memory represents a small fraction of the system's total memory, software must properly allocate memory and limit process migration for the NUMA architecture to reduce latency significantly. One obvious area for optimization is data that is private to a given process. Likewise, if code is replicated, then code misses can be arranged to be satisfied from local memory. Finally, if shared data structures are accessed primarily by one processor, allocating these locations from the processor's local memory can reduce average latency.

3.2.2 Cache-Only Memory Architecture (COMA)

In a NUMA architecture every memory line has a fixed mapping from its address to the main memory of one node. In contrast, in a cache-only memory architecture (COMA) there is no fixed mapping. Even the system main memory space is treated as a cache, known as an *attraction memory* [HLH92] (see Figure 3-3). There are two major advantages to this arrangement. First, memory lines can move around to where they are needed. Second, shared copies of a line can exist in several nodes at once, which is beneficial for read-only or mostly-read data. These advantages help primarily by reducing the capacity misses of shared data, leading to lower average memory latencies.

The downside of COMA architectures is the additional hardware complexity required to treat main memory as a cache. This entails an additional level of mapping memory lines into attraction memories and finding a copy of a given cache line somewhere in the system. There is also overhead both in space (to store the tags) and time (to find a copy of a given line). In addition, the system must make sure that at least one copy of every memory line is retained in some node, which means that lines sometimes need to be moved around as a result of a replacement in the attraction memory.

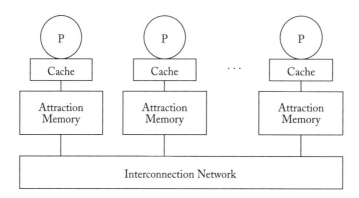

FIGURE 3-3 *Cache-Only Memory Architecture (COMA).*

Comparing the performance of COMA and NUMA architectures, we find that, on one hand, COMA machines have additional levels of caching, which reduce the average memory latency for large working sets that can be contained in the attraction memories. On the other hand, misses in the attraction memories are more expensive to service than processor cache misses in a NUMA machine, so if there is a lot of communication (which leads to attraction memory misses), the COMA machine sees larger memory latencies. Table 3-1 summarizes the comparison, which was inspired by the analysis presented by Singh et al. [SJG+93].

For each architecture we show the performance in four regimes of application behavior. The four regimes are characterized by the combinations of working set size (small or large) and communication-to-computation ratio (low or high). If the working set is small and the communication-to-computation ratio is low, both architectures do well because most references are satisfied out of the processor caches. If working sets and communication are large, both architectures do poorly: NUMA because of the poor cache performance, and COMA because of the high attraction memory miss latencies. If the working set is large and communication is low, then COMA does well because of the large attraction memories. In this regime, NUMA does medium well, unless the data can be placed locally with each processor, in which case NUMA does as well as COMA. In COMA architectures, data placement is achieved in hardware at a cache line granularity. For NUMA architectures, data placement can be attempted in software at a page granularity, which is successful for some applications, but not for all. Finally, if the working sets are small, but the communication-to-computation ratios are high, the caches of neither architecture help much. However, NUMA performs better due to the lower communication latencies.

Thus, there are different regimes of application behavior that favor either the NUMA or COMA architecture, and there is no obvious answer as to which architecture is better. It is clear, however, that COMA architectures are more expensive. In addition, COMA is relatively new, and there have been several proposals on how the overhead and complexity of the basic COMA architecture can be reduced [SJG92, HSL94]. This area of research is both active and interesting.

TABLE 3-1

Performance of NUMA and COMA Architectures

COMMUNICATION-TO-COMPUTATION RATIO	NUMA		COMA	
	SMALL WORKING SET	LARGE WORKING SET	SMALL WORKING SET	LARGE WORKING SET
Low	Good	Medium	Good	Good
High	Medium	Poor	Poor	Poor

3.2.3   Direct Interconnect Networks

Direct and indirect networks were introduced in Chapter 1. Here we look at them again in the context of latency reduction. A *direct interconnect network* [AtS88] is a switching network in which processing and memory nodes are allocated at the switch points. Indirect networks put the nodes at only the inputs and outputs of the network. Direct networks reduce latency because an average request only traverses a small number of the network switch points to reach its destination; in an indirect network every request must travel across the entire network. The disadvantage of a direct network is that distributing the network across the nodes makes the switch physically bigger, potentially slowing down the network. Furthermore, if the direct network is implemented as part of the individual nodes, it becomes difficult to change the network characteristics (e.g., additional dimensions in a mesh) as the system grows.

Direct networks can also be viewed as another level of NUMA, which can be exploited in software by allocating memory and processors that must communicate near to one another. This arrangement also permits the direct network to have increased aggregate bandwidth when communication is primarily with neighboring nodes. In many physical problems and their corresponding computational models, much of the interprocessor communication is between neighboring nodes, and a direct network can be very useful in decreasing latency and increasing bandwidth. In actual machines, both direct and indirect networks have been used. The MIT Alewife, Intel Paragon, Stanford DASH, and Cray T3D all use direct networks; the IBM RP3, the CM-5, and the University of Illinois Cedar machine use indirect networks.

3.2.4   Hierarchical Access

Since much interprocessor communication and data sharing is restricted to a subset of the processors, a hierarchical search can reduce memory latency if the locality of data sharing matches the structure of the hierarchy. Such a hierarchical search typically employs an interconnection network that maintains information about the outstanding requests or caching state of neighboring processors. A hierarchical search can reduce latency for both locally shared and widely shared data items. For local communication, searching the nearby caches retrieves data directly from the writing processor and avoids accessing a remote memory. For widely shared items, interaction between the local processors occurs indirectly when the

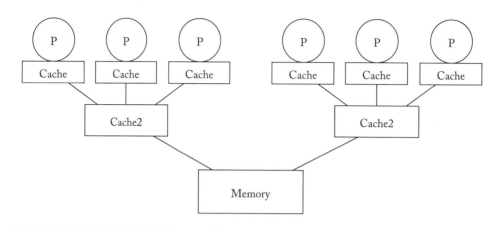

FIGURE 3-4 *Hierarchical Access.*

location is updated, and the set of nearby processors must all refetch the location. In this case, the search is likely to find a read-only copy of the updated data that has already been fetched by a nearby processor. Thus, only one of the local processors will incur a remote memory access, and the rest retrieve the data locally. In the widely shared case, a hierarchical access also increases the effective bandwidth to the shared data.

There are two general ways to structure a hierarchical search mechanism. The more common method is to have additional levels of caches that are shared by an increasing set of the processors (shown in Figure 3-4). Such schemes have been proposed for the Encore GigaMax, Stanford ParaDiGM, SICS DDM, and MIT J-Machine. Another possibility is to search in the individual caches of nearby processors (used in DASH and the KSR-1). The trade-offs in choosing the cache organization and levels of hierarchy involve both cost and performance. Large shared caches have a greater cost, but they also have a higher likelihood of containing the requested data. Similarly, searching more than one level of hierarchy increases the chance of finding the requested data. Unfortunately, the problem is that each level of hierarchy causes *increased* latency to every request not satisfied by that level, which limits the effective depth of the cache hierarchy to 2 or 3. Overall, any hierarchical access method must be carefully analyzed to ensure that it yields a net reduction in latency and that its hardware cost and complexity are warranted.

3.2.5 Protocol Optimizations

While hierarchical access can be thought of as a protocol optimization to reduce latency, there are further optimizations to reduce latency that can be used at a lower level in the protocol. One example of this type of optimization is when a remote processor cache with a dirty copy of a requested data item satisfies a memory request. While a simple coherence protocol would first update memory before returning the requested data, latency can be reduced by sending the data to the requesting processor in parallel with updating memory. This technique is used on DASH (further discussed in Section 8.3.1.1) and the J-Machine. Another example is the support of an *exclusive* request in addition to a *read-exclusive* request for memory writes that hit in the local cache, but are in the shared state. The former request can allow the processor to retire the write when the request is made, while the latter forces the processor to assume that its shared copy of the block is out-of-date and must be refreshed before it is updated. Other protocol optimizations include optimizations for migratory data [CoF93, SBS93] and producer-consumer access patterns [BCZ90b, JLG+90]. All of these optimizations rely on common sharing patterns to reduce the effective memory latency. As in hierarchical access methods, care must be taken that accesses not optimized are not penalized excessively, and that the added complexity is justified.

3.2.6 Latency Reduction Summary

Memory latency is critical to the performance of large-scale shared-memory multiprocessors. Minimizing latency is accomplished by aggressive implementation technology and architectural optimizations. The architecture-level techniques reduce latency by increasing cache hit rates or limiting the average distance within the memory system that a request must travel in order to be satisfied. The architectural techniques rely on both implicit and explicit cooperation with software to be effective. For example, employing local memory allocation and limiting process migration between processors enable NUMA architectures and direct networks to limit memory traffic to within or close by a node. Conversely, techniques such as hierarchical access and producer-consumer protocol optimizations implicitly take advantage of the typical access patterns of parallel programs.

3.3 Latency Hiding

Although it is desirable to reduce memory latency as much as possible using aggressive technology and an architecture optimized for reduced latency, nevertheless memory latencies in large multiprocessors will be larger than in uniprocessors. Fundamentally, there is the larger physical size of the machine to traverse, and also all processors must have access to all memory. In addition, with private caches and an invalidating coherence protocol, communication is demand-driven, and thus the processor consuming the data sees all of the latency. Also, the ever-increasing clock rate of processors makes memory latency expressed in processor clock cycles look increasingly longer. This is true even in uniprocessors, because the cycle time of processors is decreasing faster than the access latency of DRAM.

What can be done to hide the latency of memory operations? There are only two general choices for hiding read and write latency. The first choice is to issue the operation early, using some sort of prefetch or by pushing the data from the producer to the consumer when it is ready. Examples of this technique are software- and hardware-controlled prefetch, decoupled architectures, messages, block copy, and update operations. The second choice is to occupy the processor with something else while waiting (e.g., multiple-context processors, vector processors). One principle that both of these techniques have in common is that they attempt to hide the long latency of memory operations by overlapping communication with computation or with other communication. In general, this overlap leads to higher bandwidth requirements on the memory system.

For writes, the processor does not require any data to be returned, so the processor only has to stall if the memory consistency model requires a strict ordering of references. With a relaxed memory consistency model, write buffers can be used, and the latency seen by the writes is decoupled from the processor.

The techniques considered in this section are weak consistency models [DSB86, DSB88, GLL+90, AdH90], prefetch [Lee87, Por89, GGV90, MoG91], multiple-context processors [Smi81, HaF88, Ian88, WeG89b, ALK+90], and producer-initiated communication techniques. These techniques tend to exploit parallelism at different levels and may be used in a complimentary fashion [GHG+91]. Weak consistency models primarily hide write latency by allowing buffering and pipelining of memory references. Prefetching techniques hide latency by bringing data closer to the processor where they will be needed in the future. Multiple-context processors hide latency by switching from one context to another when a high-latency operation is encountered, thus overlapping computation with communication. Producer-initiated communication is faster than consumer-initiated communication because the communication is started as soon as the data is ready.

In this section we explain these techniques in detail and quantify the performance gain achievable with each of them. These results were previously reported [GHG+91]. Details of the architecture simulated and assumptions made can be found in that paper. In summary, an execution-driven simulator of a multiprocessor architecture similar to DASH is used. The study uses 16 processors, each with a 64-KByte write-through primary cache, a 256-KByte write-back secondary cache, and a 16-entry deep write buffer between them. The caches are lockup free [Kro81], direct mapped, and use 16-byte lines. The cache coherence protocol and contention effects are all simulated in detail. Memory latencies are on the order of those encountered in DASH (see Chapter 8).

The study looks at three different applications: MP3D, PTHOR, and LU. The first two have already been described in detail in Chapter 2. The third application, LU, is a program that performs dense matrix LU factorizations. Each of the applications was chosen because it exhibits certain interesting memory access characteristics. MP3D suffers greatly from a very high cache miss rate and is therefore a good candidate for any latency hiding technique. PTHOR is a very irregular symbolic application, which makes compile-time insertion of prefetch instructions very difficult. LU is a very regular scientific application.

3.3.1 Weak Consistency Models

Memory consistency refers to constraints imposed on the ordering of memory accesses as observed by both the issuing processor and by other processors sharing the same address space. In uniprocessors, the definition of memory consistency is relatively straightforward. A read of a memory location returns the last value written to the location. Likewise, a store operation binds the value returned by subsequent reads of the location. Unfortunately, when there are multiple processors the definitions of "last written" and "subsequent reads" become unclear. For example, consider the cache-coherent multiprocessor system shown in Figure 3-5. Assume that all processors start with a read-only copy of a given data item in their cache. If processor P1 now writes to this data item, and the write succeeds in its cache, a potential memory inconsistency exists. Until the new value written by P1 is propagated to processors P2 and P3, a read of the data item by processors P2 or P3 will return the stale data found in their caches. Another example is that when processors P1 and P2 both write a new

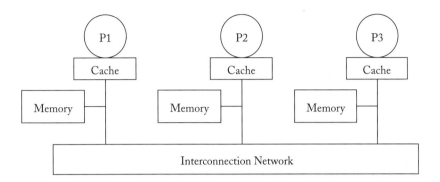

F I G U R E   3 - 5   *Memory Consistency Model Example.*

value simultaneously, we must be sure that some order is established between the two writes so that a single value persists in the entire system.

In a system with no caches and a single memory, an absolute order of reads and writes can be established by their arrival at memory, but such a system is not scalable. The most widely accepted multiprocessor consistency model, however, states that memory should have these semantics. As defined by Lamport [Lam79], a *sequentially consistent* (SC) memory model requires that the values observed by all processors represent some valid interleaving of the memory accesses issued by the individual processors, which essentially amounts to the "single memory with no caching" model. A distributed memory system can be made sequentially consistent, but this action eliminates much of the pipelining that would otherwise be possible because it requires memory references to complete one at a time, in strict order.

A simple example of how caching can break sequential consistency is the following code executed on two different processors. Assume variables A and B start out initialized to 0.

Proc 1

```
write A, 1
read B
```

Proc 2

```
write B, 1
read A
```

To satisfy sequential consistency, at least one of the values A and B read by the two processors must be 1. Yet if B is cached in Proc 1's cache and A is cached in Proc 2's cache, we can imagine the two writes being followed immediately by the two reads without the new write values having propagated to the other processor's cache. Thus both reads could return the cached value 0, which is not legal under sequential consistency.

To relax the restrictions of sequential consistency, several alternative consistency models have been proposed [DSB86, Goo89, AdH90, GLL+90]. These models support the uniprocessor consistency model for accesses made by a single processor, but relax the ordering constraints on how a processor's accesses are observed by other processors. The basis for these weaker models is that ordering is usually required only when accesses are made to synchronization variables. For example, operations to variables within a critical region need not be ordered because mutual exclusion already guarantees that only one processor is manipulating the set of data items. In our previous example, if processor P1 writes the shared data item while in a critical region, the mutual exclusion of the critical region assures that processors P2 and P3 will not attempt to read the data item until it is assured that the new value has propagated to all processors. When P1 does exit the critical region, all other processors see the updated data structure before they are allowed to enter the critical section. The main advantage of the weaker models is the potential for increased performance. The main disadvantages are increased hardware complexity and a more complex programming model.

Let us now take a look at a specific consistency model and show what the performance advantages of using such a model are. We focus on *release consistency* (RC) [GLL+90], one of the most relaxed memory models. This model is an extension of the *weak consistency* model originally proposed by Dubois, Scheurich, and Briggs [DSB86]. In weak consistency, the ordering of normal reads and writes is only maintained for the issuing processor. The order in which other processors observe accesses, is only guaranteed across synchronization accesses. Release consistency distinguishes between *acquire* and *release* synchronization operations to further reduce the ordering constraints of weak consistency. In particular, an acquire synchronization operation must complete before the completion of any other operations issued by this processor after the acquire. Thus, locks are acquired in program order, and protected data is not accessed before the associated lock is acquired. Correspondingly, a release synchronization operation is only made visible to other processors after operations issued before the release have completed. The constraint on acquire operations usually delays the issuing processor, but releasing operations need not stall the processor if there is sufficient buffering to hold the writes that are outstanding before the release operation. In any case, only processors doing synchronization are exposed to the delays associated with assuring that outstanding writes have completed.

Release consistency does not constrain the order in which ordinary accesses complete, allowing for the use of high-performance write buffers. Writes can be retired into the write buffer while the issuing processor continues. Writes to different locations can be retired from the write buffer in any order. The net effect is that given sufficient write buffering, the latency required to retire writes is completely hidden from the processor. In addition, any reads issued by the processor can bypass writes in the write buffer (as long as they are to different addresses). Thus, multiple read and write requests can be outstanding, and there is a large amount of communication latency overlapped with computation. This situation is not possible with a stricter memory model that imposes more ordering constraints on memory references.

While there is generally much greater flexibility in the ordering of memory accesses in a multiprocessor that uses a memory model such as release consistency, we still need the ability to enforce order at synchronization boundaries. For example, we must be able to assure that all outstanding memory operations have completed before a release can succeed. Therefore, a machine that implements a weakly consistent memory model must have an explicit mechanism for ordering accesses when a stronger order is required. An example is the *fence* operation of RP3 [PBG+85]. A typical fence operation explicitly asks that the write buffer or processor be stalled until all previous operations have completed. Fences allow the programmer or compiler to emulate any consistency model. Similar mechanisms are making their

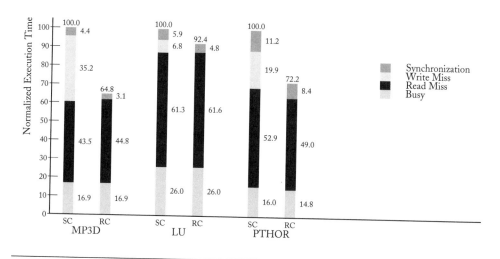

FIGURE 3-6 *Effect of Relaxing the Consistency Model.*

way into microprocessor architectures. Examples can be found in the DEC Alpha [DEC92] and in the SPARC V9 [Spa94] architectures.

3.3.1.1 Comparison of SC versus RC

Several studies have been done to quantify the performance gains that are achievable by relaxing the memory model used [GGH91, GHG+91, ZuB92]. In order to obtain quantifiable results, these studies must assume a target architecture and simulate different consistency models on that architecture. Naturally, the results are then somewhat limited by the assumptions made in the studies. Nonetheless, these studies observed some interesting behavior and drew worthwhile conclusions. We present results of the Stanford study [GHG+91] to accompany the discussion of different memory hiding techniques in this section and start by looking at the results obtained for different memory models.

Figure 3-6 shows the comparison of SC versus RC. (The architectural assumptions of these simulations were stated earlier in Section 3.3.) For each of the three applications, execution time is shown for both consistency models. Each bar is broken down into busy time, idle time due to read and write misses, and idle time due to synchronization. The execution times are normalized to show SC as 100%. As can be seen from the results, RC removes all idle time due to write miss latency. The gains are large in MP3D and PTHOR since the write miss time constitutes a large portion of the execution time under SC (35% and 20%, respectively), while the gain is small in LU because of the relatively small write miss time under SC (7%). The achievable gains depend on the frequency of shared write misses in the parallel application.

The pipelining of writes under RC provides another way in which RC can outperform SC. If there is a release operation (e.g., unlock) behind several writes in the write buffer, then a remote processor waiting at an acquire (e.g., lock on the same variable) can observe the release sooner under RC, thus spinning for a shorter amount of time. Figure 3-6 shows that synchronization times also decrease under RC. Overall, the release consistency model provides speedup over sequential consistency of about 1.5 for MP3D, 1.1 for LU, and 1.4 for PTHOR. The study by Zucker and Baer [ZuB92] found very similar gains achievable by moving from sequential to release consistency.

3.3.2 Prefetch

Prefetching is a technique that moves data that is expected to be used by a given processor closer to that processor before it is actually needed. When prefetching is successful, a large fraction of the memory latency can be hidden. Prefetching can be classified into binding and nonbinding, as well as software- versus hardware-issued.

With binding prefetch, the value returned is bound when the prefetch returns. For example, in the case of a register load, the prefetched value is actually written into the register. Binding prefetch places restrictions on its use because the bound value could become stale between the prefetch and the actual use if another processor writes to the same location in that interval. These restrictions make the safe placement of prefetches extremely difficult, negating most of the benefits obtainable through prefetch [LYL87]. We will instead focus on nonbinding prefetch. In nonbinding prefetch, the value is also brought closer to the processor, but it remains visible to the coherence protocol. For example, the prefetched value is placed into the processor cache. Any write that occurs between the prefetch and the actual use of the value invalidates the prefetched value out of the processor cache. For this case, the prefetch is useless, but correct semantics are preserved. Nonbinding prefetch has no effect on the memory consistency model, and prefetch operations can be safely placed anywhere in the application code.

Examples of hardware-issued prefetches are long cache lines, instruction look-ahead, and techniques that attempt to find regular access patterns (such as vector strides) in the data reference stream and then prefetch data accordingly [Smi78, Jou90]. The effectiveness of these techniques is reduced by the limited knowledge that hardware has concerning access patterns of the application. With software-issued prefetching, prefetch instructions are inserted into the application code, either explicitly by the programmer or automatically by the compiler. The advantage of software-issued prefetching is that it can be done more selectively and that the interval between prefetch and use can be greatly extended, thus allowing even large latencies to be hidden. The downside of software-issued prefetching is that it uses instruction bandwidth for the actual prefetch instructions and potentially redundant address calculations. In addition, it requires extra work from the application programmer, or a sophisticated compiler. We focus on software-issued nonbinding prefetch. The latency reductions seen with software-issued prefetch are likely to represent close to the upper bound of what could be achieved with any kind of prefetch because the software can be sophisticated about what to prefetch and because prefetches can be moved well before the actual use of the data, neither of which is possible with hardware prefetch.

The latency reduction due to prefetch derives from several sources. The obvious one is that if a prefetch is issued far enough in advance, most of the memory latency can be hidden when the actual use occurs. But even if the prefetch did not go out early enough, there is still some benefit. The latency is partially hidden, and more importantly, several prefetches can be in progress at any given time. This additional pipelining of memory references can be a significant advantage. For example, if a data structure needs to be accessed, but its address is not known until right before the access, prefetches can be issued to all parts of the structure. While almost none of the latency to obtaining the first part of the structure is hidden, most of the latency to accessing the remaining parts of the structure is hidden. The third advantage to prefetching in multiprocessors is due to the use of a simple invalidating cache coherence protocol. In such a system, a read followed by a write of a given location requires two long-latency operations: one to fetch the data for the read and a second to obtain ownership for the write. For this common access pattern, we can issue a *prefetch-exclusive*, a special flavor of prefetch that requests ownership as well as data. We thus save one of the long-latency operations, even if no latency is hidden for the first reference. Use of prefetch-exclusive also reduces network bandwidth since fewer network messages are required.

Nonbinding software-issued prefetch was first implemented in DASH [LLG+90]. Increasingly, microprocessor architectures now support prefetch. Prefetch is implemented in the DEC Alpha, and prefetch instructions are defined in the SPARC V9 architecture. The SPARC architecture defines prefetch for single and multiple reads as well as prefetch for single and multiple writes. The single read and write prefetch instructions are included to allow for support of a small prefetch buffer next to the processor cache. If large amounts of data are to be moved by the processor, the data can be kept out of the cache by using these special prefetch operations. In this manner, latency is hidden and the cache contents are preserved.

3.3.2.1   Benefits of Prefetch

In the Stanford study, prefetches were inserted manually at the source code level using macro statements. Later work by Mowry automates this process with a prefetching compiler [Mow94]. For the three applications studied, the type of prefetching that can be taken advantage of is very different. In MP3D, there is a large loop that moves particles within the space array. The behavior is very deterministic, and the required data for the particle and from the space array can be prefetched several loop iterations ahead of time. The result is good prefetch coverage—the number of misses in the original application that can be covered by prefetches. In LU, the computation takes place on columns of the matrix being factored. Prefetch of columns is very effective because once it is known which column to prefetch, the entire column can be fetched. In addition, prefetch-exclusive is used on columns that are going to be modified. In PTHOR, however, prefetching is very difficult. Application execution is driven by the connectivity of the underlying circuit being simulated and is very irregular and unpredictable. In addition, several important data structures are based on linked lists, which further complicate the use of prefetch. In order to prefetch an element that is at the end of a linked list, link list elements have to be prefetched and evaluated one at a time. Prefetch is thus limited to the circuit element structures and the first few elements of some of the linked lists.

In order to study prefetching, a 16-entry prefetch buffer is inserted in parallel with the write buffer between the primary and secondary caches. The results of the prefetch experiments are shown in Figure 3-7. Comparing the execution time bars of Figure 3-6, we see that an additional category has been added: prefetch overhead. This category represents processing overhead to issue the prefetch and includes time to execute code to determine

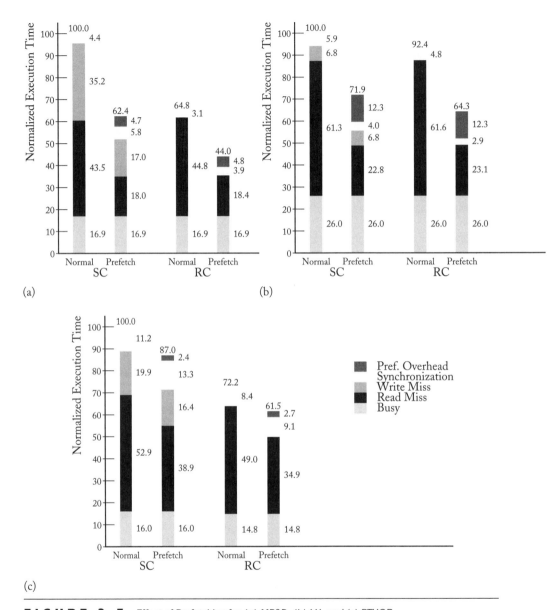

F I G U R E 3 - 7 *Effect of Prefetching for (a) MP3D, (b) LU, and (c) PTHOR.*

whether to prefetch or not, for redundant address calculations as well as for the prefetch itself. It also includes the time the processor is stalled because the prefetch buffer is full or because of prefetch operations locking the processor out of the cache when the prefetched value is returned and placed into the cache. The graph shows prefetch gains for sequential and for release consistency.

For sequential consistency, most of the benefits of prefetch result from reduced read latencies. The gains are larger than the additional prefetch overhead. For MP3D

(Figure 3-7(a)), there is also a significant reduction in write latency due to the success of prefetch-exclusive instructions. The result is a reduction of execution time by 38%. Prefetch overhead is large for LU (Figure 3-7(b))because there is very little computation for each prefetched data item. Nonetheless, a reduction of execution time of 28% is achieved.

The main difference we see when release consistency is used is that most of the write latency is already hidden, so the benefits of prefetching are limited to the elimination of some of the read latency. Nonetheless, the benefits of release consistency and prefetch are complementary. For each application running under RC, adding prefetch reduces the execution time further.

Mowry [Mow94] mentions several reasons that limit the gains achievable through prefetching. First, for some applications (such as PTHOR) it is very difficult to determine what and when to prefetch (i.e., prefetch coverage is low). Second, there can be cache interference that knocks a prefetched value out of the cache before it can be used. This interference can be induced by the processor itself because of replacements, or by remote processors in the form of invalidations. Third, the cost of prefetching can offset some of the gains achievable with prefetching.

Thus, prefetch takes advantage of parallelism within a single process by overlapping communication latency with computation and other communication. Software-issued prefetch can achieve execution time reductions in the 30–40% range without relying on sophisticated prefetch hardware.

3.3.3 Multiple-Context Processors

While prefetching is a mostly software solution to hiding latency, using multiple context processors [Smi81, WeG89b, ALK+90, SCE90, LGH92] is a mostly hardware solution. The basic idea is that when a long-latency operation such as a cache miss is encountered, the processor switches to another context and continues computation while the long-latency operation is in progress. Multiple-context processors take advantage of intercontext parallelism to hide latency. Several processes are assigned to each processor and are switched in hardware when a long-latency operation is encountered. With processor caches, the interval between long-latency operations becomes large enough for just a handful of contexts to effectively hide most of the latency [WeG89b]. This situation is in contrast to the early cacheless multiple-context processors such as the HEP [Smi81], where context switches occurred on every cycle and thus a large number of contexts were required to keep processor utilization high. More recent work by Laudon et al. [LGH92] shows that these two schemes can be effectively combined. The result is a processor that is able to switch contexts on every cycle, but does not force a context switch on every cycle. Latency tolerance is good, yet single-context performance is not compromised.

The performance gain to be expected from multiple-context processors depends on several factors. First, there is the number of contexts. With more contexts available, the processor is less likely to be out of ready-to-run contexts. The number of contexts, however, is constrained by hardware costs and available parallelism in the application. Using more contexts also leads to a less desirable point on the speedup graph of an application. Second, there is the context switch overhead. If the overhead is a sizeable fraction of the typical run length (time between misses), a significant fraction of time may be wasted switching contexts. Shorter context switch times, however, require a more complex and possibly slower processor. Laudon covers the trade-offs in multiple processor design in detail [LGH92]. Third, the performance depends on the application behavior. Applications with clustered misses and irregular miss latencies make it difficult to completely overlap computation of one context with memory accesses of other contexts. Multiple context processors thus achieve a lower processor utilization on these programs than on applications with more regular miss behavior. Fourth, multiple contexts themselves affect the performance of the memory system. The different contexts share a single processor cache and can interfere with each other, both constructively and destructively. Also, as is the case with weaker consistency models and prefetching, the memory system is more heavily loaded by multiple contexts, and thus latencies may increase.

Another practical issue is that there are no commercially available multiple-context processors. The only microprocessor with multiple contexts is SPARCLE, a modified SPARC processor that uses a register window for each context and is used in the MIT Alewife multiprocessor [ALK+90]. Unless multiple contexts are implemented in a state-of-the-art microprocessor, their performance will remain of primarily academic interest. And since the benefit to uniprocessor performance is limited, the addition of multiple context to state-of-the-art microprocessors is not very likely.

3.3.3.1 Benefits of Multiple-Context Processors

In the Stanford study [GHG+91], multiple-context processors with two and four contexts and a context switch overhead of four and 16 cycles are considered. The four-cycle overhead corresponds to the flushing of a short RISC pipeline, while the 16-cycle overhead corresponds to a less aggressive implementation that requires explicit save and restore of processor state for each context.

Figure 3-8 shows the results obtained under sequential consistency. Each execution time bar is broken down into the following components: *busy time*, which represents actual work done by the processor; *switching time* incurred when switching from one context to another; *all idle time*, which represents the time when all contexts are idle waiting on memory references; and *no switch time*, which represents time when the current context is idle but is not switched out. This last case occurs mostly because of the processor being locked out of the cache while the fill of another context's memory reference completes.

MP3D (Figure 3-8(a)) does very well with multiple contexts. The median run lengths are about 11 cycles long, and latencies are about 50 cycles. We thus expect to need about five contexts to hide most of the latency. With the low context switch overhead of four cycles, two contexts save a substantial amount of the *all idle time*, and with four contexts even more is hidden. For the larger switch overhead of 16 cycles, there are also substantial savings in *all idle time*. However, there is a significant increase in idle time due to context switching, especially when we go to four contexts.

LU (Figure 3-8(b)) does not benefit as much from multiple contexts, because there is significant cache interference between the different contexts. Even though some idle time is

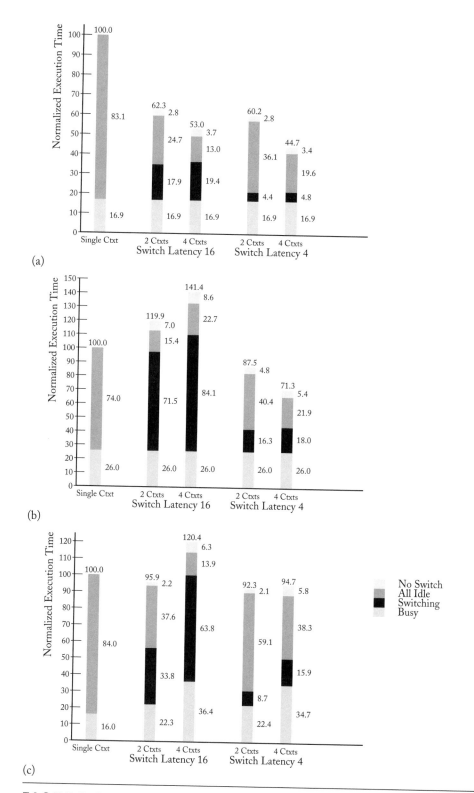

FIGURE 3-8 *Effect of Multiple Contexts under Sequential Consistency for (a) MP3D, (b) LU, and (c) PTHOR.*

hidden, there is also significant overhead due to context switching. For the case of 16-cycle context switches, the gains are completely offset by the additional overhead.

PTHOR (Figure 3-8(c)) shows another interesting effect of multiple contexts—reduced processor efficiency due to limited parallelism. Although the average run lengths and latencies (7 and 60–80 cycles, respectively) suggest good multiple-context behavior, the gains actually seen are small because multiple contexts push us to a less desirable point on the speedup graph. The additional contexts spend most of their time busy-waiting on an empty task queue and hold up real work being done. This time shows up as additional *busy time* in the graphs and together with context switch overhead negates the positive effects due to reduced *all idle time*.

Thus, multiple contexts can reduce execution time significantly. The amount of execution time reduction varies by application and depends greatly on the context switch overhead and the number of contexts. With a context switch overhead of four cycles and four contexts, execution times were reduced by 5–55%. With a context switch overhead of 16 cycles, execution time was increased for some applications.

3.3.3.2 Interaction of Multiple Contexts with Other Memory Latency Hiding Techniques

We have seen that multiple contexts with sequential consistency can increase performance substantially. An interesting question is whether multiple contexts can gain any extra performance when combined with relaxed consistency models. The left and middle sections of the graphs in Figure 3-9 show the performance of multiple contexts with SC and RC, respectively. We only show results for a context switch overhead of four cycles. The major difference between release consistency and sequential consistency is that write misses are no longer considered long-latency operations from the processor's perspective, since writes are simply put into the write buffer. (A decomposition showing write latencies with single contexts can be found in Figure 3-6.) We thus find that median run lengths between switches have increased (from 11 to 22 cycles for MP3D and from 6 to 14 cycles for LU; PTHOR is unchanged) and that fewer contexts are required to eliminate most of the remaining read miss latency. As a result, the gains achieved with four contexts over two contexts are also diminished. As is apparent from the results, there is some benefit from relaxing the consistency model with multiple contexts. For the four-context case, performance improved by a factor of 1.32 for MP3D, 1.23 for LU, and 1.21 for PTHOR when going from SC to RC.

Finally, let us consider the combined effect of multiple contexts and prefetching (see the right portion of the graphs in Figure 3-9). The main benefit of combining the two, of course, is that each scheme can compensate for the other scheme's weaknesses. For example, prefetching can increase the hit rate, thus increasing the run lengths and ensuring that a small number of contexts suffice. Similarly, multiple contexts can ensure that the processor does not remain idle for misses where prefetching was not effective. However, the two schemes also have negative interactions. First, both prefetching and multiple contexts add overhead. So if the latency of a reference could be totally hidden by one scheme alone, the second one only contributes overhead. Second, the two techniques may interfere with each other. For example, when multiple contexts are used, the time between issue and use of a

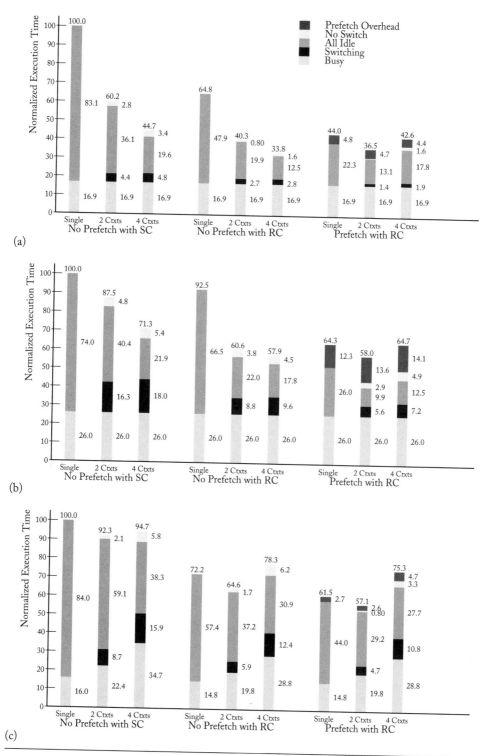

FIGURE 3-9 *Effect of Combining Schemes on (a) MP3D, (b) LU, and (c) PTHOR Performance (Multiple Context Uses Four-Cycle Switch Latency).*

prefetch may increase substantially, thus increasing the chance of the prefetched data being invalidated or replaced from the cache before being referenced. Depending on the relative magnitudes of the above effects, the performance of an application may increase or decrease when both schemes are used. Our data show that when four contexts are used, the negative effects overwhelm the positive effects (see Figure 3-9) for all applications. However, when only two contexts are used, additional use of prefetching helps achieve higher performance than when only a single context with prefetching is used or when two contexts without prefetching are used.

Although prefetching and multiple contexts both attempt to hide the same latency, there are several distinguishing features. The major advantage of prefetching is that it does not require a special processor. Also, it allows many more accesses to be outstanding at any given time, thus permitting their latencies to be overlapped. With prefetching, each processor can issue an essentially unlimited number of prefetch requests. Multiple contexts, on the other hand, are limited by the total number of contexts, which is expected to be a small number. One advantage of multiple contexts is that they can handle very irregular access patterns that cannot be prefetched efficiently. Another significant advantage is that multiple contexts do not require compiler support.

In the Stanford study, prefetching was added to the applications without multiple contexts in mind, which the authors believe has had some negative impact on the results for combined prefetching and multiple contexts. For example, for a single-context processor, it is reasonable to be quite aggressive and add prefetches in situations where we expect only a small portion of the latency to be hidden. However, for a multiple-context processor, this aggressive use of prefetch may be a bad decision. If the multiple-context processor would have hidden the latency anyway, prefetch overhead has been added without any benefit.

Release consistency helps multiple contexts because it eliminates writes as long-latency operations, thus increasing run lengths and allowing the remaining latency to be hidden with fewer contexts. The benefit of adding prefetching to multiple contexts is small, and may even be negative, especially when little latency is left to hide. Inserting prefetches with more awareness of their effect on the performance of multiple contexts may achieve better results.

3.3.4 Producer-Initiated Communication

An invalidation-based coherence protocol inherently requires consumer-initiated communication. Data transfer proceeds as follows: The producer writes a new value to the location. If the consumer has a cached copy, then it is invalidated at that time. When the consumer wants to read the new value, it must first pull it out of the producer's cache and across the network. Communication can become more efficient if the production and consumption of the data are far apart because then the likelihood that the producer still retains the value in its cache is reduced. Most likely the new value has already been written back and has thus moved closer to the consumer. If production and consumption of the data closely follow one another, such as in the case of a contended lock, invalidation protocols slow communication significantly.

The problem can be alleviated by mechanisms that allow for producer-initiated communication. One example is an update protocol, where a write to a shared data item causes updates to be sent to all remote copies rather than invalidations. The advantage of update protocols is that communication from producer to consumer is faster. The downside is that there is typically much more coherence traffic [GDF94] because all shared copies have to be updated on every write. In terms of network bandwidth, this situation is analogous to the comparison of a write-through versus a write-back cache. While one requires transfers of single words for every write, the other can collect multiple writes to the same location and multiple writes to nearby locations into efficient transfer units (cache lines).

Other examples of producer-initiated communication mechanisms are message-passing support and block-copy engines. In message passing, the producer bundles up the data and sends it to the consumer. Message-passing support is usually provided instead of shared memory. Block-copy support is a similar mechanism in shared-memory architectures. It allows a portion of memory to be copied from one address range to another, usually on a physically distant part of the machine.

Several schemes have been proposed for combining the advantages of invalidation-based coherence protocols (lower network bandwidth) and update-based protocols (lower communication latency). One idea is to use a hybrid coherence protocol that can use both invalidation and updates and to switch between them dynamically using some kind of competitive algorithm [KMR+86, BCZ90b]. A different idea, embodied in DASH, is to have both protocols implemented in the system and to allow the programmer/compiler to use whichever is more efficient for the task at hand. One obvious choice is to use update operations for most synchronization operations such as locks, barriers, and event notifications, while sticking to invalidation-based coherence for the majority of the data in the application.

DASH supports three types of producer-initiated communication mechanisms. They are discussed in detail in Chapter 6. *Update-writes* implement the classic update protocol, where the producer writes a data item and copies of this word are distributed to all caches that currently hold a copy of the item. This mechanism is useful for communicating small amounts of data to consumers that are already waiting. For example, update-writes are very efficient for barrier release and event notification. While update-writes only send single words of data, and only to caches that already have a copy, *producer prefetch* operations are used to send entire cache lines to prospective consumers of the data. A cache line of data is sent by the producer to a list of consumers. In this manner, a producer can efficiently send large amounts of data, and the communication is initiated as soon as the data has been produced. The third update mechanism built into DASH is *granting locks*. When a granting lock is unlocked, the lock is sent to exactly one of the waiting processors. This processor receives the unlocked value of the lock and can immediately acquire the lock locally. Thus, release-to-acquire times are reduced to a minimum. We present quantitative data on the performance advantage of these three mechanisms in Chapter 8.

Thus, producer-initiated communication is most useful when data sizes are small and communication latency is important to achieving good application performance. A common special case of this requirement is found in many multiprocessor synchronization mechanisms.

3.3.5 Latency Hiding Summary

There are two general mechanisms for hiding memory latency: issuing the operation early and doing something else while waiting on the operation. For hiding write latency, there is the additional mechanism of using a relaxed memory consistency model. In this section, we discussed four different techniques for hiding memory latency in multiprocessors. Prefetching and producer-initiated communication issue memory operations early, multiple-context processors switch to another context while waiting on the operation, and relaxed consistency memory models hide write latency. All of these techniques take advantage of application parallelism to overlap communication with computation or with other communication.

Relaxing the consistency model provides performance gains by a factor of 1.1 to 1.5, arising mainly from the hiding of write latencies. This gain requires no special software effort as long as programs use explicit synchronization. The main hardware requirement is lockup-free caches, since the relaxed models allow multiple outstanding references. Lockup-free caches, however, are also necessary for prefetching and for multiple-context processors, and thus form a universal requirement for latency hiding techniques.

Prefetching is very successful in reducing the stalls due to read latencies (26–63% less). Prefetching is less effective in reducing write latency under the strict consistency model, but it combines well with the relaxed consistency model to eliminate both read and write latency. The speedups of relaxed consistency and prefetching over sequential consistency alone are 2.3 for MP3D, 1.6 for LU, and 1.6 for PTHOR. Although prefetching has the drawback that it requires compiler or programmer intervention, a significant advantage is that it requires no major hardware support beyond that needed by RC, and it can easily be incorporated into systems built using existing commercial microprocessors.

Multiple-context processors require significant hardware support. They provide reductions in execution times of between 5 and 55% when the context switch overhead is four cycles. The results are much less impressive when the context switch overhead is 16 cycles. In cases where the concurrency is low (e.g., PTHOR) or where there is substantial cache interference (e.g., LU), the use of multiple contexts makes the performance worse. The use of relaxed consistency helps multiple-context performance by hiding write latencies and increasing the run lengths. Under an aggressive implementation, with use of four contexts and a context switch overhead of four cycles, the combined performance benefit was a factor of 3.0 for MP3D, 1.7 for LU, and 1.3 for PTHOR. The interaction of multiple contexts with prefetching is complex, and often the performance becomes worse when the two are combined together. To achieve better results, it appears that the prefetching strategy must become more sensitive to the presence of multiple contexts.

Producer-initiated communication requires a coherence protocol that is different from the invalidation-based protocols that are most efficient for regular data coherence in large-scale shared-memory multiprocessors. Although it may be costly to add the additional hardware mechanism to support producer-initiated communication, the rewards are reduced communication latencies—especially important in situations where communication latency is critical to operation scalability, such as for synchronization operations. Producer-initiated communication is especially well suited to locks, barriers, and event-notifications.

We have seen that a number of methods can be used to hide the latency of memory accesses in large-scale shared-memory multiprocessors. Some are more hardware intensive (relaxed consistency memory models, multiple-context processors, and producer-initiated communication), while one is more software intensive (prefetching). The schemes can offer substantial gains in performance and often work well in combination with one another. Overall, execution time reductions by factors of 2–3 were found in the comparative simulation study [GHG+91], and results are likely to be even more impressive for larger machines with longer memory latencies.

3.4 Memory Bandwidth

A scalable system must increase memory bandwidth in proportion with the number of processors if it is to achieve linear performance growth. In NUMA systems with distributed processors and memory nodes, total bandwidth to private data increases linearly with system size if private data is accessed from the local node's memory. For shared data, scalable bandwidth is achieved if the processors are connected to global memory through a scalable interconnection network. A scalable interconnection network, however, does not guarantee scalable memory bandwidth if individual accesses generate traffic that grows in communication distance or number of messages with system size. In particular, in a direct or hierarchical interconnection network, the locality of communication affects the achievable bandwidth. The greater the locality of communication, the greater the aggregate bandwidth. For example, the aggregate bandwidth achievable for a communication pattern that requires each message to cross only one link is 4 times that of a pattern that requires each message to traverse four links, even for the same underlying network. An example of increasing number of messages with increasing system size is the traffic generated by snoopy-based cache coherence schemes. Every memory access is broadcast to each processor cache. As more processors are added, the number of messages sent for each memory access increases, and this traffic eventually saturates the scalable system interconnect. Directory-based cache coherence avoids broadcasts because coherence traffic consists of point-to-point messages to nodes that have already fetched the memory block. If an invalidation-based coherence protocol is used, then there is at most one invalidation message for every fetch of a data item. In the worst case, coherence increases the total number of messages by a factor of two.

Another potential limit to memory bandwidth arises if bandwidth is sensitive to internode latency. As the system grows, internode latencies grow, and if intranode resources cannot service additional memory requests while a remote request is pending, then bandwidth will degrade proportionally to the increase in latency. In a memory system without caching, this coupling does not occur because requests are only serialized by the access time to the memory array itself, as long as the processor can have a large number of outstanding requests. In cache-based systems, however, not all memory requests can be satisfied immediately. For example, if the memory controller is blocked while fetching data from a dirty cache in a remote node or waiting for acknowledgments of invalidations, then its overall bandwidth will degrade substantially. To avoid this problem, the coherence protocol must be designed not to block memory when processing remote requests, or the memory controller

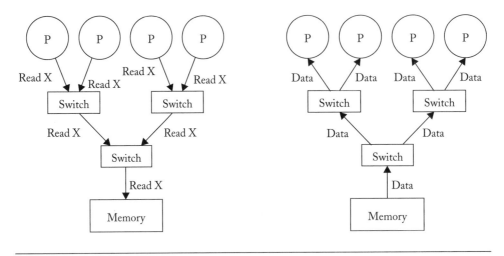

F I G U R E   3 - 1 0   *Hardware Combining.*

must have sufficient buffering so that accesses that are dependent on internode communication do not block subsequent requests.

3.4.1 Hot Spots

The above discussion of memory bandwidth assumes that accesses are uniformly distributed across the address space. For highly contended synchronization objects and heavily shared data objects, this assumption does not hold [WeG89a]. Such concentrated accesses during a short time duration represent a *hot spot* [PBG+85]. Under hot spot conditions, the effective bandwidth of the memory system is reduced because only a fraction of the distributed resources are in use. Caching eliminates some classes of hot spots, in particular, those where read sharing is dominant. In these cases, the processor caches dynamically increase the bandwidth to individual memory locations. An example can be found in a dense LU decomposition application. The pivot column needs to be broadcast to all processors and applied to all remaining columns. Without caches, the memory module holding the pivot column could become a hot spot. With caches, each processor can obtain its own copy of the pivot column, and the effective memory bandwidth is much larger.

Unfortunately, not all hot spots can be eliminated via caches. If precautions are not taken, hot spots can limit scalability. The solution to the hot spot problem requires the load on the hot spots to be distributed. Distribution can be done either through software restructuring or through hardware logic that supports the combining of memory accesses. An example of software restructuring is the distribution of a barrier synchronization as individual gather and release trees with separate entry counts and spin locations. An example of hardware combining is present in the NYU Ultracomputer [GGK+83] and IBM RP3 [PBG+85]. In hardware combining, references to the same memory location are combined at every level of the network (see left side of Figure 3-10), and each switch point remembers the combined requestors to allow it to fan-out the data when it is returned (right side of Figure 3-10).

Distributing the load on a hot spot requires a hierarchical access method to the logical data structure. If each level of the hierarchy combines n requests, then no level will see more than n simultaneous requests. The problem in using hierarchy to remove a hot spot is the same as using it to reduce memory latency. The gain in bandwidth and latency on hot spot locations must be balanced by the added latency for non–hot spot accesses.

3.4.2 Synchronization Support

Synchronization accesses can frequently lead to hot spots. For example, when a highly contended lock is released, a large number of waiting nodes rush to grab the lock. Furthermore, when a synchronization variable passes from one processor to another it represents a small interprocessor message. As discussed before, invalidation-based coherence protocols are not optimized for interprocessor communication because they force the consumer to refetch the data after it is updated from the producer's cache. Consequently, specialized operations can substantially improve synchronization performance. These specialized operations increase performance and reduce hot spots by taking advantage of the higher-level semantics of the synchronization primitives.

Some of the more common synchronization operations (already discussed in Chapter 2) are the following:

1. Mutual exclusion

2. Dynamic work distribution

3. Event notification

4. Global serialization—barriers

Of course, mutual exclusion can be used to build any of the other synchronization primitives, but the associated data manipulations force the serialization of any contended mutual exclusion region to be greater than or equal to the latency of a remote memory access (e.g., see Section 8.3.2.1). Thus, although mutual exclusion is an important primitive to support, additional operations can improve the performance of fine-grained parallelism [Her91].

In most small-scale systems, hardware support for mutual exclusion is through an atomic test&set instruction, and the use of a test-and-test&set protocol for spin waiting. Ideally, spin locks should meet the following criteria: (1) minimal amount of traffic generated while waiting for a lock; (2) low-latency release of a waiting processor; and (3) low-latency acquisition of a free lock. Cached test&set schemes satisfy the above criteria for low-contention locks, but fail for locks with higher contention. Figure 3-11 shows an example using test-and-test&set spin waiting. In part (a) we see one processor executing a critical region, and two others spinning on a shared copy of the locked lock. In (b) the leftmost processor exits the critical region and releases the lock by writing to it. The lock is invalidated out of the waiters' caches. Each of the contending processors now experiences a cache miss in its spin loop and rereads the lock. Depending on the timing, several processors may see the lock in its unlocked state (c). All of these now execute a test&set instruction to acquire the lock (d). As shown in (e) this causes further invalidation and interference in the caches. After some time, all unsuccessful lock contenders have a cached copy of the locked lock again, and the system returns to a quiescent state (f). We see that test-and-test&set spin

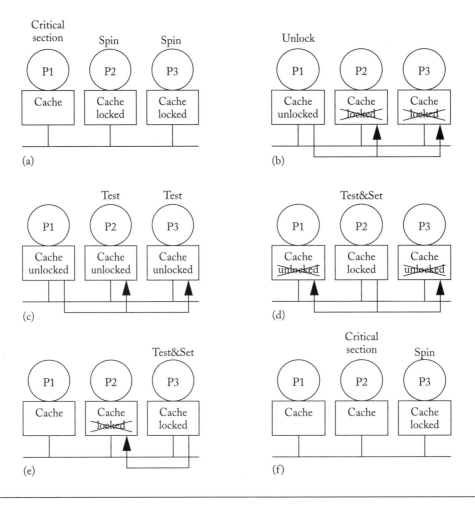

F I G U R E   3 - 1 1   *Test-and-test&set Spin Lock. (a) Lock is locked, other requestors are spinning locally. (b) Unlock operation. (c) Requestors test. (d) One requestor wins with test&set. (e) Later requestors also try test&set but only invalidate the lock from the caches. (f) Lock is locked, other requestors are spinning locally (like (a)).*

waiting exhibits excessive traffic and latency when releasing and acquiring contended locks using a simple invalidation-based protocol.

The problem with contended test&set spin locks is that they release all waiting processors, but there is only one processor that will be successful in acquiring the lock. Spin locks can be optimized by notifying just a single waiting processor of the released lock. The QOLB (queue on lock bit) operation proposed by Goodman, Vernon, and Woest [GVW89] and incorporated in the IEEE SCI protocol is such a primitive. It supports single waiter notification by keeping a list of waiters in the cache tags of the spinning processors. When a lock is released, only the head of the waiter list is notified. There is only O(1) traffic for the ownership to be passed to a new processor. In a directory-based system such as DASH, the directory pointers can be used to keep an approximation of the QOLB waiting list (see

Section 6.4.1). When a lock is released, one of the waiting processors is chosen at random and granted the lock. A grant request is sent only to that node and allows the processor to acquire the lock with a local operation. This mechanism greatly reduces the traffic for highly contended locks, and reduces the latency when there is modest contention. The grant mechanism also includes a time-out to insure that lock grants will eventually invalidate all cached copies of the lock if there is no longer anyone waiting on it.

Dynamic work distribution is used to allocate work to processors at run time in order to better load-balance a system. It is generally based on dynamic allocation of loop indices, or the use of task queues. If a task queue is implemented as an array, then manipulation of the queue also requires allocation of unique queue indices. Thus, both of these operations require a counting variable to be updated atomically. If mutual exclusion and normal variables are used, then multiple remote memory accesses must be made for every update. A simple solution is to support a Fetch&Op operation that is implemented directly in memory. Fetch&Op operations [GGK+83] return the current value of a memory location and perform the given operation on the location (usually a simple add/subtract or increment/decrement). Using Fetch&Op at memory can reduce the serialization for a series of updates by more than an order of magnitude in a large system (i.e., reduce latency from P to $P/10$–$P/20$, see Section 8.3.2.1).

Combining Fetch&Op operations have the potential to reduce serialization and latency from P to $\log P$ by merging Fetch&Op accesses in a tree manner through the interconnect before they reach memory. When the number of processors accessing a common variable is between 100 and 1,000, latency is reduced from P to $P/10$–$P/50$, depending upon the number of processors and the delay of the combining logic compared to memory. The question is whether the additional improvement relative to an in-memory Fetch&Op is worth the complex combining hardware. Another alternative to hardware combining is to use software restructuring to eliminate the hot spots that involve very large numbers of processors. For example, multiple local work queues can be used instead of one large global queue. Similarly, a software combining tree can be used to update different memory locations instead of updating a single Fetch&Op variable.

Task queues are also often based on linked-list structures. In a similar fashion to Fetch&Op, an in-memory Compare&Swap [IBM, Spa94] instruction can be used to reduce the serialization of linked-list manipulations to that of a memory read-modify-write. Systems such as the MIT Alewife [ALK+91], the active-message system proposed by Culler [VCG+92], and the Stanford FLASH system [KOH+94] generalize in-memory operations by providing a general mechanism to perform local computation on a memory location on behalf of remote processors.

Global event notification arises in two contexts. As a synchronization primitive, it is often used by the producer of data to indicate to a set of consumers that new data has been generated. Notification can also be used by itself to communicate new global data to a set of consumers—for example, updating a new minimum or maximum value for a parallel optimization problem. For both types of notifications, the data is frequently read and potentially frequently written. If the frequency of writes is low, then normal caching with invalidation-based coherence is sufficient. If the frequency of writes is high, then an update coherence protocol reduces the latency of communication and increases the utilization of the consuming processors since they do not incur remote read misses.

Globally serializing sections of code is a very common occurrence in parallel programs, especially when parallelism is exploited across loop iterations. After execution of a parallel loop, synchronization is achieved by a barrier, before continuing on to the next section of code (see Section 2.1 for an example of barrier usage). Barriers consist of two phases. In the first phase, all of the processes enter the barrier and wait for the last process to arrive. In the second phase, the processes are informed that global synchronization has been achieved and continue execution in parallel. Some systems implement barrier synchronization in dedicated hardware [LoT88, Cra93a], but such hardware can have significant overhead in a large system. Alternatively, the first phase of the barrier can be implemented using the Fetch&Op primitive discussed above. Assuming the counter of processes entering the barrier starts at zero, the last process recognizes itself by fetching a value equal to the number of processes synchronizing minus one. That process then resets the counter value and begins the second phase of the barrier. The second phase of the barrier amounts to a global event notification and can be implemented with an invalidating or updating write as discussed above. For both phases of the barrier, if the number of processes synchronizing is very large[1], then the processes can be collected/released in a tree fashion to reduce the risk of hot spots. See Section 8.3.2.2 for further discussion of barrier performance.

3.5 Chapter Conclusions

The memory system is the most critical part of the design of a scalable single address space multiprocessor. The memory system must support scalable bandwidth and low latency without a large overhead in hardware costs.

Memory bandwidth ultimately limits system scalability, but this limit does not appear to be significant for systems that use several hundred or even a few thousand processors. Systems of this size can take advantage of scalable direct interconnection networks to achieve sufficient bandwidth for memory access. The most severe bandwidth problems are caused by hot spot references, which are likely to be to synchronization variables. Hardware combining structures could be used to reduce the hot spot problems, but their negative impact on latency for non–hot spot locations limits their effectiveness. A combination of limited hardware support such as in-memory Fetch&Op operations and software techniques is the most suitable solution.

As far as overall performance is concerned, long memory latency is much more limiting than low memory bandwidth. Without good cache and memory locality, demand-driven cache misses can severely impact processor utilization. In the design of a large-scale memory system, careful attention has to be paid to reduce memory latency at every level. In addition, techniques for hiding memory latency, such as the use of a relaxed memory consistency model and prefetching, can reduce the impact of memory latency and improve performance.

---

[1]*The actual number of processors to justify using a gather (or release) tree is determined by the ratio of the Fetch&Op (notification) serialization time versus the latency of a remote memory operation.*

CHAPTER **4**

System Implementation

This chapter details the issues that are key to implementing a scalable shared-memory multiprocessor. The discussion is divided into two major parts. In the first part, the issue of scalability of hardware costs is discussed. Scalability of costs is important for two reasons. First, overhead costs often grow greater than linearly and, together with the non-ideal increases in performance, set the upper limit on the practical size of a parallel system. Second, the marginal costs of providing scalability establishes the lower limit on when a scalable system is competitive with a uniprocessor system. If marginal costs are low, then a greater volume of the common components can be used in building a wide range of systems. Providing a scalable directory structure is the major issue to be discussed. The second part of this chapter is an outline of common implementation problems for scalable shared-memory machines. Although these problems are not comprehensive nor all unique to SSMP systems, they are aggravated by the sophisticated coherence protocols and sheer size of these systems.

4.1 Scalability of System Costs

While the effectiveness of highly parallel systems can be limited by the scalability of the algorithms and memory performance, the size of a particular implementation is also limited by practical issues related to system cost. For example, the CM-5 [Thi93] can theoretically scale to over 16,000 processors, but the cost of the system is in excess of $50 million in 1994. Furthermore, the overhead costs of a large system can make it untenable since its delivered performance does not scale ideally. As technology increases the level of integration, absolute cost will be less of a limit on system size, but the fundamental issue of increasing marginal cost with decreasing performance growth will remain.

All SSMP systems must address three important issues related to system costs and scalability. The first is the overhead of a general interconnect and coherence mechanism on top of the base uniprocessor system. The second is the marginal growth in system overhead as the system grows. The third issue is the balance between optimizing a system for a particular size versus support for a wide range of system sizes.

The overhead of the interconnection between processors will clearly degrade the cost-performance of a multiprocessor relative to a uniprocessor. Although there is potential savings from resource sharing (e.g., memory, disks, and power supplies) in a multiprocessor, these savings can be quickly overrun by the costs of the interconnect and coherence mechanism. Even though a large impact on cost-performance is acceptable in situations where absolute performance is paramount, most situations will only allow a slight decrease in cost - performance relative to state-of-the-art uniprocessor systems. This problem is compounded by the fact that added processors always give less than linear increases in performance. Thus, a system that hopes to achieve near-ideal scalability of cost and performance relative to a uniprocessor can only use a modest fraction of system resources for scalability itself. As demonstrated by the DASH prototype detailed in Part II of this book, keeping the overhead of the directory and the interconnect network low is a challenge, but it can be achieved.

The second limit to scalability in costs is the growth in overhead as the system grows. In a scalable shared-memory system, increases in overhead arise primarily from the costs of the interconnect and coherence mechanism. In Chapter 1, a number of interconnection schemes were described that limit interconnect cost growth to within a factor of $\log N$ of linear. Assuming that the base overhead of the interconnect is small, scaling the interconnect to hundreds or thousands of nodes is possible without large impact on cost-performance. For example, the 16-node fat tree interconnect shown in Figure 1-10(e) can be extended to 1,024 processors by adding three more levels of switches. If the cost of the interconnect for 16 processors was 5%, then the overhead for the 1,024-processor system would be $5\% \cdot \log_4(1024/16) = 15\%$, and the degradation in cost-performance would be 10%.

Unfortunately, the simple bit vector directory organization outlined in Chapter 1 scales as N^2 since memory is added in proportion to processors and the number of bits of directory state per entry also increases with N. For the same example given above, if main memory represents 40% of system cost, then a directory with two state bits, 16 presence bits, and 32-byte memory blocks has a directory overhead of $40\% \cdot 18/(32 \cdot 8) = 2.8\%$. For a 1,024-processor system, however, this overhead grows by a factor of 1026/18, to an overhead of 160%, which degrades cost-performance by over 100%. Thus, alternative directory structures are required for large-scale systems.

The third issue that limits the scalability of a given system implementation is the trade-off between optimizations for a given system size and flexibility of supporting a large range of sizes. These trade-offs arise throughout a design. For example, while a 2-D mesh interconnect has sufficient bandwidth for a 64- to 256-processor system (e.g., DASH), a 3-D mesh is more appropriate for a 1,000- to 2,000-processor system (e.g., Cray T3D or Tera-DASH). Obviously, the 3-D network could be used in the smaller systems, but not without an increase in overhead costs. Similar issues arise in the packaging of a system. Systems targeted for larger configurations tend to use larger cabinets that amortize power, cooling, and cabling resources, while smaller systems use smaller cabinets that have less overhead in smaller configurations and allow finer increments of system growth. Likewise, the physical size of large systems often dictate the use of a different interconnect technology (e.g., fiber optics) whose costs and complexity would not be warranted in smaller systems. Finally, the mean time to failure of a large system with many components dictates that a greater support

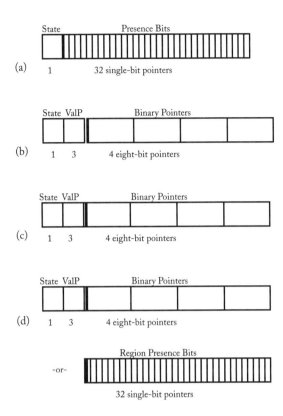

FIGURE   4-1   *Limited-Pointer Directory Entries. (a) Full-bit-vector entry for 32 nodes (Dir$_{16}$).*
(b) Limited-pointer entry with broadcast for 256 nodes using four pointers (Dir$_4$B). (c) Limited-pointer entry
with no broadcast for 256 nodes using four pointers (Dir$_4$NB). (d) Coarse-vector scheme for 256 nodes
using four pointers (Dir$_4$CV$_8$).

for fault tolerance and high availability is required than in smaller systems, where the mean
time to failure is higher and the impact of downtime is smaller. Overall, these practical considerations tend to limit the scalability of a given system implementation to two orders of
magnitude or less. Thus, systems that support 2–8 processors cost-effectively will be far from
ideal when using more than 500 processors, while systems supporting thousands of processors would rarely be configured with less than 32–64 processors.

4.1.1 Directory Storage Overhead

Directory-based cache coherence solves the bandwidth problem of snoopy schemes, but
introduces a scaling problem in the memory overhead of the directory that can grow faster
than linearly with the number of processors. In the following sections, we analyze the various alternative structures that have been proposed to limit the storage requirements of the
directory. The alternatives address the two dimensions of directory growth: the size of each
directory entry and the number of entries. We first discuss different options in implementing
entries: the full-bit-vector scheme, limited-pointer schemes, and extended-pointer schemes.

We then present the sparse directory organization, which reduces the number of entries by using a cache structure for the directory. This technique can be used in conjunction with any of the directory entry organizations listed above. Finally, we outline hierarchical schemes that use a hierarchy of directories to reduce both entry size and the number of entries.

4.1.1.1 Full-Bit-Vector Scheme (Dir$_P$)

A full-bit-vector directory is the simplest directory scheme. It was first proposed by Censier and Feautrier [CeF78] as an alternative to snoopy schemes for small-scale multiprocessors. This scheme associates a bit vector that has one bit per processor for each block of main memory. The directory also contains a dirty bit for each memory block to indicate if one processor has been given exclusive access to modify that block in its cache. Each bit indicates whether that memory block is being cached by the corresponding processor. Thus, the directory has exact knowledge of the processors caching a given block. When a block has to be invalidated, messages are sent to all processors whose caches have a copy. Because it has complete knowledge of who is caching a given block, this scheme produces the minimum coherence traffic.

The structure of a directory entry for a 32-node full-bit-vector scheme is shown in Figure 4-1(a). In this structure the presence bit for a particular processor is set if that processor has a cached copy of the corresponding memory block. If the block is in a shared state then multiple presence bits may be set. If dirty, then the state bit is set and a single presence bit will indicate the owning processor.

Unfortunately, for a multiprocessor with P processors, M bytes of main memory per processor, and a memory block size of B bytes, the directory memory required for presence bits is $P^2 \cdot M/B$ bits, which grows as the square of the number of processors. Thus, full-bit-vector schemes become unacceptable for machines with a very large number of processors.

Although the asymptotic memory requirements look formidable, full-bit-vector directories can be quite attractive for machines of moderate size. For example, the Stanford DASH multiprocessor consists of 64 processors organized as 16 clusters of 4 processors each. A full-bit-vector directory scheme is used for intercluster cache coherence. The block size is 16 bytes and a 16-bit vector per block is required to keep track of all the clusters. Each block also needs a valid and a dirty bit. Thus, the overhead of directory memory as a fraction of the total main memory is 14%,[1] which is comparable to the overhead of an ECC code on memory. Note that if the cache block size is increased from 16 bytes to 64 bytes, then this same overhead could be maintained on a system of up to 256 processors. Beyond a certain point, however, this approach is not very practical because increasing the cache block size can have other undesirable side effects such as false sharing.

4.1.1.2 Limited-Pointer Schemes

Our study of parallel applications in Chapter 2 has shown that most kinds of data objects are cached by only a *small* number of processors at any given time. We can exploit this knowledge to reduce directory memory overhead by restricting each directory entry to a small fixed number of pointers, each pointing to a processor caching that memory block [ASH+88]. In

---

[1] 14% = 18 bits / (16 bytes · 8 bits/byte).

limited-pointer schemes we need $\log P$ bits per pointer, while only one bit sufficed to point to a processor in the full-bit-vector scheme. Thus, the full-bit-vector scheme makes more effective use of the bits. However, by keeping only a small number of pointers, we can reduce the total number of bits kept in each directory entry. If we ignore the state bits, the directory memory requirement for a limited-pointer scheme with i pointers is $(i \cdot \log P) \cdot (P \cdot M/B)$, which grows as $P \log P$ with the number of processors. The storage growth rate of the limited-pointer schemes is thus much more favorable.

An important implication of limited-pointer schemes is that there must exist some mechanism to handle blocks that are cached by more processors than the number of pointers available in the directory entry. Several alternatives exist to deal with this *pointer overflow*, and we discuss three of them below. Depending on the alternative chosen, the coherence and data traffic generated may vary greatly.

Limited pointers with broadcast (Dir$_i$B). The Dir$_i$ B scheme [ASH+88] solves the pointer overflow problem by adding a broadcast bit to the state information for each block. When pointer overflow occurs, the broadcast bit is set. A subsequent write to this block causes invalidations to be broadcast to *all* caches. Some of these invalidation messages go to processors that do not have a copy of the block and thus reduce overall performance by delaying the completion of writes and by wasting communication bandwidth.

The structure of a Dir$_4$B directory supporting 256 nodes and four pointers is shown in Figure 4-1(b). In this scheme, each pointer is a binary number. The ValP field denotes how many pointers are valid. If this field is greater than four, then more than four processors are caching the block and a broadcast invalidate will be sent on the next write. As before, if the state bit is set, then there is one valid pointer, which is the cache holding the block dirty. Note that the directory overhead for this 256-node system is almost identical to that of the 32-node full-bit-vector directory scheme.

Limited pointers without broadcast (Dir$_i$NB). One way to avoid broadcasts is to disallow pointer overflows altogether. In the Dir$_i$NB scheme [ASH+88], room for an additional requestor is made by invalidating one of the caches already sharing the block. In this manner a block can never be present in more than i caches at any one time, and thus a write can never cause more than i invalidations.

The structure of a Dir$_4$NB directory entry supporting 256 nodes is illustrated in Figure 4-1(c). The format of a Dir$_4$NB directory entry is identical to the Dir$_4$B. The only difference is when there are four valid pointers and the directory receives a read, one of the caches pointed to in the directory will be invalidated in order to keep the number of pointers at four.

The most serious degradation in performance with this scheme occurs when the application has read-only or mostly-read data objects that are actively shared by a large number of processors. Even if the data is read-only, a continuous stream of invalidations results as the objects are shuttled from one cache to another in an attempt to share them between more than i caches. This situation results in an increased number of misses and an increase in the data and coherence traffic in the machine. Without special provisions to handle such widely shared data, performance can be severely degraded.

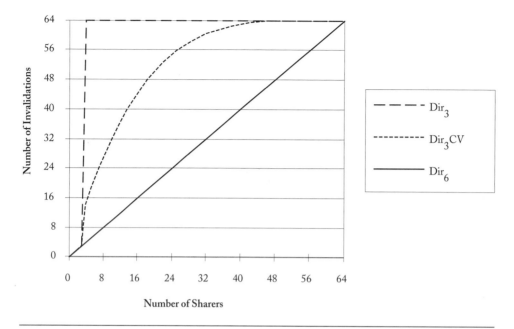

FIGURE 4-2 *Invalidation Messages as a Function of Sharers.*

Coarse-vector scheme (Dir_iCV_r). Another solution to the overflow problem is the coarse-vector scheme (Dir_iCV_r). In this notation, i is the number of pointers and r is the size of the region that each bit in the coarse vector represents. Dir_iCV_r is identical to the other limited-pointer schemes when there are no more than i processors sharing a block. Each of the i pointers stores the identity of a processor that is caching a copy of the block. However, when pointer overflow occurs, the semantics are switched, so that the memory used for storing the pointers is now used to store a coarse bit vector. Each bit of this bit vector stands for a region of r processors. The region size r is determined by the number of directory memory bits available. While some accuracy is lost over the full-bit-vector representation, we are neither forced to throw out entries (as in Dir_iNB) nor to go to broadcast immediately (as in Dir_iB).

The structure of a Dir_4CV_8 coarse-vector directory for 256 processors using four pointers and eight-node regions is given in Figure 4-1(d). When the number of sharers is four or less, then the format is identical to the Dir_4B scheme. If there is a fifth read, however, the coarse-vector scheme resorts to a presence bit encoding of the directory pointers. Since there are only 32 bits to represent 256 processors, however, each bit represents a region of eight nodes. Once in region mode, subsequent reads set the appropriate region bit if it is not already set. Upon a write, invalidates are sent to groups of eight nodes designated by the set region presence bits, and the directory returns to the binary pointer format used in Dir_4B. Note that since there can be no more than one dirty cache, a pointer to a dirty cache is always a full binary pointer.

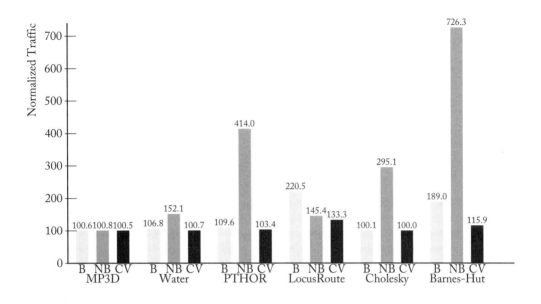

FIGURE 4-3   *Memory System Traffic with Different Limited-Pointer Directory Structures.*

Limited-pointer scheme performance. Figure 4-2 makes the different behavior of the broadcast and coarse-vector schemes apparent. We consider a machine with 64 processors and assume that the limited-pointer schemes each have three pointers. Since each pointer is 6 bits wide, there are 18 bits per directory entry, which means that the region size r for the coarse-vector scheme is 4. The graph shows the average number of invalidations sent out on a write to a shared block as the number of processors sharing that block is varied. For each invalidation event, the sharers are randomly chosen and the number of invalidations required is recorded. After a very large number of events, these invalidation figures are averaged and plotted.

In the ideal case of the full-bit-vector scheme (stipple line), the number of invalidations is identical to the number of sharers. For the other schemes, we do not have full knowledge of who the sharers are, and *extraneous* invalidations need to be sent. The area between the stipple line of the full-bit-vector scheme and the line of a scheme represents the number of extraneous invalidations for that scheme. For the Dir$_3$B scheme, we go to broadcast as soon as the 3 pointers are exhausted, which results in many extraneous invalidations. The coarse-vector scheme, on the other hand, retains a rough idea of which processors have cached copies. It is thus able to send invalidations to the *regions* of processors containing cached copies, without having to resort to broadcast. Hence, the number of extraneous invalidations is much smaller.

Figure 4-3 shows the normalized memory system traffic that the Dir$_i$B, Dir$_i$NB, and Dir$_i$CV$_r$ schemes produce for each of the applications studied in Chapter 2. These simulations use 64 processors and assume 4 pointers per directory entry. Traffic is calculated as described in Section 2.7 and is normalized such that a traffic value of 100 corresponds to the traffic produced by the full-bit-vector scheme. For applications that are well-suited to lim-ited-pointer schemes (such as MP3D), the traffic is uniformly low for all directory entry organizations. In applications with a large fraction of mostly-read data (such as Barnes-Hut), the nonbroadcast scheme has an explosion in memory system traffic. Furthermore, the invalidations in the nonbroadcast scheme actually remove data from the target cache and lead to additional misses. Large increases in traffic are also seen for the broadcast scheme in applications where broadcasts are relatively frequent (such as LocusRoute). The coarse-vec-tor scheme is more robust and outperforms the other limited-pointer schemes for all appli-cations. In addition, the traffic produced by the coarse-vector scheme is very close to the ideal traffic of the full-bit-vector scheme for most applications. The broadcast scheme is closest to the coarse-vector scheme, but we expect the performance gap to widen with increased number of processors because broadcast invalidations become increasingly more expensive.

4.1.1.3 Extended Pointer Schemes

While the previous directory schemes use extra invalidations when their pointer storage is exhausted, other schemes extend the base number of directory entry pointers by various mechanisms so that precise information about caching is always maintained.

LimitLESS Directory. Agarwal et al. [ALK+91] have proposed the LimitLESS directory scheme for the MIT Alewife machine. This scheme is a standard limited-pointer scheme, but it uses a software mechanism to handle pointer overflow. When a pointer overflow occurs in a directory, the processor in the same node is interrupted and stores the hardware pointers to memory, thus freeing up the storage for more pointers.

The structure of a 256-node LimitLESS directory entry with four hardware pointers is shown in Figure 4-4(a). Again, the format is similar to the Dir_4B and Dir_4NB schemes. The only difference is what happens on the fifth read operation and subsequent writes. Upon the fifth read, a trap is taken and software copies the hardware pointers to a dedicated portion of memory. The hardware directory can then accept four more reads before a trap must be taken. While the format of the main memory extension to the directory could take many forms, a hash table is proposed by Agarwal et al. [ALK+91]. If any pointers have been cop-ied off to memory, then any write must trap to software in order to send invalidates to the processors whose pointers are stored in memory. After the write, the LimitLESS directory will have the dirty bit set and be in the same format as the Dir_4B or Dir_4NB schemes.

The LimitLESS scheme is very flexible since pointer overflows are handled in software. This scheme also reduces hardware complexity since it minimizes the hardware support for overflows. However, to work efficiently, LimitLESS requires a special-purpose processor that has a fast context switch mechanism to support fast interrupt handling of directory overflows. Even with fast trap handling, the performance penalty of pointer overflow is large because of both the overhead on the local node processor and the latency of the software mechanism.

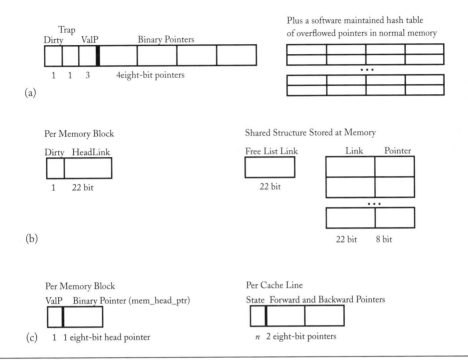

FIGURE 4-4 *Extended-Pointer Directory Entries. (a) LimitLESS pointer scheme for 256 nodes using four pointers (LimitLESS$_4$). (b) Dynamic pointer scheme for 256 nodes. (c) Doubly linked list cache-based scheme for up to 256 nodes.*

Dynamic Pointer Directory. Simoni has proposed a dynamic pointer allocation directory [SiH91, Sim92]. In this scheme, a short directory entry is associated with each memory block. This entry contains the state of the block and a head pointer to a list containing pointers to processors with cached copies of the block. The linked list is made up of entries that are dynamically allocated from a directorywide pool of entries.

The structure of the dynamic pointer scheme is shown in Figure 4-4(b). In this structure, there is only a head link and a state bit associated with each memory block. The head pointers are null if the block is uncached, or point into a dedicated scratch memory that contains pairs of links and cache pointers. There is also a free list link that points to the head of a list of currently unused link/pointer pairs. On reads, a new cache pointer is allocated from the free list and spliced into the head of the sharing list for that block. Upon a write, the sharing list for the specific block is traversed and invalidates are sent to each processor currently caching the block. The block is marked dirty and the head link points to an entry that has a pointer to the dirty cache. If any link/pointer entries are freed in the process, they are added to the free list.

The dynamic pointer allocation scheme solves the directory storage overhead problem of the basic full directory scheme because its storage requirements are a function of the number of cached blocks in the machine, which grows linearly with machine size. One issue with this scheme is that without replacement messages (i.e., messages to the directory indicating a clean block has been replaced), the linked lists will fill with stale pointers and the free list will often be empty. If replacement messages are used, then they will trigger list walking to remove the processor from the sharing list, a process that increases the bandwidth demands on the directory. The lists also have to be walked at invalidation time. The performance impact of these operations depends on the implementation of the directory controller.

This scheme can be viewed as a hardware implementation of LimitLESS pointers. Both schemes have the advantage of keeping perfect information about the caching of every memory block and never generating any extra invalidation traffic. The disadvantage of these schemes is that their directory entry extension schemes require additional processing time and complexity in the directory controller (or processor).

Cache-based linked-list schemes. A different way of addressing the scalability problem of full-bit-vector directory schemes is to keep a list of pointers in the processor caches instead of in a directory next to memory [Kni87, Wil88]. These schemes are similar to Simoni's, but distribute the linked list in the processor caches. One such scheme has been formalized as the IEEE 1596-1992–Scalable Coherent Interface (SCI) standard [JLG+90]. Related work has been done by Thapar and Delagi [ThD90]. In SCI, each directory entry is made up of a doubly linked list. The head pointer to the list is kept in memory. Each cache with a copy of the block is one item on the list with forward and back pointers to the remainder of the list.

The structure of a cache-based linked-list directory is shown in Figure 4-4(c). When a cache wants to read a shared item, it uses the pointer in memory to find the current head of the list and adds itself as the new head. When a write to a shared block occurs, the list is unraveled one by one by sending messages sequentially to each processor in the list. The benefit of maintaining the doubly linked list is that it simplifies leaving a sharing list when a processor replaces a cache line.

The advantage of this scheme is that it scales naturally with the number of processors. As more processors are added, the total cache space increases and so does the space in which to keep the directory information. Unfortunately, there are also disadvantages to distributed directory schemes. First, the protocol required to maintain a linked list for each directory entry is more complicated than the protocol for a memory-based directory scheme because directory updates cannot be performed atomically. Second, the maintenance of the lists requires several messages to be sent at each cache replacement, which increases overall coherence traffic. Third, a write of data that is shared by even a small number of caches takes longer to complete because the sharing list has to be unraveled one element at a time. In contrast, invalidations in a memory-based directory scheme are serialized only by their injection rate into the network.

Extended-pointer scheme performance. Comparing the performance of the extended-pointer directory organizations to each other and the limited schemes is difficult. While the papers referenced in the previous sections compare their proposed scheme to the full-bit-vector scheme, there has not been a comprehensive study that includes all of the options with the same system and application assumptions. The closest is a survey by Chaiken et al. [CFK+90], but it does not include the broadcast or region-bit schemes and only covers a small set of applications.

In the extended schemes, the effects on performance are not due to extra invalidations; they are tied primarily to the performance of the directory controller when trapping to software (LimitLESS) or doing complex list manipulation (dynamic pointer). For the cache-based schemes, the performance degradation depends upon the size of the sharing lists and the serialization time to traverse each node of the sharing list. For the typical case where the average number of sharers is small, one would expect all of the memory-based directory schemes to perform similarly (the possible exception being the behavior in the nonbroadcast scheme for widely shared objects), with the coarse vector and dynamic pointer schemes having the least performance degradation when the number of sharers exceeds the hardware pointer count. Of course, these last two schemes rely on more complex hardware. The cache-based linked-list schemes are likely to have somewhat lower performance relative to the other schemes in all cases because of the extra network traversals that they require even when sharing lists are short.

4.1.2 Sparse Directories

The previously described schemes attempt to reduce the size of each directory entry, but still retain a directory entry per memory block. We now turn to the other dimension of directory memory growth: the number of entries. Typically, the total amount of cache memory in a multiprocessor is much less than the total amount of main memory. If the directory state is kept in its entirety, we have one entry for each memory block. Most blocks are not cached anywhere, and the corresponding directory entries are empty. To reduce this waste of memory, we can use a cache of directory entries. If we also enforce a rule that all directory entries not in the cache are empty (i.e., their corresponding memory blocks are uncached), then the cache is the only directory storage required. We refer to a directory cache without backing store as a *sparse directory* [GWM90, Web93]. Similar caching directories have been proposed by O'Krafka and Newton [OKN90] as well as Lilja [LiA94].

As an example of directory storage inefficiency, a machine with 64 MBytes of main memory per processor and 1 MByte of cache memory per processor has no more than 1/64 or about 1.5% of all directory entries active at any one time. By using a directory cache of suitable size, we are able to drastically reduce the directory memory. This reduction allows for either a lower machine cost, or for each directory entry to be wider. For example, if the Dir_iCV_r scheme were used with a sparse directory, more pointers i and smaller regions r would result.

The ratio of main memory blocks to directory entries is called the *memory size factor* of the directory. Thus, if the directory only contains 1/16 as many entries as there are main memory blocks, it has a memory size factor of 16. The other important parameter of sparse directories is the ratio of directory entries to cache lines, the *directory size factor*. A directory size factor of 1 indicates that the total number of directory entries is the same as the total number of cache blocks in the system. This is the minimum useful sparse directory size because the directory is just big enough to be able to keep track of all cached lines.

Table 4-1 shows some sample directory configurations for machines of different sizes. For these machines, 64 MBytes of main memory and 1 MByte of cache were assumed per processor. A directory memory overhead of around 13% has been allowed throughout. Pro-

TABLE 4-1

Directory Configurations and Directory Memory Overhead

NUMBER OF CLUSTERS	NUMBER OF PROCESSORS	TOTAL MAIN MEMORY (GBytes)	TOTAL CACHE MEMORY (MBytes)	BLOCK SIZE (bytes)	DIRECTORY SCHEME	DIRECTORY MEMORY OVERHEAD (%)
16	64	16	64	16	Dir_{16}	13.3
64	256	64	256	16	sparse Dir_{64}	13.1
256	1024	256	1024	16	sparse Dir_8CV_4	13.3

cessors have been clustered into processing nodes of 4 — similar to DASH. If there are 64 processors arranged as 16 clusters of 4 processors, then a full-bit-vector scheme Dir_{16} is easily feasible. As the machine is scaled to 256 processors, we keep the directory memory overhead at the same level by switching to sparse directories. The sparse directories contain entries for 1/4 of the main memory blocks (memory size factor is 4). As we shall see in the next section, even much sparser directories still perform well. For the 1,024-processor machine, the directory memory overhead is kept constant and the entry size is kept manageable by using a coarse-vector directory entry scheme (Dir_8CV_4) in addition to using a sparse directory with a memory size factor of 8. Note that this is achieved without having to resort to a larger cache line size.

Although there are some similarities between sparse directories and caches, there are some important differences. We already mentioned that unlike regular caches, a sparse directory does not require a backing store. A second difference between sparse directories and processor caches is that caches typically have a line size that is larger than a single item (word). A sparse directory only has one directory item per entry. The issue of spatial reference locality thus does not arise in sparse directories. Third, a sparse directory handles references from the entire machine. Thus, the reference stream it sees is very different from a primary or secondary processor cache. The directory sees the interleaved stream of misses from all the processor caches.

Lastly, when looking at the performance of caches we are interested in the performance impact of the cache *misses*. In contrast, when looking at the performance of a sparse directory in relation to a full directory, we are interested in directory *collisions*. A collision occurs when requests to distinct memory lines map into the same directory entry. The collision is resolved by invalidating all cached copies of the memory line that is currently occupying the directory entry, thus making room for the new request. As with caches, the rate of collisions in a sparse directory can be decreased by having more entries (i.e., a smaller memory size factor) or by adding associativity. Figure 4-5 shows the structure of a four-way set-associative sparse directory entry. This structure supports a 64-cluster, 256-processor configuration given in Table 4-1. The structure is identical to a normal full-bit-vector Dir_{64} structure, but has the addition of a cache tag for each entry. Read and write operations using the sparse directory proceed as if there was a normal full-map directory except when there is a sparse directory

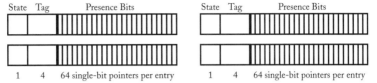

Four directory entries for every 64 memory blocks

F I G U R E 4 - 5 *Four-Way Set-Associative Sparse Directory with Memory Size Factor of 4.*

miss. When a miss occurs and there is a free entry within this directory entry set, then the entry is allocated and the request is processed as if the block was uncached. If a miss occurs and there are no unused entries within the set, a collision has occurred and an entry must be freed. If the victim block is in a shared state, then it can be freed simply by invalidating the processors caching the block. If all the entries are dirty, then one block must be forced back to memory. These invalidations cause additional coherence traffic and processor cache misses, and thus degrade overall system performance. We focus on the causes and effects of directory collisions and their impact on performance in the next section.

4.1.2.1 Sparse Directory Collisions

How many directory entries are required in a sparse directory? If there was a single central memory and directory, and each directory entry could be used for any memory line, then having exactly as many directory entries as there are cache lines in the whole system (directory size factor = 1) would suffice. In practice, the directories and memories must be separated into different banks in order to increase bandwidth. This can create an imbalance in directory memory requirements if an unusually large fraction of the cached blocks correspond to a given bank. In addition, the mapping of memory references to sparse directory entries can cause conflicts. Also, cache replacements without notification of the directory (replacement hints) increase the apparent number of cached lines. All of these factors cause directory collisions if the directory size factor is 1, so we need to increase the directory size factor to reduce the likelihood of collisions.

Weber [Web93] has developed an analytic model of collisions for a sparse directory of associativity a, directory size factor d, memory size factor m, and number of processors P. Assuming accesses are uniform and replacement hints are used, it is shown that the probability that a particular request causes a directory collision is

$$\text{Pr(collision)} = \text{Pr(sparse directory entry is full)} \cdot \text{Pr(request to new block)}$$

$$\text{Pr(collision)} = \left(\sum_{x=a}^{P} \text{Pr}(x \text{ requests}) \cdot \left(1 - \binom{ma}{a-1} \left(\frac{a-1}{ma} \right)^{x} \right) \right) \cdot \frac{m-1}{m}$$

$$\text{Pr}(x \text{ requests map to this entry}) = \frac{\lambda^{x} e^{-\lambda}}{x!} \qquad \text{where } \lambda = \frac{a}{d}$$

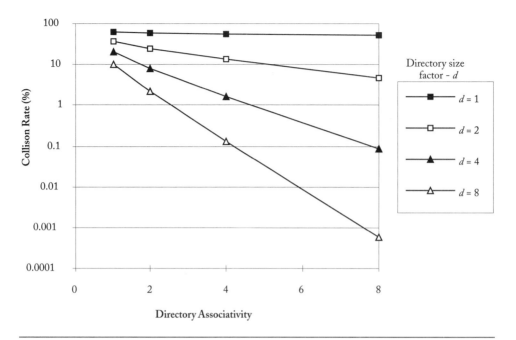

FIGURE 4-6 *Combined Effect of Associativity and Directory Size Factor (m · d = 64).*

where the last equation makes a Poisson approximation of the exact binomial distribution for the probability that there are exactly x requests to this directory entry. Since the probability of a collision goes down with $x!$, the collision probability is not a strong function of the number of processors in the system.[2] Likewise, the memory size factor m is not a strong factor when the directory is really organized as a cache (i.e., $m \geq 8$). The model assumes that memory size is proportional to processor count and that replacement hints are used, so the only active directory entries are for locations that are actually cached. The dominant factors in determining the collision rate is the directory size factor d and the directory associativity a. Figure 4-6 shows the collision rates obtained with different combinations of associativity and directory size factor. We see that the collision rate can be high if a or d are 1, but it is greatly reduced by using larger values. With both a and d at 4, the collision rate is only 1.8%, and with both values at 8, the collision rate is down to nine per million.

As shown in Figure 4-7, an actual application does even better than the model predicts. In this simulation, we use MP3D because its data set is large enough to fill all of the available main memory. The total data set of the simulated problem (50 K molecules) encompasses 32 KBytes per processor for a 64-processor run. We assume a ratio of main memory size to cache size of 64, which leads to scaled caches of 512 bytes (see Section 2.7 for more details on cache scaling). With a line size of 4 bytes, a directory associativity of 1 and directory size factor of 1, there are 128 directory entries per processing node. The simulation

---

[2] This observation results from the assumption that memory and directory entries are added in proportion to the number of processors.

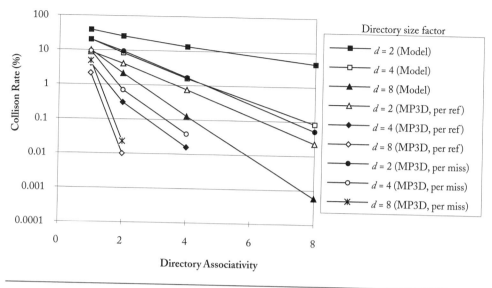

FIGURE 4-7 *Model and Simulation Comparison for MP3D.*

results confirm the basic conclusion that the lowest collision rates are achieved when taking advantage of both a larger directory size factor and an associativity greater than 1. The graph also indicates that the model predictions are quite conservative. For some configurations there are no collisions. There are a number of reasons why the simulations are better than the model predictions:

1. The model assumes all requests are uncorrelated. For variables that are read and then modified, there will be memory requests to transition from the shared to exclusive state. Unless the block is invalidated before it is written, the write request is guaranteed to hit in the sparse directory.

2. The effective directory size factor is greater than the number of directory entries divided by the number of cache lines because shared data is held in more than one processor cache.

3. The processor caches are not fully utilized because of invalidations and conflicts within the cache.

4. Private data requires no directory entries if it is allocated from local memory.

Overall, the analytic collision model appears very conservative and indicates that collisions will have a minimal impact on performance if directory associativity and size factor are greater than one. This analysis assumes that replacement notifications for clean blocks are sent to the directory. If they are not used, then the directory will tend to fill up with stale entries that point to blocks that have been replaced in the processor caches. The net effect is similar to having much larger processor caches or a reduced directory size factor: collisions are more frequent. However, note that collisions that require the replacement of a stale entry are relatively cheap because the invalidations do not actually remove anything from the cache.

Weber [Web93] shows that if a FIFO or LRU replacement policy is used for the sparse directory, and the directory size factor and associativity are both greater than one, then the rate of *real* collisions (i.e., those that actually cause a cache invalidation) is similar to the rate of collisions when replacement hints are used.[3] This result implies that performance and traffic will be no worse if replacement hints are not used (i.e., the number of stale directory collisions and implied invalidation messages will be about the same as the number of replacement hint messages). Thus, sparse directories perform equally well with or without replacement hints, and the decision to use such hints would be based on whether the processor provides them and the details of the coherence protocol.

4.1.3 Hierarchical Directories

In the directory schemes we have discussed so far, each memory line has a home node that is queried first on a miss. One of the potential problems of these schemes is that the home can become a bottleneck in very large multiprocessors. If a given memory block were to become a hot spot, with a large fraction of all processors requesting the line within a short time interval, the read latency would become very large for most processors because a single directory is processing all requests. This problem can be alleviated with hierarchical directory schemes because requests are combined on their way to the top of the hierarchy and replies are fanned out as they descend the hierarchy.

The hierarchy of the directory structure can be reflected in the interconnect topology itself [Wil87, WWS+89, CGB91, HLH92, Bur91], or it can be embedded in a more general interconnect [Wal90, Sco91]. For hierarchical interconnects the higher levels of the hierarchy may require larger interconnect bandwidth, depending on how well an application can be partitioned to fit the hierarchy. For directory hierarchies that are embedded in a more general interconnect, this problem can be avoided by embedding a number of different hierarchies in the interconnect and using a different hierarchy for each portion of the address space. While the bandwidth requirements for these two variations of hierarchical directories may differ, the directory storage requirements are the same. The directory overhead scales as $P\log^2 P$ with the number of processors, because each of the $O(P)$ cached memory lines requires directory information at $O(\log P)$ levels of the hierarchy [Sco91], and each directory entry requires $O(\log P)$ bits for tag storage.

Directory size has to increase towards the top of the hierarchy because there are more items to keep track of higher up in the hierarchy. A practical way to deal with the increased directory size towards the top of the hierarchy is to manage it as a cache (i.e., a sparse directory). This approach makes contention for directory entries possible and leads to replacement of directory entries from the cache. There are two ways of dealing with missing entries in the directory hierarchy. In the more common approach (known as *multilevel inclusion*), a cache line is removed from the subtree below the directory when it is evicted from a direc-

---

[3] For MP3D with $a = 2$, $d = 2$, Real Collision% = 4.6%, 5.0%; $a = 4$, $d = 4$, Collision% = 0.12%, 0.08%; $a = 8$, $d = 8$, Collision% = 0.03%, 0.00% for FIFO and LRU replacement, respectively.

Per memory block => 16 pointers to groups of 16 processors

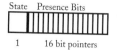

Lower-level directory => 16 pointers to groups of 16 nodes

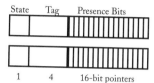 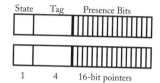

FIGURE 4-8   *Two-level Hierarchical Directory Structure for a 256-processor NUMA System.*

tory. In contrast, Scott [Sco91] proposed a pruning cache scheme that does not require the cache line to be removed from the subtree when the corresponding directory entry is evicted. The downside of this scheme is that a missing entry has to be treated conservatively. Thus, for writes, invalidations have to be propagated to all members of that subtree, even if none of them contain a cached copy.

The structure of a two-level hierarchical directory structure supporting 256 processors is shown in Figure 4-8. In this structure it is assumed that the system is organized with all memory at the top of the tree or set of trees, and all processors at the leaves of the tree. At memory, operations proceed as if there was a full directory supporting just 16 nodes. At the lower level of the hierarchy, there are sparse directory entries that filter both upward and downward traffic. Memory requests travelling toward memory are satisfied within a particular subtree if the sparse directory indicates that the block is cached within the subtree. For interventions coming down the tree (e.g., invalidations or requests to dirty blocks), the lower directories filter this traffic and pass it on to only the particular processors caching the block.

4.1.4   Summary of Directory Storage Overhead

A simple full-bit-vector directory storage organization does not scale well because its size grows as P^2 with the number of processors. While the full-bit-vector scheme is adequate for medium-size machines (i.e., up to 64 or 128 processors depending upon cache line size and number of processors per node), a more scalable scheme is needed for larger systems. Scalable directory storage schemes take advantage of the size difference between the processor caches and main memory, which insures that most directory pointers are null. Thus, savings can be had by not dedicating a directory entry per memory block (i.e., sparse directories). Furthermore, even when a block is cached by some processors, it is usually cached by only a small number of processors, so one need not reserve a pointer per processor in each directory entry. There are many options for organizing a scalable directory entry. The limited and hierarchical schemes produce extra invalidations when the number of pointers becomes inadequate. The extended pointer schemes use overflow storage, so precise information is always maintained, but they suffer degraded directory performance when overflow occurs.

The analysis presented here (and [Web93]) suggests that the limited-pointer schemes (especially with region bits) perform very close to the full-bit-vector scheme. Thus, the extended and hierarchical schemes do not appear to warrant their complexity. If an additional reduction in directory overhead is needed (for example, in order to cost-effectively use static RAM instead of dynamic RAM for the directory storage), then sparse directories can be used to help eliminate null directory entries. However, sparse directories add the complexity of managing the directory as a cache and dealing with sparse directory entry replacements.

4.2 Implementation Issues and Design Correctness

Although scalability and low latency are desirable properties of a system, correct operation is a necessity. Correct operation implies more than just the maintenance of cache coherency and memory consistency. Operations must be guaranteed to complete in a finite amount of time, and the system as a whole must make forward progress. Thus, the memory system must be free of deadlock and livelock, and individual requests must not starve. In addition, it is desirable that a large-scale system be able to detect and respond to error conditions. Correct operation is made difficult by several problems inherent in a large-scale distributed system. Some of the more difficult issues are the following:

1. Unbounded number of requests to each node

2. Distributed memory operations

3. Request starvation

4. Error handling and fault tolerance

For performance reasons, these issues must be resolved directly in hardware. Thus, the solutions must not be too complex nor compromise performance. The following sections detail these problems and their potential solutions. The section concludes with a brief discussion of design verification, a very important aspect of implementing a complex memory system.

4.2.1 Unbounded Number of Requests

The minimum communication protocol in a distributed memory system is a strict request-reply protocol between the processors and memories, and between the processors themselves. For example, processors make cache fill requests to memory, and memory replies with the requested data. Likewise, processors receive invalidation requests and reply with acknowledgment messages. In general, a node can guarantee sufficient buffering for reply messages by limiting the number of requests it has outstanding. However, it is usually impractical to provide enough buffering to receive all incoming requests because multiple requests might be received simultaneously from every processor in the system. For example, in a system with 256 processors and two 64-byte write-back messages outstanding from each processor, a particular memory would need 32 KByte of incoming request buffering to hold the maximum amount of message traffic it might receive.[4]

---

[4] One exception to this rule would be an overflow mechanism that extends the hardware queues into a main memory buffer as in Alewife [ALK+91].

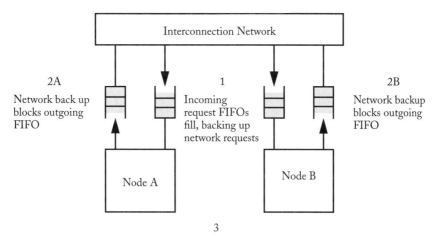

If head of request queue for A requires reply to B and vice versa, then no progress can be made => deadlock.

FIGURE 4-9   *Network Deadlock Due to Unbounded Number of Request Messages.*

A more robust network interface would support a flow control mechanism that allows a receiver to limit new incoming requests. However, the flow control mechanism must not block network resources needed to reply to messages or deadlock may result. Figure 4-9 illustrates how such a deadlock could arise. First assume that nodes A and B have a number of pending requests and are currently blocking requests on their incoming network request inputs. If the requests back up to the reply output ports of A and B, then A and B will never be able to process the head of their respective request queues if they require replies to be sent to each other. Other deadlock scenarios can also arise whenever a circular dependency between the nodes exists because of their need to send outgoing replies in order to satisfy incoming requests.

Assuming that request and reply messages do not block one another within a node, there are several possible solutions to the problem of network deadlock. In systems with direct connections between nodes (e.g., a crossbar or other fully interconnected system), flow control can be used to limit requests at their source without blocking the network. Unfortunately, most scalable networks do not have such direct connections due to the N^2 complexity of such schemes. Alternatively, if direct communication is limited to a fixed set of nodes (e.g., nearest neighbor), and a store-and-forward communication protocol is used along with separate request and reply buffers, then intermediate nodes can flow control requests messages without blocking replies. Store-and-forward is undesirable, however, because the delay in traversing intermediate nodes significantly increases latency. The simplest solution is to have two completely separate networks for requests and replies. Note that the two networks need not be physically separate, but must contain dedicated resources (e.g., buffers, handshake lines, etc., as in Dally's virtual channels [DaS87]) so that blockage of the request network does not affect the reply network.

In a system that supports a deadlock-free request-reply protocol, it is also possible to allow more complex communication patterns by having more dedicated network channels or by restricting when such communication is done. For example, a memory controller might forward an incoming request for a block dirty in a remote node if its output port is not blocked, but revert to the simpler request-reply protocol whenever the port is blocked. In a more aggressive system (e.g., DASH) request forwarding can be attempted even when the output request blockage, as long as this node's input request buffer is not full. Deadlock is still avoided because no circular dependencies involving this node can exist if the node is currently accepting incoming requests.

4.2.2 Distributed Memory Operations

In a system without cache coherence, operations on a single memory location complete after accessing memory and can be ordered by their arrival at memory. Likewise, in small-scale cache-coherent systems, requests are serialized by their issue on the common bus, and all cache updates are synchronous to the bus access. In a distributed system with caches, however, some memory operations cannot complete within one node. For example, a read request for a location held dirty in a remote cluster must be sent to that cluster. Likewise, updating shared copies of a line requires that each caching node be updated. Distributed execution of memory operations results in three problems. First, it complicates the problems of serializing accesses to a location, both in determining when requests are accepted and insuring that once an order is chosen, it is consistent throughout the system. Second, distributed cache coherence creates buffering problems for requests that must be delayed until a remote portion of the operation completes. Third, distribution complicates the coherence protocol by creating numerous transient states that must be managed and their interaction with other requests specified and verified.

Looking at the serialization problem in more detail, maintaining coherence and a memory consistency model requires that at least a partial ordering be placed on all memory references. Since read operations are idempotent, ordering is most important between write operations themselves and between write and read operations. These problems are akin to the read-after-write (RAW), write-after-write (WAW), and write-after-read (WAR) hazards found in pipelined CPUs [HeP90]. Examples of these serialization problems are shown in Figure 4-10. The figure uses the labeling conventions and directory protocol described in Chapter 6 (see Section 6.3.1). To summarize the conventions, the circles represent nodes with **Cx** being a CPU and **H** being the home memory node (i.e., the node that contains the memory/directory for a particular address). The arrows in the figure represent messages sent between nodes.

The first requirement to deal with the serialization problem is that at any one time, there is a single entity that determines the order of operations on a location. The memory of the block can serve this role, but in a distributed system, it may need to delay and buffer requests while data is returned from a remote dirty cache. This blockage can lead to deadlock within the memory since there may be an unbounded number of requests for a given block.

Read-after-write memory hazard example.
- CPU 1 issues read to home node containing the directory and memory for the given location (1).
- CPU 2 issues read-exclusive to home (2).
- Home receives CPU 1's read request and sends reply data (3) and sets directory presence bit.
- Home receives CPU 2's read-exclusive request, sends an invalidate to 1 (4a), and reply to CPU 2 (4b).
- Due to reordering in the network (e.g., due to adaptive routing), CPU 1 receives the invalidate (4a) before its reply and sends acknowledge (5).
- CPU 1 receives and caches its read reply (3) from memory.
- CPU 2 receives the invalidate acknowledge (5) and read-exclusive reply (5) and completes its write.
- A RAW hazard now exists since CPU 1 can read the stale value of the location until it is displaced from its cache.

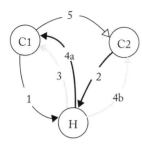

Write-after-write memory hazard example.
- Assume CPU 1 has an exclusive copy of the given location.
- CPU 2 issues read-exclusive to home (1).
- CPU 2 message is forwarded to CPU 1 (2).
- CPU 1 receives exclusive request, replies to CPU 2 (3a), and sends transfer message to directory (3b).
- CPU 2 receives exclusive reply and completes write.
- CPU 2 issues write-back of given location (4).
- CPU 2's write-back (4) received at home memory before transfer request (3b).
- Once transfer request is received, directory and memory state are corrupt since CPU 2's write-back has been lost and the directory points to CPU 2 for the latest copy of the given location.

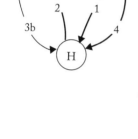

Write-after-read memory hazard example.
This hazard only occurs between processor accesses to memory when one considers writes to different locations that are supposed to be ordered.
- Assume CPU 1 writes location A, which is cached by CPU 2. This generates a read-exclusive message (1).
- CPU 2 reads location B (2), which is dirty in CPU 1's cache. This is forwarded to CPU 1 (3).
- CPU 1's request is received, which generates an exclusive reply (4a) and invalidate to CPU 2 (4b).
- If CPU 1 proceeds after receiving the exclusive reply (4a), then it can complete a write to location B, which is already exclusive in its cache.
- CPU 2 read of B is received by CPU 1, which replies with the new value of B (5a) and a write-back to the directory (5b).
- If the read reply to CPU 2 with the new value of B (5a) is received before the invalidate (4b), then CPU 2 could read the new value of B, but the old value of A from its cache even though they were written in the opposite order by CPU 1.

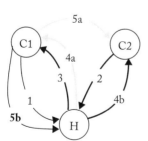

FIGURE 4-10 *Memory Operation Serialization Hazards on Individual Memory Locations.*

CPU 2 completes write even though invalidates are pending.
- Assume line is in shared state in cache of CPU 3.
- CPU 1 issues read-exclusive (1), while CPU 2 issues read-exclusive another location in same cache line (2).
- CPU 1 is given exclusive access (3a) and invalidate is sent to CPU 3 (3b).
- CPU 2 request is forwarded to CPU 1 (4).
- CPU 1 receives exclusive reply and completes write.
- CPU 2 request reaches CPU 1, and it generates an exclusive reply (5a) and a transfer request to directory (5b).
- Even if CPU 2 waits for the directory update acknowledge (6), but then completes another write in its cache that CPU 3 subsequently reads before receiving the invalidate (3b), then the ordering of writes issued by CPU 2 may not be maintained.
- Note that this case is similar to Figure 4-10(c), except it's the pending invalidate generated by CPU 1's write that causes an ordering problem for CPU 2. For CPU 2, even if it delays the request from CPU 3 until the directory update acknowledge is complete, it could still have a problem.

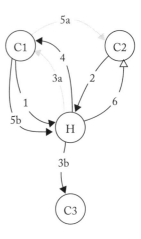

FIGURE 4-11 *Potential Ordering Problem Caused by False Sharing.*

A number of approaches can be used to solve the ordering problem without causing deadlock. Simoni [Sim90, Sim92] suggests a protocol and a set of dedicated queues within each node to avoid blocking requests that are dependent upon one another. In the IEEE SCI protocol [JLG+90], the solution is to serialize all requests at memory and to form a distributed *pending queue* that serves as a buffer for the requests. The advantage of this scheme is that it provides fairness for requests and has a fixed overhead (i.e., one pointer) per node regardless of the size of the pending list. The disadvantage of this scheme is that it forces additional latency and serialization for requests when such delay is not needed. For example, if a number of read requests are made for a block, servicing these requests will be limited by the rate that each processor can receive a memory block and then pass it on to the next requestor in the pending list. In reality, memory could respond to all of these requests directly. The approach used in DASH is to forward requests and serialize them in the cluster that currently owns the block. Thus, if a block is in a clean state, order is determined by memory. If it is dirty, then order is determined by the dirty cluster. While the DASH scheme reduces latency and buffering, it does lead to complications. For example, a request may be forwarded to a dirty cluster, but when it arrives the block may have been already written back to memory. In this case, the request must be retried by the originating cluster, which will receive a negative acknowledgment.

The second requirement to insure ordering of requests is that requestors complete their operations before allowing access to another requestor. For example, if completing a write requires invalidating a number of shared copies, then the writing processor should not satisfy requests for the now dirty block until all invalidate acknowledges have been received. If it does not, then it can cause problems for subsequent reads, as illustrated by Figure 4-10(c), or by writes, as illustrated by Figure 4-11. Similarly, in a system like DASH where order is sometimes determined outside the home node containing the corresponding directory entry, the update to the directory must take place before any new requests are satisfied (see Figure 4-10(b)). Further problems can arise if the network does not guarantee ordering of messages between nodes. For example, to prevent a read from creating a stale cache copy and a subsequent RAW hazard, invalidates to nodes that have outstanding reads for the given block must either be held until the read reply is received (insuring that the write is complete when it receives the acknowledge), or the invalidate can be acknowledged immediately and the read conservatively retried when the read reply is received (see Section 6.3.2.1 for more details on this case).

Note that it is possible to relay pending status for an operation instead of delaying the response or forcing a retry, as indicated above. For example, if invalidates are still pending, the data block can be passed to a new writer as long as it is informed about the pending invalidates. The problem is when all the invalidate acknowledgments are received, the new writer must be informed, requiring additional complexity in the form of new coherence messages and transient states. It also requires the processor with the pending operation to track the indentity of anyone who has been given a partial response. In most cases, this additional complexity is not justified.

4.2.3 Request Starvation

As illustrated above, distributed memory operations cannot always be immediately serviced, creating the need to delay or retry pending requests. Queuing is difficult because an arbitrary number of requests may need to be delayed, and the potential buffer of outstanding requests could be very large. Retrying requests is much simpler, but can lead to request starvation, as illustrated in Figure 4-12.

There are two potential solutions for this problem. The conservative approach is to build a distributed buffer, or queue, using pointers distributed throughout the system as in SCI's pending list. Thus, if an operation cannot be satisfied by memory, the reply is a pointer to the last node queued for this block. This approach guarantees FIFO ordering of the requests with fixed resources per node (i.e., one queue pointer), but it has the drawback of increased complexity and potentially increased latency for the queued requests. A second approach relies on retries. In the simplest form of retry, as used in DASH, the system relies on statistical variance in the request stream to avoid starvation. However, for the case illustrated by Figure 4-12, the probability of a request taking longer than any given period is still finite. A retry scheme that incorporates a retry priority can be used to reduce this probability to zero without the full complexity of a distributed queue. See Section 9.2.2.1 for a further discussion of this issue.

4.2.4 Error Detection and Fault Tolerance

Assuring the correctness of complex parallel programs is difficult. Thus, further complications caused by undetected data corruption by the hardware can be extremely hard to diagnose. Compounding this problem is that a large-scale multiprocessor contains thousands of physical components. All the components have finite failure rates, which implies the system as a whole will have a low mean time between failure (MTBF). To counter this problem, it is

CPU S gets starved by continuous exclusive requests from CPU 1 and CPU 2.

- Assume CPU 1 starts with the line dirty in its cache.
- CPU 2 issues read-exclusive (1), while CPU S issues read to same location (2).
- CPU 2 request is forwarded to CPU 1 (3), and CPU S request is forwarded to CPU 2 (4).
- CPU 2 reaches CPU 1, receives ownership of line, receives an exclusive acknowledge for its request (5a) and also a transfer request to directory (5b).
- CPU S reaches CPU 1 and finds no copy of the line, so it receives a negative acknowledge (6).
- The transfer acknowledge updates the directory and issues a final acknowledge (7) to CPU 2.
- At this point, ownership of the line has moved from CPU 1 to CPU 2, and CPU S will retry its request.
- If CPU 1 re-requests exclusive access to the line and its request is received before the retry from CPU S, the same sequence can occur where ownership moves back to CPU 1, and CPU S is told to retry again.
- If we assume that CPU 1 and CPU 2 continue to write to the given line, then they will continue to make progress, but CPU S may starve.

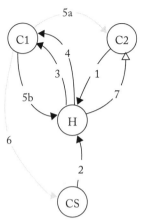

FIGURE 4-12 *Example of Potential Request Starvation in DASH Protocol.*

desirable that a large-scale system provide recovery from faults, or at least an explicit indication of failure, so faults do not lead to undetected data corruptions.

There are many techniques that can be used to add resilience to a large-scale system. Probably the most straightforward is the use of an error-correcting code (ECC) over the memory components, especially main memory. Such protection is important since large-scale shared-memory systems are likely to have tens of gigabytes of main memory. Furthermore, alpha-particle induced soft errors can be quite frequent,[5] but can be virtually eliminated by the use of a SEC-DED ECC code [SiJ82].

After ECC on memory, data integrity and fault tolerance of the interconnection network is most important for three reasons. First, the interconnect ties the system together, and being able to isolate failures in the network is key to being able to pinpoint failures to a given module. Second, the interconnect of a scalable system will run through connectors and cables both internal and external to system cabinets. Such components are much more prone to damage and electrical interference which makes the network more susceptible to errors than logic within a node itself. Third, regardless of the location of error, reconfiguration around a failing node will be made at the network level and requires support by the interconnection network.

The remaining portion of the system consists of the processor logic, the directory and memory control logic, and the I/O system. Fault tolerance in the I/O system can take

---

[5] The frequency is something greater than 500 failures per megabyte of DRAM per billion hours [MaW79, Sch94], implying a failure rate of one bit per 500 hours (21 days) in a 4-GByte memory system.

advantage of the distributed nature of the system to provide multiple paths to communication and disk subsystems. At the I/O device level, techniques such as disk mirroring and RAID [PGK88] are applicable. Likewise, retry and switchover techniques for communication lines are already used extensively.

The processor, directory control logic, and other data manipulation logic (e.g., ALUs) are the most complicated and costly areas to add data integrity or fault tolerance to. Straightforward data integrity schemes for general logic functions and state machines usually take the form of duplicate and compare, used in many highly reliable systems [WeB91, BBC+92]. To provide fault tolerance once an error is detected, a statically or dynamically allocated spare can be used. In a static scheme, sometimes called *pair-and-spare* (e.g., Stratus [WeB91]), if a lockstepped pair detects an error, its hot standby takes its place. In a dynamic scheme (e.g., Sequoia [Ber88] and Cache-Aided Rollback [WFP90]), the caches are used to maintain state whose write-back to memory is treated as a transaction that takes place atomically. While a complete discussion is beyond this text, both schemes are costly. Static sparing nearly doubles system costs, while the dynamic schemes incur only a 10–30% overhead. Unfortunately, the dynamic schemes add much more complexity and can negatively impact performance.

Whether a system requires a high degree of data integrity and fault tolerance in its CPU and directory logic depends upon its application. For mission critical space [SiJ82] and financial [BBC+92, WeB91] systems, it may be required. For more typical scientific and commercial systems, it usually is not justified. Furthermore, the reliability of the software running on the system must also be measured relative to the hardware. In many systems, software failures are dominant [Gra90], and adding additional tolerance at the hardware level may add little. Overall, the most important fault tolerance attribute to support is to simply maintain the potential for high availability inherent in the redundancy of a scalable system. This requires that the system be able to reliably isolate failing components and reconfigure around these components. Thus, particular attention must be paid to the interfaces between nodes in order to minimize the propagation of errors and allow portions of a system to be partitioned off. Furthermore, defensive techniques such as time-outs on outstanding requests and consistency checks on incoming requests can be used to isolate problems.

4.2.5   Design Verification

The design of a distributed coherence protocol is difficult, and verification is necessary to insure that the protocol and implementation are correct. Unfortunately, the verification of a highly parallel coherence protocol is even more challenging than its specification. Proofs of protocol and system correctness are desirable, but they are difficult given the highly parallel and complex nature of the protocols. Proving techniques are improving, however, and correctness proofs for simplified versions of various protocols have been made [McS91, GMG91, GjM91].

Proving techniques are likely to play an important role in the future, but extensive system simulation with monitoring is also important. As in many complex systems, both systematic corner case testing and tests involving machine randomized sequences are useful. For the DASH prototype, a protocol verifier [Kle89, OKN90] was used that provided both deterministic and random accesses from multiple processors. Within a test, deterministic controls allowed for the exact sequencing of references between all processors. Random controls allowed processors, memory modules, cache offsets, and sequencing to be automatically varied. The verifier could also combine tests by creating false sharing within the cache lines referenced by different tests to create interactions not envisioned by the test writer. Since actual locations are not mixed between tests, the memory semantics of the individual tests are unchanged. Overall, the DASH verification effort was successful. While there were still approximately 25 bugs out of 100,000 gates found in the lab, none of these involved internode protocol errors, and the majority of the bugs were in logic that could not be fully simulated.[6]

4.3 Chapter Conclusions

To support scalability to a large number of processors, overhead costs must be constant or grow only slowly with the total number of processors. The primary constraint on overhead costs in a directory-based system is the directory storage itself. A number of extensions to the base full-vector directory scheme have been proposed that reduce the size of each directory entry and dedicate less than one directory entry per memory block. The scalable directory schemes can provide scalable directory storage without compromising system performance.

Many practical issues tend to limit the dynamic range of a system. In many cases, optimizations such as the use of a full-bit-vector directory can limit system size. Likewise, packaging and cabling of a system tends to bias it towards a small or large size. For example, a small system may use a 2-D mesh network that is easy to make modular, but it may not provide adequate bandwidth for a system with thousands of processors. Oppositely, a large system is likely to be made out of large cabinets that can hold 32–64 processors, but they would not be cost-effective for a system with only 8 or 16 processors. In most cases, optimizations for a given size are likely to limit the practical range of any implementation to a factor of 100.

The design of a truly scalable shared-memory system is a difficult task. Correct operation of the memory system requires support of a memory consistency model and freedom from deadlock, livelock, and request starvation. In addition, the distributed environment of a scalable memory system adds the problems of an unbounded number of requests, distributed memory operations, and reorderings of events. Finally, a large system will experience faults. These faults should not go undetected. Instead, the system should tolerate faults or, at least, gracefully indicate to the affected process that an error has occurred.

---

[6] The DASH prototype was implemented primarily in PLDs and FPGAs. Thus, the number of simulation cycles was not as extensive (approximately 250,000) as would be the case in a custom or semicustom implementation technology.

5

Scalable Shared-Memory Systems

E ven within scalable shared-memory MIMD architectures, there is much diversity in system organizations and memory operations supported. This chapter surveys many of the important SSMP systems that have been proposed and highlights their unique features. The survey is not intended to be wholly encompassing, but rather to give examples of machines representing the diverse approaches to SSMP. The discussion emphasizes machines that have been built, or for which serious implementation efforts have been made. The focus is on these real designs because they are more complete and have faced the constraints of actual implementation.

The systems studied are broken into the following categories: directory-based, hierarchical, reflective memory, non-cache-coherent, vector, and virtual shared-memory architectures. Directory-based systems have the basic SSMP structure outlined in Chapter 1. Hierarchical systems utilize a tree-structured system organization. Reflective memory systems rely on replicated memory pages maintained by update messages instead of invalidations. Non-cache-coherent systems support a scalable memory interconnect, but do not support hardware cache coherence. Vector machines use a very high-speed, pipelined main memory to build a high-performance shared-memory multiprocessor without caches. Finally, virtual shared-memory systems create the illusion of shared-memory on top of a message-passing system.

5.1 Directory-Based Systems

Systems in this category are distinguished by using directories as the primary mechanism for cache coherence. Some of the hierarchical systems described in the next section also use directories, but differ in that their coherence protocols rely on the hierarchical nature of their system structure. Directory-based systems in this section use a relatively flat interconnection hierarchy, or support a protocol that is independent of any such hierarchy. Since these systems support cache coherence and typically have a nonuniform memory structure, they are generally referred to as CC-NUMA systems.

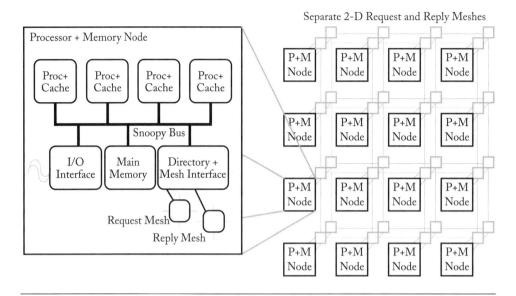

FIGURE 5-1 *Organization of the DASH Multiprocessor.*

5.1.1 DASH

DASH [LLG+92] is a directory-based system developed at Stanford University. The organization of DASH is shown in Figure 5-1. DASH uses a full-bit-vector directory, but extends the basic directory organization given in Figure 1-11 in two ways. First, it uses a NUMA organization where memory is distributed with the processing nodes. As discussed in Chapters 1 and 3, the NUMA organization reduces average memory latency. It also naturally expands memory bandwidth as processing nodes are added. Second, each node employs multiple processors that maintain coherence with snoopy caches. Using multiprocessing nodes within DASH helps reduce the overhead of the directory and network logic. It also improves performance since it permits sharing of remote data between the local processor caches.

DASH also supports many of the memory access optimizations given in Chapter 3, including release consistency, nonbinding prefetch, invalidation and update coherence, and specialized synchronization operations. Since the detailed design of DASH is the topic of Part II of this book, we will defer further discussion of these optimizations until then.

5.1.2 Alewife

Alewife [ALK+91] is a large-scale directory-based cache-coherent system developed at MIT under Anant Agarwal. Its architecture is similar to DASH in that it uses directories, a mesh interconnection network, and processing nodes that include a portion of the globally shared memory. Unlike DASH, Alewife has only one processor within each node and a single mesh network, as shown in Figure 5-2. Alewife also differs from DASH in that its SPARCLE processor supports multiple contexts and a fast switch between contexts. Multiple contexts are used primarily to hide the latency of remote cache misses and when a

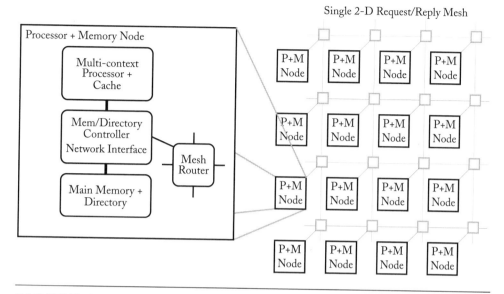

FIGURE 5-2 *Organization of the MIT Alewife Multiprocessor.*

synchronization attempt fails. The fast context switch also helps reduce hardware complexity by allowing software to handle corner cases in the coherence protocol. For example, Alewife can employ a single logical mesh network because network deadlocks between requests and replies can be broken in software by extending the incoming request queue into main memory (see Section 4.2.1).

As discussed in Chapter 3, multiple contexts allow latency to be hidden without any modifications to the applications. However, multiple contexts do rely on additional application parallelism to hide latency, and they require a special multiple context processor. Multiple-contexts complement rather than replace other latency hiding techniques. Multiple contexts hide latency with task-level parallelism, while mechanisms such as release consistency and prefetch exploit parallelism within a single thread.

Alewife uses limited pointers in its directory hardware with a software trap mechanism that stores additional pointers in a section of normal main memory (LimitLESS directories). This flexible mechanism allows Alewife to precisely track all cache copies, but it causes additional latency and processor overhead when pointer overflow occurs. As discussed in Chapter 4, other directory structures provide scalability at the expense of imprecise caching information. Given the application statistics presented in Chapter 2, any of these directory entry extension mechanisms should perform equally well since pointer overflow is rare. Alewife's software scheme is simpler to implement, but it is only practical when used with a processor that has a very low overhead trap mechanism.

Alewife has also generalized its access mechanism to the network and made it accessible to user code in the form of a message-passing interface. This allows Alewife to use producer-initiated communication to help hide system latency and improve interprocessor messaging efficiency. Since Alewife has a base level of cache coherence, the programmer can selectively

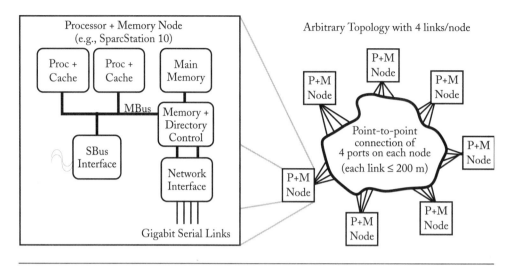

FIGURE 5-3 *Organization of S3.mp.*

use message-passing as a performance enhancement similar to prefetch or release consistency. Of course, if used extensively, then the difficulty of programming the machine will be the same as a traditional message-passing system.

5.1.3 S3.mp

S3.mp is a scalable multiprocessor research project ongoing at Sun Microsystems [NMP+93, NoP93]. It is similar to DASH in that it uses directory-based coherence and multiprocessor nodes. As shown in Figure 5-3, the most distinguishing feature of S3.mp is that it is intended for use in a looser confederation of distributed systems (e.g., workstations) that still support a coherent shared-memory space. Distribution impacts S3.mp in a number of ways:

1. S3.mp must support an arbitrary interconnect topology.

2. Each S3.mp node runs its own kernel, or a distributed kernel that can deal with node failures. Mechanisms are included to support protection and fault tolerance between nodes.

3. Facilities are provided for dynamic changes in system configuration such as adding and deleting nodes.

A significant contribution of the S3.mp has been the development of a very high-speed serial link technology with supports greater than 1 Gbit/sec performance using 0.8μ CMOS. Each S3.mp node supports four serial ports that can be tied directly to other nodes in a variety of topologies with links up to 200 meters long. Thus, an S3.mp system can be configured like a set of LAN connected systems, but with remote memory latency and bandwidths much closer to that of centralized systems.

S3.mp supports an address translation mechanism for physical addresses. This mechanism translates local 36-bit Mbus addresses to a global 64-bit address space that consists of a

12-bit node ID and a 52-bit local address. The 36 least-significant bits of a global address are subject to another local-to-global translation when they are received, which provides the basis for node autonomy (i.e., protection) and replicated memory on multiple nodes. Memory replication can be used for fault tolerance and the distribution of real-time multimedia data.

S3.mp technology could be used to create a centralized server that would be similar to DASH in that an interface board would be used to extend a snoopy bus-based multiprocessor node to a full SSMP. However, the most intriguing concept in S3.mp is the notion of forming a distributed SSMP system. As an alternative to today's networking technology, S3.mp offers exceptional node and network bisection bandwidth. Furthermore, direct shared-memory access support in S3.mp offers a significant reduction in communication latency and software overhead. When viewed as a single SSMP system, though, the question is whether the limits of wiring a distributed system overly restrict the achievable network bisection bandwidths compared to more centralized approaches. For example, wiring even a 2-D mesh in a LAN-like, distributed environment would be difficult. For large-scale systems, it is clear that the fault tolerance and dynamic configuration features of S3.mp would be useful in increasing the availability of both centralized and distributed systems.

5.1.4   IEEE Scalable Coherent Interface

The IEEE 1596-1992–Scalable Coherent Interface (SCI) is an interconnection standard that addresses the scalability problems of existing buses [JLG+90]. The model of a typical SCI system consists of a large set of nodes connected to one another through bidirectional SCI interfaces. Nodes can include CPUs, memories, I/O interfaces, or any combination of these. In small systems, the SCI interfaces can be directly connected to form a ring. In larger systems, active switches connect the nodes, but their topology and design is not specified by the SCI standard. The block diagram for a small SCI system is shown in Figure 5-4(a), but it is also possible to build an SCI system that uses multiprocessor nodes that include portions of memory as in Figure 5-1.

A key part of SCI is the definition of a cache coherence mechanism based on distributed directory entries. Instead of storing all directory pointers with their associated main memory blocks, SCI only keeps a head pointer and state information at memory. As shown in Figure 5-4(b), fields associated with the tag of each processor cache line are used to form a doubly linked list that contains all processors caching a memory block. The main advantage of the SCI scheme is that directory pointer storage grows naturally as processor caches are added.

The primary disadvantage of the SCI coherence scheme is that the distribution of directory pointers increases the latency and complexity of memory references because additional update messages must be sent between the processors to maintain the sharing lists. For example, a processor wishing to write a block shared by N processors including itself must (1) detach itself from the sharing list, (2) determine the current sharing list head from main memory, (3) relink itself to the head of the list, and (4) serially purge the other processors by traversing the sharing list. Altogether, this amounts to $2N + 6$ messages, of which $2N + 2$ must be processed serially as members of the sharing list are individually invalidated while

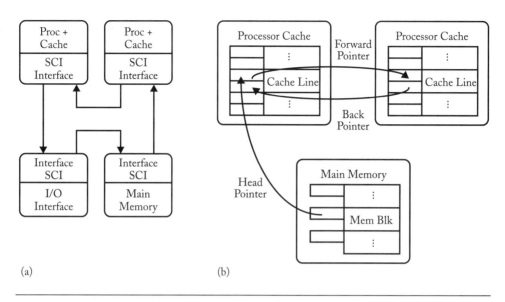

FIGURE 5-4 *(a) Simple ring-connected IEEE SCI system and (b) Distributed linked-list directories.*

returning a pointer to the next node in the list. Latencies are increased further by the use of a strict request-response network protocol in SCI (see Section 4.2.1). In a centralized directory system, all pointers are found in a single directory lookup and $2N$ of its $2N + 2$ messages can be processed in parallel and are serialized only by the time needed to launch them into the network.

From the statistics in Chapter 2, N is typically 1 or 2, implying that distributed directories require 50–100% more messages. More importantly, the time to send, remotely process, and then receive a reply across a system is typically 5–20 times the time to simply launch a message into the network.[1] Thus, the latency of a write miss in SCI would be 33% longer if one invalidate is needed (4 versus 3 serialized network traversals), 100% longer if two are required (6 versus 3 serialized network traversals), and continue to increase with higher N. SCI includes extensions that reduce latencies to being proportional to $\log N$ for large sharing lists [Joh93], but they add complexity and are only effective on large sharing lists. The request-response protocol of SCI simplifies network hardware and helps support network error recovery, but it adds latency to other common memory requests.

Given the goals of a general-purpose interface standard, the SCI directory structure and coherence protocol are very sensible in that they allow for standard processor and memory boards that can be used in anything from a simple uniprocessor to an MPP system with thousands of nodes. The issue is whether the compromises in complexity and performance

---

[1] In DASH for example, the time to launch an invalidate message is approximately 175 ns, while the minimum time to send and then receive a reply from a remote node is about 1 µs (i.e., factor of 5.7). For TeraDASH, the estimated delays are 28 ns and 400 ns, respectively (14.3 times longer).

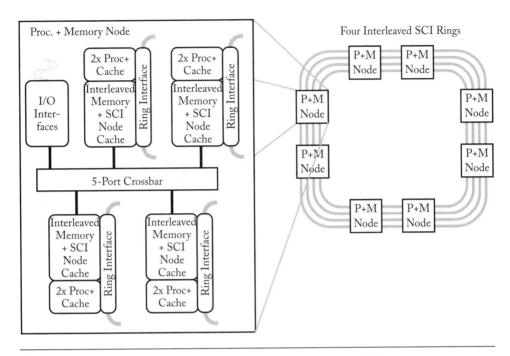

FIGURE 5-5 *Organization of a 64-Processor Convex Exemplar Multiprocessor.*

needed to stretch over this large range of systems can be contained so that SCI is effective for the smaller range that a particular system implementation would be designed for. Of course, the benefits of the standardization inherent in SCI (e.g., the potential of off-the-shelf components, boards, and network switches) may outweigh the disadvantages. It will all depend on the amount of support SCI receives.

5.1.5 Convex Exemplar

The Exemplar multiprocessor was introduced in 1993 by Convex Computer Corporation [Con94]. The most distinguishing aspect of the Exemplar is that it is the first commercially available directory-based multiprocessor. As shown in Figure 5-5, the structure of the Exemplar is a set of ring-connected nodes. Each node is a tightly coupled shared-memory multiprocessor with eight CPUs, local memory, and an I/O interface connected by a five-port crossbar. Up to 16 nodes can be connected to form a 128-processor system. The nodes are connected by four unidirectional rings that implement the SCI electrical and network protocols. The rings run in parallel with accesses interleaved across the rings on cache block boundaries.

Coherence within a node is implemented with a full-bit-vector directory, which also indicates whether there are remote cached copies of a local portion of the global memory. Between nodes, Exemplar uses the SCI cache coherence protocol implemented on top of large node caches. The node caches maintain inclusion over (i.e., are a superset of) remote memory cached by the local processors. The node caches are built from a portion of each node's local memory.

The two-level hierarchy of the Exemplar has a number of advantages, some of which are common to other cluster systems like DASH and S3.mp. First, this structure provides for lower latency and finer-grain sharing for processors within the same cluster. In Exemplar, latency to local memory is 500 nanoseconds, while remote memory latency is 2 microseconds. Second, the hierarchy amortizes the cost of the SCI interfaces over more processors. Other benefits are more particular to the use of SCI in Exemplar. First, the eight-way node reduces the length of the SCI linked list directories by up to a factor of eight. This reduces the number of linked list directory traversals discussed in the previous section. Second, the node cache provides a convenient place to provide SCI compliance. Without it, the SCI link-list cache tags would have to be placed in parallel with the processor-supplied caches. Since extra SCI tag state is necessary, providing data storage as well enables the size of the cache and cache lines to be increased. This helps improve cache hit rates and compensate for the longer latency of remote memory.

Exemplar also extends the SCI protocol with a number of optimized memory operations, including support of nonbinding software prefetch, optional weak memory ordering, a direct message-passing interface, and support for at-memory noncombining Fetch&Op operations.

5.2 Hierarchical Systems

Hierarchical systems differ from directory-based systems in two respects. First, their coherence protocols use a logical (and often physical) tree structure to communicate with other nodes. Second, system expansion is accomplished by adding layers of hierarchy to the system. Hierarchical systems are recursive: the same coherence protocol that manipulates processors and caches at the bottom of the hierarchy, manipulates groups of processors and caches at higher levels.

Hierarchical systems are appealing because of the conceptually simple recursive coherence protocols, and the ease with which they can be extended. They do not have the problem of limited pointers found in the flat systems because the system is expanded by adding depth to the hierarchy. If the tree structure is physical, then another advantage of a hierarchical system is that assumptions can be made about the ordering of memory references since there is only one path between any two processors. Hierarchical access methods also provide for merging of requests, responses, and caching states. For example, if many processors simultaneously fetch a value, these requests can be merged in the hierarchy to form a smaller number of requests at the memory. Likewise, invalidation acknowledges from a write to a widely shared variable can be merged before they are returned to the writing processor. Finally, intermediate caches in the hierarchy permit the exchange of cache ownership of remote memory between clusters beneath them without traversing the entire hierarchy.

Unfortunately, hierarchical systems also have disadvantages. Most important, each level of hierarchy adds latency when it is traversed. Access to each hierarchical level adds considerable delay, comparable to the latency required to access another node's memory or cache.

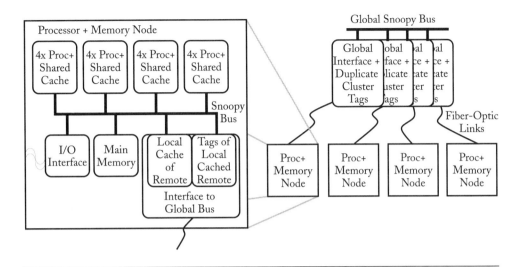

FIGURE 5-6 *Organization of a 64-Processor Encore GigaMax.*

Furthermore, in systems with a single physical root, the root can become a performance bottleneck if communication patterns do not match the tree structure.

Looking at the latency issue in more detail, consider a small hierarchical system with two levels of shared buses and 16 to 64 total processors, as shown in Figure 5-6.[2] Assuming memory is distributed with the processors, an access to remote memory requires three bus transactions to access memory, and two more bus transactions to return the response data. Each of these transactions is comparable to a remote access in a system without hierarchy such as DASH or Alewife. Thus, remote latency would be approximately 5/3 times as long as these other systems. Alternatively, if all memory is placed at the top of the hierarchy, then latency for data stored in memory would be comparable to a system without hierarchy, but there would be no local memory support (i.e., a dance-hall architecture with processors and memory on opposite sides of the interconnect). Larger systems with deeper hierarchies only worsen the latency problem by adding at least two additional units of delay for each level of hierarchy.

5.2.1 Encore GigaMax

The GigaMax system was developed by Encore Computer Corporation. Its architecture is an extension of the work done by Andrew Wilson on hierarchical snoopy cache coherence [WWS+89, Wil87]. The GigaMax architecture supports a hierarchy of buses and snoopy caches, each with inclusion of the caches below. In the actual GigaMax machine, there are two levels of hierarchy, as shown in Figure 5-6. The bottom layer is a bus-based multiprocessor with 16 processors. Each cluster contains a large cluster cache that enforces the inclu-

---

[2] Assuming a 16-processor system consists of 4 clusters attached to a root bus and 4 processors within each cluster, and a 64-processor system has the same structure, but with each processor replaced by 4 individual processors sharing a common cache.

sion property over the processor caches. The cluster cache has duplicate tags stored at the top level in the hierarchy that snoop on the root bus. This snooping allows the cluster to perform the invalidations and interventions needed for requests by other clusters to data cached within this cluster.

Main memory in GigaMax is distributed among the individual clusters. This arrangement complicates the system structure and protocol because accesses by local processors to local memory need to know about the presence of remote cached copies. In GigaMax, this is determined by another snooping cache on the local bus that indicates the remote caching state of local memory. This cache must enforce inclusion over all remote caching of local memory, but it does not need to store the remotely cached data, only the cache tag and state. The remote cluster cache is used to determine whether an access to local memory must be propagated to the root bus. Once propagated to the root bus, snooping at this level determines which clusters are holding a copy of the block. The remote cluster cache can be viewed as a sparse directory that contains only state information, not pointers, that indicate that a local request must be propagated outside of the local cluster.

As mentioned previously, the key issues in a hierarchical system such as GigaMax revolve around the latency of remote memory, root bandwidth, and the hardware overhead and complexity of the coherence scheme. Average memory latencies in GigaMax will be large due to the cache accesses[3] required at each level of the hierarchy. Unless the pattern of sharing closely matches the structure of the machine, latency and contention will lead to low processor utilization. Furthermore, the memory overhead to support the dual-ported snooping cluster caches and the remote cache will be at least as large as a sparse directory. Finally, while the GigaMax machine may seem conceptually simpler than a directory-based system because it extends the abstraction of the snoopy bus, the complications of implementing the memory in the processing nodes negates most of this potential advantage.

5.2.2 ParaDiGM

ParaDiGM is a hierarchical directory-based system currently under development in the Distributed Systems Group at Stanford University [CGB91]. A ParaDiGM system (Figure 5-7) combines several processors with individual first-level caches to a common second-level cache, all on a single board (referred to as a *multiple-processor module* or MPM). MPMs then interface on a common bus with other MPMs to form an MPM group that includes a common third-level cache (an interbus caching module or ICM). MPM groups are interconnected through the ICM to the root bus, which contains main memory and associated directories. Each level has a fan-out from 4 to 8, resulting in a system supporting 64 to 512 processors. A network connects MPMs to each other. Coherence is maintained by enforcing inclusion on the caches and by having the higher levels of the hierarchy maintain directory pointers to the caching entities below them. Thus, the structure of ParaDiGM is similar to GigaMax, but without local cluster memory, and with the snoopy caches replaced by directories.

---

[3] Note that the cluster caches are made of DRAM.

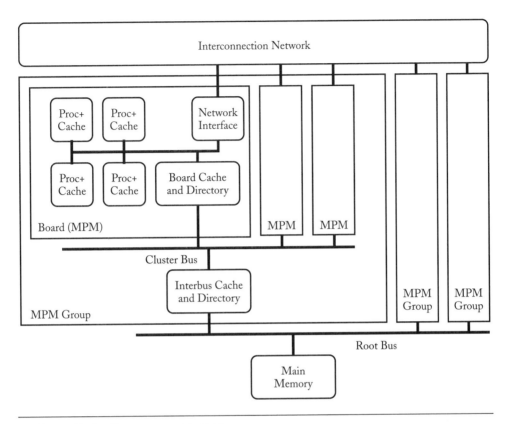

FIGURE 5-7   *The ParaDiGM Multiprocessor.*

The directory state required for the coherence mechanism on the MPM board bus is also used for two interesting synchronization mechanisms. The first is fine-grained locking at the level of a cache line. The second is an efficient message exchange protocol. Processors can write to a cache line and then notify all processors with a copy of the line. The notify operation issues an interrupt to each recipient processor.

ParaDiGM relies heavily on application locality matching the hierarchy of the architecture. As pointed out earlier, the trade-off in having main memory at the top of the hierarchy is reduced latency for remote data versus longer latency for local data. Without local memory, however, the ICM cache at the MPM group level must be large so it can satisfy the majority of processor requests. Thus, the ICM cache will need to be even larger than GigaMax's cluster cache. In addition, if the ICM caches hold a large fraction of memory, the latency gain from the centralized memory will be lost because most writable locations will be held in an exclusive state in or below an ICM. Thus, the latency and root bandwidth issues for ParaDiGM will be similar to the GigaMax for applications that do not match the hierarchy well.

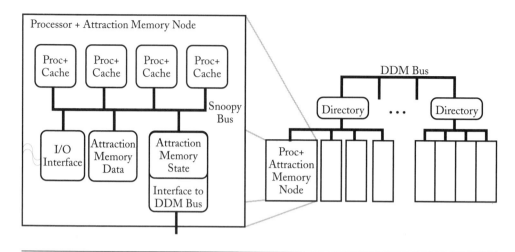

FIGURE 5-8 *Organization of the Data Diffusion Prototype Machine.*

5.2.3 Data Diffusion Machine

The Data Diffusion Machine (DDM) [HHW90] is currently under development at the Swedish Institute of Computer Science. Its architecture is a combination of ParaDiGM and GigaMax together with its own unique features (Figure 5-8). Like ParaDiGM, it uses directories to locate which nodes are caching a particular memory block. Like GigaMax, however, DDM places memory local to each processing node. The most unique feature of DDM is that the local memories are structured as caches. Recognizing that hierarchical systems hold most of their data in their large cluster caches, DDM removes main memory and replaces its cluster caches with attraction memories (AM) that implement a cache-only memory architecture (COMA) described in Section 3.2.2. Structurally, the AMs are similar to cluster caches, but they support additional protocol features that insure that the last copy of a memory block is never deleted.

Besides the memory savings from combining the cluster caches and main memory, the primary advantage of COMA is the decoupling of physical memory addresses from fixed memory homes. Data can be allocated anywhere, and it migrates to the processors that use it. In a CC-NUMA system, dynamic migration and replication only takes place when data is cached. Allocating data in memory and any subsequent migration is the responsibility of software in a CC-NUMA system. Thus, COMA offers a performance advantage in two situations. First, when the data set is larger than a cache and is not subject to frequent writes, then the attraction memories can change a remote miss into a local miss. Second, if it is difficult for the software to determine where to place data that has affinity to a certain processor, then the COMA structure will migrate it as needed.

The question is how much performance is gained in these cases compared with the additional complexity and potential performance loss due to COMA. The complexity in COMA arises from the need to turn main memory into a cache. Organizing memory as a cache requires tags for each memory block. Furthermore, since the AMs act as second- or third-level caches and are shared by multiple processors in DDM, it is desirable to organize

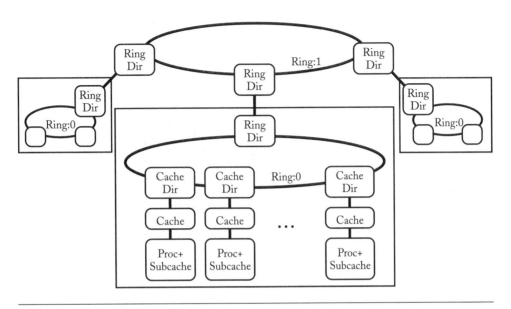

FIGURE 5-9 *The Kendall Square Research KSR-1.*

them as associative caches to reduce conflict misses [Prz90]. An associative cache requires either additional datapath width to access an entire set, or an associative tag match before the data access. DDM uses the latter approach, in which the tags are stored in fast static RAMs.

The potential performance losses in DDM arise in two areas. First, since DDM uses a hierarchical search to find a copy of the requested block, there is increased latency for remote cache misses as in other hierarchical systems. Second, searching and allocating locations within the AM when there is a remote miss implies that there are at least two or three slow DRAM accesses per remote access: one to determine that the local AM does not contain the value,[4] one to fetch the latest value from the remote AM, and one to allocate the data into the AM. In a directory-based NUMA machine, there need only be one DRAM memory access and two faster cache accesses.

Overall, the COMA structure of DDM is appealing since it reduces the need for software to optimize memory allocation due to nonuniform memory structures. While there are difficult trade-offs in implementing COMA, the structure raises the interesting question of what hardware support a NUMA system should have to assist software in optimally allocating and migrating memory.

5.2.4 Kendall Square Research KSR-1 and KSR-2

The Kendall Square Research KSR-1 machine [Bur91, FRB93, KSR93a] was introduced in 1991. It is a multiprocessor built as a two-level hierarchy of slotted rings (see Figure 5-9).

---

[4] In DDM, the first of these is relatively fast because the AM tags are stored in SRAMs.

Each of the lower level rings (Ring:0) connects up to 32 processor nodes with a bandwidth of 1 GByte/s. Each processing node consists of a 20 MHz two-way superscalar processor, 512 KBytes of cache memory (subcache) and 32 MBytes of DRAM memory (cache), and a 30 MByte/sec I/O channel. Up to 34 of the Ring:0s can be connected by another ring (Ring:1), yielding a machine with up to 1,088 processors. More bandwidth can be provided at this level by running multiple rings in parallel, yielding the bandwidth profile of a fat tree [Lei85]. The KSR-2 [KSR93b], introduced in late 1993, improves processor speed to 40 MHz and increases the system hierarchy to three levels, allowing for systems with more than 5,000 processors.

The KSR machines support a sequentially consistent memory model, which means that all invalidations of shared copies have to be accomplished before a write can complete. Support for prefetch is provided to help hide memory latency. Locking is provided on the granularity of each subpage (128 bytes), which allows for fine-grained distributed locking.

As with DDM, the most interesting part of the KSR machine is that its memory system is organized as a set of caches into a COMA structure. KSR refers to it as the ALLCACHE architecture. In KSR, the movement of memory blocks around the machine is controlled by large directories. When a processor's local subcache misses, it first looks for the block in the cache. If it is not found there, the request goes out on the Ring:0. As it passes each node on the ring, a directory lookup at each node determines whether the block may be found in that node. A node that contains the block replies to the request. For reads, a copy of the block is sent, and for writes the block is moved to the requestor. If no node on the local Ring:0 has a copy of the block, the request moves up to Ring:1, where the search is continued among all of the connected Ring:0 directories. The movement and replication of memory blocks is controlled in hardware.

The advantage of allowing memory blocks to dynamically move around the machine without any software intervention is that the memory will naturally move to take advantage of any reference locality in the parallel application. If a given processor regularly references a piece of data, the data will move into that processor's cache and subcache. If a set of processors is referencing a region of memory, that region will move to the lowest level of hierarchy shared between those processors. This all happens without the programmer being explicitly aware of data reference locality. The programmer only has to make sure that cooperating processors are located close to each other (i.e., on the same ring).

On the downside, there is a fair amount of hardware associated with the dynamic management of memory blocks. For each cache, there is a large directory that records the contents of each memory slot. To save on tag space, blocks are allocated in 16 KByte pages, each of which is broken into 128-byte subpages. There is a trade-off between the amount of tag space versus the utilization of memory. Having the unit of allocation in the cache be a 16 KByte page saves on tag space but can dramatically reduce memory utilization if data accesses have a large stride. Also note that the directories for each Ring:0 on the Ring:1 have to include information on all of the memory on that ring, which is 1 GByte.

As discussed earlier, the general disadvantage of hierarchical architectures is the latency incurred if many levels of the hierarchy have to be traversed. On the KSR machines, latencies seem to be particularly long. On the KSR-1, a miss that can be satisfied from another node on the same ring is 7.5 μs (150 cycles). When a cache miss occurs in one node, and the memory is actually found on another ring, several directory lookups have to be accomplished before the data is found and can be passed back. The latency for this kind of miss is as long as 28.5 μs (570 cycles). For the KSR-2, doubling the speed of the processors further increases memory latencies in terms of processor cycles.

5.3 Reflective Memory Systems

Reflective memory systems attempt to minimize the processor stalls caused by read misses by satisfying all read misses from a local copy of shared memory. Shared memory is replicated on each node that accesses a location, and all writes to shared locations perform updates to all replicas. These systems use write-through cache coherence for reflected pages and trade off memory and network bandwidth for reduced read latency. Replication is controlled by software on a page basis and is normally done statically at program load time because of the overhead of creating replicas (i.e., the time to copy an entire page).

Small-scale reflective systems have been available for some time. Systems offered by Gould (now Encore Computer) first introduced the notion of reflective memory in 1984 [Gou84]. The Scramnet system designed by Systran, Inc., allows a reflective memory to be added to a standard bus such as VME [Boh94, Sys94]. Both of these systems are aimed at real-time applications where the worst-case processor latency for reading local replicas is very valuable. In October 1994, Digital Equipment announced that it will incorporate the Gould/Encore reflective memory technology into their clustered workstation systems [Ora94]. While these commercial systems all use reflective memory technology, we study two academic systems in this section because they are aimed at larger-scale systems.

5.3.1 Plus

The Plus system has been developed at Carnegie-Mellon University [BiR90]. It supports a set of uniprocessor nodes that are connected by a mesh interconnect (Figure 5-10). Memory locations are either local or remote (i.e., NUMA), but remote locations can be locally replicated. If replicas are not used, Plus becomes a non-cache-coherent NUMA system supporting fast local memory and slow remote memory. A local replica can only satisfy read requests. Write requests are always sent to a master (home) node to serialize writes. Writes update replicas by following a linked list distributed across the nodes holding the replicas. After an update has traversed the replica list, the writing processor is sent a single acknowledgment that allows it to order references using fences. Support for both remote and replicated access allows Plus to tune applications for a balance between replication update overhead and remote access stalls.

In comparison with cache-coherent systems, writing a replica is similar to using update coherence. The major difference is that an update will only satisfy a subsequent remote read miss if the location is cached at the time of the write. In Plus, a replica will always be present at the consuming node if it has been allocated. Depending upon the size and usage of the data structure, the Plus scheme can be much more effective at eliminating remote memory misses than a CC-NUMA system using an invalidation-based protocol. Oppositely, if data sharing is migratory (i.e., blocks have affinity over time to a single processor) as discussed in

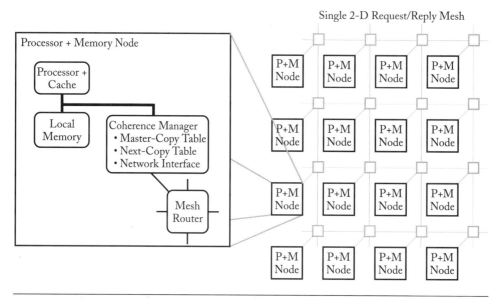

FIGURE 5-10 *Organization of the CMU Plus.*

Chapter 2, then the strict update protocol in Plus can lead to excessive coherence traffic. An invalidation protocol eliminates this traffic since the first write to location will invalidate any *replica* in a remote cache. As with all systems that enforce coherence at the page level, the other problem with replicas is false sharing. For example, in Plus, if items shared by disjoint pairs of processors are allocated on the same page, then every node will receive every update, but it will only consume (i.e., read) the updates from one other processor.

The key trade-offs depend on what access patterns are most frequent. If there is frequent read-write sharing between applications, then the update writes and replicated pages of Plus will greatly increase processor utilization. If shared data is migratory, however, then replication and a write-through update coherence policy will degrade performance with unnecessary network and remote memory traffic.

For the applications shown in Chapter 2, most nonsynchronization locations exhibited the migratory access patterns that would favor invalidations. Furthermore, for large data structures the cost of replicating the memory image in multiple nodes may be prohibitive. If replicas are made of the data structures shared by all processors at some point in time, then the system will surely not scale due to the resulting write broadcasts (i.e., the system will be equivalent to a snoopy scheme using write-through). Thus, for Plus to achieve good performance, the programmer must control data replication explicitly to achieve a balance between performance loss due to remote latency and performance loss due to network saturation.

5.3.2 Merlin and Sesame

Merlin [MaW90] and its follow-on Sesame [WHL90] have been jointly investigated by researchers at Sandia National Laboratories and SUNY–Stony Brook. The goal of these systems is to combine high-performance workstations with reflective memory interfaces to form multiprocessor supercomputers. The interconnection between the nodes is assumed to be gigabit fiber optic links. The reflective memory replicas are similar to Plus, but there is no support for remote accesses. All shared pages are replicated at each node requiring access to locations in that page. However, to reduce traffic, Sesame supports the temporary disabling of replica updates. Another difference between Sesame and Plus is that Sesame allows update messages to be split at nodes to provide $O(\log N)$ delay for update propagation. Sesame includes the notion of a home to provide serialization, but it does not support the acknowledgment of write completions. Instead, it only guarantees that writes from the same processor to variables with the same home memory node will be seen by all processors in the order in which the writes were issued.

Sesame exposes more of the underlying machine to the programmer than Plus. For example, since ordering is only guaranteed for writes with the same home, the compiler or programmer must carefully place all data that have ordering constraints in the same home module. Alternatively, the programmer must use multiple synchronization variables per logical synchronization variable to assure ordered access to a set of distributed data items. Likewise, Sesame's ability to turn off replica update is a form of software cache coherence that must be managed by the programmer.

As with Plus, the scalability of Sesame beyond a modest number of nodes is not clear because of network saturation and the overhead of replicas. The use of write-through multicasts (or broadcasts) will eventually saturate the memory interfaces of the processing nodes if the number of writes in a program is constant, and an increasing number of processors are used to solve the problem in a shorter period of time. While selective updates and limited replication may relieve this problem, programming such a machine is much closer to message-passing than shared-memory. As with S3.mp, having nodes distributed like workstations will limit the bisection bandwidth of the system. Thus, any problems with network saturation may occur earlier in Sesame than in Plus.

5.4 Non-Cache-Coherent Systems

The traditional approach to scalable shared-memory systems connects processors to memory through a scalable interconnection network that does not support global cache coherence. Systems such as the IBM RP3 [PBG+85] have clearly demonstrated that large-scale systems of this type are feasible. The only question is whether they can support high-performance individual processors. The fundamental problem is that without cache coherence, the latency of accesses to shared data items can severely impact processor throughput.

5.4.1 NYU Ultracomputer

The NYU Ultracomputer [GGK+83] was one of the early large-scale shared-memory multiprocessors. It has influenced the design of such machines as the IBM RP3 and BBN Butterfly and TC2000. Work on the latest incarnation of the Ultracomputer architecture (Ultra III [DiK92, GBD+93, FRB93]) is ongoing at NYU. The architecture of the Ultracomputer consists of an equal number of processor elements and memory modules connected by an Omega network (see Figure 5-11).

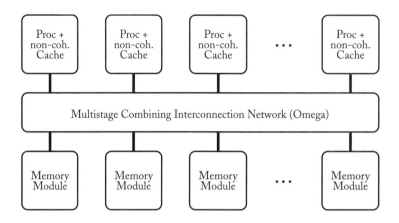

F I G U R E   5 - 1 1   *The NYU Ultracomputer.*

The Ultracomputer network has the additional feature of being a combining network (i.e., memory requests to the same location are combined in the network). This feature alleviates hot-spots in memory reference traffic. Another novel feature of the Ultracomputer is the support of an atomic Fetch&Add operation at the memory modules as well as in the combining network. As discussed in Section 3.4.2, Fetch&Add is a useful primitive for distributing parallel work, and combining minimizes the serialization of such accesses. Although the designers have consistently claimed that the addition of combining hardware does not slow down their network chips because combining is not on the critical path, other combining network designs might well incur added latency for the majority of accesses that do not benefit from combining.

The major system limit to achieving high performance in the Ultracomputer is the latency to memory. All memory is equally far away on the other side of the interconnection network. Local caches help reduce memory latency for private data and code, but there is no hardware cache coherence, so all shared data must remain uncached and suffer the long latencies across the network. Memory latency counted in processor cycles will further increase with the addition of network stages to accommodate more processors and/or with the use of higher-performance processors.

5.4.2 IBM RP3 and BBN TC2000

The IBM RP3 [PBG+85] is similar to the Ultracomputer in its architecture. It also supports access to globally shared memory without cache coherence. The main difference is that in RP3 the network wraps back on itself, so that processor elements and memory modules live in combined nodes. The memory on each node can be partitioned into local memory and global memory. The global portion of memory can be interleaved in different ways across all nodes.

Having memory close to the processing elements dramatically cuts memory latency for private data and instruction cache misses. All shared data accesses, however, encounter the long latency of crossing the network. Having global memory finely interleaved across the

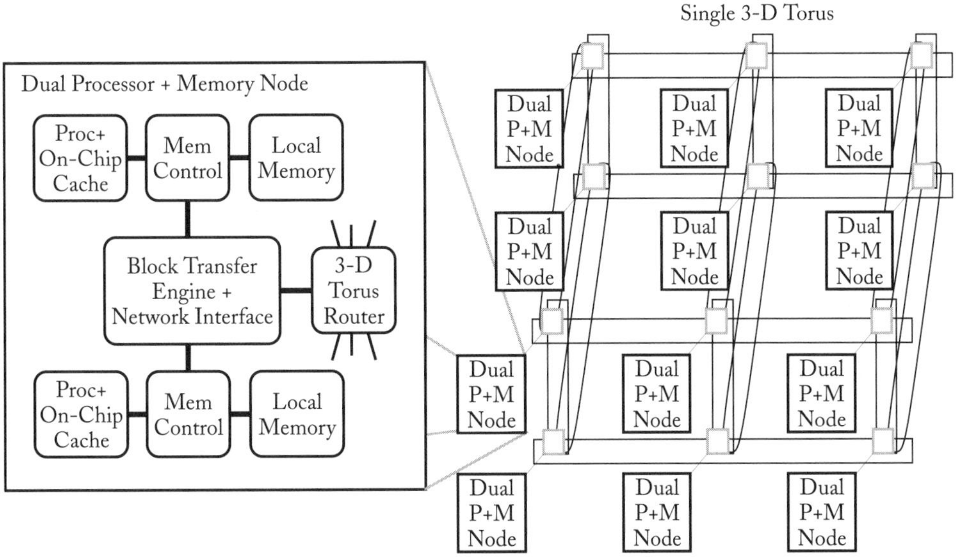

FIGURE 5-12 *A Cray T3D Node and a Portion of the 3-D Torus Network.*

nodes reduces the danger of hot-spotting one of the modules. On the downside, fine inter-leaving makes it very difficult to take advantage of any memory locality. In other words, all global memory is equally far away. If the interleaving of memory across nodes is coarse, it is possible to reduce the average access latency to shared memory by allocation of shared data in the node of the processor that uses it the most. The disadvantage is that poor allocation leads to memory module hot-spotting and reduced aggregate memory bandwidth.

There are two main differences between the architecture of RP3 and the BBN TC2000 [BBN89]. First, memory cannot be finely interleaved across nodes in the BBN machine and is coarsely mapped in a fashion similar to the NUMA structure of Alewife or DASH. Second, the TC2000 does maintain coherence between its local memory and processor cache. Thus, while remote caching of data is not supported in hardware, the local processor's cache is fully coherent with its local memory.

5.4.3 Cray Research T3D

Cray Research's T3D [Cra93a] first shipped in late 1993. This system is aimed at massively parallel applications with support for up to 2,048 processors. Using 150 MHz Alpha proces-sors from Digital Equipment [Sit93], the T3D provides a peak of 300 GFLOPS. The sys-tem block diagram of the T3D is shown in Figure 5-12. It consists of uniprocessor nodes that are connected in pairs to switch points of a 3-D torus. Each node supports up to 64 MBytes of local memory, which is globally accessible to every processor. As in the BBN TC2000, shared memory in the T3D is only kept coherent with the local processor's cache.

The T3D includes a number of latency hiding mechanisms. The first is remote stores. These are simply uncached writes to a memory location in another node. These stores can be viewed as a degenerate case of a reflective memory since they allow the producer to push data close to the consuming processor, which can then access the data with a local memory read. There is no replication, however, so this must be done in software with multiple writes if there is more than one consumer of the data. The second latency hiding mechanism is a software-controlled prefetch operation. In T3D, prefetch operations return one 64-bit word of data and bind the value they return to a memory-mapped register (i.e., they are equivalent to a nonblocking register load). Binding reduces the benefits from prefetching because the prefetch cannot be done speculatively, as with coherent cache line prefetching. Further, each prefetch operation returns a small amount of data, which increases the overhead of issuing the prefetch. The third mechanism is the block transfer engine (BLT). The BLT is a general purpose memory-to-memory copy engine with scatter-gather capability. There is one BLT for every two processors.

The T3D also includes two mechanisms for fast synchronization. The first is a set of fetch and increment registers (one per processing node). The second is support for fast barrier synchronization using 16 dedicated hardware AND trees. The AND trees have limited flexibility, but they provide global synchronization with very little latency or overhead.

With the other latency reduction and latency tolerating features, it is surprising that the T3D does not include a global cache coherence mechanism. This seems to be an outgrowth of Cray's background in vector supercomputers. In a vector-like mode, remote locations would be copied to the local, possibly using the BLT, and then the processor would use local DRAM memory and on-chip cache as a set of vector registers. From the application data in Chapter 2, it is clear that leaving out cache coherence will force T3D programmers to be much more cognizant of locality and interprocessor communication than in a cache-coherent system. For some users, it is likely that the BLT and other latency hiding mechanisms will be used to implement low-overhead message-passing. In this mode, the T3D should be quite effective relative to message-passing machines such as the Intel Paragon, but relative to machines with cache coherence we would expect lower processor utilization.

5.5 Vector Supercomputer Systems

Vector supercomputers have dominated the high end of the computing market for the last 20 years. High performance in vector systems has come from a number of factors. First, these systems have been built with the highest performance technology (bipolar ECL and GaAs IC technology along with exotic packaging). Second, operating on vectors (one-dimensional arrays, usually 64–128 words (64 bits each) in length) in a pipelined fashion allows these systems to exploit fine-grain parallelism. Third, vector machines utilize a high-speed interconnect to directly attach the processors to an interleaved SRAM main memory system. Fourth, these systems support limited scalability on the order of 16 processors. To maximize performance, these systems rely on hiding memory and operation latencies by pipelining operations on entire vectors. Realized performance depends heavily on the percent of code that is vectorizable.

In recent years, many of the performance advantages of vector machines have diminished. The CMOS technology used in microprocessors supports higher integration levels and has closed the gap in terms of individual gate delays. For example, the DEC Alpha at 300 MHz operates faster than the 240 MHz of the Cray Research C90. Today's highest-performance microprocessors outperform the vector machines on scalar code. The very high-speed memory interconnect of the vector machines is not as critical if most references can be satisfied by a cache integrated near the microprocessor. Furthermore, since most vector machines do not include data caches, effective memory access time will be smaller in a cache-based system if the code is not highly vectorizable. Almost all high-performance microprocessors have access times to their first-level cache of less than 20 ns, which is five times less than the 96 ns access time for global memory in the C90. Finally, SSMP systems described in this book can support a larger number of processors with a shared-memory model than the vector machines. Vector machines have limited scalability due to their physical size, which is constrained in order to achieve a very low latency to global memory.

5.5.1 Cray Research Y-MP C90

Since the first Cray 1 was introduced in 1976, Cray has been synonymous with supercomputing. They have set the standard for vector processing. The first multiprocessor Cray was the four-way Cray X-MP introduced in 1983. The latest Cray Research system is the Cray Y-MP C90 [Rob92], which supports up to 16 processors, each capable of a peak 1 GFLOPS.

A block diagram of a 16-processor C90 is shown in Figure 5-13. Each processor contains eight 128-word vector registers and dual vector pipelines capable of producing four floating-point multiplies and adds per clock. Each processor can issue six 64-bit data references per clock. A multistage interconnect with an aggregate of 246 GByte/sec of bandwidth connects the processors to 1,024 banks of memory. The highly interleaved main memory system consists of high-speed static RAMs capable of supplying data to the processors with a round-trip latency of 96 ns (23 processor clocks) for the first 64 bits. Vector memory references support arbitrary constant or vector index scatter/gather. The system also supports very high-performance I/O attachments providing two memory ports per processor. An individual I/O port can provide up to 1.8 GByte/sec of bandwidth.

Vector machines like the C90 retain advantages relative to other forms of high-performance computing. First, there is high-speed access to all of main memory. If a cache-based machine does not get good cache line reuse, then the vector machine will outperform it. The fast global memory also allows for high-speed processor-to-processor communication. In a more typical SSMP, communication usually results in an access to a slower DRAM main memory. Finally, because of the limited scale of the vector machines, they can include hardwired logic that allows high-speed synchronization between the processors. Overall, if a problem is limited to a small degree of parallelization and vectorizes well, a vector supercomputer still offers the highest absolute performance.

Overall, the niche for large vector supercomputers is shrinking due to the narrowing performance difference between vector machines and supermicros, and the much poorer cost-performance of the vector machines. Furthermore, the effort needed to extract maximum performance through vectorization could alternatively be used to block an algorithm for better cache performance. Blocking provides payback on many classes of machines from PCs through supermicros. Finally, the larger amount of parallelism afforded by SSMP and other MPP systems implies that many applications can achieve higher aggregate performance on these machines than a vector machine.

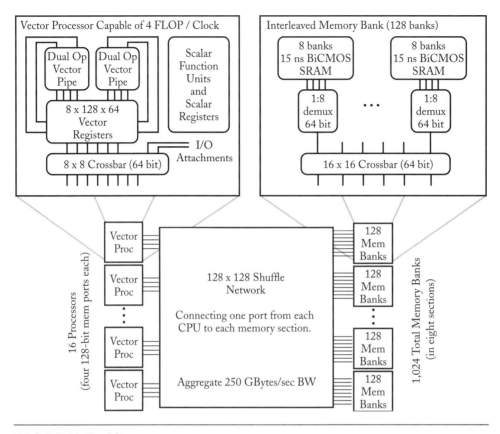

F I G U R E 5 - 1 3   *Organization of the 16-Processor Cray Y-MP C90.*

5.5.2 Tera Computer MTA

An alternative approach to vector processing and memory latency hiding is used in the MTA machine being developed by Tera Computer [ACC+90]. The Tera computer is a high-performance multiprocessor (2.8 ns cycle time) based on GaAs technology. MTA supports up to 256 processors with additional memory nodes embedded in a multistage interconnection network. It has no local memory or caches, but instead relies on multiple hardware contexts (threads) per processor to hide memory latency. Context switching between up to 128 active contexts per processor occurs without a pipeline refill penalty because the processor switches context on every cycle. To achieve 100% utilization, the processor requires 16 or more active threads, and a single thread sees no more than 1/16 the raw performance of the processor. MTA's memory latency is typically 70 clocks, implying that additional parallelism is needed to hide memory latency. Each thread is allowed to issue up to 8 instructions before waiting for its value to return. To maintain 100% utilization during memory operations, either parallelism within a thread is needed, or more than 16 threads are required.

As with the C90, the MTA requires a very high-performance memory system to keep its processors running efficiently. To prevent the interconnection network from becoming a bottleneck, the system is designed to support the maximum offered load from the 256 pro-

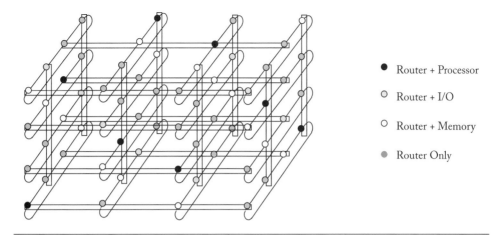

● Router + Processor

○ Router + I/O

○ Router + Memory

● Router Only

FIGURE 5-14 *The 8-Processor Tera Computer MTA with its Sparsely Populated 3-D Torus.*

cessors if traffic is uniformly distributed. As shown in Figure 5-14, the network in the MTA is a 3-D torus using 64-bit data links running at the same speed as the processor. To increase bandwidth per processor further, the N^3 cube switch points are only populated with N^2 processor and memory nodes. The partial population of the torus keeps the bisection bandwidth per processor constant as processors are added, since the 2-D bisection of the 3-D torus increases its bandwidth as N^2. In a full 256-processor configuration, the MTA supports over 1.4 Terabyte/sec of bisection bandwidth.

The MTA relies on fine-grain parallelism to achieve high performance. Fine-grain parallelism is supported by a very low-cost task spawning mechanism using the multiple hardware contexts. Spawning tasks in the MTA is analogous to issuing a vector operation. The start-up costs are higher than a vector machine, but each thread can execute a different set of operations on its assigned data. Using a large MTA system on a single problem requires a huge amount of parallelism. In particular, assuming a typical mix of 20% load instructions, each thread will reference memory every five instructions. Since a single MTA instruction can perform three operations (i.e., an arithmetic, memory, and branch operation), this implies that a load will be issued every other thread dispatch. Thus, a 256-processor MTA will only reach peak performance when the number of active threads is more than 8,960.[5] Processor utilization will fall to less than 50% if average parallelism over the program's execution falls to less than 4,480. Some of this parallelism can be achieved by multiprogramming the machine since there is no difference between switching context between a set of related tasks working on one job and those working on entirely different jobs. While this approach increases the utilization of the system, a particular job will only see a fraction of the power of the machine.

From the discussion in Chapter 1, it is clear that if the MTA cannot effectively exploit fine-grained, vector-level parallelism, its utilization will be low compared with machines

---

[5] 8,960 equals 256 processors each running 35 threads to cover the 70-cycle memory latency incurred every other thread issue due to loads from memory.

that rely on less parallel tasks and higher task throughput through latency reduction (i.e., global cache coherence) or vector operations. Assuming the flexibility of the separate threads makes up for the higher overhead of thread creation compared with vector machines, then the comparison of the MTA to cache-coherent machines is similar to that of vector multiprocessors to cache-coherent machines. Namely, when blocking and other techniques can be used to achieve good reuse of cache data, then the reduced memory access time of the cache-coherent system allows the cache-coherent system to achieve similar performance to the MTA with substantially less threads. Furthermore, the cache-based machine will achieve higher performance on scalar code. However, if there is little cache reuse, then the MTA and vector machines with their low-latency and high-bandwidth memory subsystems will perform better. This observation is true even when prefetch operations are used in the cache machine because of the added overhead of the cache and the generally larger main memory latencies in these machines.

In terms of absolute performance, the comparison between the two classes of systems depends on whether an application can achieve reasonable cache hit rates. In terms of cost-performance, however, it is clear that MTA and vector machines are not competitive because of their specialized use and exotic technology. In practice, the rising cost of processor developments and economies of volume may make the question of which class of system achieves the highest performance on the most applications irrelevant.

5.6 Virtual Shared-Memory Systems

Virtual shared-memory systems provide the illusion of shared memory on a set of networked or message-passing machines with distributed address spaces. These systems utilize techniques similar to those used to maintain coherence on cache lines in hardware, but they implement the coherence algorithms in software and manipulate blocks at the page level. Page or translation lookaside buffer (TLB) faults are used to trigger the coherence mechanisms. The main advantages of virtual shared-memory schemes is their low hardware overhead and the ability of these systems to be built on top of existing large-scale message-passing machines. Another advantage of using software for coherence is that coherence algorithms can be more sophisticated and better at tailoring the coherence mechanism to the user's data access patterns. The major disadvantage of these schemes is the large performance overhead in supporting data sharing. Shared pages that are actively updated will have tens, if not hundreds, of times more latency than comparable systems with hardware coherence. Furthermore, the large granularity of a page can lead to problems with false sharing.

5.6.1 Ivy and Munin/Treadmarks

Ivy and other virtual shared-memory systems have been developed by Kai Li at Yale and Princeton Universities [LiH86, Li88]. This early work described numerous distributed coherence protocols, some of which have been used in subsequent software and hardware implementations of distributed shared memory [LiH89]. Software implementations of the protocols were made on standard workstations and message-passing multicomputers. Obviously, on standard workstations with a LAN interconnect, only applications with the extremely low sharing and large grain sizes can be supported. Likewise, most message-passing multicomputers have latencies of over 100 microseconds to migrate an entire page. Thus, except in cases where shared data updates are very rare, the performance of virtual shared-memory systems is lower than non-cache-coherent machines because of the large cost of shared data accesses.

The Munin systems [BCZ90a, BCZ90b] are similar to Ivy in implementing shared virtual memory on a set of networked workstations. This work has refined the data access classifications given in Chapter 2 to include *write-once, write-many, producer-consumer, private, migratory, result, read-mostly,* and *synchronization*. Given the larger overheads of maintaining coherence with software, the further optimizations of the coherence mechanism can be beneficial. Simulation studies have shown that on a number of kernels (e.g., quick-sort, FFT, Gaussian elimination), the optimized coherence algorithms reduce traffic by over 50% compared with an invalidation protocol.

Another contribution of Munin and its follow-on Treadmarks was the introduction of *lazy release consistency* (LRC) [KCZ92]. LRC is equivalent to normal release consistency, but it differs from the normal hardware implementation in the way write invalidates or updates are propagated. LRC delays propagating writes to the time when a lock is acquired, as opposed to before the corresponding lock release. This delay reduces the number of messages and data transferred between processors because the effects of multiple writes are collapsed into a single invalidate or update when the processor can legally (by the definition of release consistency) access the data. Together with a multiple writer protocol that minimizes the effects of false sharing within a page, LRC can improve virtual shared-memory performance significantly [CDK+94].

Of course, in a hardware implementation, these optimizations will have a smaller performance impact because the latency of coherence actions is much lower. The other significant issue in incorporating more sophisticated coherence algorithms in hardware is their impact on complexity and performance of the more common access patterns.

5.6.2 J-Machine

The J-Machine [DCF+89] developed by Dally et al. at MIT includes primitives to allow it to function as a shared-memory machine, a message-passing machine, or even a data flow machine. The basis for the J-Machine is the message-driven processor (MDP) chip, which together with three DRAM chips forms a complete processing node. The MDPs are connected in a 3-D mesh network as shown in Figure 5-15. The MDP supports low-overhead context switch and message-passing directly in the instruction set. Using this hardware, each MPD acts as an application processor while also emulating the cache and directory controllers. As envisioned by Wallach [Wal90], when emulating a shared-memory machine, the J-Machine supports a hierarchical directory tree for each memory block. Unlike the hierarchical machines discussed in Section 5.2, however, the tree hierarchy in the J-Machine is logical; physically it is embedded in a 3-D mesh that does not have a single root. Thus, the J-Machine retains the combining and directory storage advantages of other hierarchical machines, but it does not incur the root bottleneck problem.

There are many issues to consider when comparing the J-Machine to systems with direct hardware support cache coherence. The first is whether the latency of the emulated hardware will be sufficiently low to provide comparable performance to dedicated hardware; furthermore, the J-Machine's hierarchy and remote latencies are larger than those of Para-

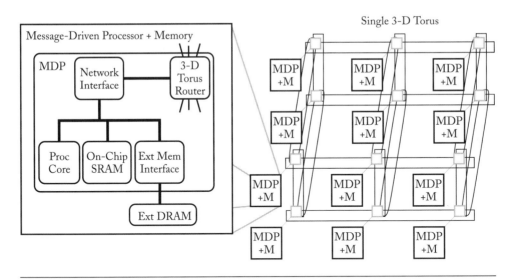

FIGURE 5-15   *A J-Machine Node and a Portion of the 3-D Torus Network.*

DiGM or GigaMax because of the larger number of processors used in the J-Machine and the lack of any clustering. Second, since the J-Machine does not directly support cache coherence on its local memory, it must use its primitive address translation mechanism to trigger coherence operations. Thus, the J-Machine must make the difficult choice between large or small coherence blocks. If large blocks are used, then there can be problems with false sharing. If small blocks are used, then there can be a significant time overhead for translating accesses and a space overhead for translation table memory.

Another potential problem for the J-Machine is that the lower performance of its individual processors will lead to problems on applications with limited parallelism. While the J-Machine could theoretically use the same processors as other systems, the J-Machine tends to have lower per-processor performance because of a number of design choices. First, to improve message-handling and context-switching speed, the J-Machine supports a very small number of registers. Second, to provide a better balance between the silicon area used for logic versus memory, the J-Machine uses a relatively small amount of silicon for its processor and a very simple memory hierarchy. Third, by using the processor as a memory/directory controller for the local memory, the effective processing power seen by the user is smaller than it would otherwise be.

As with a SIMD machine, the J-Machine has the benefit of more processor elements than other designs for a fixed system cost. The advantage of this style is its high peak performance and design simplicity. Each node consists of a single VLSI part and a small number of DRAMs. This integration reduces the design time and complexity of the J-Machine and increases the total number of processors by 50–75% when compared to a similar system with dedicated directory hardware. The potential power of the extra processors, however, may be lost in many cases due to Amdahl's Law, the overhead of larger system latencies, and dual use of the processors for both application and directory functions.

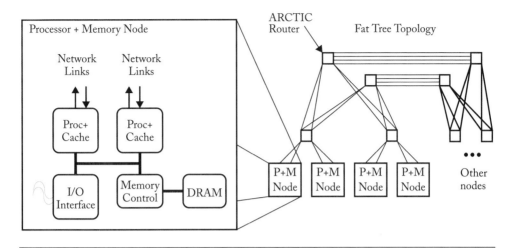

FIGURE 5-16 *The *T System.*

5.6.3 MIT/Motorola *T and *T-NG

*T [NPA92, Bec92] is a joint project between MIT and Motorola. It is a hybrid data flow/ von Neumann machine using commercial microprocessors (Motorola 88110) that are modified to provide a tightly coupled message interface and thread dispatch mechanism. The basic architecture of *T is shown in Figure 5-16. Two processors, a memory controller, and an optional I/O controller are integrated onto a multichip module. Each 88110MP is a 50-MHz 88110 with a special message and synchronization unit (MSU) added. This unit provides the interface to the network, which consists of an incoming and an outgoing 200 MByte/sec network link. The network links connect the processors to a fat tree network made up of ARCTIC [Bou94] router chips and links.

Messages are dispatched by writing into special registers on the MSU, making message launch as efficient as register access. Similarly, messages can be received via special register reads. The message interface is thus directly exposed to the compiler and user applications. A microthread dispatch mechanism using a continuation stack allows multiple threads to share the processor. Given a global virtual address space, threads can be passed around as continuations in messages. *T is thus a platform that can efficiently execute active messages [VCG+92].

*T is certainly very efficient at sending messages, receiving messages, and dispatching threads. Short threads that do not require registers can execute directly on the MSU. Longer threads that require the use of registers need to run on the main processor and must save and restore any registers they use because there is no automatic switch of register sets on thread switch. The hope is that the multithreading nature of the *T architecture is an efficient way to hide the long memory latencies that are typical of large-scale multiprocessors. Whether the primitives of remote thread execution and fast dispatch are sufficiently powerful to layer a high-performance implementation of globally shared physical memory on top of the base architecture is unclear.

In late 1993, the *T project was cancelled due to a swing of emphasis in favor of the PowerPC architecture at Motorola. A new cooperative project between MIT and Motorola, known as *T-NG (*T the next generation) is now underway. This architecture plans to make do with completely unmodified PowerPC processors. Fast message dispatch will be achieved with a memory-mapped network interface on the secondary cache port. At least two processors will get paired in a node: one to be the main data processor, and one to receive messages and access memory on behalf of remote processors. This arrangement alleviates the main processor from the burden of frequent disturbances due to message reception. *T-NG also plans to have global cache coherence, which will be achieved with the aid of a snoopy memory bus and a directory-based cache coherence protocol running in software on the message processor.

5.7 Chapter Conclusions

As shown in this chapter, there is a wide diversity in the architecture of large-scale shared-memory multiprocessors. Many of these machines incorporate concepts that could be combined. Some of the more promising functions are the following:

- Scalable hardware support for global cache coherence (directory-based, hierarchical, and reflective memory systems)
- Software-controlled, nonbinding prefetch operations to help hide communication latency (DASH, Alewife, Exemplar, S3.mp, and KSR)
- Multiple-context processors to help hide latency and exploit intertask parallelism (Alewife and MTA)
- Alternative memory operations that traverse the system hierarchically and avoid hot-spots through combining (Ultracomputer, hierarchical systems, and SCI)
- Large cluster caches or COMA to help capture the migration of large data sets and reduce capacity misses to remote memory (DDM, KSR, GigaMax, ParaDiGM, and Exemplar)
- Integrated message-passing support for fast message launch and efficient transfer of large blocks (J-Machine, Alewife, *T, Exemplar, and T3D)

The problem with simply incorporating all of these features is that scalable shared-memory processing is not mature enough to quantify the gains of these features over a large set of diverse applications. Parallel architectures are in a similar position to instruction set architectures in the 1970s. Many mechanisms can be seen as superior given certain reference behavior and programming paradigms. Thus, architects are apt to build machines with additional features that support a wide variety of application behavior. These additions inevitably lead to compromises in the performance of common operations. As with CISC architectures, many of the mechanisms will be difficult or infrequently used. Eventually, a "RISC" memory system will emerge with the core mechanisms supported with maximum performance. With the hindsight of the CISC/RISC debate, architects will hopefully be more cautious about adding unproven functionality, and a smaller number of machine generations will be needed to identify the features that optimize cost-performance.

P A R T 2

EXPERIENCE
WITH DASH

C H A P T E R

6

DASH Prototype System

The DASH prototype system was an outgrowth of research into scalable shared-memory multiprocessing in the Computer Systems Laboratory at Stanford University. The primary goal of building the machine was a better understanding of the design issues and feasibility of this class of machine. The existence of a real machine would also aid in the development and characterization of parallel processing software including new applications, automatically parallelizing compilers and parallel languages, and multiprocessor operating systems. Another indirect benefit of building the machine was to provide a realistic set of performance metrics (e.g., obtainable latencies and bandwidths) for use in related architecture simulation studies.

Work on the prototype system began in the fall of 1988 and resulted in the initial 16-processor configuration in the spring of 1991 and a 48-processor system one year later. The design and implementation were carried out by a small group of graduate students (including the authors) under the direction of Professors John Hennessy and Anoop Gupta. Professors Mark Horowitz and Monica Lam were also part of the larger DASH project and gave valuable input in the prototype design.

This chapter summarizes the system-level organization and coherence protocol used in the prototype system. Details of the actual hardware structures and implementation costs are given in Chapter 7. While the prototype was not necessarily optimal in implementing all aspects of the DASH architecture, the description in this chapter is based on the prototype because it represents a complete and consistent design. A high-level description of a more ideal implementation of DASH is given in Chapter 9.

The discussion in this chapter begins with a description of the system-level organization of the DASH prototype. The discussion then moves down to the level of the individual clusters. The structure of a cluster is given with emphasis on the directory and network logic that execute the directory-based coherence protocol. The protocol is then discussed, starting with the basic invalidation-based coherence protocol. The protocols for the alternative memory operations (prefetch, update write, and synchronization) are then given. The chapter ends with a summary of the prototype organization and the protocol features.

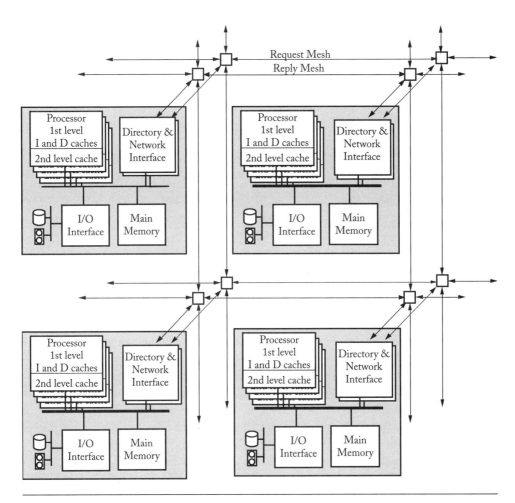

F I G U R E   6 - 1   *Block Diagram of the DASH Prototype System.*

6.1 System Organization

A block diagram of the DASH prototype system is shown in Figure 6-1. As a specific instance of the more general picture given in Figure 1-4(a), this diagram retains the three important attributes of the DASH architecture. First, the processing nodes and memory are interconnected by a scalable network. In the prototype, a pair of 2-D mesh networks are used. Second, the global shared memory is distributed among the processing nodes. Third, each processing node is a small-scale multiprocessor cluster. Each cluster contains four processors, a portion of global memory, and local I/O devices. The following sections examine the structure of the individual clusters and the interconnection meshes in more detail.

   The prototype system is limited to a 4 × 4 configuration with 16 clusters and 64 processors. This limit was chosen due to the constraints in memory addressing of the base cluster hardware, which supports no more than 256 MByte of total memory. Thus, with 16 clusters the size of each cluster's local memory partition is only 16 MByte. While the system could have been extended to support 32 or 64 clusters, the amount of memory per cluster would become too small. Support of 64 high-performance processors still gives the prototype much more power than would be possible on a single bus, and it provides a valuable platform for evaluating the architecture and experimenting with parallel software.

6.1.1 Cluster Organization

The individual shaded boxes in Figure 6-1 represent a single DASH cluster. Each cluster contains a set of processors, a section of the global memory, the directory and intercluster interface, and optional local I/O devices. These modules are interconnected by a bus supporting snoopy cache coherence. The directory tracks caching information at the cluster level, while bus snooping keeps the individual processor caches coherent.

A practical benefit of the prototype's structure is that a single cluster without its directory logic is a small-scale bus-based multiprocessor. This allows the cluster to be based on an existing commercial multiprocessor and helped reduce development time and effort. The clusters in the prototype are based on Silicon Graphics POWER Station 4D/340s [BJS88]. Although leveraging available hardware has constrained the coherence protocol and performance in some areas, the prototype retains the fundamental features of high-performance and scalable memory bandwidth.

The SGI 4D/340 system consists of four MIPS R3000 processors and R3010 floating point coprocessors running at 33 MHz. Each processor is nominally rated at 25 VAX MIPS and 4.9 DP LINPACK MFLOPS. Figure 6-2 shows a block diagram of a processor and its two levels of cache. The first-level caches consist of a 64-KByte instruction cache and a 64-KByte write-through data cache. The data cache interfaces to a 256-KByte, second-level write-back cache through a four-word write buffer. The write buffer allows the processor to continue executing instructions and accessing its first-level cache while writes are outstanding. Both the first- and second-level caches are direct-mapped and use 16-byte cache lines. The first-level caches are synchronous with their associated processor, and the second-level cache is synchronous to the 16 MHz cluster bus. The second-level caches are responsible for bus snooping and maintaining coherence among the data caches within the cluster. Coherence is maintained by an Illinois (MESI) protocol [PaP84, SwS86]. The Illinois protocol is especially useful in DASH since it specifies that processor caches should satisfy all reference possible (i.e., read requests if they have a shared copy of the requested line, and a read-exclusive request if they have a dirty copy). Such transfers do not reduce the latency of local memory, but they can short-circuit accesses to remote memory by sharing data between processor caches. Effectively, the set of processor caches act as a cluster cache for remote memory, similar to the shared multilevel caches proposed for other scalable systems [WWS+89, CGB91] (see Section 5.2 for details).

Local I/O devices within the cluster support scalable bandwidth to disks and communication channels. The I/O interface supports direct memory access (DMA) to memory. DMA access differs from normal processor access in that the DMA requestor does not contain a cache. Thus, DMA read operations must return coherent data, but this data is not subsequently kept coherent. Likewise, DMA write operations need to update all cached data, but they do not request exclusive ownership. The semantics of a DMA write amounts

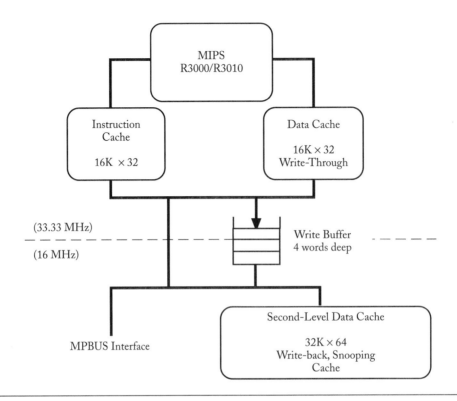

F I G U R E 6 - 2 *Block Diagram of a Processor in the DASH Prototype.*

to an update coherence protocol. In the prototype, DMA transfers are supported across the system and are integrated into the support for processor update writes. Thus, support for DMA operations improves both I/O and interprocessor communication performance.

The cluster bus (MPBUS) of the 4D/340 is a synchronous bus that consists of separate 32-bit address and 64-bit data buses running at 16 MHz. While the MPBUS is pipelined, it is not split-transaction. The bus protocol is a problem for DASH because remote accesses must not occupy the bus while the request is outstanding. If such accesses did occupy the bus, then memory bandwidth would be reduced considerably, and deadlock could result. As shown in Figure 6-3, deadlock could occur when two processors in different clusters make accesses to the memory in the other's cluster (steps 1 and 2). If both processors continue to hold their local bus while attempting to acquire the bus in the other cluster (steps 3 and 4), then the system will deadlock.

The deadlock problem is solved in the prototype by adding a bus retry mechanism to the MPBUS, which effectively creates a split-transaction protocol for remote accesses. When a remote access is first made, the processor is forced to retry, and a request is sent to the remote cluster for service. To limit the loss in bus bandwidth while the remote request is outstanding, the bus arbiter is modified to accept a mask from the directory logic. The mask is set while the request is outstanding and keeps the processor from doing unnecessary retries. When the remote reply is received, the arbitration mask is released and the processor

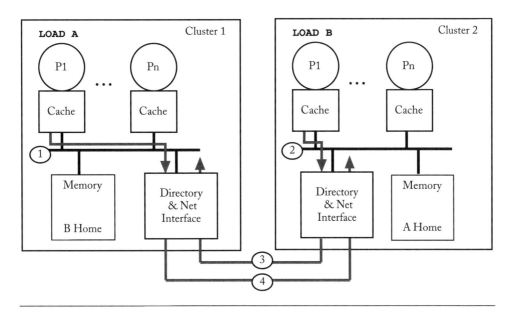

FIGURE 6-3 *Deadlock Example on Two Non-Split-Transaction Cluster Buses. (1) P1 in Cluster 1 loads A (generates local bus transaction). (2) P2 in Cluster 2 loads B (generates local bus transaction). (3) P1's read request can't be issued on Cluster 2 bus because of P2's outstanding request that is holding the bus. (4) P2's read request can't be issued on Cluster 1 bus because of P1's outstanding request that is holding the bus.*

retries the access. This time, the directory logic can satisfy the request, and the processor completes its memory access.

To use the 4D/340 in DASH, we have had to make minor modifications to the existing system boards and design a pair of new boards to support the directory and intercluster interface. The primary modification to the existing boards is support for the bus retry and arbitration masking outlined in the previous paragraph. Other minor modifications to the standard 4D/340 include changing the memory board to accept a local/remote decode signal from the directory logic and reducing the read miss fetch size from 64 bytes to 16 bytes. Reducing the fetch size to 16 bytes was done because the 64-byte fetch is actually done as four separate 16-byte bus transactions on the 4D/340. While this same technique could have been used across clusters in DASH, these accesses could not be pipelined. Thus, any hit rate improvement from the larger fetch size was likely to be nullified by the increase in miss penalty.

6.1.2 Directory Logic

The directory logic in DASH is responsible for implementing the directory-based coherence protocol and interconnecting the clusters within the system. A block diagram of the directory boards is shown in Figure 6-4. The logic is partitioned between the two boards roughly into the logic used for outbound and inbound portions of intercluster transactions. The boards are called the directory controller (DC) and reply controller (RC) boards, respectively.

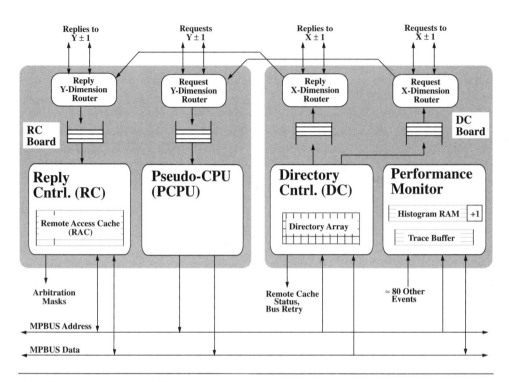

The DC board contains three major subsections. The first section is the *directory controller*, which includes the directory memory associated with the shared memory contained within this cluster. The DC logic is responsible for keeping the directory updated and sending all outbound network requests and replies. The second section is the request and reply outbound *network logic* together with the horizontal dimension of the network itself. Included in this logic are FIFOs that isolate the local bus from congestion on the global network. The final section of the DC board is the *performance monitor*. The prototype is intended as an experimental machine, and the performance logic aids in the analysis of the system by tracing and counting a variety of low-level intra- and intercluster events.

The directory memory is organized as a simple bit vector with one bit for each of the 16 clusters. In addition to the bit vector, each directory entry contains two state bits and two parity bits. One state bit indicates whether the memory block is held dirty in some remote cluster. The other bit is the logical OR of directory vector and provides a quick indication of whether the block is cached in a remote cluster. While the bit vector structure is not scalable, its memory overhead is similar to more scalable schemes given the limited size of the prototype. In addition, the full bit map allows more direct measurements of the caching behavior of the machine. Scalable extensions to this structure and their effects on the prototype protocol are outlined in Chapter 9.

The directory memory is accessed on each bus transaction. The directory information is combined with the type of bus operation, address, and the result of snooping the local caches to determine what network messages and bus controls the DC will generate. The directory is implemented in DRAM technology and always accessed in read-modify-write cycles. Performing the DRAM read-modify-write cycles on the directory in the time that DRAM main memory reads a 16-byte block is difficult. In the prototype, the directory cycle time matches that of main memory. In other systems, the need for the read-modify-write may limit memory cycle time (see Section 9.1.4 for a further discussion of this issue).

The RC board's major responsibility is processing incoming network messages. The RC contains three major sections. The first is the *reply controller*, which tracks outstanding requests made by the local processors. It also receives and buffers replies from remote clusters using the *remote access cache* (RAC). The second section is the *pseudo-CPU* (PCPU). The PCPU is a simple translator that receives network messages and issues them on the local bus for remote CPUs. Issuing all remote requests to the bus compromises performance slightly, but the effect is minor because most remote requests must access main memory or the directory. Since both of these are single ported, the bus serves as an arbiter for these RAM arrays. Issuing remote requests on the bus also keeps the processor caches coherent for the local portion of global memory. The final section of the RC board is the vertical dimension of the mesh network and the inbound network receive logic. This logic includes FIFO buffers to provide isolation of the network from congestion on the cluster bus.

The RC and RAC coordinate and buffer replies to intercluster requests. This function ranges from the simple buffering of reply data to the accumulation of invalidation acknowledgments and the enforcement of memory consistency. The RAC is organized as a 128-KByte direct-mapped snoopy cache with 16-byte cache lines. One port of the RAC services the in-bound reply network while the other snoops on the bus. The RAC is a specialized lockup-free cache in which numerous outstanding requests from each of the local processors can be pending. RAC entries are allocated when a remote request is issued by a local processor and persist until all intercluster transactions relative to the request have completed. If there is a conflict for a RAC entry, the subsequent request is delayed and then retried after the previous request has finished with the entry.

The snoopy cache structure of the RAC has several benefits. First, when a remote reply is received, the RC releases the processor's arbitration mask and allows it to repeat its access. Snooping by the RAC transfers the remote data to the processor in the same way that a local processor cache might service a remote access with a cache-to-cache transfer. Second, the snoopy structure also allows the RAC to detect when the local processors are accessing the same remote location. In this case, the RAC merges the later request and satisfies both requests when the first reply is returned. The third, and most important, benefit of the RAC structure is that it supplements the function of the local processor caches. This function is critical in supporting memory consistency because the processor caches respond to remote requests without regard to the global state of the line. For example, a processor cache will relinquish a dirty line while remote invalidations are still pending. The RAC detects this case and takes ownership of the cache line. The RAC also supplements the processor caches to improve performance. For example, the RAC supports a shared owning state that allows the local processors to read-share a dirty cache line without losing ownership of the block. Adding this shared ownership state converts the processor's MESI protocol to a MOESI

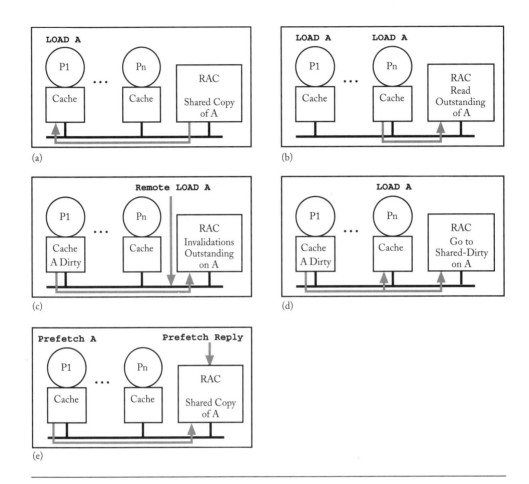

FIGURE 6-5 *Example Interactions of the RAC with the Processor Caches. (a) After receiving reply data, the RAC supplies data to the processor through a cache-to-cache transfer. (b) The RAC merges multiple requests to the same remote location. (c) The RAC enforces memory consistency by holding off remote requests if invalidates are pending. (d) The RAC allows read-sharing of remote dirty data without losing local cluster ownership. (e) The RAC holds result data from prefetch operations.*

protocol at the cluster level [SwS86]. Likewise, the RAC improves performance by accepting data from prefetch requests and adding to the overall cluster cache formed by the processor caches. These multiple uses of the RAC are summarized in Figure 6-5.

The RC also contains the RCPU function that generates bus transactions. The RCPU performs bus cycles for local processors. As outlined in the following sections, these cycles include translation of CPU I/O accesses into DMA operations and retrying bus cycles that the originator has not waited for completion (see Section 6.3.4.2 on update writes).

6.1.3 Interconnection Network

As stated earlier, the primary design requirement for the intercluster network is that it provide scalable bandwidth and low latency. It must also provide deadlock-free routing for requests and replies. Work by Dally and Seitz [DaS87] has shown that low-dimension *k*-ary *n*-cubes along with *wormhole* routing meet the goals of scalable bandwidth and low latency. Wormhole routing breaks packets into smaller words (16-bit words or *flits* in the prototype network), and it allows packets to be forwarded after the first few flits have been received. Wormhole routing reduces the latency of each hop in the network in the prototype to approximately 50 ns. The network uses unidirectional links that are asynchronous and self-timed. Bandwidth is limited by chip I/O delay and the round-trip delay of the request-acknowledge signals on the cable that connects a given pair of clusters. Each link has a cycle time of approximately 35 ns and the maximum transfer rate of approximately 60 MByte/sec. Since each cluster can transmit and receive requests and replies simultaneously, each cluster has a maximum global throughput of 240 MByte/sec.

Unfortunately, a single mesh network cannot meet the requirement for deadlock-free routing of requests and replies. As discussed in Section 4.2.1, deadlock because of request buffer overflow can be avoided only if there are two logical paths for request and reply messages. In the prototype, messages can back up in the PCPU's input FIFO into the request network. To process requests at the front of the FIFO, the DC may need to send additional requests and replies. With a single network, requests and replies may be blocked by the congestion at the input of the PCPU FIFO. With two networks, replies will always be delivered eventually. Replies do not have the problem of buffer overflow because RAC entries are always preallocated at the time when the original remote request is made on the MPBUS. Thus, with two mesh networks, there is never a problem with deadlock between requests and replies, or within the reply network itself. There is still a potential for deadlock due to requests that generate new requests. For example, an incoming write request may be blocked because it needs to send outgoing invalidation requests. These potential deadlocks in the request mesh are broken by a back-off mechanism.

Conservatively, a cluster assumes deadlock could occur if its output request FIFO is full and its PCPU input request FIFO is also full. This condition implies there is blockage on the cluster's outgoing network, and this cluster is also blocking the reception of incoming messages. The potential deadlock is broken by taking requests at the head of the PCPU FIFO that require request forwarding and rejecting them with negative acknowledgment replies. This process continues until enough input requests are removed to stop blocking the input network port or the congestion on the output FIFO is cleared. Rejected requests are retried by the issuing processor. The deadlock-breaking mode is not actually the same as the back-off mechanism proposed in Section 4.2.1 because forward progress is not made by the rejected requests. On the prototype, however, this difference is not a problem because the FIFOs are large (each can hold at least 300 requests) and the number of processors is limited. Thus, the need for deadlock-breaking is reduced, and retried requests are guaranteed to eventually make forward progress.

6.2 Programmer's Model

Generally, the programmer sees DASH as a large-scale shared-memory multiprocessor. While the detailed address map and register definitions are beyond the scope of this book, there are a number of interesting high-level issues in programming DASH. The first, of

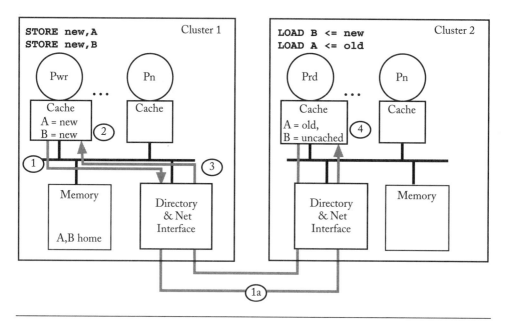

FIGURE 6-6 *Out-of-Order Writes in Release Consistency Mode. (1) Pwr writes to A, which generates invalidate to Prd. Pwr is allowed to continue and updates B. (2) Prd's outstanding load of B reaches Pwr just after update of B by Pwr. (3) Reply from Pwr of new B value passes invalidate and is returned to Prd. (4) Prd reads old value of A from cache since invalidate hasn't arrived yet.*

course, is that the system supports a cache-coherent nonuniform memory architecture (CC-NUMA). The most important performance issue is that a cache miss satisfied within the cluster has one-third the latency of a remote miss (approximately 30 versus 100 processor clocks). Additional detailed memory system performance data are given in Chapter 8.

The second major programming issue is the memory consistency model. DASH supports two modes that are controllable on a per-processor basis. The operating system sets the mode based on an attribute of the running process. The two modes are processor consistency and release consistency (see Section 3.3.1). In the processor-consistent mode, it is guaranteed that all writes issued by a processor are seen by every other processor in the same order. This guarantee is implemented by only allowing one write operation to be outstanding from each processor at a given time. Strong ordering is not guaranteed because the processor does not stall when the write is issued since the write can be buffered in its write buffer (see Figure 6-2). In the prototype, the other consistency mode, release consistency, is exactly like processor consistency, except a processor can retire a write after receiving exclusive access to a block but before all associated invalidates are completed. Thus, writes issued by the same processor can be seen out-of-order if a subsequent write is issued and completed while the first write still has invalidates pending. This difference is illustrated in Figure 6-6. In this figure, the writes from processor Pwr are observed out of order by processor Prd because processor Pwr is allowed to issue its second write before its first write has been globally performed (i.e., all of its invalidates have been completed). In processor consistency mode, processor Pwr would not be allowed to complete its first write until all of its invalidate acknowledgments have been received. To further support release consistency, DASH supports "releasing" synchronization primitives that automatically stall for all previous memory operations to globally complete before allowing the release to become visible to any other processor.[1]

The next major programming issue is gaining access to the alternative memory operations. These operations include synchronization primitives, prefetch operations, update operations, and diagnostic access to the directory memory. Because the MIPS I architecture does not define synchronization primitives, all synchronization is done on a distinct portion of the physical address space that is decoded by the hardware. Corresponding to these physical addresses, the programmer must allocate distinct virtual memory pages that map in portions of the synchronization memory.

Access to the alternative memory operations for regular variables is more complicated because simultaneous user access to these different modes is required. These operations are specified by partitioning physical memory into large regions where the high-order address bits indicate the memory operation, and the low-order address bits specify the location's address. Access to these alternate physical regions is made available by the OS by establishing corresponding redundant virtual addresses. This scheme is illustrated by Figure 6-7. For a given location, there are four potential virtual addresses that refer to that location. These addresses vary only in high-order address bits. The operating system maps each virtual address (operation) region to a corresponding physical address (operation) region through separate TLB entries. The hardware then accesses the location (or its directory) and applies the operation specified by the high-order physical address bits.

This scheme has the benefit of allowing selective user mode access to alternative memory operation. It also allows a simple interface for the run-time system that must generate the necessary alternative virtual addresses. The scheme requires only one physical page table entry per location, but it does require redundant TLB entries to support the parallel mappings. Note that when a TLB miss occurs, especially on an alternative operation such as prefetch, the potential cost of extra TLB misses can be reduced by loading both the alternative operation translation and the normal translation.

The prototype only supports 256 MByte of main memory, which is then redundantly mapped three times to trigger the alternative memory operations. Had the base cluster supported more memory, or the DASH prototype supported a larger number of clusters, then one would quickly run out of physical address bits. In fact, even on today's 64-bit processors there is often a limit on the number of physical address bits (e.g., the DEC Alpha 21064 only supports 34 physical address bits). This limitation can force system designers to add additional segmentation registers outside the processor to enable it to generate the larger range needed by a SSMP system. For example, the Cray T3D, which uses the Alpha 21064, requires at least a 38-bit address range (2,048 nodes · 64 MByte/node). Likewise, the Convex Exemplar, which is based on a 32-bit HP-PA processor, requires at least 35 address bits

---

[1] The update write operation, if used, is always executed in a release consistency mode. Actually, for implementation reasons, these operations do not even obey consistency with respect to the processor that issued them unless the processor issues a full fence after the write.

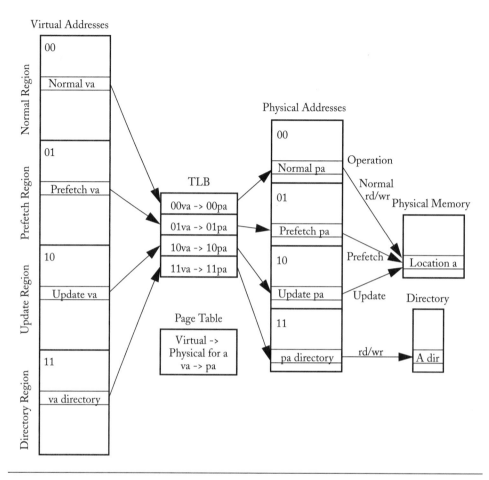

FIGURE 6-7 *Issue Addresses and Translation of Alternative Memory Operations.*

(16 nodes · 2 GByte/node). Hopefully, future 64-bit processors will support 44 or more physical address bits to enable processes to directly address all memory on a large SSMP that might include 2,048 nodes, each with 1–4 GByte of memory.

One final programming issue for the prototype is extended addressing of I/O across clusters. The directory boards fully support I/O DMA originating in any cluster accessing memory in any other cluster. For a number of reasons, however, making programmed I/O accesses from a processor to an I/O device in another cluster is not allowed. Thus, the OS is responsible for migrating any process that attempts to access a physical I/O device to a processor within the same cluster as the I/O device.

6.3 Coherence Protocol

The memory operations in DASH are broken into the following categories: (1) the base memory operations that support normal cached reads and writes, (2) nonblocking prefetch operations, (3) update and DMA operations, and (4) synchronization operations. The following sections give an overview of these operations, specifying the messages that flow between clusters to satisfy the request and maintain cache coherence. In the next section, the terms and symbols used in these definitions are given. The definitions are given for the typical cases; Section 6.5 discusses exceptions that can occur that are not illustrated with the individual operations.

6.3.1 Nomenclature

In describing the DASH protocol, three types of clusters and two types of memory are distinguished. The *local* or *requesting cluster* is the cluster that includes the CPU that issued the memory request. The *home cluster* is the cluster that contains the physical memory associated with a given memory address, and a *remote cluster* is any other cluster. Similarly, *local memory* is the memory whose home is in the local cluster; *remote memory* is memory whose home is in any other cluster.

The base cache coherence protocol used in DASH is based on invalidations. As represented by the directory, a memory block may be in one of three states:

1. Uncached: not cached by any remote cluster

2. Shared-Remote: held in an unmodified state in the cache of one or more remote clusters

3. Dirty-Remote: held in a modified state in a single remote cluster

The directory stores only the caching state of remote clusters. The caching state of the home cluster is not stored because the processor caches in the home are kept coherent by snooping on the bus. Although storing the caching state of the processors in the home is possible, it would complicate accessing the directory memory because of the nature of write-back operations on the Silicon Graphics' MPBUS (see Section 7.1.1).

The coherence protocol maintains the notion of an *owning cluster* for each memory block. The owning cluster is the home cluster unless the block is held dirty-remote. In this case, the dirty cluster is the owner. Except read misses satisfied by cache-to-cache transfers within a cluster, only the owning cluster can satisfy a memory reference. As discussed in Section 4.2.2, the owning cluster serializes accesses to determine their global order. Even though the owning cluster is not always the home, the directory entry for a block always resides in the home cluster. When a dirty cluster changes ownership of a block, it sends a message to the home to update the directory.

Roughly corresponding to the directory states, cache lines in the processors' second-level caches can be in one of four states:

1. Invalid: not valid in the cache

2. Shared: unmodified in the cache, valid for reads only; may be cached by other processors

3. Dirty: modified in the cache, valid for reads and writes; block is held only by this cache; must be written back to memory if replaced

4. Private-Unmodified: unmodified in the cache, valid for reads and writes; block is held only in this cache

The purpose of the first three states listed above are relatively straightforward. The processors respond to the bus cycles by the other CPUs, the PCPU, and RCPU as specified by the MESI protocol. The private-unmodified state is somewhat less clear. This state is only supported for processors in the home. It is entered on a read miss when no local or remote processor holds a copy of the block. This state allows the processor to transition to the dirty state on a later write without doing another bus cycle. If another processor reads the block before such a write, the cache transitions to the shared state. This transition is detectable by processors in the home since they see all accesses to local memory blocks that were not cached at the time they entered the private-unmodified state. Because processors outside the home are not guaranteed to see all such accesses, they cannot support this cache state.

The coherence protocol is executed in a distributed manner by a set of state machines associated with the processor caches, directory controllers, reply controllers, and PCPUs. The primary state machines that carry out the intercluster coherence protocol reside in the directory and reply controllers. These state machines are based on a set of programmable read-only memories (PROMs). The actual definition of the protocol is specified by ASCII tables that are automatically translated to a form suitable for PROM programming. Although precise and convenient for the hardware implementation, the protocol is hard to extract from these tables.[2] As an alternative, the protocol is defined in the following sections through a set of graphs that illustrate the flow of intercluster messages for the common cases of each operation. The actual hardware state machines can be determined by the decode of each step in the normal and exception cases for each request, and their corresponding network messages, bus transactions, and state transitions.

The message flow graphs are divided into cases by three attributes. The first distinction is whether the request is made by a processor in the home or a remote cluster. Requests originating in the home are different because the directory information is available on every local bus access. Thus, extra network messages and bus cycles can be eliminated. The second distinction is made on the basis of the directory state when the access reaches the home cluster. The directory state determines whether the home or some dirty-remote cluster is the current owner of the requested block. Third, the cache state of the other processors and RAC in the same cluster as the issuing processor separates the flow of requests for remote locations because a local cache can satisfy a remote memory request by a local cache-to-cache transfer.

The flow diagrams in the following sections use the notation given below:

(L) Local Cluster: Cluster that contains the processor that initiated the memory access.

(H) Home Cluster: Cluster that contains the physical memory and directory corresponding to the requested address.

---

[2] There are five major tables that define the actions of the DC and RC. The two DC tables decode approximately 500 valid bus operation/current state pairs. The RC tables decode roughly the same number of valid bus input conditions and approximately 150 reply message/RAC state pairs.

Ⓓ Dirty Cluster: A remote cluster that currently caches the requested memory block in a modified state.

Ⓢ Shared Cluster: A remote cluster that currently caches a shared, read-only copy of the requested memory block.

Ⓠ Queued Cluster: A cluster that currently caches a locked value of the requested lock and is assumed to be spinning on that lock.

— i ⟶ Request Message: An intercluster request message that traverses the request mesh and is issued by the PCPU on the destination cluster's bus.

— i ⟶ Normal Reply: An intercluster reply message that traverses the reply mesh and is received by the reply controller. The reply will release a local CPU to retry the access and fetch the reply data from the RAC.

— i ⟶ Ack Reply: An intercluster acknowledge reply message that traverses the reply mesh and received by the reply controller. These replies are handled within the reply controller by updating the RAC. They do not generate a bus cycle on the destination cluster.

6.3.2 Basic Memory Operations

Processor load and store instructions in the normal physical memory address space maintain cache coherence through an invalidation-based protocol. Most memory operations are satisfied by the processor's first- or second-level caches. A load of a location not already in the caches generates a read request on the bus to fetch the corresponding 16-byte memory block. Store operations write through the first-level cache and are held in the four-entry write buffer. Writes can be satisfied by the second-level cache if it has ownership of the memory block. Otherwise, a read-exclusive request is issued on the bus to retrieve the block and invalidate all other cached copies of the block. The processor does not wait for completion of stores; it only stalls if there is no space in its write buffer. Memory reads that are not satisfied by the first-level cache must wait for the write buffer to empty before accessing the second-level cache. Write-back requests are generated by cache fills that replace dirty blocks in the second-level cache.

6.3.2.1 Read Requests

Normal processor load instructions that are not satisfied by the first- or second-level cache generate read requests on the bus. The possible flows of a read request are illustrated in Figure 6-8. This figure demonstrates many of the protocol features mentioned previously. For example, the protocol supports cache-to-cache sharing between the local processors and RAC to reduce the latency of remote accesses (Figure 6-8(c)). If the source cache holds the line dirty, then the RAC will keep ownership of the block within the cluster by storing the block in the RAC in a shared-dirty state. Another protocol feature illustrated in (Figure 6-8(b, d, and e)) is that read requests not satisfied by a local cache-to-cache transfer are always satisfied by the owning cluster (i.e., the home cluster unless the block is dirty-remote). Finally, if a request is forwarded to a dirty-remote cluster, the dirty cluster replies directly to the local cluster (Figure 6-8(e)). Forwarding removes the latency of one network

(a) Home request to uncached or shared-remote block.
  - CPU reads from main memory; directory unchanged.

(b) Home request to dirty-remote block.
  - CPU issues read and is forced to retry.
  - Allocate RAC entry and send read request (1) to dirty cluster.
  - Dirty cache supplies data and goes to shared state; dirty cluster sends read reply(2) to home.
  - CPU repeats read; RAC supplies data, which is also written back to main memory; directory entry to shared-remote.

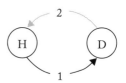

(c) Remote request satisfied by local cache.
  - CPU issues read and dirty or shared cache supplies data. If dirty, the RAC takes sharing ownership if RAC entry is free, otherwise, a sharing write-back request is sent to home.

(d) Remote request to uncached/shared-remote block.
  - CPU issues read and is forced to retry.
  - Allocate RAC entry and send read request (1) to home cluster.
  - Main memory supplies data for read reply(2); Directory entry to shared-remote.
  - CPU repeats read and RAC supplies data.

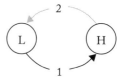

(e) Remote request to dirty-remote block.
  - CPU issues read and is forced to retry.
  - Allocate RAC entry and send read request (1) to home cluster.
  - Home forwards request to dirty cluster(2).
  - Dirty cache supplies data and goes to shared state. read reply(3a) sent to local cluster and sharing writeback req(3b) sent to home cluster.
  - CPU repeats read, RAC supplies data.
  - PCPU issues sharing writeback in home; directory entry to shared-remote.

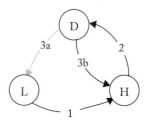

FIGURE 6-8 *Read Request Flows.*

and cluster hop over a simpler scheme that would first write-back the block to memory. Forwarding also removes the need for the home cluster to retain any state about requests that it cannot satisfy immediately.

There is one exception that occurs only for read requests, when the cluster has a remote read outstanding and an invalidation request is received for the requested block. The invalidation may be due to a read-exclusive request that logically precedes or follows the outstanding read. In the former case, the read-exclusive is invalidating an older copy of the block, and it is safe to accept the read reply. In the latter case, the invalidation is for a shared copy of the block that is currently in transit on the reply network. Reordering of events between the home and local cluster is possible because of the independent request and reply meshes. Since these two cases are ambiguous from the local cluster's perspective, the conservative action is to treat whatever reply is received for the pending read as a negative acknowledge (NAK). As a result, the processor must retry the read. This case is illustrated by Figure 6-9.

- CPU 1 issues read and is forced to retry; allocate RAC entry and send read request (1) to home.
- CPU 2 issues read-ex and is forced to retry; allocate RAC entry and send read-ex request to home (2).
- Main memory supplies data for read reply (3); directory entry to shared-remote.
- Main memory supplies data for read-ex reply (4a); invalidation requests sent to shared clusters (4b); directory entry to dirty-remote.
- PCPU of cluster 1 issue invalidations; RAC entry marked as needing retry reply with invalidation ack reply (5).
- Upon receipt of read reply, RAC treats data as stale and forces CPU 1 to reissue its initial request.

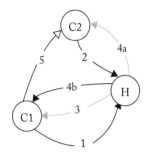

This case could also arise if CPU 2's read-exclusive reached the home first. In this case the CPU 1 would only receive an invalidate if it has previously dropped a shared copy of the line. In this case, CPU 1 would be receiving a fresh copy of the location from CPU 2's cache. CPU 1 can not distinguish this case from the above and would conservatively assume that the reply is stale.

FIGURE 6-9 *Out-of-Order Read Reply and Invalidation Forcing Retry of the Read Request.*

6.3.2.2 Read-Exclusive Requests

Processor store operations write-through the processor's first-level cache and are buffered in the write buffer. The write buffer then retires writes, in order, into the second-level cache. If a block is not dirty in the second-level cache, then the second-level cache issues a read-exclusive request on the local bus. A read-exclusive will retrieve the cache block and eliminate all other cached copies of the block. The possible flows of a read-exclusive request are illustrated in Figure 6-10. The flows are similar to read requests if the block is uncached or dirty-remote, but differ when the block is in the shared-remote state.

Read-exclusive requests stall the write buffer until the request is satisfied by the local bus or an exclusive reply is received from a remote cluster. Receiving exclusive ownership, however, does not imply that the operation has completed systemwide (Figure 6-10(b and f)). Invalidations of the other cached copies may still be in progress if the block was in the shared state when it reached the home. In these cases, the exclusive reply contains a count of the pending invalidations. The RAC entry will persist in the *busy* state until all invalidation acknowledges have been received. If the processor is in processor consistency mode, the data is not given to the processor until all invalidations have been received. If the processor is in release consistency mode, then the processor does receive the data early, but it is not allowed to issue a releasing synchronization operation. Other local processors can cache the block while the busy state persists, but they also become responsible for the pending invalidations on the block. The result is that no processor will release a lock while data they have accessed is not consistent systemwide. While this sharing of invalidation responsibility during the

(a) Home request to uncached-remote block.

- CPU issues read-ex and main memory supplies data; directory unchanged.

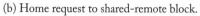

(b) Home request to shared-remote block.

- CPU issues read-ex and main memory supplies data; directory entry to uncached; allocate RAC entry; send invalidation requests (1) to shared clusters.
- PCPUs issue invalidations on shared clusters; reply with invalidation ack reply (2).
- Deallocate RAC entry after all acks received.

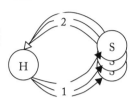

(c) Home request to dirty-remote block.

- CPU issues read-ex and is forced to retry; allocate RAC entry and send read-ex request (1) to dirty cluster.
- Dirty cache supplies data and goes to invalid state; dirty cluster sends read-ex reply (2) to home.
- CPU repeats read-ex and RAC supplies data; directory entry to uncached.

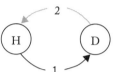

(d) Remote request satisfied by local cache.

- CPU issues read-ex and local dirty cache supplies data and goes to invalid state.

(e) Remote request to uncached-remote block.

- CPU issues read-ex and is forced to retry; allocate RAC entry and send read-ex request to home (1).
- Main memory supplies data for read-ex reply (2); directory entry to dirty-remote.
- CPU repeats read-ex and RAC supplies data.

(f) Remote request to shared-remote block.

- CPU issues read-ex and is forced to retry; allocate RAC entry; send read-ex request to home (1).
- Main memory supplies data for read-ex reply (2a); invalidation requests sent to shared clusters (2b); directory entry to dirty-remote.
- CPU repeats read-ex and RAC supplies data.
- PCPUs issue invalidations on shared clusters; reply with invalidation ack reply (3).
- Deallocate RAC entry after all acks received.

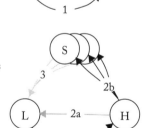

(g) Remote request to dirty-remote block.

- CPU issues read-exclusive and is forced to retry; allocate RAC entry; send read-ex request to home (1).
- Home forwards read-ex request to dirty cluster (2).
- Dirty cache supplies data and goes to invalid state; send read-ex reply to local cluster (3a) and dirty transfer request to home (3b).
- CPU repeats read-ex and RAC supplies data.
- PCPU in home issues dirty transfer; directory entry to dirty-remote; sends ack to local (4).
- RC deallocates RAC entry upon receiving ack.

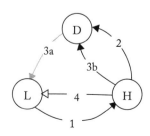

FIGURE 6-10 *Read-Exclusive Request Flows.*

busy state could be extended to remote processors, it would add considerable complexity. In particular, local storage would be needed to store the identity of the remote processors who have accessed the busy data. They would eventually need to be informed when all invalidation acknowledgments have been received. The complexity arises because there is no limit, a priori, on the number of remote processors that could request the busy block. Because of this complexity and the minimal performance gain, remote requests are rejected with NAK replies if the corresponding RAC entry is in the busy state.

Another noteworthy aspect of read-exclusive requests is the need for the final acknowledgment (message 4) in Figure 6-10(g). This extra acknowledgment is needed to remove the race condition that results from the message that gives the local cluster ownership (3a), and the one that updates the directory (3b). Without this acknowledgment, it would be possible for the local cluster to issue a write-back for the block before the directory is updated. If the write-back arrived before the dirty-transfer message (3b), then the dirty-transfer message would corrupt the directory. This condition is inhibited by preventing any write-backs until the RAC receives the directory update acknowledgment and leaves the busy state.

One other feature of a read-exclusive request is that if a cluster held a shared copy of the line at the time the read-exclusive request reached the home, then an invalidation will be sent to the writing cluster. This invalidation is not needed to eliminate the other local shared copies, because the read-exclusive issued on the bus by the writing processor eliminates these. However, stale copies of the block may be in transit in the request network, so the invalidation is sent to eliminate these copies (discussed in more detail in Section 6.3.3.2). The PCPU on the local cluster recognizes the invalidation request is on behalf of the local cluster and converts the request to a special *self-invalidation*. The self-invalidation does not affect the processor caches, but it does decrement the count of invalidation acknowledgments expected by the RAC and insures that all copies of the block that might have been in the request network are eliminated before the RAC leaves the busy state.

6.3.2.3 Write-Back Requests

Write-back requests are generated as a side effect of processor read and read-exclusive transactions. As will be shown in the MPBUS timing diagrams in Figure 7-2, write-backs are actually embedded in the same bus transactions as the read and read-exclusive requests that replace the dirty line. These embedded write-backs are part of the reason that the home cluster does not maintain the caching state of the local cluster. To do so would require two directory updates per bus transaction when a read and write-back request were for the local cluster. Because the caching state of the home is not kept in the directory, a local write-back never affects the directory; it always stays uncached-remote. A write-back to remote memory generates a write-back request message. The write-back request is issued by the PCPU in the home cluster along with a dummy read request for the write-back block. This bus transaction causes main memory to be updated and the directory to be marked uncached.

Write-back requests issued during a read or read-exclusive request that must be retried because of remote service are initiated on their first bus transaction. The dirty line being replaced goes to a clean state while the request is pending, and the write-back is not repeated when the primary request is retried. A final complication of write-back requests is that a write-back may occur for a block that is still busy (i.e., remote invalidations pending). In this case the processor proceeds, but the write-back data is stored in the RAC instead of being sent to the home.

6.3.3 Prefetch Operations

An invalidation-based cache coherence protocol works well for most data objects [EgK88, WeG89a]. However, performance can degrade substantially if data objects exhibit poor cache behavior. The degradation results primarily from read misses that fetch data on demand and force the processor to stall during the cache fill. Prefetch operations allow the processor to fetch data without waiting for the memory response. Prefetch relies on intratask level parallelism to hide memory latency. To be effective, prefetch also requires there to be sufficient memory bandwidth to accept the increased memory reference rate.

DASH supports prefetch commands that move a shared or exclusive copy of a memory block closer to a processor or send a shared copy out to other clusters. The first type of prefetch is called a *consumer prefetch*; the latter, a *producer prefetch* or *deliver*. Prefetch operations in DASH are nonbinding; data remains visible to the cache coherence protocol and is kept consistent until the processor reads the value. Prefetch operations are specified by processor stores within a prefetch region of the physical address space. These store operations do not stall the processor if there is space in the processor's write buffer. The prefetch type is specified by the cache offset portion of the address.

6.3.3.1 Consumer Prefetch

Ideally, consumer prefetch would bring data into the processor's first- or second-level cache. Furthermore, prefetch of data already in the processor's cache would be filtered out by the cache. In the prototype, both of these features would have required extensive modifications of the existing processor board. Consequently, prefetch data in the prototype is only brought into the issuing cluster's RAC, and unnecessary prefetches are only filtered by snooping after they are issued on the local bus.

As mentioned previously, a read-prefetch is issued as a store operation that bypasses the processor caches. The store operation is issued on the bus and generates a cache read request message if the block is not held in any of the local caches or RAC. Outside of the cluster, the prefetch is treated as a normal cache read, so only the RAC knows that a processor is not waiting. Upon receiving the reply, the RAC entry goes to a valid state. On a subsequent processor read, the RAC supplies the block through the normal cache-to-cache transfer mechanism. If a normal load operation is issued before the data is available in the RAC, the request is merged into the outstanding prefetch. Read-exclusive prefetches are issued like a read-prefetch except they use a different cache line offset. Outside the cluster, they are translated into read-exclusive requests. When complete, the read-exclusive prefetch leaves an exclusive copy of the memory block in the RAC.

Prefetch data in the RAC is kept coherent in the same manner as normal cache data. Outside the issuing cluster the request is literally a read or read-exclusive request. Once the prefetch reply is received, the RAC performs the normal cache snoop operations that invalidate a shared cache line or source an exclusive cache line. Since prefetch operations are only hints, it is also permissible for the memory system to ignore a prefetch request. The prefetch will be ignored if it conflicts with an active RAC entry, or the prefetch request receives a NAK reply. In the former case, it is assumed that stalling the write buffer until the RAC is freed will cancel any gain from the prefetch. In the latter case, it is assumed that the block is a hot-spot and eliminating the prefetch will reduce the load on it.

6.3.3.2   Producer Prefetch

Producer prefetch (PPREF) allows the producer of a data item to push the item closer to consuming processors. PPREF is useful when multiple consumers require a block, or when the consumer needs data as soon as it is produced. PPREF operations also improve the efficiency of emulating message-passing within a shared-memory machine. In the prototype, the destination of the producer prefetch is specified as a bit vector in the data of the store operation that initiates the PPREF. Each cluster specified in the bit vector is sent a shared copy of the block. If the vector is null, the operation simply flushes any dirty-remote copy of the data item back to memory. Producer prefetch is optimized for the case where the PPREF block is dirty in the issuing processor's cache. In particular, unlike the consumer prefetch operations, the PPREF is always translated by the RCPU on the local bus. The RCPU cycle will flush any dirty copies of the PPREF block held locally back to memory before the PPREF is sent to the home. This optimization, however, does not restrict when or where a PPREF can be issued. PPREFs can be issued by any processor at any time. They are only hints that affect the caching of the given memory block.

Figure 6-11 shows the flow of producer prefetch operations. One item of note is that the actual deliver messages are sent as requests to the PCPU, not as replies to the RC. Although not as efficient as sending a reply, it is important that the deliver follow the same network path as any later invalidation. Unlike a normal read reply, the deliver does not have an associated RAC entry to detect possibly stale replies caused by a race between the two networks. Because a single mesh guarantees in-order delivery of messages between any two nodes, the deliver and later invalidation will be issued at the destination in the same order that they are issued in the home. Similarly, it is important that an invalidation (actually a self-invalidation) be sent to a writing node if the directory indicates that the issuing cluster is in the shared state. The sharing state might be the result of a pending deliver, and the self-invalidation guarantees that such a deliver has been purged from the request network before the RAC leaves the busy state. This problem is illustrated in Figure 6-12.

Another unique attribute of the PPREF flows shown in Figure 6-11 is that deliver requests do not require acknowledgments because deliver operations have guaranteed ordering given the network restrictions mentioned above. If in-order message delivery cannot be guaranteed, then deliver requests require acknowledgments, and pending producer prefetches require a busy condition similar to read-exclusives.

6.3.4   DMA/Uncached Operations

DMA operations made by I/O devices are similar to uncached processor memory operations. In both cases no caching is desired for reads, and ownership is not requested for writes. Caching is not desired for reads because the resulting memory value is leaving the

(a) Home request to uncached or shared-remote block.

- CPU issues producer-prefetch (PPREF) to bus with a bit-vector of destination clusters.
- RCPU repeats PPREF in the normal cache space with the destination bit-vector and main memory supplies data; send deliver request to specified clusters (1); directory entry to shared-remote.
- PCPUs on destination clusters issue deliver; destination RCs take shared data into RAC.

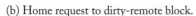

(b) Home request to dirty-remote block.

- CPU issues PPREF to bus; allocate RAC entry; send PPREF request to dirty cluster (1).
- Dirty cache supplies data and goes to shared state; dirty cluster sends sharing write-back request and PPREF request to home (2ab).
- PCPU issues sharing write-back in home; directory entry to shared-remote.
- PCPU issues PPREF in home; main memory supplies data; send deliver request to specified clusters (3a); send acknowledge reply to home (3b).
- PCPUs on destination clusters issue deliver; destination RCs take data into RAC.

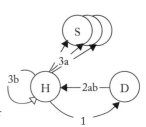

(c) Remote request satisfied by local dirty cache.

- CPU issues producer-prefetch (PPREF) to bus.
- RCPU repeats PPREF in the normal cache space and local dirty cache supplies data; allocate RAC entry; send sharing write-back request and PPREF request to home (1ab).
- PCPU issues sharing write-back in home; directory entry to shared-remote.
- PCPU issues PPREF in home, main memory supplies data; send deliver request (2a) to specified clusters; send acknowledge reply to local RC (2b)
- PCPUs on destination clusters issue deliver; destination RCs take data into RAC.

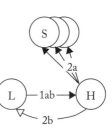

(d) Remote request to uncached or shared-remote block.

- Same as above except sharing write-back request does not precede producer prefetch request sent to the home.

(e) Remote request to dirty-remote block.

- CPU issues producer-prefetch (PPREF) to bus.
- RCPU repeats PPREF in the normal cache space; allocate RAC entry; send PPREF request to home (1).
- PPREF request forwarded by home to dirty cluster (2).
- Dirty cache supplies data and goes to shared state; dirty cluster sends sharing write-back request and PPREF request to home (3,4).
- PCPU issues sharing write-back in home; directory entry to shared-remote.
- PCPU issues PPREF in home; main memory supplies data; send deliver request to specified clusters (5a); send acknowledge reply to home (5b).
- PCPUs on destination clusters issue deliver; destination RCs take data into RAC.

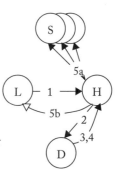

FIGURE 6-11 *Producer Prefetch Request Flows.*

- CPU in home issues producer-prefetch (PPREF) to bus with a bit-vector of destination cluster.
- Send deliver request to specified cluster (1);
  directory entry to shared-remote.
- CPU in destination cluster issues read-ex and is forced to retry;
  allocate RAC entry; send read-ex request to home (2).
- Main memory supplies data for read-ex reply (3a); invalidation request sent to sharing cluster (3b);
  directory entry to dirty-remote.
- CPU repeats read-ex and RAC supplies data.
- PCPUs issue self-invalidate on home cluster;
  decrement invalidate count to zero;
  deallocate RAC entry.

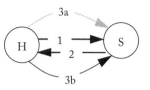

- Since messages are delivered in order between any two nodes, the deliver message (1) must arrive at S before the self-invalidate. Without the self-invalidate, the deliver might arrive after the read-ex reply and leave a stale copy of the location in the RAC of writing processor.

FIGURE 6-12 *Producer Prefetch Need for Self-Invalidate.*

domain of memory coherence (i.e., an external I/O device or processor register). Thus, while the most up-to-date value of a location is required, no caching is implied. For DMA writes, caching is not desirable because the operations are typically large and sequential, and they are referenced only once by the writer. Similarly, processor writes used for interprocessor communication and event notification are more likely to be referenced by other processors before the issuing processor re-requests the data. As with uncached reads, update writes must maintain coherence, but they use cache updates instead of invalidations to do so.

The prototype supports DMA and uncached operations through extensions of the DMA bus transactions supported on SGI's MPBUS. DMA reads return coherent data, and DMA writes update all cache and memory copies of a block. Neither operation affects the cache state of the block. DMA reads and writes are issued directly by the I/O interfaces in the 4D/340. Ideally, uncached and update operations would be issued by the processor in the same way, but the processor boards do not support these transactions. Instead, an alternate physical address region is used. These accesses are then translated by the directory hardware into DMA operations in the normal cachable memory space.

6.3.4.1 Uncached/DMA Reads
DMA or uncached reads are identical to normal cache reads except the caching and directory state is unaltered by the read. Figure 6-13 shows the request flow for DMA read operations. Uncached reads are similar, but require translation between uncached I/O space and normal cache space. The translation is done by the RCPU if the request is issued and satisfied by the home. Otherwise, the outgoing network request logic performs the translation on the way to the network. Since uncached reads are translated after issue on the bus, they are never satisfied by the requesting processor's cache or by local cache-to-cache sharing.

(a) Home request to uncached or shared-remote block.

- IO issues DMA read on bus and main memory supplies data; directory entry unchanged.

(b) Home request to dirty-remote block.

- IO issues DMA read on bus and is forced to retry; allocate RAC entry; send uncached read request (1) to dirty cluster.
- Dirty cache supplies data and stays in dirty state; dirty cluster sends uncached Read reply (2) to home.
- IO repeats DMA read and RAC supplies data.

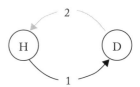

(c) Remote request satisfied by local cache.

- IO issues DMA read on bus and local shared or dirty cache supplies data.

(d) Remote request to uncached or shared-remote block.

- IO issues DMA read on bus and is forced to retry; allocate RAC entry; send uncached read request (1) to home.
- Main memory supplies data for uncached dead reply (2); directory entry unchanged.
- IO repeats DMA read and RAC supplies data.

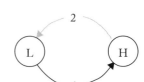

(e) Remote request to dirty-remote block.

- IO issues DMA read on bus and is forced to retry; allocate RAC entry; send uncached read request (1) to home.
- Home forwards request to dirty cluster (2).
- Dirty cache supplies data and stays in dirty state; dirty cluster sends uncached read reply (3) to local cluster.
- IO repeats DMA read and RAC supplies data.

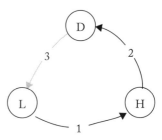

FIGURE 6-13 *DMA/Uncached Read Request Flows.*

6.3.4.2 DMA/Update Write Operations

DMA and update write operations update all cached copies of a memory location with a new value. DMA write operations are nonblocking in the sense that the I/O interface can continue as soon as the request is issued on the local bus. Retry is only required if allocation of a RAC entry is not possible. As in DMA reads, DMA write operations are issued directly by the I/O interface logic, but processor update writes must be translated by the directory logic. Translation of update writes complicates memory consistency for the issuing processor. In particular, it is possible that the processor issues an update write and then reads an old value of the location from its own cache. To prevent this, a full-fence operation (see Section 6.4.3) must be issued before any read of the location by the writing processor. The fence insures that the write has updated any copies of the location in the processors' caches before the read completes. Figure 6-14 shows the flow of update write operations. Note that update writes, like deliver operations, rely on in-order message delivery between any two nodes

(a) Home request to uncached-remote block.

- IO issues DMA write on bus updating main memory and local caches; directory entry unchanged.

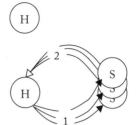

(b) Home request to shared-remote block.

- IO issues DMA write on bus updating main memory and local caches. allocate RAC entry; send update request (1) to all shared clusters.
- PCPUs issue updates on shared clusters; reply with update ack replies (2).
- Deallocate RAC entry after all acks received.

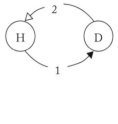

(c) Home request to dirty-remote block.

- IO issues DMA write on bus; allocate RAC entry; send DMA write request (1) to Dirty cluster.
- DMA write issued in dirty cluster;
  dirty cache updated;
  dirty cluster sends DMA write ack (2) to home.
- Deallocate RAC entry when ack received.

(d) Remote request satisfied by local cache.

- IO issues DMA write on bus updating local dirty cache.

(e) Remote request to uncached-remote block.

- IO issues DMA write on bus; allocate RAC entry; send DMA write request (1) to home.
- DMA write in home updates main memory;
  DMA write ack (2) sent to local cluster.
- Deallocate RAC entry when ack received.

(f) Remote request to shared-remote block.

- IO issues DMA write on bus; allocate RAC entry; send DMA write request (1) to home.
- DMA write in home updates main memory;
  DMA write ack (2a) sent to local cluster and update request (2b) sent to shared clusters.
- PCPUs issue updates on shared clusters;
  reply with update ack reply (3).
- Deallocate RAC entry after all acks received.

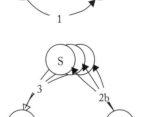

(g) Remote request to dirty-remote block.

- IO issues DMA write on bus; allocate RAC entry; send DMA write request (1) to home.
- Home forwards DMA write request to dirty cluster (2).
- DMA write issued in dirty cluster;
  dirty cache updated;
  dirty cluster sends DMA write ack (2) to local cluster.
- Deallocate RAC entry when ack received.

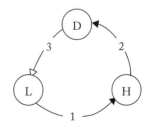

FIGURE 6-14   *DMA/Update Write Request Flows.*

within a single mesh. In-order delivery insures that multiple update writes do not leave different values within the caches of different clusters or the memory home.

6.4 Synchronization Protocol

Synchronization variables have different access and sharing patterns than normal variables [WeG89a]. In particular, synchronization is often associated with interprocessor communication, and an invalidation-based protocol is not likely to be optimal. Furthermore, if lock operations are recognized by the hardware, then the higher semantic content of these operations can be used to increase performance. The DASH prototype supports four different synchronization operations. The first set supports efficient spin locks. The second set performs atomic Fetch&Op operations. The third is the update write operation outlined in the previous section, and the final set of operations are explicit fences that control memory consistency.

6.4.1 Granting Locks

Spin locks provide the basis for low-level protection of mutual exclusion regions. Most cache-coherent systems integrate support for spin locks with the caching mechanism. Waiting processors spin in their cache on a locked value of the lock and atomically read-modify-write the lock to acquire it. DASH supports efficient spin waiting with granting locks. Granting locks use the pointer information in the directory and hardware-recognizable lock and unlock operations to improve performance. When processors are spinning in their cache, an unlock operation causes invalidations only in a single waiting cluster. Subsequently, a processor in the *grant* cluster can acquire the lock with a local bus operation. This arrangement reduces the latency in passing the lock between processors and eliminates the unnecessary traffic of invalidating all the waiting clusters. Furthermore, RAC merging implies that even when multiple processors within the grant cluster requeue for the lock, only a single remote request is sent to the home. Finally, granting locks do not require exclusive ownership to acquire a lock (i.e., a complete test&set), thus no extra invalidations are generated when the processor acquires a lock.

Locks in the prototype reside in an alternate memory space, separate from normal variables. Separating locks is required because the MIPS I architecture does not support any atomic read-modify-write operations. Within the address range of locks, only one lock is provided per memory block, and any read of the block is an attempt to acquire the lock. The processor caches are not capable of atomic updates, so the atomic action is done at the memory site. Lock storage is actually done in the corresponding directory entries, which takes advantage of the normal read-modify-write accesses used by the directory and the fact that only one lock is supported per cache line. When a locked lock is read, a shared copy is brought into the processor's cache and the processor receives the locked value. Spin waiting on the lock then occurs locally in the processor's cache. If free, the lock is atomically updated in memory, and the unlocked value is returned to the processor. A special unlock reply inhibits the processor from caching the unlocked value.

Lock release is done through an alternate memory address space which bypasses the processor caches. The flow of remote unlocks is shown in Figure 6-15. Unlocks in the home

(a) Remote granting/invalidating unlock to remote unlocked/
   locked lock.

- CPU issues unlock on bus; allocate RAC entry;
  send granting unlock request to home (1).
- Granting/inv unlock in home unlocks lock;
  send unlock ack to local cluster (2).
- Deallocate RAC entry when ack received.

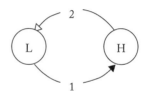

(b) Remote granting unlock to remote queued lock.

- CPU issues unlock on bus; allocate RAC entry;
  send granting unlock request to home (1).
- Granting unlock causes a lock grant (2) to be sent to one of
  queued clusters chosen at random;
  grant cluster is removed from the directory queue.
- PCPU on grant cluster issues the lock grant;
  cached value of lock invalidated and granted lock placed in
  RAC.
- First processor to read the lock receives unlocked value, but
  caching inhibited; an unlock ack reply (3) is sent to local.
  Subsequent requests for the lock by other processors will
  requeue the grant cluster in the directory.
- Deallocate RAC entry when ack received.

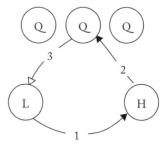

(c) Remote invalidating unlock to remote queued lock.

- CPU issues unlock on bus; allocate RAC entry;
  send invalidating unlock request to home (1).
- Invalidating unlock in home causes invalidation requests (2a) to
  be sent to all queued clusters and invalidation ack reply (2b) to
  be sent to local cluster; lock is changed to unlocked state.
- PCPUs issue invalidations on queued clusters; these clusters
  reply with invalidation ack replies (3).
- Deallocate RAC entry after all acks received.

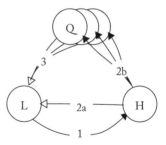

FIGURE 6-15 *Remote Unlock Request Flows.*

---

are similar, but avoid the extra request and reply between the local and home cluster. As
shown in the figure, there are two basic types of unlocks, which differ only when there are
waiting processors. The first type of unlock, the *granting unlock*, treats the directory entry as
a list of clusters wanting to acquire the lock. The grant cluster is chosen at random based on
the priority set by a free-running hardware counter. Granting unlocks are usually preferred
because they minimize latency and traffic. The second unlock type is the more typical *invalidating unlock*. This type of unlock is more efficient if processors do not spin-wait on the lock
or processes migrate while spinning. In these cases, the granting lock will be less efficient
because it invalidates each cluster serially until the lock is reacquired. The serial invalidation
uses a time-out of the grant that rejects it after approximately 8 μsec. After the time-out,
the RCPU repeats the granting unlock on behalf of the releasing processor, and this returns
control of the lock to the home and causes a grant to a new cluster. Each grant eliminates a
single cluster from the directory queue, so a series of time-outs will eventually leave the lock

unlocked in memory and acknowledge the unlock operation. While correct, serial invalidations with time-outs are much less efficient than a simple invalidating unlock.

6.4.2 Fetch&Op Variables

While spin locking is a very general mechanism, it does not remove the latency of the memory system from serializing access to critical regions. This serialization can only be significantly reduced if the mutual exclusion region is reduced to the time of a local operation. If the mutual exclusion region is contended by processors throughout the system, then restricting it to a local operation requires that the *mutex* region be specified in a single remote operation. While it is difficult to specify general mutual exclusion in a single operation, one useful set of operations are Fetch&Op primitives. These primitives have been shown to be quite effective in several common parallel algorithms [FRB93]. For example, Fetch&Op primitives can be used to build efficient distributed work queues and barrier arrival counters.

The DASH prototype restricts its Fetch&Op primitives to simple Fetch&Increment and Fetch&Decrement operations. Only these operations are supported because it is difficult to provide the data operand for a more general Fetch&Op given a normal processor instruction set. The prototype maintains Fetch&Op variables in the same directory storage area used for spin locks. One 16-bit Fetch&Op variable is available per cache block. Access to these variables is uncached, and values are always returned from the home. The particular Fetch&Op is specified by the word offset within the cache block. The flow for Fetch&Op operations is very simple because there are only two cases. For access to local Fetch&Op variables, the directory supplies the data to the processor directly over the MPBUS. Access to remote variables follows the normal flow of a local bus cycle, remote request, home bus cycle, reply, and local bus repeat. The only exception for Fetch&Op variables is that the RAC cache index (i.e., address) is based in part on the processor ID. Using the processor's ID removes the interference that would otherwise occur between two Fetch&Op accesses by different processors in the same cluster to the same variable. Since Fetch&Op requests cannot be merged, allocating unique RAC entries insures that serialization for Fetch&Op accesses is minimized.

6.4.3 Fence Operations

As discussed in Chapter 3, fence operations are useful in controlling the ordering of processor accesses. In DASH, ordering is assured by delaying operations until previous operations have completed. Unlock operations optionally include a write-fence that will delay the unlock until all previous writes have completed systemwide. These write-fences together with blocking processor loads insure that release consistency is supported by the base hardware.

If a stricter consistency model is required, explicit fence operations can be used. There are three types of fences. The first is an explicit *write-fence*. A write-fence simply delays later write operations until all RAC entries allocated for this processor (usually pending writes or invalidation acknowledgments) have completed. If the processor itself must be stalled, then a *stall-fence* can follow the write-fence to create a *full-fence*. This operation stalls the processor until all RAC entries for this processor have been eliminated.

6.5 Protocol General Exceptions

In addition to the various request flows illustrated in the previous sections, there are six exceptions that can occur while satisfying any request. The first two are related to allocating a RAC buffer when a remote request is first issued. The third and fourth occur because of serialization constraints and the potential interleaving of requests. The fifth exception is the deadlock-breaking mode discussed in Section 6.1.3, and the final set of exceptions occur when a hardware error is detected. These exceptions can occur for any of the operations discussed in the previous sections. Most exceptions cause delays in initiating a request or force a request retry.

The first two exceptions occur when a remote request tries to allocate a RAC entry. Since the RAC is a cache, a bus request can conflict with an earlier request that is still pending. If the entry is in use for an access to a different cache block, then the new request *conflicts* with the old request and must be delayed. After the RAC entry is deallocated for its current use, the new request is allowed to retry. The second exception occurs if the RAC entry is in use for a compatible reference to the same block by another processor.[3] In this case, the new request is *merged* with the old request. Like a conflict, a merged request does not generate any outgoing requests. Unlike a conflict, however, a merged request is satisfied along with the original request when the reply to the original is received.

Two additional exceptions arise from the potential for operations and their associated intercluster messages to be interleaved. In general, a request for a block that is held dirty in a remote cluster can only be satisfied by that cluster. However, if a request is forwarded to a remote dirty cluster, that cluster may not hold the block dirty when the message arrives. It may have written it back to memory, or some other request might have changed the cache state of the block. In these cases the request will not find the dirty block, and a negative acknowledge (NAK) reply is sent to the requesting cluster. Likewise, even if a cluster does own a cache line, it may be unable to satisfy the request because of pending operations on the block. In particular, if invalidation acknowledgments are pending (i.e., busy RAC state), then the block cannot be released and a NAK is returned. This case is illustrated in Figure 6-16.

Another exception case, as mentioned in Section 6.1.3, results from the need to reject incoming request messages due to deadlock avoidance. If the PCPU queue is blocking its incoming request network port, and the cluster's outgoing request port is also full, then the requests at the head of the PCPU input FIFO will be rejected with NAK replies. As with all NAK replies, this will force the issuing processor to retry its access.

The final set of exceptions arise when there is an error detected in the system. The system includes a variety of error checking mechanisms such as parity on the directory, an error correcting code on main memory, network message length and command type checking, illegal bus operation checking, and operation time-outs. Errors that arise in operations for which the requesting processor is known (e.g., uncorrectable memory errors) are returned

---

[3] A compatible reference would be a read or read-prefetch while a read or read-exclusive was outstanding, or a read-exclusive or exclusive-prefetch while a read-exclusive was outstanding.

- CPU issues read and is forced to retry. Allocate RAC entry and send read request (1) to home.
- Home forwards request to dirty cluster (2).
- Dirty cache write-back data to home (3) before read request is received.
- Dirty cluster receives read request, issues on bus and then responds with a NAK (4) to requesting cluster since no dirty copy is found.
- CPU will retry request and will receive clean data from home if its request reaches the home after the write-back. Otherwise, it will get forwarded and be NAK'd again.

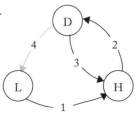

A NAK would also be sent from the dirty cluster if it had not done a write-back, but had invalidates pending for a previous write to the location.

F I G U R E 6 - 1 6   *Request NAK Because of Write-Back or Invalidations Pending.*

directly to the processor as bus errors. Errors for which the requesting processor is not known (such as a corrupted network message) are dropped after setting an error register or error state in a RAC location. These type of errors generally result in a time-out error. The reply controller maintains a time-out counter on the number of RAC entries in use by each processor. If a processor has an allocation greater than zero, and the count does not change for more than a time-out period (25–50 milliseconds on the prototype), the processor's arbitration mask is released and the processor is given a bus error on its next bus access. Bus errors are fatal to the process that is currently running on the processor, but the hardware provides diagnostic paths that can be used to recover from the error if the fault does not happen when running the OS kernel.

6.6 Chapter Conclusions

The DASH prototype is a compromise between an ideal DASH implementation and the desire to minimize development time. While embodying the major scalability features of a larger system, the prototype is restricted to 64 processors. Using the 33 MHz MIPS R3000, this configuration still provides for up to 1.6 GIPS and 600 DP MFLOPS of performance. This is a high level of absolute performance, and one that is clearly not possible without a scalable memory system. The size is also large enough to provide a base for the development of and experimentation with software for large-scale shared-memory machines.

The prototype consists of a set of commercially available small-scale multiprocessors, which are supplemented by a pair of directory and network boards. The system is interconnected by a pair of wormhole-routed mesh networks that provide low latency and scalable bandwidth. The key state machines that execute the directory-based coherence protocol are the directory and reply controllers. The directory controller interprets local bus cycles and the directory state to determine the set of intercluster messages and directory updates that are necessary. The reply controller uses the remote access cache to coordinate the outstanding requests made by local processors.

The prototype coherence protocol is based on invalidations and write-back caching. The basic read and write operations are optimized to reduce latency though local cache-to-cache sharing and request forwarding. Alternative memory operations are supported to help hide latency. Prefetch operations can be used to request or transmit cache lines without stalling the processor. Uncached-read and update-write operations are useful for interprocessor communications and can be integrated into support for I/O DMA accesses. Another area for protocol optimization is synchronization references. DASH supports granting locks, which reduce the latency and traffic associated with spin locks. Additionally, support of simple Fetch&Op variables is used to reduce the serialization of synchronization primitives.

Overall, the prototype attempts to optimize a rich set of memory operations that execute in a complex, distributed environment. Each operation can encounter a variety of different cache states, and exceptions can occur when these states dynamically change. Although further optimizations and operations are possible, the protocol is already complex and additional features would add still more complexity. Furthermore, the prototype already includes some features (e.g., producer prefetch) that may be of marginal performance benefit, but that have been included because the prototype is an experimental machine. Thus, we expect future large-scale shared-memory systems, which must already deal with additional scalability issues (e.g., limited pointer directories), to include less rather than more operations and protocol features than the DASH prototype.

C H A P T E R

7

Prototype Hardware Structures

T his chapter summarizes the hardware structures of the DASH prototype. These details serve two purposes. First, the hardware overhead of supporting directory-based cache coherence can be derived from the logic complexity of the base cluster hardware and the added directory logic. Second, the detailed implementation issues of the directory logic and network interface can be examined. The material in this chapter is aimed at those designing or analyzing directory-based coherence hardware. Except for the concluding section, it can be skipped by those not interested in hardware details without creating any discontinuities with the rest of the text.

This chapter begins with a summary of the bus timing and hardware of the base cluster. A description of the major sections of the directory logic is then given, including the timing and structure of the major hardware components. The chapter concludes with an analysis of the proportion of logic dedicated to each section of the prototype.

The DASH prototype consists of a set of Silicon Graphics 4D/340 systems interconnected by a pair of mesh networks. Figure 7-1 shows the internals of a 64-processor DASH system with its intercabinet ribbon cables. Note that two clusters are housed in each cabinet, making this a 4 × 4 configuration. The inset in Figure 7-1 shows the outside of a 48-processor system in a 3 × 4 configuration. Each cluster uses eight ribbon cables to connect with its four neighbors. The logic within a cluster is implemented on six printed circuit boards (each board is a standard 9U400 size, 14.437" × 15.499"). The processor caches and their support logic are implemented in surface-mount technology. All other logic is implemented in through-hole DIP and PGA packages. The hardware consists of three major logic types: CMOS VLSI and ASICs, CMOS static and dynamic memories, and CMOS and bipolar MSI (PAL) logic and buffer parts. The vast majority of the approximately 1,700 ICs that make up a cluster are memory or MSI parts.

F I G U R E 7 - 1 *The Internals of a 64-Processor DASH Prototype System. The inset is the outside of a 48-processor system.*

7.1 Base Cluster Hardware

The base SGI hardware implements a complete bus-based multiprocessor. The logic used to support four-way multiprocessing is implemented on four printed circuit boards (PCBs): two processor boards with two CPUs each, a memory board, and an I/O interface board. These boards interface with one another over two buses. The primary MPBUS supports snoopy cache coherence and connects the processors to memory and I/O devices. The second bus (SYNCBUS) is used to distribute I/O and inter-CPU interrupts and supports 64K test&set spin locks. In DASH, only the MPBUS memory functions and I/O transfers to the directory board itself are supported between clusters. The only SYNCBUS function supported between clusters is the mapping of certain MPBUS I/O cycles to SYNCBUS interrupt cycles, which allows CPU-to-CPU interrupts between any pair of CPUs in the system.

7.1.1 SGI Multiprocessor Bus (MPBUS)

As stated previously, the SGI MPBUS consists of a 32-bit address bus and a separate 64-bit data bus running at 16 MHz. The bus supports three types of bus cycles. *Cache cycles* transfer 16-byte memory blocks between a CPU cache and memory; these cycles optionally include an embedded 16-byte write-back transfer. *DMA cycles* read and write from 1 to 16 bytes of contiguous data within a memory block. *I/O cycles* transfer up to 8 bytes of data between a CPU and an I/O device or the directory.

The timing of bus cycles is shown in Figure 7-2. Bus cycles are pipelined into three stages: arbitration, address, and data transfer. A minimum bus transaction has a latency of seven bus cycles, but occupies the bus for only four cycles. These cycles are nominally labeled with respect to the data transfer cycles as CC1–CC4. Arbitration and address cycles occur before the data phase and are labeled PC1–PC4 since they correspond, potentially, to the data transfer phase of a previous bus cycle. Cycles after the data transfer are similarly labeled NC1–NC4. Arbitration between bus masters is based on a fair, round-robin priority and takes a single cycle (PC2). The address transfer phase takes three cycles. The first two cycles (PC3–PC4) hold the primary address, and the last cycle (CC1) holds the address of the optional embedded write-back transfer. The address phase always ends in a tristate cycle to minimize the delay for a new address to stabilize on the bus. The data transfer stage is delayed two cycles from the address transfer and starts with the bus master issuing write or write-back data on the bus during CC1 and CC2. The last two cycles (CC3 and CC4) contain read data from memory, a processor cache, or an I/O device. One other significant bus timing issue is that all bus snooping results must be presented by bus slaves during CC2 and CC3.

One unique aspect of the MPBUS is that all memory transactions have the fixed, seven-cycle timing shown in Figure 7-2. I/O transfers can be extended through *wait* cycles, but these are not used in the I/O transactions handled by the directory logic. While the fixed bus timing simplifies bus interfacing, it implies that any entity that may not be able to respond to a specific bus cycle must delay all bus activity. Thus, even though the memory board gets write-back data during CC1–CC2, the bus must be idled for four bus clocks after each write-back. This time allows the actual write-back (which takes place after the primary read access) to complete before any new access that might read the same memory bank. The bus hold-off is accomplished through signals to the central arbiter that delay all arbitrations. To keep bus bandwidth high, it was important that the directory logic supply sufficient bandwidth so hold-offs due to the DASH logic were rare.

7.1.2 SGI CPU Board

Each SGI CPU board contains two complete processors, including their two-level caches and bus interfaces. In addition, each processor includes a variety of miscellaneous logic including EPROMs, UARTs, and interrupt and general control/status registers. The processors and the first-level caches run synchronously at 33.33 MHz. The second-level caches and bus interface logic run synchronous to the central 16 MHz bus clock. The read and write buffers between the first- and second-level caches (shown in Figure 6-2) serve as an asynchronous boundary between the two clock regimes. Activity on the processor board is initiated by memory cycles from the R3000 processor and write cycles issued by the write buffer. In addition, the second-level cache is responsible for snooping on bus cycles from other masters on the MPBUS. A complete description of the timing of CPU internal activities is beyond the scope of this work, but the timing of major bus activity is given in Figure 7-2.

The approximate gate count and IC equivalent of each section of a single CPU is given in Table 7-1. A processor board includes two such CPUs, and a cluster has two processor

PC2	PC3	PC4	CC1	CC2	CC3	CC4	NC1

Request bus / arbitrate

Arbiter drives bus grant to selected master

Drive request type and address

Cache Read, Read-Ex Transaction

If needed, drive write-back request and WB address

If needed, drive 16 bytes of WB data

Fill data into 2nd-level cache

Slave caches snoop and update state

Drive snoop results to bus

Read main memory, ECC correct

DRAM Ras Precharge

Memory or CPU cache drives 16 bytes of read data to bus

DMA Read, Write Transaction

Continue drive of DMA address

Drive up to 16 bytes of DMA write data

Slave caches snoop DMA

Update second-level cache on DMA write hit

Drive snoop results to bus

Read main memory, ECC correct

DRAM Ras Precharge

Memory or CPU cache drives 16 bytes of DMA read data to bus

I/O Read, Write Transaction

Continue drive of I/O address, repeat CC1 cycle until ack.

Drive up to 8 bytes of I/O write data

Selected I/O slave acknowledges transfer

Selected I/O slave drives up to 8 bytes of I/O read data to bus

F I G U R E 7 - 2 *Basic Timing of the MPBUS.*

TABLE 7-1

Logic Used for a Single Processor With Cache and Bus Interface

SECTION	GATES	IC EQUIVALENT	LOGIC TYPE
CPU, cache and 2nd-level interface	55,000	15.1	MIPS R3000, R3010
	240 KB	45.0	1st-level inst. and data caches—SRAM
	11,000	12.2	Read/write buffers—CMOS gate arrays
	5,594	67.9	PAL, MSI overhead logic
2nd-level cache and bus interface	1,857	18.0	PAL control logic
	4,590	55.4	Bus and other buffering logic
	280 KB	19.8	2nd-level data cache—SRAM
SYNCBUS and misc.	9,703	6.8	UARTs, timer VLSI
	4,000	4.5	SYNCBUS controller—CMOS gate array
	128 KB	5.2	Boot EPROM
	752	25.5	Miscellaneous control logic
Total	92,496	275.4	2-input gate equivalents
	520 KB		SRAM
	128 KB		EPROM

boards. The gate counts given in Table 7-1 are based on two-input gates in a gate array style of design. This number was derived from the schematics and design files for each board. For each logic type the following methods were used to estimate the gate count:

- Custom VLSI: Estimates based on part complexity and specifications. The MIPS R3000 and R3010 are the major parts in this category.
- CMOS gate arrays: Estimates directly from design documentation or estimated from the size of the master slice and design complexity.
- Xilinx FPGAs: Minimized Xilinx logic translated into gate array equivalents.
- PALs: This is the dominant logic type on the DASH boards and also heavily used in base cluster logic. The gate counts were derived directly from minimized programming files.
- PROMs: Software EPROMs were not counted as gates. The primary state machines in the directory and reply controllers, however, were converted to PLA equivalent and minimized by Espresso.
- FAST TTL: Converted using gate count for equivalent gate array macros.

The counts are a slight overestimate for the PALs and PROMs because no multilevel minimization was assumed. Furthermore, the counts assume no product sharing within the two-input gate trees used to make up separate outputs. The counts of memory are in bytes and include the overhead of cache tags, parity, and error correcting codes.

TABLE 7-2

Logic Used for a 56 MByte Main Memory Board

SECTION	GATES	IC EQUIVALENT	LOGIC TYPE
Memory array	63 MB	140.0	Memory array w/ ECC, DRAM SIMMs
and interface	1,194	11.6	PAL, MSI DRAM timing control logic
	3,510	101.2	Address and data buffering logic
ECC	10,000	18.0	2 CMOS gate arrays
	597	15.2	ECC datapath logic
Bus interface	897	10.7	PAL, MSI control logic
	1,668	33.5	Bus and other buffering logic
Total	17,866	330.2	2-input gate equivalents
	63 MB		DRAM

"IC equivalents" is a measure of board area based on a 16-pin DIP component (0.36 sq. in.). With two exceptions, all components in the system use normal through-hole DIP or PGA packages. One exception is that some memories use higher density packaging (SIMMs, ZIP, and VDIP modules). Their IC equivalent is taken as the actual footprint of the module mounted on the board. The other exception is the approximately 1/4 of the processor logic that uses surface-mount technology. The IC equivalent of this logic is based on the corresponding area assuming DIP packages. This adjustment was made so that all area comparisons are fair because it is possible to surface mount all sections of the logic.

7.1.3 SGI Memory Board

The SGI main memory board is a relatively simple board that includes up to 64 MByte of ECC (SEC/DED) protected data. In DASH, the maximum memory supported on the memory board is 56 MByte since the top 8 MByte is reserved for locks stored in the directory. The memory array is made up of 512K × 36 SIMMs based on 256K × 4, 100 ns DRAMs. The memory board responds to all three types of bus cycles (cache, DMA, and I/O). I/O cycles bypass the processor caches and are used for diagnostic and boot-up purposes. To the memory board they are virtually identical to DMA cycles. All bus transactions begin with a 4-clock memory read followed by zero, one, or two 4-clock memory write cycles. A read takes place even for DMA or I/O write cycles to merge the write data into one or both of the 72-bit ECC data words. Cache cycles can generate a single write cycle to retire write-back data or dirty data shared between two processor caches. In this latter case, there may be two write cycles generated by a single bus transaction because the access may include a replacement write-back and a dirty-sharing write-back. As mentioned previously, the fixed bus timing implies that each write cycle holds off bus arbitration for four bus clocks. In addition, refresh of the main memory DRAMs holds off bus arbitration for six bus clocks every 15.6 μsec. A summary of the logic used in a 56 MByte memory board is shown in Table 7-2.

7.1.4 SGI I/O Board

The I/O interface board supports several I/O interfaces and overall control of the MPBUS and SYNCBUS. The board's functions include the following:

1. MPBUS and SYNCBUS control, arbitration, and clock distribution

2. SCSI disk and tape interface

3. Ethernet interface

4. DMA control and virtual DMA memory mapping

5. Interface for programmed I/O and DMA access between the MPBUS and VME

For DASH, only the first item is required in every cluster. Furthermore, support for scalable I/O bandwidth requires that at least some clusters contain SCSI disk interfaces and DMA control. The VME function of the I/O board could be used to attach additional disk devices, but it is not required. The DMA interface of the I/O board includes a mapping RAM that permits DMA transfers to cross virtual page boundaries.

The timing of the I/O board is complex given the variety of interfaces that it supports. Typically, the board responds passively to MPBUS I/O cycles that map to its I/O ports or the VME bus. In addition, it responds to DMA requests from the local SCSI controller or VME bus by issuing DMA MPBUS cycles, and it responds to interrupt messages from local and VME devices with interrupt cycles on the SYNCBUS. A summary of the logic of the I/O board is given in Table 7-3.

7.2 Directory Controller

The directory controller (DC) is responsible for three major functions:

1. Maintaining the directory for the local cluster memory

2. Initiating outbound network request and reply messages

3. Responding to bus transactions with MPBUS cache status and retry signals

A block diagram of the DC is shown in Figure 7-3. The DC acts as a bus slave responding to bus transactions given the transaction type, home cluster, directory state, and the result of processor cache and RAC snooping. Its response includes asserting bus control signals (e.g., bus retry), updating the directory, and generating network messages. The timing of major DC activities is shown in Figure 7-4. The directory controller logic is divided into three major sections: the control pipeline, the directory DRAM array and update datapath, and the outbound network request and reply datapaths.

The DC control pipeline centers on two sets of PROMs that control the coherence protocol. Embedding the protocol in PROMs was not strictly required from a gate complexity standpoint, but it provided a flexible structure that minimized the impact of protocol changes on the hardware. The DC control pipeline contains four stages. In PC4, a decode of the MPBUS address and control signals is combined with additional signals from the PCPU and RCPU to form an MPBUS control PROM index. In CC1, the MP Control ROM and Directory Update PAL use this index to determine the DC's bus response and the update of

TABLE 7-3

Logic Used in SGI I/O Interface Board

SECTION	GATES	IC EQUIVALENT	LOGIC TYPE
MPBUS and SYNC arbiters and control	3,354	29.4	PAL and MSI logic
SCSI interface	3,500	3.8	SCSI interface VLSI chip
	962	9.9	PAL and MSI control logic
Ethernet interface	7,300	7.2	Ethernet interface VLSI chip
	1.128 MB	8.8	1 MByte DRAM transfer buffer w/ parity
	2,584	38.5	PAL and MSI control logic
DMA master and mapping logic	8,000	9.0	CMOS gate array
	1,549	28.5	PAL and MSI control logic
VME Interface	3,303	31.1	PAL and MSI control logic
	3,092	29.6	Bus buffering
MPBUS interface	1,852	12.0	PAL and MSI control logic
	2,918	23.8	Bus buffering
SYNCBUS interface	643	9.2	PAL and MSI control logic
	490	13.0	Bus buffering
Miscellaneous	256 KB	10.4	Additional 64K x 8 monitor EPROMs
	4,671	88.5	PAL and MSI status/control/error logic
Total	44,218	352.7	2-input gate equivalents
	1.128 MB		DRAM
	256 KB		EPROM

the directory. During CC2, the CC1 index is combined with the directory state to determine the network control PROM index. At the end of CC2, the actual network control signals are generated as a combination of the PROM outputs and the results of cache snooping. During CC3, the network PROMs are reindexed to determine the network messages to send out relative to any embedded cache write-back transfer.

The directory DRAM consists of 4 M directory entries and supports up to 56 MByte of globally shared memory and 512 K lock or Fetch&Op variables per cluster. Each entry consists of a state bit, a zero vector bit, 16 directory vector bits (DIRV), and two parity bits. The state bit indicates whether a normal memory entry is dirty-remote, or whether a lock entry has queued clusters. The zero vector bit is the logic OR of the directory vector and is maintained to speed the decode of the directory state. The directory vector includes one bit for each of the 16 clusters. The directory vector parity bits support even parity error checking over the two bytes of the directory vector.

The directory DRAM array is accessed by a read-modify-write cycle on every bus transaction. This access method was used because the directory state must always be read first to determine if the block is dirty. If not, then the directory state is usually updated. The direc-

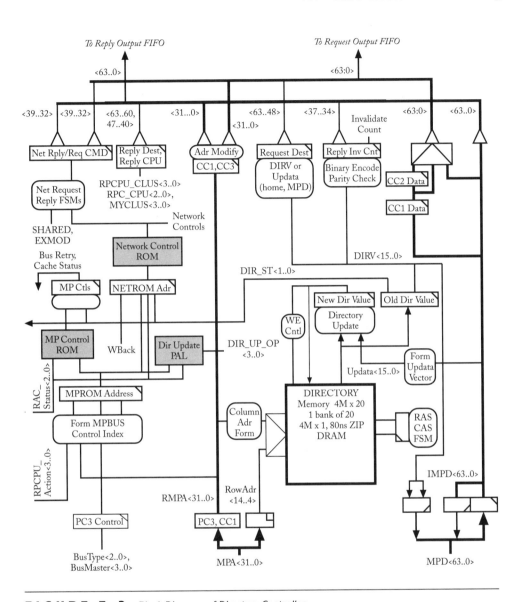

FIGURE 7-3   *Block Diagram of Directory Controller.*

tory vector must also be read before written in some cases. Using read-modify-write cycles unified the DRAM timing for the state and vector and allowed the directory memory to support locks and Fetch&Op variables. Performing the read-modify-write cycles (including DRAM precharge) during the 240 ns allowed for main memory access and error correction was challenging. To speed the directory update, individual write enables are used on the state and parity bits and each nibble of the directory vector. At the end of CC1, each section predicts their updated state based on the update operation and the current directory state. At the beginning of CC2, sections are selectively written based on the value of all sections (nibble carry, zero detect, parity change, etc.). The directory datapath supports 11 update opera-

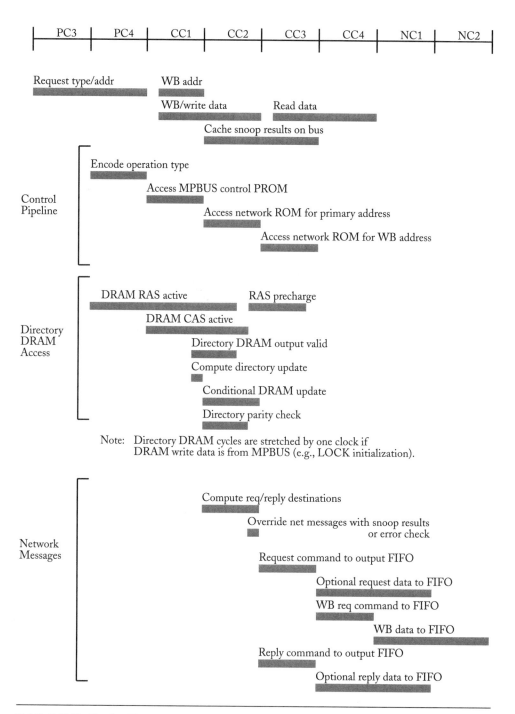

FIGURE 7-4 *Timing Diagram of Major Directory Controller Activity. Write-back requests are delayed 1 or 2 clocks if primary request includes network request data (e.g., sharing write-back).*

TABLE 7-4

Directory Update Operations

OPERATION	DESCRIPTION
SREM	Reset dirty bit and OR in the new requesting cluster to DIRV.
DREM	Set dirty bit and DIRV to new requesting cluster.
UNC	Reset dirty bit and DIRV.
SHST	Reset dirty bit, no change in DIRV.
LOAD	Load the dirty bit and DIRV from MPBUS write data.
PSEM†	If lock value > 0, decrement DIRV; otherwise set queue bit and OR in new queued cluster.
DCRZ†	If lock value > 0, decrement DIRV; otherwise NOP.
GRNT†	If queue bit set, reset single DIRV corresponding to highest priority queued cluster; otherwise set DIRV = 1.
SET†	Reset queue bit and set DIRV = 1.
DCR*	Decrement DIRV.
INC*	Increment DIRV.

† Used only for Fetch&Op variables.
* Used only for locks.

tion, as shown in Table 7-4. All operations can be made conditional on the directory state bit.

The network interface datapath is responsible for buffering the MPBUS address and data buses into the outbound network FIFOs. All outbound messages consist of one 64-bit command word and 0, 32, or 128 bits of data (zero, one with half valid, or two 64-bit data words). The type and format of outgoing messages are shown in Figure 7-5. As shown in the DC timing diagram, a single bus cycle can generate a single reply transfer and one or two request messages. The second request message, if present, is associated with an embedded cache write-back request. Reply messages are always unicast, but request messages support a 16-bit multicast destination vector. One complication of the network interface is the difference in the timing of primary bus address and data (PC3 and CC3–CC4, respectively), versus the potential write-back address and data (CC1 and CC1–CC2, respectively). A two stage buffer holds the write-back data and allows the primary request to bypass the write-back request and be sent to the network before the less critical write-back.

The DC also includes miscellaneous logic to support a control and status register, which is used during system boot, and an error capture register. Finally, the DC contains the SYN-CBUS interrupt generation logic that posts CPU interrupts to the SYNCBUS based on an I/O write cycle on the MPBUS. The gate costs of the DC are summarized in Table 7-5; a directory board is shown in Figure 7-6.

The structure and timing of the DC were driven by a number of factors. First, the definition of the MPBUS and our desire to minimize the modifications to the SGI boards

Request Command Word:

63	47	43	39	33	31	0
Destination Bit Vector	REQ Clus	REQ Proc	Request Command	Len	Address	

Requests Types	Encoding	Length		Requests Types	Encoding	Length
Read	000000	00		DMA Read	001010	00
Read-Exclusive	000001	00		Corrupted Mem.	001011	00
IO Read	000010	00		Producer Prefetch	001100	10
IO Write	010xxx	1x		Deliver	001101	01
Lock Grant V	000100	00		DMA Write	10xxxx	01, 1x
Lock Grant Set	000101	00		DMA Update	11xxxx	01, 1x
Invalidate	000110	00				
Write-back	000111	01		xxxx in IO Write and DMA Write/Update is		
Sharing Write-back	001000	01		the byte offset of the last valid byte within		
Dirty Transfer	001001	00		block being written.		

Reply Command Word:

63	47	43	39	33	31	0
Dest Clus		Src Clus	REQ Proc	Reply Command	Len	Address

Reply Types	Encoding	Length		Length Field Interpretation
Acknowledge	001110	Any		00 => No data
Negative Ack	001100	00		01 => Full 128 bits in two 64-bit data words
Ack w/ Inv Count	01vvvv	00,01		follow command word
Supplemental Ack	001111	00		10 => 32 bits of valid data in one 64-bit data word
Error Ack	001101	00		follow command word. Data on bits 63–32.
Locked Ack	000000	10		11 => 32 bits of valid data in one 64-bit data word
Unlocked Ack	000001	10		follow command word. Data on bits 31–0.

vvvv in Ack with Invalidate Count is the
number of invalidates acknowledgments
to expect minus 1.

FIGURE 7-5 *Format of Network Messages Generated by the Directory Controller.*

restricted the design. Likewise, minimizing complexity and gate costs drove many decisions. Achieving maximum performance, however, usually required added complexity or changes to the SGI hardware. These conflicting goals led to several design trade-offs as outlined below.

The first important trade-off is the delay (until CC3) for the DC to generate network messages. In some cases, the DC could send a request message as soon as the home cluster was decoded (CC1 or possibly PC4). While this could reduce the latency to generate some messages, it was not done because it would only apply to a few cases. In particular, reply messages containing data from memory or another cache, or that rely on the directory state or snooping, must be delayed until this information is available (i.e., beginning of CC3, see Figure 7-4). The only important bus transaction that could be accelerated is the initial bus request for a remote location. This case was not optimized because it would have compli-

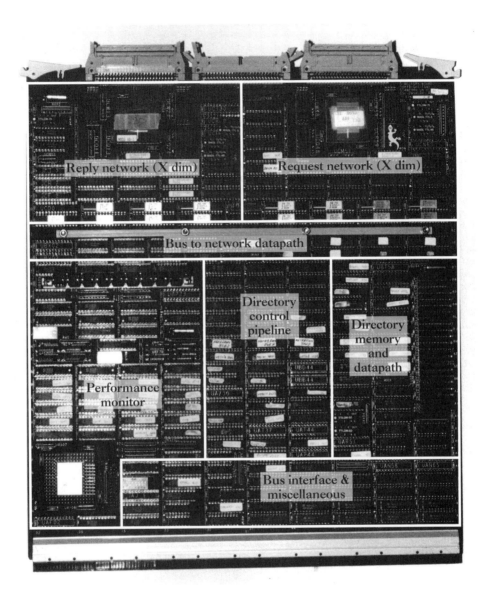

FIGURE 7-6 *DASH Directory Controller Board*

TABLE 7-5

Logic Used in Directory Controller.

SECTION	GATES	IC EQUIVALENTS	LOGIC TYPE
DC control pipeline	2,757	10.5	7 high-speed 8K x 8 EPROMs (30 ns)
	4,859	29.1	PAL and MSI decode and control logic
Directory array and update datapath	10 MB	12.0	20 4M x 1 DRAM (80 ns)
	4,453	38.3	PAL and MSI update/control logic
Network request/reply datapaths	3,087	18.6	PAL and MSI control logic
	3,975	40.3	Datapath registers and buffers
MPBUS interface	2,862	28.7	Bus interface registers
Miscellaneous	1,606	36.3	PAL and MSI control, status and error registers
Total	23,599	213.8	2-input gate equivalents
	10 MB		DRAM

cated the hardware structure. Furthermore, it would have made it impossible to cancel unnecessary network messages when remote requests were satisfied by local cache-to-cache transfers.

Another trade-off in the DC is the use of two full 64-bit-wide outbound FIFOs to the network. This wide structure was dictated primarily by the "no wait" bus protocol of the MPBUS. The 64-bit paths were required so the common network messages could be sent in four or less bus clocks. Otherwise, additional buffers would be required, or the bus would have to be held off because the MPBUS protocol does not support a wait signal to extend a bus cycle. Likewise, the need to keep up with the bus dictated that the multicasting of invalidation and update requests be carried out on the network side of the output FIFOs.

Using the directory DRAM for Fetch&Op and lock variables was prompted by two factors. The first factor was the desire to minimize changes to the SGI logic boards. Second, the directory already required support for read-modify-write operations and a diagnostic path to access the directory DRAM. Thus, supporting these additional operations added little complexity to the directory datapath. The disadvantage of this scheme is that software could not use an arbitrary memory location for a lock. Thus, a lock is separate from its associated data, and acquiring a lock cannot bring the associated data into the cache in a single transaction. While efficiently handling both lock and data acquisition in one cycle presents other complications (e.g., updates to the locked data while a requestor is spinning in its cache), having a special lock address range precludes any optimizations.

7.3 Reply Controller

The reply controller (RC) supports several functions. The most important of these functions is the coordination of remote requests made by the processors in the local cluster using the remote access cache (RAC). The RC also controls the processor's arbitration masks and releases processors when their pending requests have been satisfied. The RC maintains per-processor RAC allocation counters, which, together with acknowledge counts in individual RAC entries, are used to enforce release consistency. The cache structure of the RAC is also used to supplement the function of the processor caches. It does this by taking dirty-sharing ownership of remote cache lines when necessary, and by holding prefetch data. In addition, the RC performs other functions using the RCPU, including translating uncached reads, update writes, and prefetch operations; timing out granted locks; and retrying nonwaited operations. The design of the RC was the work of James Laudon.

The structure of the RC is shown in Figure 7-7. The logic is centered around the RAC and the datapaths that maintain the RAC's state and data arrays. The RC includes two control pipelines. One is similar to the DC's control pipeline; it decodes the current bus cycle and directory and RAC states to determine the new RAC state and processor arbitration masks. The second control pipeline services the reply network; this logic combines reply messages and the selected RAC state to determine the update of the RAC and processor arbitration masks. The other major structures of the RC are the RCPU, the per-processor RAC allocation counters, and the granted lock time-out counters.

The decision to structure the RAC as a cache was driven by several factors. The most important was the need to distinguish between dirty cache blocks that have pending invalidations and those that do not. If a cache line has pending invalidations, the hardware enforces release consistency by retaining ownership of the block within the writing cluster. The RAC structure supports this by snooping all bus transactions and providing the status of pending invalidations on a cache line basis. Local requests to such blocks can be satisfied, but the new sharing processor becomes responsible for the outstanding invalidations. Remote requests for such busy blocks are forced to retry. Furthermore, the RAC's data array provides storage for cache lines that have pending invalidations but are invalidated from the processor's cache by a read-exclusive request issued by the local PCPU. Once the cache structure was chosen for the RAC, it proved very useful in unifying the storage needed for the other RAC functions mentioned previously.

RAC entries are accessed by one of two types of indices. The first type corresponds to the processor caches and consists of the MP address bits 16 through 4. It is important that the address mapping for cachable items match between the RAC and processor caches, which insures that the RC needs to do only one RAC access for both the primary and any embedded write-back operation. The second indexing mechanism uses an exclusive OR on address bits 16 and 15 and the issuing processor's ID. This address mechanism insures that Fetch&Op accesses to the same variable by different processors do not conflict in the RAC and increase serialization. Oppositely, the first address method guarantees that normal cache accesses can be merged. The second index also inverts bit 14 of the RAC address so that a granting unlock operation (second index type) never conflicts with the granted lock itself (first index type), if the lock happens to be granted to the unlocking cluster.

The format of RAC tag/state entries is shown in Figure 7-8. A tag/state entry contains seven major fields. The first is the cache address tag. The next is the RAC state field, which holds the current state of the line. There are 37 unique states, which indicate both the state

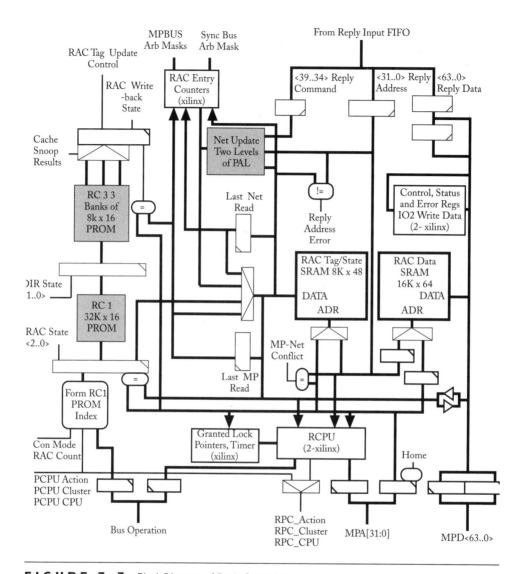

FIGURE 7-7 *Block Diagram of Reply Controller.*

of the line and the operation type that is pending. Most of these states are self-explanatory given the protocol description in Chapter 6, but some are less obvious. In particular, the RRD and RPRD states are used when a cache or prefetch read is pending, but the cluster has received an invalidation for the outstanding request. These states allow the RC to distinguish this exception case and treat both a normal or NAK replies as a NAK (see Section 6.3.2.1). The WRDO, DRDO, WPRDO, and DPRDO states are used only in the home cluster's RAC to distinguish outstanding read requests that take ownership away from a remote dirty cluster. Unlike the case of a remote processor receiving ownership from a dirty cluster, there is no sharing write-back request when a processor in the home acquires dirty

44	40	36	31	26	21	15	0
Start Byte	End Byte	Inval. Count	Wait	Conflict	State	RAC Tag	

RAC Entry States

Used with:	Name	Description	Used with:	Name	Description
——	INVAL	Invalid	UpdateWr	WUPDW	Waiting for acknowledge
——	ERR	Error states (5 total)	UpdateWr	WUP	Waiting for update acks
CacheRd	WRD	Waiting for reply	DMARd	WDMAR	Waiting for reply
CacheRd	DRD	Reply data	DMARd	DDMAR	Reply data
CacheRd	WRDO	Waiting for ownership reply	DMAWr	WDMAW	Waiting for acknowledge
CacheRd	DRDO	Reply data with ownership	DMAWr	WUP	Waiting for DMA acks
CacheRd	RRD	Waiting for inval. reply	CacheLck	WLCK	Waiting for reply
CacheRdEx	WRDX	Waiting for reply	CacheLck	DLCK	Locked reply data
CacheRdEx	DRDX	Reply data	CacheLck	DULCK	Unlocked reply data
CacheRdEx	WINV	Waiting for invalidate acks	CacheLck	RLCK	Waiting for inval. lock
PrefRd	WRD	Waiting for reply	CacheLck	DGNTS	Granted lock (set)
PrefRd	DPRD	Reply data	CacheLck	DGNTV	Granted lock (inc)
PrefRd	WPRDO	Waiting for ownership reply	Unlock	WDIRW	Waiting for acknowledge
PrefRd	DPRDO	Reply pref. data with own.	Unlock	WINV	Waiting for inval. acks
PrefRd	RPRD	Waiting for inval. reply	Fetch&Op	WDIRR	Waiting for reply
PrefRdEx	WPRDX	Waiting for reply	Fetch&Op	DDIRR	Reply data
PrefRdEx	DPRDX	Reply data	MiscRd	WMISR	Waiting for reply
PrefRdEx	WINV	Waiting for invalidate acks	MiscRd	DMISR	Reply data
ProdPref	WDLVR	Waiting for acknowledge	MiscWr	WMISW	Wating for acknowledge
UncacheRd	WUPDR	Waiting for reply			
UncacheRd	DUPDR	Reply data			

FIGURE 7-8 *Format of RAC Tag Entries.*

data. Thus, the reply itself has implicit ownership of the line. This status must be relayed to the directory controller when the processor completes its request. Furthermore, the reply controller cannot drop such a line if the entry is needed for other purposes. The wait and conflict fields in the RAC tag hold a bit vector of the processors (and I/O DMA master) currently waiting for a reply, or waiting to use a RAC entry. Generally, a processor in the wait field will have its arbitration released when the reply is received, and its RAC allocation count will be decremented. If the RAC entry is in use for a nonwaited access, then the allocation counters are decremented when the entry is deallocated. The conflict field points to the processors whose request conflicted with an ongoing request mapped to the same RAC entry. These processors are freed when the RAC entry becomes available. The invalidation count field holds the number of invalidation or update acknowledgments that are expected for a given read-exclusive or DMA write. Finally, the start and end byte fields contain the cache offsets of the first and last byte of data written in an outstanding DMA or update write. The RAC retains the data for these unwaited accesses so it can repeat these requests if they are negative acknowledged. These two fields are also used to hold the cluster and processor to acknowledge when the entry holds a granted lock (DGNTS and DGNTV states). While the RAC tag format can be compacted, the encoding used provides a relatively orthogonal structure that allows for quick decoding and simple interfacing.

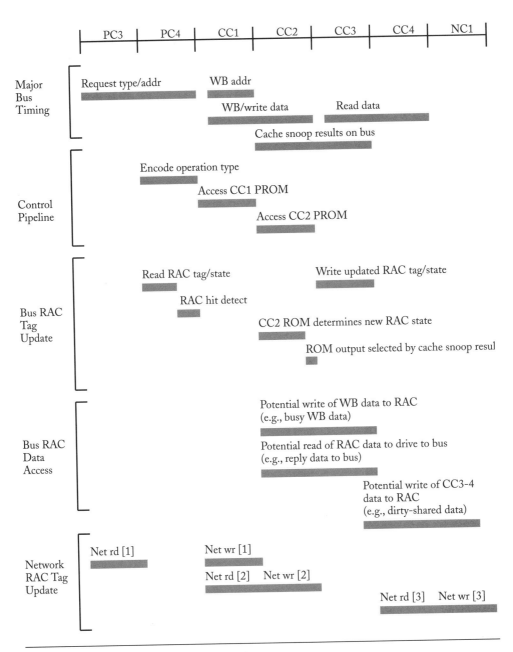

FIGURE 7-9 *Reply Controller Bus Timing.*

The timing of RAC operations is shown in Figure 7-9. The RAC tag is read during PC4, in parallel with a decode of the bus operation. During CC1, the RC-CC1 PROMs are accessed. These PROMs control the driving of bus signals by the RC, the movement of CC1–CC2 data into the RAC, and the re-encoding of the bus operation to minimize the size of the CC2 PROMs. During CC2, the second bank of PROMs is accessed to deter-

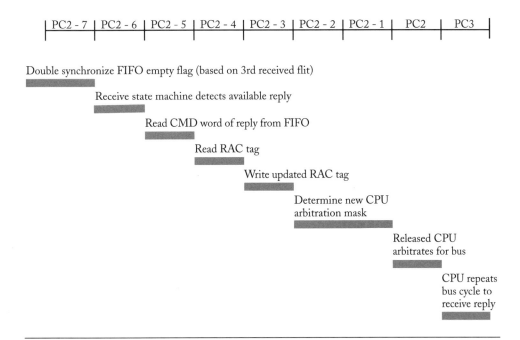

| PC2 - 7 | PC2 - 6 | PC2 - 5 | PC2 - 4 | PC2 - 3 | PC2 - 2 | PC2 - 1 | PC2 | PC3 |

Double synchronize FIFO empty flag (based on 3rd received flit)

Receive state machine detects available reply

Read CMD word of reply from FIFO

Read RAC tag

Write updated RAC tag

Determine new CPU arbitration mask

Released CPU arbitrates for bus

CPU repeats bus cycle to receive reply

FIGURE 7-10 *Reply Controller Network Reply Timing.*

mine the updated RAC tag/state fields. Similar to the DC, the hot results of cache snooping are used late in CC2 to determine the final RC controls. During CC3, the RAC tag/state array is written. The timing of accesses to the RAC data array is more complicated than the tag array because of the varying timing of data movement into and out of the RAC. As shown in Figure 7-9, the data array may be read or written during CC2–CC3, or written during CC4–NC1. Furthermore, for some RCPU operations the RAC data array must be read during PC4 and CC1. When accesses to the RAC data array conflict, the RC stalls the bus. The timing of network tag access to the RAC is also shown in Figure 7-9. These accesses are usually done on two adjacent clocks, except when interrupted by a bus access. The three allowed bus and network interactions are shown in Figure 7-9. If a network access is interleaved with a bus access to the same RAC entry, then the network update is delayed to assure atomicity.

The timing of reply message processing is shown in Figure 7-10. A reply must first be synchronized to the local RC clock. The RAC is then accessed and updated in two cycles (assuming no ongoing bus activity). The RC then takes two clocks to determine the update to the arbitration mask, which allows the processor to retry the bus cycle. If the reply contains data, this will be read out of the receive FIFO on every other clock after the initial command word is read. A separate state machine is responsible for filling data into the RAC data array during idle cycles.

The timing of RCPU operations is similar to other bus masters, but the timing to begin these cycles varies based on the source of the RCPU operation. First, RCPU operations can be initiated in response to a local processor operation. For example, a RCPU bus cycle will

TABLE 7-6

Logic Used in Reply Controller

SECTION	GATES	IC EQUIVALENT	LOGIC TYPE
RC control pipeline	10,807	12.0	High-speed 6 - 8K x 8, 2 - 32K x 8 EPROMs
	8,176	62.2	PAL and MSI decode and control logic
RC network control	2,844	23.7	PAL and MSI decode and control logic
RAC tag RAM and	48 KB	9.0	6 - 8K x 8 SRAM (15 ns)
datapath	4,074	48.8	Datapath registers and buffers
RAC data RAM and	128 KB	13.6	4 - 16K x 16 SRAM module (28 ns)
datapath	511	9.6	Pipeline registers
RAC allocation counters	2,929	9.0	Xilinx counters and update logic
RAC MPBUS interface	1,934	15.5	Bus interface registers
RCPU FSM and control	4,100	33.8	Control state machine and decode
RCPU MPBUS interface	1,493	12.9	Additional bus interface registers
Lock time-out counters	2,737	7.0	4 pending granted lock timers in Xilinx
Miscellaneous	5,427	54.0	Control, status, and error registers
Total	45,032	297.5	2-input gate equivalents
	176 KB		SRAM

occur if a prefetch request requires translation to the cache space, or a dirty RAC line must be written back to memory due to a conflict. In these cases, the RCPU bus transaction will immediately follow the generating bus cycle. RCPU operations are also generated by NAK reply messages for unwaited operations (such as update or DMA writes). For these cases, the RCPU will retry the operation for the requesting processor before servicing another reply. Finally, the RCPU will issue a bus cycle to reject a granted lock if it is not acquired during the lock time-out period. These cycles start asynchronous to any bus transaction or network reply messages.

The gate costs of the RC are shown in Table 7-6. As in the DC, the PROM logic of the RC has been converted to an equivalent number of gates needed to implement the PROM in a PLA minimized by Espresso. An RC board is shown in Figure 7-11.

7.4 Pseudo-CPU

The PCPU is responsible for issuing requests from remote processors onto the local MPBUS. Separating this function from the RC and the RCPU is important because the coherence protocol relies on independent paths for request and reply messages to avoid deadlock. The implementation of the PCPU is relatively simple because it only translates network requests to bus transactions. The DC and RC are responsible for interpreting the response to these bus cycles. This bus-issuing function could be done by the RCPU, but this

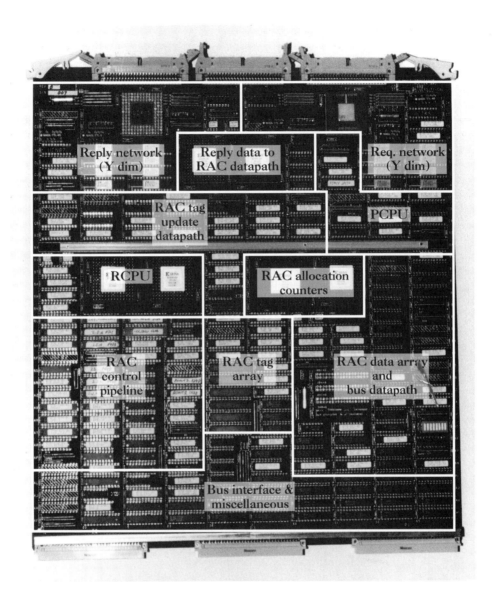

FIGURE 7-11 *DASH Reply Controller Board.*

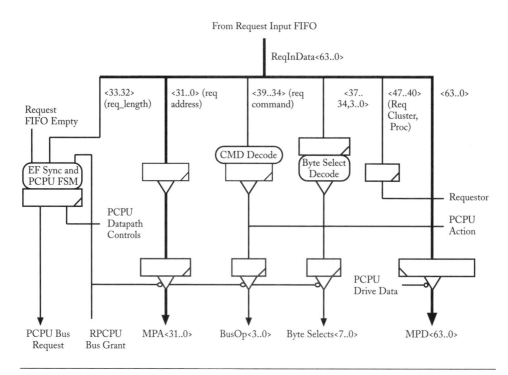

From Request Input FIFO

ReqInData<63..0>

Request FIFO Empty

<33.32> (req_length)

<31..0> (req address)

<39..34> (req command)

<37.. 34,3..0>

<47..40> (Req Cluster, Proc)

<63..0>

EF Sync and PCPU FSM

CMD Decode

Byte Select Decode

Requestor

PCPU Datapath Controls

PCPU Action

PCPU Drive Data

PCPU Bus Request

RPCPU Bus Grant

MPA<31..0>

BusOp<3..0>

Byte Selects<7..0>

MPD<63..0>

FIGURE 7-12 *Block Diagram of the Pseudo-CPU.*

would not reduce logic significantly and would complicate the RCPU design. The detailed logic design of the PCPU was the work of David Nakahira.

A block diagram of the PCPU logic is shown in Figure 7-12. The logic with outlined boundaries is shared with the RCPU. Timing for PCPU operations is given in Figure 7-13. The gate count is given in Table 7-7.

7.5 Network and Network Interface

The network and network logic interfaces are difficult to separate in the prototype because both are distributed on the directory boards within each cluster. The network itself consists of modified versions of the Caltech Mesh Routing Chips (MRC) [Fla87]. Each MRC is responsible for routing network messages in one dimension. These chips allow cascading of node outputs to inputs to support grids with an arbitrary number of dimensions. In the prototype, the mesh input MRCs are located on the DC board and are responsible for horizontal routing. Once a message has been routed to its destination column, it exits the MRC on the DC board and crosses over to the RC board, where it is routed vertically. The detailed logic design of the network logic was the work of David Nakahira. The modifications to the Caltech MRC were the work of Tom Chanak, John Maneatis, and Mark Horowitz.

A detailed block diagram of a single cluster's request network and interface logic is shown in Figure 7-14. The reply network is similar. Entry and exit from the network is through a pair of 1K × 64-bit wide FIFOs. The size of these FIFOs is larger than needed

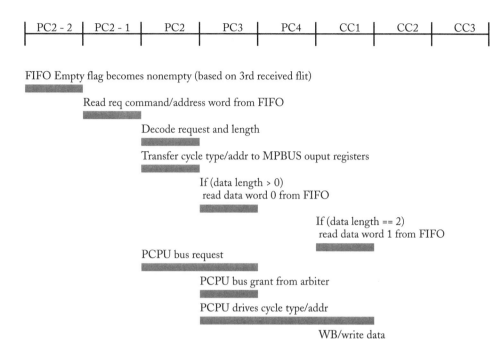

| PC2 - 2 | PC2 - 1 | PC2 | PC3 | PC4 | CC1 | CC2 | CC3 |

FIFO Empty flag becomes nonempty (based on 3rd received flit)

Read req command/address word from FIFO

Decode request and length

Transfer cycle type/addr to MPBUS ouput registers

If (data length > 0)
read data word 0 from FIFO

If (data length == 2)
read data word 1 from FIFO

PCPU bus request

PCPU bus grant from arbiter

PCPU drives cycle type/addr

WB/write data

FIGURE 7-13 *Timing Diagram for the Pseudo-CPU.*

TABLE 7-7

Logic Used in PCPU

SECTION	GATES	IC EQUIVALENT	LOGIC TYPE
PCPU control FSM	556	4.2	PAL logic
Request decode	637	6.0	PAL and MSI logic
Input request datapath	1,538	21.0	Pipeline registers
MPBUS interface	—	—	Shared with RCPU logic
Total	2,371	31.2	2-input gate equivalents

simply to isolate the network and the cluster bus. Their size was chosen to address two other issues. First, to avoid deadlock, the RCPU must always be able to repeat nonwaited write operations that are NAK'd. These repeats may generate new outgoing request messages. Half of the outbound request FIFO is reserved as a buffer for these messages. The size of this buffer constrains the total number of nonwaited local requests that the RC can allow. Second, the PCPU detects a potential network deadlock (see Section 4.2.1) when the out-

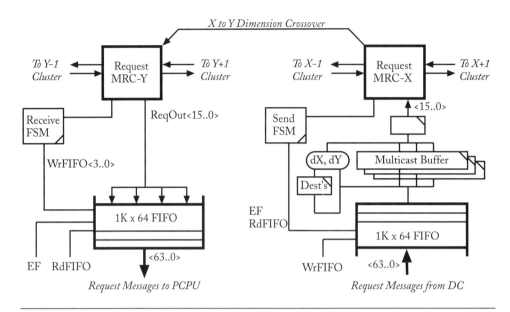

FIGURE 7-14 *Block Diagram of a Single Cluster's Request Network Interface.*

bound request FIFO is more than half full and the incoming request FIFO is completely full. Thus, the larger the FIFOs, the less likely deadlock avoidance will force the PCPU to reject requests.

In addition to the FIFOs, the network interface logic consists of asynchronous state machines and pipeline registers that are responsible for converting the 64-bit FIFO outputs to the 16-bit MRCs inputs and vice versa. The outgoing network interface is also responsible for providing the routing information for the MRCs (horizontal and vertical offsets from the sending cluster) and supporting the multicast of request messages. Multicasting requires extra buffering by the outgoing logic since some multicast requests (e.g., DMA updates) contain more than just a command word.

All network messages begin with two 16-bit words that give the X and Y offset from the current node to the destination. They are followed by three words that hold the command and a 32-bit address (see Figure 7-5). Based on the length specified in the command, these words are followed by zero, two, or eight 16-bit data words. Because of problems in the MRCs, each message is also terminated by a word with a fixed zero value and an end-of-message designation. In future systems, the zero value could be replaced with a cyclic-redundancy-check for error checking. In total, all network messages include 6, 8, or 14 words.

The timing of messages through the network is shown in Figure 7-15. The diagram shows a case where the packet encounters no blockage and must travel two network hops in both the X and Y dimension. The latency of messages is primarily due to the fall-through time in the MRCs that the message must traverse. The network cycle time also plays a part in latency because the PCPU and RC will not recognize the message until a complete 64-bit word is written to the receive FIFOs. In the prototype, the fall-through times are approximately 50 ns when entering or exiting a dimension and 45 ns when traveling through a node

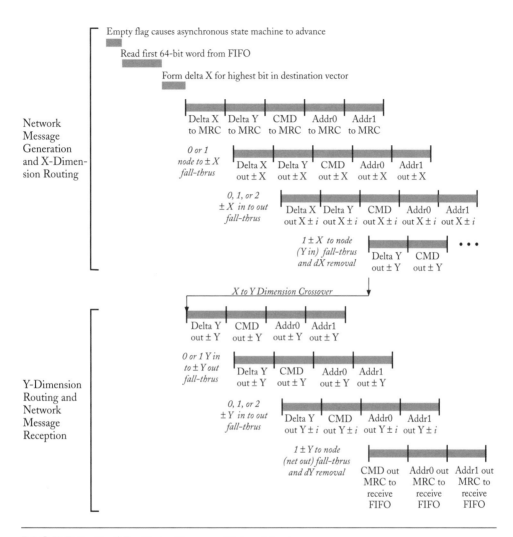

FIGURE 7-15   *Timing Diagram of Network Logic.*

in the same dimension. The network cycle time is approximately 35 ns, limited by both the network send and receive logic, and the MRC cross-chip cycle times (including 5 feet of cable). A summary of the logic used in the network and network interfaces is shown in Table 7-8.

7.6 Performance Monitor

As an experimental machine, it was important that the detailed performance characteristics of the prototype be easily measured. To this end, we have dedicated over 20% of the DC board to a hardware performance monitor. Integration of the performance monitor into the base directory logic allows noninvasive measurements of the complete system with no test hardware setup and few, if any, software modifications. The performance hardware provides

TABLE 7-8

Logic Used in Network and Network Interface per Cluster

SECTION	GATES	IC EQUIVALENT	LOGIC TYPE
Req. outbound FIFOs	9 KB	14.4	8 high-speed 1K x 9 FIFOs
Req. outbound control	1,994	20.8	PAL FSMs and control logic
Req. outbound datapath	3,612	17.4	Pipeline registers
Req. X-dim. MRC	2,000	9.0	1-D, 16-bit-wide Mesh Routing Chip
Reply outbound FIFOs	9 KB	14.4	8 high-speed 1K x 9 FIFOs
Reply outbound control	1,641	16.3	PAL FSMs and control logic
Reply outbound datapath	3,612	17.4	Pipeline registers
Reply X-dim. MRC	2,000	9.0	1-D, 16-bit-wide Mesh Routing Chip
Req. Y-dim. MRC	2,000	9.0	1-D, 16-bit-wide Mesh Routing Chip
Req. inbound control	1,002	10.9	PAL FSMs and control logic
Req. outbound FIFOs	9 KB	14.4	8 high-speed 1K x 9 FIFOs
Reply Y-dim. MRC	2,000	9.0	1-D, 16-bit-wide Mesh Routing Chip
Reply inbound control	1,002	10.9	PAL FSMs and control logic
Reply outbound FIFOs	9 KB	14.4	8 high-speed 1K x 9 FIFOs
Total	20,863	172.5	2-input gate equivalents
	36 KB		SRAM (FIFOs)

low-level information on software reference characteristics and hardware resource utilizations. The monitor hardware can trace and count a variety of bus, directory, and network events. Event selection is controlled by a software down-loadable Xilinx field programmable gate array (FPGA) [Xil91], which allows flexible event selection and sophisticated event preprocessing.

A block diagram of performance logic is shown in Figure 7-16. It consists of three major blocks: (1) the FPGA, which selects and preprocesses events to be measured and controls the rest of the performance logic; (2) two banks of 16 K $\times$ 32 SRAMs and increment logic that count event occurrences; and (3) a 2M $\times$ 36 trace DRAM, which captures 36 or 72 bits of information on each bus transaction.

The counting SRAMs together with the FPGA support a wide variety of event counting. The two banks of SRAM can be used together to count events that change on a cycle-by-cycle basis. Alternatively, the banks can be used independently to monitor twice as many events. In the simplest use of the SRAM, each address bit is used as an independent event. By summing over all addresses with a particular address bit high or low, the number of occurrences of that event can be determined. Likewise, the conjunction or disjunction of any set of events can be determined by summing over the appropriate address ranges. Another use of the count SRAM is as a histogram array. In this mode, certain events are used to start, stop, and increment a counter inside the FPGA. The stop event also triggers the count value

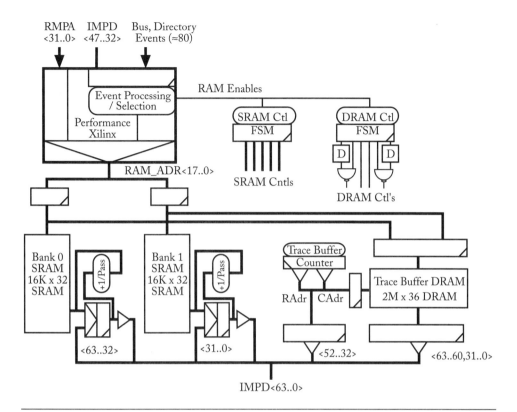

FIGURE 7-16 *Block Diagram of Performance Monitor Logic.*

to be used as an address to the increment SRAM. The resulting values stored in the SRAM are a histogram of the count events between the start and stop events.

A typical use of the counting SRAM in the prototype increments the two banks of SRAM independently on each bus transaction. The address of the first bank is the directory controller's state machine PROM address. The resulting SRAM values give a complete distribution of bus transaction types and initiators, directory states, RAC states, and locality. From this data, access type distributions, bus utilization, access locality, RAC performance, remote caching statistics, and the distribution of network messages can be calculated. The second bank of SRAM is addressed with the local cache snoop results and histogram counters of remote latency. The remote latency histogram dedicates an internal FPGA counter to each CPU. An individual counter is reset until its corresponding processor is forced to retry for a remote access. When the processor is released the counter value is used to index the SRAM and increment a histogram bucket. The result is a distribution of remote access latencies. These results can also be used to calculate an estimate of processor utilization.

The other component of the performance monitor is bus transaction tracing. The exact information traced can be varied based on programming of the FPGA, but the normal use of the trace logic supports two modes. In the first configuration, up to 2M addresses along with

TABLE 7-9

Logic Used in Performance Monitor

SECTION	GATES	IC EQUIVALENT	LOGIC TYPE
Event selection/control	3,352	9.0	Xilinx 3090-100 FPGA
Count RAM	128 KB	13.6	4 - 16K x 16 SRAM modules (28 ns)
Count RAM control/inc.	3,644	32.5	PAL and MSI pipeline and update logic
Trace RAM	9 MB	5.0	2M x 36 DRAM SIMM (80 ns)
Trace RAM control	2,296	26.8	PAL address counter and control
Miscellaneous	458	3.0	PAL Xilinx programming/control
Total	**9,750**	89.9	2-input gate equivalents
	128 KB		SRAM
	9 MB		DRAM

the issuing processor number and read/write status are captured. The second mode captures only 1M addresses, but adds the directory controller's PROM address and a bus idle count to each trace entry. The trace information can be used to do detailed analysis of reference behavior or as input to another memory simulator. The only restriction is that only bus references are captured, not references satisfied by the processor cache. If a complete address trace is desired, it can be generated by using uncached memory spaces. Of course, this may distort the results somewhat due to the differences in memory timing. A breakdown of the performance monitor costs is given in Table 7-9.

7.7 Logic Overhead of Directory-Based Coherence

One important result of building the DASH prototype is that it provides a realistic cost model of directory-based cache coherence and a general memory system interconnect. While some of the costs are tied to the specific prototype implementation (e.g., the full DRAM directory vector), they provide a picture of one complete system. At a high level, the cost of the directory logic can be estimated by the distribution of the logic boards in a DASH cluster. Two of the six boards are used for directory and intercluster coherence, so the overhead is roughly 50%. This estimate is very conservative, however, because some of the SGI logic, in particular the MIPS R3000 and R3010 chips, are much more integrated than the directory logic. A more accurate picture of the overhead is given in Table 7-10 and Figure 7-17. Table 7-10 summarizes the cost of each subsystem in terms of gates, kilobytes of SRAM, megabytes of DRAM, and IC equivalents. Figure 7-17 shows these same costs as a percentage of the total of each type. As expected, only when measured in terms of IC equivalents (i.e., board area) is the overhead of the directory logic 50%. When measured in terms of gates, the overhead is approximately 24%. In SRAM and DRAM, the overhead is 16% and 30%, respectively.

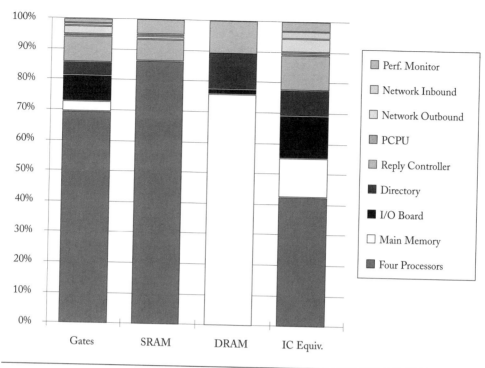

FIGURE 7-17 *Percentage of Logic in a DASH Cluster.*

TABLE 7-10

Summary of Logic Used in a DASH Cluster

SECTION	GATES	SRAM (KB)	DRAM (MB)	IC EQUIVALENT
Processor/cache (4x)	369,984	2,080	0	1,101.6
Main memory	17,866	0	63	330.2
I/O board	44,218	0	1	352.7
Directory	23,599	0	10	213.8
Reply controller	45,032	176	0	311.1
PCPU	2,731	0	0	31.2
Network outbound	14,859	18	0	111.3
Network inbound	6,004	18	0	61.2
Performance monitor	9,750	128	9	89.9
Total	534,043	2,420	83	2,603.0

The DASH prototype also contains logic in each cluster that is not strictly necessary. The major extraneous functions are the following:

1. The SGI I/O board's Ethernet and VME bus interfaces

2. The diagnostic UARTs and timers attached to each processor

3. The performance monitor logic on the directory board

Table 7-11 summarizes the core logic of a cluster (i.e., without the extra functions), and Figure 7-18 gives the corresponding percentages. Looking just at the core logic, the gate overhead is 25%, and the SRAM and DRAM overhead are 10% and 16%, respectively. While it is somewhat difficult to combine the different costs, the overall overhead to support directory-based coherence and a scalable memory system interconnect is in the range of 15–20%.

Looking in more detail at the prototype's implementation, there are some areas where directory overhead might be improved. In particular, the prototype's simple-bit-vector directory grows in direct proportion to the number of clusters in the system and in inverse proportion to cache line size. Thus, increasing cache line size from 16 to 32 or 64 bytes would reduce the directory DRAM overhead to 8% and 4%, respectively. Conversely, this increase in line size could allow the system to grow to 128 or 256 processors while maintaining the same 16% overhead. For even larger systems, one of the more scalable directory structures discussed in Chapter 3 could be used to keep directory overhead at or below the level in the prototype.

The prototype's SRAM overhead could also be improved. The RAC is the dominant user of SRAM in the DASH logic. The size of the RAC was primarily driven by its use in supplementing the function of the processors' second-level caches (e.g., destination of prefetch and support of dirty-sharing cache state). If the second-level caches were enhanced to support these functions, then the RAC could be reduced to a fraction of its current size. The primary need for the RAC would become collecting invalidation acknowledgments and receiving granted locks. It could shrink by at least a factor of 4 or 8, and reduce the SRAM overhead to less than 3%. Likewise, better integration of the base cluster logic into the inter-cluster coherence protocol might reduce the directory logic by as much as 25%. Thus, the core of the current prototype is a conservative estimate of directory overhead. A more integrated system would have a logic overhead of 20–25%, an SRAM overhead of 3–10%, and a DRAM overhead of 4–16%. This overhead is still significant, approximately equal to an extra processor, but when amortized over the multiprocessor cluster the overhead is less pronounced.

The prototype logic distributions can also be extrapolated to consider other system organizations. For example, if the DASH clusters were replaced by uniprocessor nodes, the overhead for scalability would be very high. Ignoring the potential growth in directory storage, the logic overhead for scalable coherence would grow to more than 75%. Thus, a system based on uniprocessor nodes loses almost a factor of two in cost-performance relative to a uniprocessor system, even if linear speedup is achieved. Another system option is support for a scalable memory interconnect, but without hardware cache coherence (as in the Cray T3D,

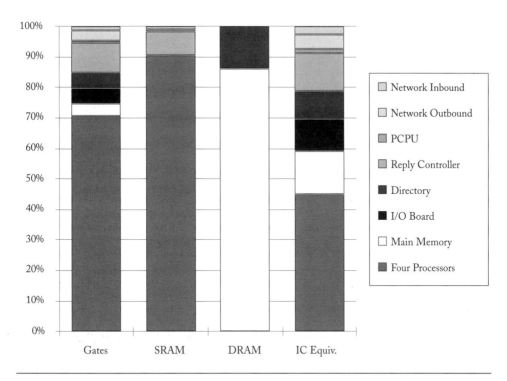

FIGURE 7-18   *Percentage of Core Logic in a DASH Cluster.*

TABLE 7-11

Summary of Core Logic Used in a DASH Cluster

SECTION	GATES	SRAM (KB)	DRAM (MB)	IC EQUIVALENT
Processor/cache (4x)	323,172	2,080	0	1,054.4
Main memory	17,866	0	63	330.2
I/O board	23,169	0	0	244.7
Directory	23,599	0	10	213.8
Reply controller	45,032	176	0	311.1
PCPU	2,731	0	0	31.2
Network outbound	14,859	18	0	111.3
Network inbound	6,004	18	0	61.2
Total	456,432	2,292	73	2,357.9

IBM RP3, BBN TC2000—see Section 5.4.2). An optimistic assumption for such a system is that this option would remove all the directory DRAM and support, the RAC and its datapath, and 90% of the RC and DC control pipelines. Under these assumptions, the logic overhead falls to 11% of a cluster, and memory overhead becomes negligible. Therefore, if a performance gain of more than 10% is realized by adding hardware cache coherence, then overall cost-performance will improve. Our work with DASH indicates that caching improves performance by far more than 10%, and support for scalable cache coherence is well worth the extra cost.

7.8 Chapter Conclusions

The DASH prototype consists of a set of modified Silicon Graphics 4D/340 systems, each supplemented by a pair of intercluster interface boards. The 4D/340 system consists of four boards. There are two processor boards containing a total of four 33 MHz R3000s along with their first- and second-level caches. The first-level cache is write-through; the second-level cache is write-back and supports the Illinois snoopy coherence protocol. The memory board supports up to 56 MByte of SEC/DED error correcting DRAM, and the I/O interface board supports DMA transfers to its VME, SCSI, and Ethernet interfaces.

The DASH logic resides on two printed circuit boards. The main intercluster coherence protocol state machines reside in the directory and reply controllers. The directory controller is responsible for maintaining the directory state and initiating outbound network traffic. Timing of the directory memory is tight because each bus access results in a read-modify-write cycle. Higher-speed designs may need to use more interleaving in the directory than in main memory, or some amount of static RAM, so that the directory update rate matches that of block main memory reads. The reply controller is responsible for tracking outstanding remote requests made by the local processors. It maintains the state of these requests in the remote access cache (RAC). The RAC is a snoopy cache that supports updates from both the cluster bus and the reply network. The RAC's structure was primarily motivated by the need for it to enforce release consistency on a per cache line basis. The cache structure also allows the RAC to supplement the function of the processor caches.

The other functions of the DASH logic include the PCPU, the mesh networks, and the performance monitor. The PCPU is a simple translator of network request messages to bus transactions. The pair of mesh networks are used to interconnect the clusters. The mesh's wormhole routing keeps network latency low. Traffic on the meshes are isolated from the cluster buses by transmit and receive FIFOs. The performance monitor logic built into each directory board supports flexible counting and tracing of bus, directory, and network events.

The directory logic adds an overhead of 25% in logic gates, 10% in SRAM, and 16% in DRAM to the core logic of a DASH cluster. This overhead is comparable to the complexity of a complete processor with its caches and bus interface. While this overhead is reasonable when amortized over a cluster, it may become unacceptable if clustering was not used. About half of the directory logic, excluding the DRAM, is necessary simply to support a scalable memory system interconnect. Thus, for approximately 10% more in hardware overhead, a scalable memory system can be enhanced to support cache coherence.

8

Prototype Performance Analysis

T he previous chapter outlined the basic cost of directory-based cache coherence as exhibited in the DASH prototype. This chapter quantifies the performance of such systems. The analysis is based on measurements of the DASH prototype machine, which includes 48 processors partitioned among 12 clusters.[1]

The performance analysis in this chapter is broken into three major sections. The first section summarizes the basic memory system performance metrics of bandwidth and latency. Bandwidth is given for the system as a whole and as seen by the individual processors. Latencies are given in terms of the response time for the issuing processor and the delays for operations to become visible to other processors. The second section summarizes the performance of parallel applications on the prototype and relates the memory reference statistics of the applications to their resulting speedup. The final section examines in detail the performance benefits of the major protocol optimizations in DASH (e.g., request forwarding, prefetch, and granting locks). These performance gains are examined in the context of the parallel applications and simple atomic tests that stress protocol features.

8.1 Base Memory Performance

The performance of a memory system can be examined from a number of perspectives. For the system as a whole, performance can be characterized by the bandwidth provided by each of the major shared resources (e.g., cluster buses, mesh networks, and PCPUs). As seen by the processor, the important metric is the latency for operations that cause the processor to stall (i.e., reads) and the issue rate for operations for which the processor does not wait (i.e., writes). For some operations, both the issue rate and latency are important (e.g., prefetch). Finally, when examining the performance of interprocessor communication, the latency between the issue of a memory operation and its effect on other processors becomes critical.

---

[1] Reliability problems with the mesh network have prevented the creation of a stable configuration with the maximum 64 processors.

The following sections outline the performance of the prototype against the global memory system metrics listed above. The data is based on unloaded (i.e., no contention) timing of a 4×4, 64-processor system. The base parameters were measured with a logic analyzer on the 2×2 prototype and extrapolated for the various operations and the larger system configuration. The asynchronous self-timed clocking of the meshes makes it difficult to give definitive timing for the network. In this chapter, the reported network timings are based on conservative estimates of the measured cycle times and logic delays.

8.1.1 Overall Memory System Bandwidth

In a cache-based system such as DASH, peak memory bandwidth is determined by the product of the number of processors and the bandwidth to their individual caches. Because cache bandwidth is high, and there is little interference on individual caches, cache bandwidth usually does not limit system performance. Rather, throughput is limited by either the processor's computation rate (including the effects of cache miss stalls) or the rate that the memory system can satisfy cache misses. This section focuses on the issue of memory bandwidth, while Section 8.1.3 focuses on memory latency and its effect on processor throughput.

In DASH, the primary shared resources in the memory system are the cluster buses and the mesh networks. In the prototype the raw bandwidth of a cluster bus is 128 MByte/sec (8 bytes wide at 16 MHz). The sustained bandwidth, including the overhead of a bus transaction and memory refresh, is 62.5 MByte/sec. Likewise, the raw bandwidth of an individual network link is approximately 57.1 MByte/sec (2 bytes wide at 35 ns), which leads to a sustained rate of 32.7 MByte/sec when message overhead is considered. A summary of local and remote cluster bandwidth is given in Table 8-1. The bandwidth of remote references is based on the total load that a remote operation puts on all buses, which usually consists of three bus transactions. The remote bandwidth calculation also assumes uniform loading such that the load imposed on other buses by remote references is equal to the load that other clusters' remote references put on the local bus. The bandwidth of memory write operations is lower than reads because of the SGI memory system, which begins each memory cycle with a read, even if the operation only requires a write.

With the uniform loading assumption, total memory bandwidth is limited by either the rate at which all of the cluster buses can sustain traffic, or the rate at which the network bisection can deliver messages. If the processors drive the cluster bus to 100% utilization with a uniform load of remote requests, then the limit on system bandwidth is given by the following equation and is plotted for varying number of clusters (N) in Figure 8-1.

$$GlobalMemoryBandwidth = \min \left(\begin{array}{c} N(RemoteBusBandwidth) \\ 4\sqrt{N}(NetworkLinkBandwidth) \end{array} \right) \quad \textbf{(8.1)}$$

The upper term in Equation 8.1 is based on the cluster bus limit, while the lower term is based on the bisection bandwidth of a 2-D mesh assuming uniform loading. The factor of four in the bisection bandwidth limit arises from the fact that neighbors in the mesh are connected by full-duplex links and the uniform loading assumption, which implies that only

TABLE 8-1

Prototype Memory System Bandwidth

	OPERATION	MTRANS/SEC	MBYTE/SEC
Cluster bandwidth	Local cache fill, DMA read (Figure 6-8(a,c))	3.91	62.5
	Local DMA write (Figure 6-14(a,d))	1.95	31.3
	Local write-back	3.91	62.5
	Remote cache fill, DMA read (Figure 6-8(b,d))	1.3	20.8
	Remote DMA write (Figure 6-14(c,e))	1.30	20.8
	Remote write-back	1.74	27.8
Network bandwidth	Command packets per link	4.76	N/A
	4-byte data packets per link	3.57	14.3
	16-byte data packets per link	2.04	32.7
	Command packets across 4 × 4 bisection	76.20	N/A
	4-byte packets across 4 × 4 bisection	57.15	229.2
	16-byte packets across 4 × 4 bisection	32.66	522.4

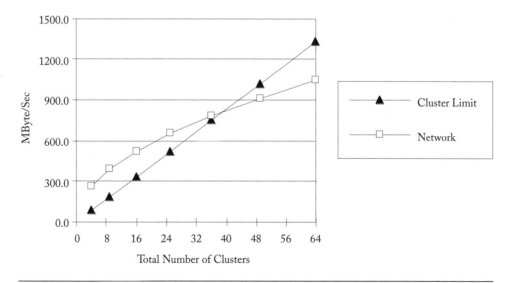

FIGURE 8-1 *Total Cluster Bandwidth and Network Bisection Bandwidth.*

half of the traffic will traverse a particular network bisection. The two meshes do not contribute another factor of two because each remote reference consists of at least one request and one reply message. Since the prototype contains no more than 16 clusters, Figure 8-1 indicates that the cluster bus is the limiting factor on prototype's memory system bandwidth.

TABLE 8-2

Cluster to Network Interface Bandwidth

INTERFACE	NETWORK MESSAGE TYPES	MTRANS/SEC	MBYTE/SEC
Directory controller	Command packets	16.00	N/A
	4-byte data packets	8.00	32.0
	16-byte data packets	5.33	85.3
Pseudo-CPU	Command packets	4.00	N/A
	4-byte data packets	4.00	16.0
	16-byte data packets	2.67	42.7
Reply controller	Command packets	4.00	N/A
	4-byte data packets	2.67	10.7
	16-byte data packets	2.29	36.6

In fact, the network will normally be only lightly loaded because not all references are remote, and it is very difficult for the processors to drive the cluster bus to 100% utilization. While not a limit on total bandwidth, the high throughput of the interconnection network does have important benefits. First, the high bandwidth of individual network links reduces congestion (tree saturation) in the network when there is hot-spotting. Second, the cycle time of network directly affects memory latency since a receiving node will not begin to process a network message until the entire command word has been received (first five flits of message—see Section 7.4).

8.1.2 Other Memory Bandwidth Limits

While the cluster bus limits overall bandwidth if uniform loading is assumed, the bandwidth to memory in an individual cluster can be limited by the network or the interfaces between the network and the cluster bus (i.e., the DC, PCPU, and RC). Table 8-2 lists the bandwidth of the DC, PCPU, and RC. Given the processing rates listed in Table 8-2, the DC and PCPU do not limit local memory bandwidth for remote requests. The limit on incoming requests is the bandwidth of the bus, and for outgoing replies, the limit is set by the network transmission rate.[2] The DC and PCPU affect the processing of remote requests to local memory, while the RC's processing rate of replies affects the bandwidth of local processors to remote memory. Thus, although the RC's processing rate for 16-byte replies is slower than the local bus, it does not limit bandwidth because replies are associated with two local bus transactions (one to initiate the request and one to receive the data). However, the RAC can be a limit when processing writes that require multiple invalidations or updates. In these

---

[2] The 16-byte network reply rate is 32.7 MByte/sec compared with the 62.5 MByte/sec bus bandwidth. Command word request arrival rate is 4.8 MTrans/sec compared with the bus service rate of 4.0 MTrans/sec.

TABLE 8-3

Cache Operation Bandwidth and Latencies as Seen By a Single Processor

CACHE OPERATION	BEST CASE		WORST CASE	
	Bandwidth MByte/sec	Latency pclocks/word	Bandwidth MByte/sec	Latency pclocks/word
Read from 1st-level cache	133.3	1.0	133.3	1.0
Cache fill from 2nd-level cache	29.6	4.5	8.9	15.0
Cache fill from local bus (Figure 6-8(a,c))	16.7	8.0	4.6	29.0
Cache fill from remote bus (Figure 6-8(b,d))	5.1	26.0	1.3	101.0
Cache fill from dirty-remote bus (Figure 6-8(e))	4.0	33.8	1.0	132.0
Write retired in 2nd-level cache	32.0	4.2	32.0	4.2
Write retired on local bus (Figure 6-10(a,b,d))	18.3	7.3	8.0	16.7
Write retired on remote bus (Figure 6-10(c,e,f))	5.3	25.3	1.5	88.7
Write retired on dirty-remote bus (Figure 6-10(g))	4.0	33.0	1.1	119.7

cases, bandwidth is limited by network serialization at the home and the RC's processing rate of acknowledgments in the writing cluster.

In addition to the globally shared resources, processors contend for resources on the processor board itself. In particular, snooping of the processor's second-level cache locks out the processor from that cache for four processor clocks. Furthermore, if snooping generates an invalidation of the processor's first-level cache, the processor is stalled for eight clocks. Finally, the processor will stall if its write buffer fills, and the processor must wait for the write buffer to empty before making any accesses beyond the first-level cache. This latter constraint of the SGI implementation can add significant delay to read misses. Thus, in general, the overhead for long-latency remote writes cannot be ignored.

8.1.3 Processor Issue Bandwidth and Latency

Although global memory bandwidth can sometimes limit the aggregate processing rate of the system, memory latency usually has a more direct effect on throughput because the processor can only overlap computation and memory latency to a limited degree. For cache-based systems, effective memory latency is determined by the cache miss rate and the penalty to fill the cache from memory on a miss. In a distributed system such as DASH, the average fill time is also affected by the ratio of local to remote accesses and the latencies of local and remote memory.

Table 8-3 lists the processor bandwidth and latency for cache memory operations. The best-case numbers assume stride-one (i.e., sequential) word access in which a 16-byte cache fill will result in one cache miss every four references. The worst-case numbers assume a stride greater than four and no reuse of blocks in the cache. Thus, the last column in this

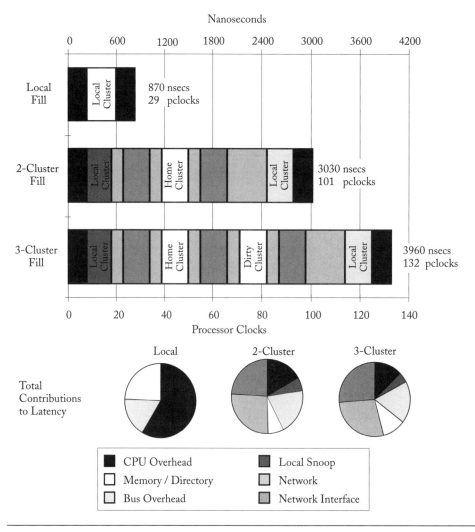

FIGURE 8-2 *Cache Fill Latencies in the DASH Prototype. For clarity four processor clocks of bus overhead per bus transaction are not shown in the bar graphs, but are included in the total contribution breakdown.*

table is the latency of a single cache miss under various conditions. Writes store-through the processor's first-level cache and are buffered in the four-word write buffer. For writes, the table lists the rate at which writes are retired by the second-level cache with, or without, a read-exclusive cache fill from the memory system. The write rates assume that release consistency is used so latency is not affected by the delay for remote cache invalidations.

The breakdown of latency for local and remote cache misses is given in Figure 8-2. The majority of the delay for a local miss (60%) is the CPU's overhead in detecting the first- and second-level misses, traversing the asynchronous processor to second-level cache interface, and filling the four words into the cache sequentially. A remote miss takes approximately 3.5

TABLE 8-4

Latency for I/O Read and Write Operations[a]

I/O READ AND WRITE OPERATIONS	MACCESS/SEC	PCLOCK/ACCESS
I/O read local bus	1.3	25.0
Uncached read local bus (Figure 6-13(a))	0.7	45.8
I/O read remote bus (Figure 6-13(b,d))	0.3	97.0
Uncached read dirty-remote bus (Figure 6-13(e))	0.3	128.0
Issue I/O write local/remote	2.0	16.7
Issue update write local (Figure 6-14)	1.3	25.0
Issue producer prefetch (Figure 6-11)	1.3	25.0

[a] Uncached reads and Fetch&Ops are issued as I/O reads. I/O writes include update writes, prefetch issues, and unlock operations. I/O writes do not require the processor to retry remote operations. Thus, local and remote issue times are the same.

times longer than a local miss. For remote misses, approximately 50% of the delay is in the DASH-specific logic including the network and bus interfaces. Another 25% of the delay is due to bus overhead (i.e., including the repeat on the local bus to complete the access) and memory access latency. The remaining 25% is the CPU overhead and the delay in sending the initial network request while the local snoop takes place. When comparing the remote to dirty-remote latency, the benefits of forwarding (see Section 8.3.1.1) become clear. The difference in latency between these two cases is 1 μsec. If forwarding was not used, an extra cluster access would be required to satisfy the dirty-remote access, and the latency would be increased by another 1 μsec (25%).

Table 8-4 gives the corresponding issue rate and latency for I/O operations. I/O operations include uncached reads, update writes, prefetch issues, and synchronization variable locks and unlocks. I/O read timing is equal to the normal cache fill time minus the small number of clocks needed to complete the cache fill. Some I/O operations also have lower performance because the RCPU must translate the I/O address issued by the processor to the corresponding physical cache address.

The processor's write buffer is stalled during the read-exclusive fetch of a cache block because of a cache write miss. In contrast, I/O writes do not fetch any data and can be issued nonwaited; that is, the processor retires the write from the write buffer as soon as the request is issued on the bus. The RC takes responsibility for completing the write operation, and maintains a RAC entry until the I/O write is acknowledged. The presence of this outstanding write (and RAC entry), however, may delay subsequent operations. For example, an unlock operation that includes an implicit FENCE will be delayed if a RAC entry is still allocated for an outstanding update write. Likewise, a cache read will see part of the latency of a prefetch if it requests the data before the prefetch has brought the data into the RAC.

TABLE 8-5

Latency to Complete Nonwaited Write Operations[a]

"NON-WAITED" OPERATION	μSEC	PCLOCKS
Read-exclusive to local shared-remote[b] (Figure 6-10(b))	2.09	69.7
Read-exclusive to rem. shared-remote[b] (Figure 6-10(f))	3.35	111.8
Prefetch of remote (Figure 6-8(b,d))	2.09	69.7
Prefetch of dirty-remote (Figure 6-8(e))	3.10	103.5
Update write to local shared-remote[b] (Figure 6-14(b))	2.09	69.7
Update write to remote (Figure 6-14(e))	2.09	69.7
Update write to rem. shared-remote[b] (Figure 6-14(f))	3.35	111.8
Update write to remote dirty-remote[b] (Figure 6-14(g))	3.10	103.5
Invalidating unlock to local queued[b]	2.09	69.7
Inv/Grant unlock to remote (Figure 6-15(a))	2.09	69.7
Invalidate unlock to remote queued[b] (Figure 6-15(c))	3.35	111.8
Grant unlock to local queued[c]	2.92	97.3
Grant unlock to remote queued (Figure 6-15(b))	3.93	131.1

[a] Numbers represent clock cycles between successive operations issued by the processor (i.e., the delay in issuing the second operation has been subtracted from the numbers given).

[b] These delays include receipt of one invalidation or update acknowledge. Add 0.25 μsec (8.3 pclocks) for each additional cluster that must be invalidated or updated.

[c] Granting unlock acknowledge latency includes the time to invalidate the grant cluster, and for a processor to immediately reacquire the lock. Latency can be considerably higher if a processor does not immediately reacquire the lock or the granted lock eventually times out.

Table 8-5 summarizes the unloaded latency for these nonwaited operations to update or deallocate their associated RAC entry.

8.1.4 Interprocessor Latency

The previous sections outlined the bandwidth of the system as a whole and the bandwidth provided to individual processors. For fine-grain computations, the latency of interprocessor communication is also important. In a cache-based system such as DASH, interprocessor communication is usually in the form of cache invalidations or updates. Table 8-6 summarizes the latency of these interprocessor operations assuming no contention.

8.1.5 Summary of Memory System Bandwidth and Latency

Memory system bandwidth, memory latency, and interprocessor latency all affect system performance. System bandwidth and cache hit rates determine the maximum system throughput. Of course, this theoretical maximum will rarely be reached because memory latency is difficult to hide in all cases. Nevertheless, bandwidth can limit performance of applications that have poor hit rates but sufficient parallelism to hide memory latency (e.g., applications that use prefetch). Likewise, bandwidth can affect performance by increasing

TABLE 8-6

Latencies of Interprocessor Operations[a]

INTERPROCESSOR OPERATION	μSEC	PCLOCKS
Invalidate/update local to local processor (Figure 6-10(a))	0.75	25.1
Invalidate/update local to remote proc. (Figure 6-10(b,e))	1.77	58.9
Inv/update remote to shared-remote proc. (Figure 6-10(f))	2.78	92.7
Producer prefetch local to remote proc. (Figure 6-11(a))	1.67	55.7
Producer prefetch remote to remote proc. (Figure 6-11(c))	2.69	89.5
Invalidating unlock of local queued	1.48	49.4
Invalidating unlock of remote queued (Figure 6-15(c))	2.50	83.2
Grant unlock of local queued	1.48	49.4
Grant unlock of remote queued (Figure 6-15(b))	2.50	83.2

[a] Numbers do not include time for the destination processor to refetch the data from its cache of memory after it has received an invalidation or update.

latency due to queuing. In the prototype, the cluster bus limits system bandwidth. The relatively low bandwidth of the prototype bus, especially for remote operations that take three bus transactions, may limit the effectiveness of the latency hiding operations.

For medium-grain applications, miss rates and memory latencies have the most direct effect on system performance. As shown in Figure 8-3, processor utilization falls off steeply with increasing miss rates given the latencies of the prototype.[3] The figure also shows that the locality of memory has a significant effect on utilization. If locality is 100%, then performance is equivalent to the base SGI hardware. With 0% locality, performance is equivalent to a system without any local memory (i.e., a "dance hall" architecture). Note that the reference rates assumed for Figure 8-3 include all memory references, private and shared. Private data is usually not a problem since the miss rates are low and locality is high. Unfortunately, shared data references have higher miss rates and lower locality. For DASH to maintain a reasonable processor utilization, shared data reference rates must be low, or shared references must exhibit reasonable cache and cluster locality. Alternatively, nonblocking memory operations can be used to hide system latencies, but their effectiveness may be limited on the prototype because of the low bandwidth of the cluster bus.

Finally, the costs of interprocessor communication limit the grain size of tasks that can be exploited on the system. In the prototype, interprocessor latency is typically 100 processor clocks per cache line. Thus, unless latency is well hidden, splitting a task into two parallel

---

[3] The graph assumes 35% of instructions reference memory. For example, 23% of instructions could be loads and 12% stores, or the reference rates might be higher if a portion of the write fill time is hidden by buffering (e.g., 30% loads and 15% stores with two-thirds of the write-latency hidden).

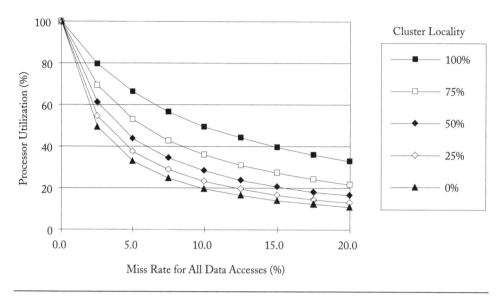

FIGURE 8-3 *Processor Utilization Versus Cache Miss Rate and Cluster Locality. Note that this assumes 100% instruction hit rate, and that 35% of instructions are loads or stores.*

tasks will only be useful if the additional interprocessor latencies can be amortized over a sufficiently large grain of work (i.e., much greater than 100 processor clocks).

8.2 Parallel Application Performance

This section outlines the performance achieved on the prototype for a number of parallel applications. We begin by describing the software environment available on the prototype and how the measurements were made. We then present the speedup for ten parallel programs representing a variety of application domains—five of the applications studied in Chapter 2 and five additional applications that were not available for the simulation studies. Four of these applications are studied in-depth using data captured by the performance monitor hardware.

8.2.1 Application Run-Time Environment

The operating system running on the prototype DASH is a modified version of IRIX, a variant of UNIX System V.3 developed by Silicon Graphics. The applications for which we present results are coded in C and use the Argonne National Labs (ANL) parallel macros [LOB+87] to control synchronization and sharing.

Before giving the speedup results in the next subsection, we first state the assumptions used in measuring the speedups. The speedups were measured as the time for the uniprocessor to execute the parallel version of the application code (i.e., not all synchronization code is removed) divided by the time for the parallel application to run on a given number of processors. Leaving in the synchronization has very small effect (< 2%) on the uniprocessor time because of the relatively low rate of sychronization in these applications when running on a single processor.[4] When possible, the execution time of the entire application is measured.

While there would be benefit to exactly matching the simulation studies given in Chapter 2 on the real machine, this would have artificially restricted our results to just the parallel portion of the code. Such a restriction is necessary for the simulation runs because of the slow rate of simulation, but it is not needed for the larger runs possible on the real machine. For five of the applications, we continue to measure just the parallel execution portion of the code. We discuss the reason for this decision when describing the applications in detail.

For our measurements, each application process is attached to a processor for its lifetime, and we fully use one cluster before assigning processors to new clusters. Physical memory pages used by the application are allocated only from the clusters that are actively being used, as long as the physical memory in those clusters is enough. Thus, for an application running with 4 processes, all memory is allocated from the local cluster, and all misses cost about 30 clocks. However, with 8 processes, some misses may be to a remote cluster and cost over 100 clock cycles. Most of the programs allocate shared data randomly or in a round-robin fashion from the clusters being actively used, but some include explicit system calls to control memory allocation. Because of restrictions in the prototype OS, all applications were run under processor consistency mode (i.e., writes were not retired from the write buffer until all invalidation acknowledgments had been received).

8.2.2 Application Speedups

The applications studied in this section are a superset of the applications studied in Chapter 2.[5,6] There are five new applications reported in this section: FMM, PSIM4, Radiosity, VolRend, and Matmult. Altogether, the applications cover a variety of domains. There are some scientific applications (Barnes-Hut, FMM, and Water), several engineering applications (MP3D, PSIM4, Cholesky, and LocusRoute), two graphics applications (Radiosity and VolRend), and one kernel (matrix multiply). The input data set and the measured run-time of the applications are summarized in Table 8-7.

Figure 8-4 summarizes the speedup of the ten parallel applications running on the prototype using from 1 to 48 processors. Looking at characteristics of each application gives insight into their achieved performance.

Matmult is a blocked matrix multiply, which uses 88×88 blocks for a roughly $1,000 \times 1,000$ matrix [LRW91]. The size of the matrix is slightly modified with the number of processors to ensure an integral number of blocks per processor. Matmult gets almost perfect speedup because there is no synchronization or producer-consumer sharing in the inner loop of the matrix multiply. On 48 processors the prototype delivers 363 double-precision MFLOPS.

---

[4] From Table 8-8 through Table 8-11, synchronization overhead can be estimated by the percent of time spent accessing synchronization variables since all of these accesses go to the bus. Conservatively, the synchronization overhead for the uniprocessor runs is given by Local Access Time · (% sync read + sync write) / Time between bus accesses. For the Water application this overhead is given as 30 · (17.6% + 17.4%) / 686.6 = 1.53%. Likewise for Barnes-Hut, MP3D, and PSIM4, the overheads are 0.22%, 0.22%, and 0.61%, respectively.

[5] Special thanks to J. P. Singh, Ed Rothberg, Andrew Erlichson, Jason Nieh, and Dave Ofelt for providing the applications and measurement data reported in this section.

[6] Machine runs of the PTHOR application were not available.

TABLE 8-7

Characteristics of Applications Run on the DASH Prototype

APPLICATION	INPUT DATA SET	UNIPROCESSOR RUN-TIME	MEASURED PORTION OF CODE
MP3D	40K molecules, test geom, (3,360 cells), 300 time steps	10 minutes	Full
Water	1,728 molecules, 45 time steps	3 hours	Full
LocusRoute	Primary2 (25.8K wiring cells, 3,817 wires)	190 seconds	Parallel
Cholesky	BCSSTK33 data set, 2.54 M nonzero elements	3.6 minutes	Parallel
Barnes-Hut	2 galaxies with 16,384 bodies ea., 30 time steps	3.2 hours	Full
FMM	2 galaxies with 16,384 bodies ea., 30 time steps	3.8 hours	Full
PSIM4	417K molecules, attack geom, (147K cells), 600 time steps	2.2 hours	Full
Radiosity	364 surface patches -> 100K final patches	10 minutes	Parallel
VolRend	$256 \times 256 \times 113$ tomography data set	22.2 sec	One rendered frame
Matrix Multiply	1056×1056 DP matrix	5 minutes	Parallel

The second application is VolRend, from the domain of computer graphics. It performs volume rendering for a $256 \times 256 \times 113$ computer tomography data set. Rendering is performed by ray tracing, casting one ray per pixel. An octree combined with early ray termination is used to reduce rendering time. VolRend is intended to be an interactive application. There is a fixed, large initialization overhead, which can be amortized over an arbitrary number of frames. Since the intention of VolRend is to allow real-time rendering and viewing of an image, we time a single frame in its entirety (including rendering and copying the image to the frame buffer). VolRend achieved a speedup of over 45 on 48 processors for this frame. With 48 processors, DASH renders this image at approximately 2 frames per second.

The next application is the FMM code [SHT+92], which represents an *N*-body galactic simulation solved using the fast multipole method. The input consists of two Plummer model clustered galaxies with 16,384 bodies each. The structure of the application and its data is complex. However, we see that caches work quite well, and we get a speedup of over 40 with 48 processors.

Immediately below is the Water code, the molecular dynamics code studied in Chapter 2. It was run with 1,728 water molecules and 45 time steps. We will discuss this application in detail later in this section.

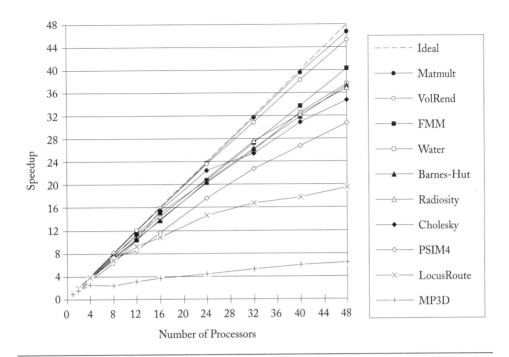

FIGURE 8-4   *Speedup of Parallel Applications Run on the DASH Prototype.*

The next application, Barnes-Hut, was also studied earlier. The input data set consists of the same two Plummer model clustered galaxies used for FMM. Again, although the structure of the program is complex, good speedups are obtained. We will discuss Barnes-Hut in detail later.

Below it is Radiosity [SHT+92], from the domain of computer graphics. It computes the global illumination in a room given a set of surface patches and light sources using a variation of hierarchical *N*-body techniques. The particular problem instance solved starts with 364 surface patches, and ends with over 10,000 patches. Radiosity has a serial initialization portion consisting primarily of generating a large array of random numbers. We do not time the initialization because, although it could be parallelized, it has not been in the current version. Radiosity achieves a speedup of 37 on 48 processors.

The next application is Cholesky factorization, as studied in Chapter 2. Here it is used to solve the BCSSTK33 problem from the Boeing-Harwell benchmark set, which contains 2.54 million nonzero matrix elements. The Cholesky numbers give speedups for the most important and most time-consuming phase of the computation, the numerical factorization. Run-times for pre- and postprocessing phases are not included because these phases have not yet been parallelized. As before, the fall off in speedup for Cholesky is due to the trade-off between large data block sizes (which increase processor efficiency, but decrease available concurrency and cause load-balancing problems) and small data block sizes. As we go to a large number of processors, we are forced to use smaller block sizes unless the problem size is scaled to unreasonably large sizes. With 48 processors, Cholesky achieves 190 MFLOPS.

Next, PSIM4, an application from NASA, is a particle-based simulator of a wind tunnel. PSIM4 is an enhanced version of the MP3D code, both in functionality and locality of memory accesses. The PSIM4 runs are done with over 415,000 particles and achieve over 32 times speedup on 48 processors. In contrast, the older MP3D code achieves a speedup of under 7 with 48 processors simulating 40,000 particles. We discuss both PSIM4 and MP3D in detail later in this section. Finally, as stated in Chapter 2, the LocusRoute application does global routing of standard cells using routed area to evaluate the quality of a given placement. LocusRoute was run over a circuit consisting of 3,817 wires and 20 routing channels. We ignore the serial initialization portion of LocusRoute, timing only the parallel routing. The serial initialization in LocusRoute consists of two portions: the reading of the design input file, and the data structure initialization. LocusRoute is intended to be the routing phase of a CAD tool, and the design would already be resident in memory.

Overall, we see that most applications achieve good speedups, even though they have not been specially optimized for DASH. More than half the applications get over 36 times improvement on 48 processors, and two of the applications get near-linear improvement.

8.2.3 Detailed Case Studies

To get a better understanding of the detailed reference behavior of these applications, we now examine the Water, Barnes-Hut, MP3D, and PSIM4 applications in more detail. These applications were chosen because they represent programs that achieved a range of good and bad speedups. Results are presented for only the parallel portions of the applications (with the exception of the speedup numbers). Statistics were ignored during the sequential initialization portion to avoid lowering the bus and network utilization.

8.2.3.1 Water

Water is a molecular dynamics code from the field of computational chemistry. The application computes the interaction between a set of water molecules over a series of time steps. For the problem size that we consider here, 1,728 molecules, the algorithm is essentially $O(N^2)$ in that each molecule interacts with all other molecules in the system. As shown in Figure 8-4, the Water application achieves good speedup on the DASH hardware.

Table 8-8 gives a detailed memory reference profile of Water running on DASH as measured by the hardware performance monitor.[7] Table 8-8 is broken into six sections: 1) overall performance and processor utilization; 2) memory request distribution; 3) issued memory request locality; 4) locality of satisfying memory references; 5) memory latency characteristics; and 6) bus and network utilization.

The first section of the table gives overall speedups and estimated processor utilizations. Unfortunately, processor utilization cannot be directly measured from the bus, so what is given is an estimate of useful processor busy time. What is actually measured is the time between processor references to the bus, and the overall time a processor waits on memory (i.e., processor memory stall time percentage). The estimated breakdown between useful

---

[7] The results given in the table are averaged over all active clusters. This implies some inaccuracies for the one- and two-processor runs due to the overhead of the idle processors running the UNIX scheduler and daemons.

TABLE 8-8

Water Memory Access Characteristics

EXECUTION ATTRIBUTE	1 PE	2 PEs	4 PEs	8 PEs	12 PEs	16 PEs	24 PEs	32 PEs	40 PEs	48 PEs
Speedup	1.00	1.98	3.85	7.13	10.42	13.95	20.27	26.05	32.58	37.57
Busy pclks between proc. stalls	686.6	620.1	486.2	425.2	432.2	453.3	412.8	440.8	442.0	428.8
Est. processor busy time (%)	96.5	95.5	92.9	86.0	83.8	84.1	81.5	78.6	78.6	75.5
Processor memory stall time (%)	3.5	3.8	4.2	8.5	9.1	10.4	11.8	12.7	12.7	13.1
Est. sync/redundant stall time (%)	0.0	0.7	2.9	5.5	7.1	5.5	6.7	8.7	8.7	11.4
Cache read (%)	60.9	67.9	62.6	60.7	58.0	54.7	58.4	56.2	58.1	58.9
Cache read exclusive (%)	3.9	2.8	15.6	20.9	23.9	25.3	23.8	24.9	24.0	23.5
Cache lock (%)	17.6	14.6	10.8	9.2	9.1	10.0	9.0	9.5	9.0	8.9
Cache unlock (%)	17.4	14.6	10.8	9.2	9.0	10.0	8.9	9.4	8.9	8.7
References to local memory (%)	99.9	99.6	99.9	56.0	37.1	29.0	20.5	16.5	12.6	11.3
References to remote memory (%)	0.1	0.4	0.1	44.0	62.9	71.0	79.5	83.5	87.4	88.7
Local refs satisfied locally (%)	98.2	99.1	99.7	52.5	33.5	24.4	17.1	13.4	10.1	8.8
Local refs satisfied dirty-rem (%)	1.7	0.6	0.2	3.5	3.6	4.6	3.4	3.1	2.5	2.5
Remote refs satisfied locally (%)	0.1	0.1	0.0	21.7	35.0	34.1	39.8	36.2	40.2	41.9
Remote refs satisfied in home (%)	0.0	0.3	0.0	20.8	26.2	32.8	34.5	38.4	37.8	37.7
Rem. refs satisfied dirty-rem (%)	0.0	0.0	0.0	1.4	1.7	4.1	5.1	8.9	9.4	9.1
Measured local cache fill (pclks)	29.2	29.2	29.5	29.6	29.7	29.7	29.8	29.8	29.8	29.8
Unloaded remote cache fill (pclks)	101.0	101.0	101.0	103.3	104.9	109.5	111.5	116.5	117.4	116.9
Measured remote cache fill (pclks)	112.8	109.9	112.0	107.5	111.3	116.1	119.6	125.5	127.8	128.3
Bus utilization (%)	4.9	6.9	11.9	16.1	16.7	17.7	19.1	19.8	19.6	19.8
Req. net bisection util. (%)	0.6	0.8	0.8	1.6	1.9	4.6	5.4	6.4	6.5	6.5
Reply net bisection util. (%)	0.5	0.7	0.7	2.0	2.2	5.2	5.8	6.4	6.3	6.4

processor busy time and synchronization and redundant parallel overhead is computed by looking at the measured speedup compared with the known difference between the single and multiple processor memory stall times. Thus, for N processors, the processor busy time and synchronization time are given by

$$\text{ProcBusy}(N) = \frac{\text{SpeedUp}(N)}{N}\text{ProcBusy}(1) \qquad \textbf{(8.2)}$$

$$\text{SyncTime}(N) = 1 - \text{ProcBusy}(N) - \text{MemTime}(N) \qquad \textbf{(8.3)}$$

and $\text{ProcBusy}(1) = 1 - \text{MemTime}(1)$ (i.e., $\text{SyncTime}(1) = 0$). This calculation method over-estimates synchronization overhead because it does not take additional causes of non-bus-related processor stalls (e.g., first to second cache misses, invalidation stalls, and extra TLB misses) into account. Further, the modeling method can only approximate the memory stall time due to processor write misses since these misses only indirectly stall the processor.[8]

For Water, cache locality is very high, and the time between processor stalls indicates that Water is not highly sensitive to memory latency. The table shows a reduction in the busy clocks between stalls as the number of processors increases from two to four processors, but this levels off afterwards. The application computes the forces on molecules one at a time and incurs misses only between force computations. The amount of work done for each force computation is essentially independent of the number of processors, which explains why the number of busy clocks between stalls does not continue to decrease.

The second section of Table 8-8 gives a breakdown on the memory reference types. This breakdown indicates the type of accesses that cause bus transactions and whether synchronization references are significant. In Water, the percentage of synchronization references is fairly high—in part because of the high cache hit rates, and in part because every successful lock acquire and release references the bus in the prototype. Given the percentage of locks and unlocks are very close, this data also indicates that lock contention is not a severe problem in Water.

The third section of Table 8-8 gives a breakdown of the locality of references issued by the processors. As expected, since the Water application has its shared data allocated in a round-robin fashion, reference locality drops off as the inverse of the number of active clusters.

The next section of Table 8-8 gives the breakdown of where cache misses are actually satisfied. The first two lines show the percentage of local references that are satisfied locally or in some remote dirty cluster. The third line shows the percentage of remote references (based on physical address) that are satisfied locally. A remote reference may be satisfied locally if another processor's cache contains that data (using a cache-to-cache transfer) or if the RAC contains that data. The fourth line in this section shows the fraction of remote ref-

---

[8] Since writes are buffered, they are not assumed to stall the processor directly. Instead, it is assumed that the processor can execute for 20 clocks before stalling. This delay is an estimate of the time for the processor to fill the other three words to the write buffer (i.e., assuming 15% of instructions are writes). In reality, the processor may not issue writes at this rate, or it may stall earlier because of a first-level cache miss.

erences satisfied by the home cluster. The last line indicates those remote references that must be forwarded to a third cluster that has the block dirty.

As can be seen from Table 8-8, the Water application does not use any specific memory placement strategy. However, nearly 50% of remote references are satisfied locally for the multiple-cluster runs. This good cluster locality results because each processor evaluates its molecules with respect to half of all the molecules. Thus, some fraction of these will be owned by the other processors within this cluster. More importantly, most of the remote molecules used by a given processor are also needed by the other processors in this cluster. Thus, if the processors stay in relative sync, then only one of the processors will fetch from the remote owning processor, and the others can share a read-only copy locally with the processor that received the remote copy.

The fifth section of Table 8-8 shows the latencies for remote and local cache read fills. The loaded latencies are measured directly by the performance monitor. The unloaded latencies are calculated by multiplying the measured ratios of remote references satisfied in the home and dirty-remote clusters by the average latencies given in Section 8.1.3. The remote reference latency figures indicate that Water does not heavily load the system; there is very little queuing. For 48 processors, less than 12 extra cycles are added due to queuing delays.

The final section of the table also shows that the memory system is not heavily loaded. With the low reference rate, both the bus and the request and reply networks have a low utilization. Bus utilization was measured directly by the performance monitor, while the network bisection utilizations were estimated assuming uniform network traffic. The bisection utilization is calculated by knowing the total number of network messages sent, assuming that half of the messages cross the midline of the mesh, and dividing by the bandwidth provided across the bisection. For Water, the bisection load is negligible.

8.2.3.2 Barnes-Hut

Barnes-Hut is a galactic N-body simulation solved using the hierarchical Barnes-Hut algorithm. The input for the runs in Table 8-9 consists of two Plummer model clustered galaxies with 16,384 bodies each.

Barnes-Hut achieves a respectable 37.2 speedup on 48 processors. The processor utilization remains essentially constant as more processors are added up to 48 processors. Excellent cache locality is achieved despite the nonuniform and dynamically changing problem domain, because the nature of the tree traversals ensures that most of the interactions computed are between bodies in the same processor's clusters, which keeps the ratio of remote references satisfied by a local processor cache high.

8.2.3.3 MP3D

The MP3D application is a particle-based wind-tunnel simulator developed at NASA-Ames. The results reported in Figure 8-4 correspond to a run with 40,000 particles and 300 time steps. The speedups are poor for MP3D because of frequent sharing of data that is actively being updated. While the particles are statically allocated to processors, the space cells (representing physical space in the wind tunnel) are referenced in a relatively random manner depending on the location of the particle being moved. Since each move operation also updates the corresponding space cell, as the number of processors increases, it becomes

TABLE 8-9

Barnes-Hut Memory Access Characteristics

EXECUTION ATTRIBUTE	1 PE	2 PEs	4 PEs	8 PEs	12 PEs	16 PEs	24 PEs	32 PEs	40 PEs	48 PEs
Speedup	1.00	1.96	3.81	7.29	10.59	13.82	20.42	26.33	31.84	37.24
Busy pclks between proc. stalls	528.9	519.8	514.1	468.8	528.4	529.0	510.4	545.4	562.5	638.9
Est. processor busy time (%)	94.7	92.8	90.2	86.3	83.6	81.8	80.6	77.9	75.4	73.5
Processor memory stall time (%)	5.3	5.4	5.3	7.1	7.2	7.4	8.0	7.8	7.6	6.9
Est. sync/redundant stall time (%)	0.0	1.8	4.5	6.6	9.2	10.8	11.4	14.3	17.0	19.6
Cache read (%)	91.8	93.8	95.3	94.3	93.6	93.4	93.6	92.7	92.5	91.7
Cache read exclusive (%)	4.2	3.9	3.3	4.4	5.0	5.1	4.8	5.4	5.5	6.0
Cache lock (%)	2.0	1.1	0.7	0.7	0.8	0.8	0.9	1.1	1.2	1.4
Cache unlock (%)	1.9	1.1	0.7	0.6	0.7	0.7	0.5	0.6	0.6	0.7
References to local memory (%)	99.1	90.5	99.5	50.5	33.6	25.7	17.6	12.7	10.6	8.7
References to remote memory (%)	0.9	9.5	0.5	49.5	66.4	74.3	82.4	87.3	89.4	91.3
Local refs satisfied locally (%)	97.8	89.9	99.3	50.2	33.4	25.4	17.5	12.6	10.5	8.5
Local refs satisfied dirty-rem (%)	1.3	0.5	0.2	0.2	0.2	0.2	0.1	0.2	0.1	0.1
Remote refs satisfied locally (%)	0.4	8.3	0.3	39.7	50.6	57.6	63.9	67.8	69.1	70.1
Remote refs satisfied in home (%)	0.5	1.2	0.2	8.4	14.6	15.7	17.6	18.6	19.5	20.2
Rem. refs satisfied dirty-rem (%)	0.0	0.0	0.0	1.5	1.2	1.0	0.8	0.8	0.8	1.0
Measured local cache fill (pclks)	29.2	29.2	29.4	29.4	29.4	29.4	29.4	29.4	29.4	29.4
Unloaded remote cache fill (pclks)	101.0	101.0	101.0	103.9	102.6	102.4	102.1	102.2	102.2	102.5
Measured remote cache fill (pclks)	111.8	110.3	111.3	107.5	109.8	113.1	114.7	118.0	118.8	122.2
Bus utilization (%)	5.2	6.9	10.1	11.5	11.1	11.2	11.5	11.1	11.0	10.2
Req. net bisection util. (%)	0.6	0.6	0.6	0.8	0.8	1.7	1.7	1.8	1.8	1.7
Reply net bisection util. (%)	0.5	0.5	0.5	0.9	1.1	2.2	2.4	2.3	2.3	2.2

more and more likely that the space cell being referenced will be in remote-dirty state. Thus, as shown in Table 8-10, cache hit rates fall (see busy clocks between processor stalls) and the average miss latencies go up.

The high miss rates together with low locality are the primary cause for the performance decrease that occurs when going from 4 to 8 processors. When all of the processors are within the same cluster, the miss latencies are 30 processor clocks. As soon as we go to two clusters (8 processors), there is a 50% chance that a space cell miss will be handled by a remote cluster, which takes over 100 clock cycles. Since the miss rates are high in MP3D, these larger miss latencies nullify the benefits of the extra processors. (As can be seen from Table 8-10, when we go to two clusters, the fraction of references to local memory goes down from 100% to 46%, and even the fraction of local references that are satisfied locally goes down from 100% to 79%.) Speedup when going from 8 to 12 processors is also poor because there is now a good possibility that a space cell cache miss will be satisfied by a dirty-remote cluster (132 versus 100 clock unloaded latency). Table 8-8 shows this is occurring; 11% (= 7.8/(13.4 + 49.6 + 7.8)) of remote references for the 12-processor run are satisfied by a dirty-remote cluster. Thus, processor utilization falls further when going from 8 to 12 processors, and speedup is poor. Interestingly enough, however, the busy time between processor stalls actually increases as more processors are added—not because the application is performing better, but because of load-balancing problems. The processors spend more time spinning in their cache, waiting on barriers, as shown in the synchronization overhead time.

Looking at Table 8-10, it is also clear that MP3D puts a heavy load on the memory system. The load on the cluster bus is very high (up to 79%) when multiple clusters are used. The load on the network is not nearly as high (up to 33%). This heavy memory system load results in large queuing delays for remote references, increasing the latency by up to 63% for the 48-processor run (while the unloaded remote reference latency should have been 125 cycles, the measured remote latency was 202 cycles). The heavy memory load also increases the amount of internal memory stalls in MP3D, meaning that the ratio of memory stall time and synchronization stall time should be more heavily weighted toward memory stalls. Having less synchronization overhead would also match the simulation results of Chapter 2 more closely.

The utilization data confirms the calculations made in Section 8.1.1 that showed that if loading is uniform, the cluster bus in the prototype limits memory system bandwidth more than the network. The high bus utilization also indicates that, in the prototype, latency hiding techniques such as prefetching will not help applications like MP3D. A better solution is to restructure the application to achieve better locality of the space cells by not strictly tying particles to processors. This restructured MP3D is called PSIM4, and from Figure 8-4 we can see that this time the speedups are significantly better (more than 30-fold with 48 processors). PSIM4 provides a good example of how a poorly performing application can be restructured to achieve much better performance on DASH, and we discuss it next.

8.2.3.4 PSIM4
PSIM4 [McD91] is an enhanced version of the MP3D code, both in terms of functionality and in terms of locality of memory accesses. The enhanced functionality includes modeling

TABLE 8-10

MP3D Memory Access Characteristics

EXECUTION ATTRIBUTE	1 PE	2 PEs	4 PEs	8 PEs	12 PEs	16 PEs	24 PEs	32 PEs	40 PEs	48 PEs
Speedup	1.00	1.60	2.48	2.33	3.12	3.74	4.42	5.27	5.99	6.42
Busy pclks between proc. stalls	82.5	46.1	43.6	44.2	38.6	49.7	56.0	58.9	61.5	84.5
Est. processor busy time (%)	73.8	59.0	45.8	21.5	19.2	17.3	13.6	12.2	11.1	9.9
Processor memory stall time (%)	26.2	32.5	38.0	65.4	75.2	72.8	73.5	73.8	73.6	67.9
Est. sync/redundant stall time (%)	0.0	8.5	16.2	13.1	5.6	9.9	12.9	14.0	15.3	22.2
Cache read (%)	98.3	72.9	67.5	57.7	56.9	54.0	51.8	52.2	53.4	51.6
Cache read exclusive (%)	0.9	26.9	32.2	42.0	42.7	45.5	47.3	46.6	45.2	46.3
Cache lock (%)	0.3	0.1	0.0	0.0	0.2	0.3	0.5	0.8	1.0	1.5
Cache unlock (%)	0.3	0.1	0.0	0.0	0.0	0.0	0.0	0.0	0.0	0.0
References to local memory (%)	100.0	100.0	100.0	46.5	29.3	23.0	16.0	11.6	8.9	8.4
References to remote memory (%)	0.0	0.0	0.0	53.5	70.7	77.0	84.0	88.4	91.1	91.6
Local refs satisfied locally (%)	99.8	99.9	99.9	36.9	21.9	15.6	10.0	7.3	5.9	5.0
Local refs satisfied dirty-rem (%)	0.2	0.1	0.0	9.6	7.4	7.4	6.0	4.2	3.0	3.4
Remote refs satisfied locally (%)	0.0	0.0	0.0	16.5	13.4	13.2	10.8	8.8	7.4	9.5
Remote refs satisfied in home (%)	0.0	0.0	0.0	36.6	49.6	48.8	49.3	54.0	59.3	48.3
Rem. refs satisfied dirty-rem (%)	0.0	0.0	0.0	0.4	7.8	15.0	23.9	25.6	24.3	33.8
Measured local cache fill (pclks)	29.4	30.8	37.0	37.2	38.1	36.6	36.0	35.7	35.2	34.1
Unloaded remote cache fill (pclks)	101.0	101.0	101.0	101.3	108.6	114.7	120.3	119.8	117.5	124.6
Measured remote cache fill (pclks)	109.5	117.5	130.4	138.7	160.9	172.2	186.8	191.3	192.7	201.6
Bus utilization (%)	16.6	42.9	78.6	77.3	78.6	73.6	71.0	69.6	67.6	62.2
Req. net bisection util. (%)	0.5	0.6	0.9	10.7	15.0	30.6	32.5	33.1	32.5	30.6
Reply net bisection util. (%)	0.4	0.5	0.9	13.7	15.6	30.1	29.6	29.3	28.7	26.3

multiple types of gases and including molecular chemistry. To improve locality, PSIM4 uses spatial decomposition of simulated space to distribute work among processors. Thus, both particles and the space cells in a large spatial chunk are assigned to the same processor, and the data are allocated from the corresponding local memory.

Although the results of PSIM4 are not directly comparable with MP3D (PSIM4 models the wind tunnel much more accurately and is solving a more realistic problem than MP3D), we can see from Table 8-11 that the spatial decomposition of PSIM4 works quite well.

There are a few interesting points to note in the reference locality of PSIM4. The first is that given the size of the data set simulated, runs that should occur in a single cluster actually do have remote accesses. Given the local-to-remote ratio of 78% to 22% for the uniprocessor, one can estimate the execution time reduction that would have occurred if all memory was local:

$$\frac{\text{UniExecTime (Local)}}{\text{MeasuredExecTime}} = \frac{166.5 + 29.2}{166.5 + 78\% \cdot 29.2 + 22\% \cdot 104.3} = 92\% \qquad \textbf{(8.4)}$$

This result implies that the speedups for the multicluster cases would be 92% of the measured speedups (e.g., speedup on 40 processors would be 28.4 instead of 30.76) if the uniprocessor case had all local memory. Another interesting reference statistic shown in Table 8-11 is that the fraction of local references stays relatively constant at 70% regardless of the number of clusters involved. This is because PSIM4 does intelligent page allocation, which attempts to keep the shared data owned by a given processor in the same cluster as that processor.

Together with the added locality, PSIM4 also benefits from a longer time between processor misses than MP3D, mainly because of improved cache usage (some gains occur from performing more computation per particle to model the different molecule types and chemistry). The improved cache and memory locality results in very good speedups. The 48-processor run achieves a speedup of around 30, in contrast to the speedup of 6.4 for 48 processors for the old MP3D code.

8.2.4   Application Speedup Summary

Overall, a number of conclusions can be drawn from the speedup and reference statistics presented in the previous sections. First, it is possible to get near-linear speedup on DASH with a number of real applications. Applications with the best speedup have good cache locality, but even those with moderate miss rates (e.g., PSIM4) can achieve reasonable speedup.

In absolute terms, the measurements confirm the results from Chapter 2 that caching shared data improves performance significantly. Table 8-12 summarizes this result for the three applications studied in depth here and also used in Chapter 2. At the top of this table, we compare the measured number of clocks between cache misses[9] to the shared-variable reference rates given in Table 2-2 to estimate the hit rate for shared variables. Using the reference rates provided in Table 2-2, we also estimate processor utilization if caching shared variables was not allowed. We also assume here the same locality and memory latencies measured on the prototype.

---

[9] Assuming all cache misses are for shared data. Actually some of the misses are for private data.

TABLE 8-11

PSIM4 Memory Access Characteristics

EXECUTION ATTRIBUTE	1 PE	2 PEs	4 PEs	8 PEs	12 PEs	16 PEs	24 PEs	32 PEs	40 PEs	48 PEs
Speedup	1.00	1.53	3.47	7.42	8.54	11.66	17.61	22.77	26.79	30.76
Busy pclks between proc. stalls	166.5	180.4	191.9	217.5	252.2	281.9	315.8	397.2	413.7	432.1
Est. processor busy time (%)	80.6	61.7	69.9	74.8	57.4	58.7	59.1	57.4	54.0	51.7
Processor memory stall time (%)	19.4	17.1	18.0	11.2	15.5	13.1	11.1	8.9	8.5	7.9
Est. sync/redundant stall time (%)	0.0	21.2	12.1	14.0	27.1	28.2	29.8	33.7	37.5	40.4
Cache read (%)	78.3	79.5	79.2	82.1	79.6	79.8	80.0	80.0	79.8	79.0
Cache read exclusive (%)	18.3	17.7	18.3	15.3	17.5	17.2	16.6	16.1	16.0	16.3
Cache lock (%)	1.7	1.4	1.2	1.3	1.6	1.6	1.8	2.1	2.4	2.7
Cache unlock (%)	1.7	1.4	1.2	1.3	1.3	1.4	1.5	1.7	1.8	2.0
References to local memory (%)	78.0	82.2	77.2	92.5	66.1	70.7	70.8	69.2	67.9	69.2
References to remote memory (%)	22.0	17.8	22.8	7.5	33.9	29.3	29.2	30.8	32.1	30.8
Local refs satisfied locally (%)	77.7	82.0	77.2	92.4	66.0	70.6	70.7	69.1	67.8	69.1
Local refs satisfied dirty-rem (%)	0.3	0.1	0.1	0.1	0.2	0.1	0.1	0.1	0.1	0.1
Remote refs satisfied locally (%)	0.2	0.3	0.2	3.6	8.3	7.2	10.9	13.7	15.8	15.8
Remote refs satisfied in home (%)	21.8	17.6	22.6	3.9	24.9	21.4	17.9	16.5	15.7	14.5
Rem. refs satisfied dirty-rem (%)	0.0	0.0	0.0	0.0	0.7	0.6	0.4	0.6	0.6	0.5
Measured local cache fill (pclks)	29.2	29.4	30.0	29.9	30.1	29.9	29.8	29.6	29.6	29.6
Unloaded remote cache fill (pclks)	101.0	101.0	101.0	101.0	101.8	101.9	101.8	102.5	102.9	102.9
Measured remote cache fill (pclks)	104.3	105.1	107.6	109.4	114.5	114.1	116.4	120.0	121.4	124.3
Bus utilization (%)	8.6	13.8	24.4	21.7	24.7	22.0	19.2	15.8	15.2	14.5
Req. net bisection util. (%)	0.1	0.2	0.4	0.4	2.6	4.1	3.0	2.2	2.1	1.9
Reply net bisection util. (%)	0.0	0.0	0.0	0.5	3.0	4.6	3.2	2.4	2.2	2.0

TABLE 8-12

Effectiveness of Caching Shared-Memory Variables

	WATER	BARNES-HUT	MP3D
Clocks between shared accesses[a]	49.4	58.1	5.8
Measured busy pclks between proc. stalls	428.8	638.9	84.5
Estimate shared variable hit rate	88%	91%	93%
Percentage of accesses to local memory	11.3%	8.5%	8.4%
Average local fill time	29.8	29.4	34.1
Average remote fill time	128.3	102.5	201.6
Estimated uncached processor utilization[b]	29.7%	37.6%	3.0%
Estimated cached processor utilization	75.5%	73.5%	9.9%
Comparison with Chapter 2 simulations			
Uncached processor utilization	27.1%	26.9%	5.2%
Cached processor util. with infinite caches	75.0%	70.6%	25.1%
Cached processor util. with scaled caches	66.6%	60.0%	20.5%

[a] As given in Table 2-2: the total number of cycles divided by the number of shared reads and writes.
[b] Estimated as $1 / (1 + ClocksBetweenSharedAccess/AverageFillTime)$.

Comparing the uncached processor utilization estimates with that measured on the proto-type indicates that caching improves performance by a factor of two to three.

Overall, this result implies that adding a scalable cache coherence mechanism improves performance much more than its 10% cost calculated in Chapter 7. As shown at the bottom of Table 8-12, the measured results also correlate fairly well with the cached and uncached simulation results given in Chapter 2. Only MP3D shows a major discrepancy in processor utilization. This discrepancy results from the large queuing delays that are not modeled in the simulation studies of Chapter 2.

Another result from the hardware measurements is that even with cache coherence, locality is important. As shown by applications like MP3D, if locality is very low and the communication misses are high, speedup will be poor. However, for many applications (e.g., FMM, Barnes-Hut, VolRend, Water) the natural locality is enough so that very good speed-ups can be achieved without algorithmic or programming contortions. Even in applications where natural locality is limited, cache coherence allows the programmer to focus on the few critical data structures that are causing loss in performance, rather than having to explicitly manage (replicate and place) all data objects in the program.

Looking at the system resource usage, the applications confirm that bus bandwidth is the primary limitation to overall memory system bandwidth in the prototype. Even without latency hiding techniques, MP3D was able to drive the buses to over 70% utilization. The network bisection, however, had a much smaller loading (2–3 times less) and does not appear to be a major contributor to queuing. Finally, the loading on the request and reply networks appears to be well balanced.

8.3 Protocol Effectiveness

This section examines in detail how the protocol features and alternative memory operations provided in DASH improve system performance. Features of the base protocol optimizations are examined in the context of the parallel applications, while the alternative memory operations are studied with stand-alone atomic tests. The atomic tests allow the alternative operations to be studied in a more controlled environment where their effects can be easily decoupled from an application's ability to utilize the operation.

8.3.1 Base Protocol Features

While there are many facets of the base coherency protocol that could be examined in detail, this section focuses on three of the most important and novel aspects of the DASH protocol: request forwarding, cache-to-cache sharing, and the use of the remote access cache. The protocol optimizations are examined on the four parallel applications on which we have made performance monitor measurements: Water, Barnes-Hut, MP3D, and PSIM4. The results in this section were derived from the reference statistics captured using the hardware performance monitor together with the measured latency of operations given in Section 8.1.3. The impact of the various features is measured as the percent improvement in average remote latency seen by having the feature. While ideally one would measure the run-time with and without the feature, this is difficult since DASH does not allow these features to be selectively shut off. Measuring effect on average latency is meaningful in the sense that reducing latency is one of the primary goals of the memory system. An efficient protocol can make a significant improvement in effective latency without greatly affecting the costs of the system (unlike brute force techniques such as using more exotic technology).

8.3.1.1 Request Forwarding

Request forwarding in DASH refers to the protocol's ability to forward remote requests from the home cluster to a third cluster that currently caches the requested memory block, and for the third cluster to respond directly to the cluster that originated the request. Two important uses of forwarding in DASH are the forwarding of memory requests to a dirty-remote cluster, and the forwarding of invalidations to clusters sharing a memory block. In both of these cases, the incoming memory request generates new outgoing request(s), and the destination cluster(s) reply directly to the cluster that originated the request. The primary advantage of forwarding is that it reduces the latency of these requests (usually by one cluster/network transaction, which is approximately 1 microsecond without contention). Fowarding also reduces hardware complexity by eliminating the need to buffer information about pending requests in the home. The home directory controller reacts to a request based on the current state of the directory, and when necessary, forwards responsibility for the request to the remote cluster(s) that should be able to complete it. The disadvantage of forwarding is that it requires a mechanism to avoid network deadlock[10] and complicates recovery from network errors. Forwarding can also lead to performance loss when requests are

TABLE 8-13

Effectiveness of Dirty-Remote Forwarding

	WATER (%)	BARNES-HUT (%)	MP3D (%)	PSIM4 (%)
Percentage remote reads, dirty-rem	51.2	4.9	76.2	6.0
Success rate	100.0	93.1	98.7	99.7
Avg. rem. read fill reduction	11.7	1.0	10.7	1.6
Percentage remote read-ex's, dirty-rem	1.1	5.3	5.1	3.4
Success rate	99.1	99.4	82.6	92.7
Avg. rem. read-ex. fill reduction	0.3	1.3	0.2	0.7

TABLE 8-14

Performance of Invalidation Forwarding to Shared-Remote Clusters

	WATER (%)	BARNES-HUT (%)	MP3D (%)	PSIM4 (%)
Percentage read-exclusive to shared	76.4	15.5	84.2	1.5
Read-ex fill reduction	16.6	3.9	11.8	0.4

forwarded to dirty clusters that cannot satisfy the requests because of pending operations or changes in block ownership (retry penalty is approximately 3 microseconds).

Table 8-13 summarizes the effectiveness of forwarding cache reads and read-exclusives to dirty-remote clusters for the benchmark applications using 48 processors. The improvement if the forward is successful is assumed to be 1 microsecond, while a retry has a cost of 3 microseconds. With these assumptions, Water and MP3D experience an improvement of approximately 11% in read fill times. Barnes-Hut and PSIM4 rarely fetch data from a dirty-remote cluster so neither of these see a large improvement from forwarding. Read-exclusive requests rarely need forwarding to a remote dirty cluster, and thus they see little benefit (two clusters writing a cache line before reading it is usually the result of false sharing).

Table 8-14 details the effect of forwarding write invalidation requests to shared-remote clusters. When release consistency is used, this type of forwarding is not as critical as dirty-remote forwarding because the receipt of invalidation acknowledgments can be overlapped with processor execution. When processor consistency is used, however, a read-exclusive request is not satisfied until all invalidations are received. Thus, in this case, invalidation forwarding saves at least 1 microsecond per write to a shared-remote location (again, one net-

---

[10]Forwarding adds a dependency between the acceptance of incoming requests on the ability of the node to send outgoing requests. Without provisions to break this dependence, there could be deadlock resulting from buffer overflow of the PCPU's input FIFO that blocks a node's outgoing requests.

TABLE 8-15

Effectiveness of Local Cache-to-Cache Sharing

	WATER (%)	BARNES-HUT (%)	MP3D (%)	PSIM4 (%)
Rem. reads satisfied locally	24.9	46.0	10.5	11.6
Read fill reduction from snoop	14.4	24.9	6.5	5.7
Rem read-ex satisfied locally	0.04	0.66	0.70	1.41
Read-ex fill reduction from snoop	–3.2	–2.7	–1.3	–2.1
Rem. rd and rd-ex fill reduct.	9.9	23.3	2.9	4.3

work and cluster hop).[11] Forwarding of invalidations has a significant effect in Water and MP3D (> 11%), but is unimportant for Barnes-Hut and PSIM4, where writes to shared variables are infrequent.

8.3.1.2 Local Cache-to-Cache Sharing

As illustrated in Figure 8-2, all remote accesses are delayed in the originating cluster until the results of the local snoop are known. Performing this local snoop has the advantage that some remote cache and cache-lock requests are satisfied by a local cache-to-cache transfer and do not incur the latency of fetching the data from a remote home cluster. Of course, it has the disadvantage of increasing latency[12] for remote accesses not satisfied by a local transfer. Table 8-15 summarizes the measured gains from the local snoop on the 48-processor benchmark runs in terms of the percent improvement of remote memory latency. As with forwarding to dirty-remote clusters, reads benefit more than writes from the local sharing. The local snoop actually results in a performance loss for read-exclusive requests, but the overall effect is a decrease in remote latency because of local cache-to-cache sharing for read requests. This performance gain, together with the hardware simplifications that result from making all the network request generation timing the same (in local, home, and dirty-remote clusters), implies that local cache sharing was well worth supporting in the prototype.

8.3.1.3 Remote Access Cache

Another design feature in DASH is the implementation of the reply controller's pending request buffer as a direct-map snoopy cache (RAC). While the RAC structure serves many purposes (e.g., enforcement of release consistency), it has two direct performance benefits. First, by serving as an additional cluster cache, the RAC supports cache-to-cache sharing

---

[11] The data in Table 8-14 also estimates the gain from release consistency over processor consistency in the prototype since the gain from release consistency is to allow a write to retire as soon as ownership is returned, even if invalidations are pending. The savings from release consistency is 1 microsecond as in forwarding, but this is compared with a nominal delay of 3 microseconds instead of 4 microseconds in the case of invalidation forwarding (implying gains are approximately 1/3 larger).

[12] The local cache snoop adds 2–4 processor clocks in the prototype.

TABLE 8-16

Effectiveness of the RAC

	WATER	BARNES-HUT	MP3D	PSIM4
Rem. reads satisfied by RAC (%)	32.6	35.9	4.3	51.9
RAC read conflicts (%)	0.00	0.12	0.05	0.32
Avg. read conflict penalty (pclk)	45.2	21.4	51.9	23.1
Read fill reduction from RAC (%)	20.0	21.4	3.4	28.3
Rem. read-ex satisfied by RAC (%)	35.1	1.0	4.7	10.5
RAC read-ex conflicts (%)	0.51	0.11	0.01	0.00
Avg. read-ex conflict penalty (pclk)	18.8	18.8	56.5	0.0
Read-ex fill reduction from RAC (%)	23.2	0.8	4.1	8.2
Rem. rd and rd-ex fill reduction (%)	20.8	20.3	3.7	24.8
Rem. reads merged by RAC (%)	0.0	0.1	0.1	0.2
Avg. read merge fill time (pclk)	85.2	80.5	89.1	86.1
Read fill reduction from merging (%)	0.0	0.0	0.1	0.1
Rem. read-ex merged by RAC (%)	0.3	1.2	0.1	0.9
Avg. read-ex merge fill time (pclk)	45.2	18.8	51.9	23.1
Read-ex fill reduction from merging (%)	0.1	0.2	0.0	0.2
Rem. rd and rd-ex fill reduction (%)	0.0	0.0	0.0	0.1
Total rem. access fill reduction (%)	20.9	20.3	3.8	24.9

and a cluster-level dirty-sharing cache state. Second, by merging outstanding requests, the RAC reduces the average latency for remote locations, and it can reduce hot-spot traffic. The disadvantage of the RAC arises from its cache structure, which can cause conflicts for individual RAC entries. In these cases, the outstanding request must be satisfied before the new request can be initiated.

Table 8-16 provides a summary of the performance impact of the RAC. The effectiveness of the RAC as a cluster cache is somewhat overstated in the table because the RAC is given credit for all requests that could be satisfied by either a local processor cache or the RAC (because of limits in the performance monitor hardware). Thus, the improvements from the cache sharing listed in Table 8-15 are understated, and the savings given in the two tables can be added. The combined savings from the two types of cluster caching are significant. Cluster caches reduce the effective remote miss penalty by 6% in MP3D, by more than 20% in Water and PSIM4, and over 30% in Barnes-Hut. Merging of outstanding remote requests by the RAC has a much smaller impact on performance. Although a number of requests are merged, they do not significantly reduce the fill time of the merged requests because latencies are not dramatically reduced. Thus, any benefits from merging are made indirectly through a reduction in hot-spot traffic.

8.3.1.4 Summary of Base Protocol Features

Overall, our performance measurements indicate that latencies can be significantly reduced by the protocol optimizations. Read operations benefit more than write operations because most of the optimizations accelerate cache-to-cache transfers, and reads can be satisfied more often than writes by another cache (e.g., producer-consumer communication with the producer or sharing with another consumer). However, writes do benefit from the forwarding of invalidation acknowledges when not using a weak consistency model, and the RAC's support of the dirty-sharing state. Altogether, on the four programs studied in detail, the optimizations reduce remote read latency by 20.6–47.3% (37.4% average), and remote write latency by 3.3–36.9% (15.5% average).

Another interesting question is whether the improvements seen on the 48-processor prototype would scale to a larger system with hundreds of processors. The benefits of request forwarding would certainly scale since the fraction of forwarded requests is only dependent on the fraction of coherency misses satisfied by processors in remote clusters. As cluster count increases, the fraction of producers who are neither in the same cluster as the consumer nor the home should increase. The scaling of cache-to-cache sharing where the producing cache is local is more difficult to predict. Intuitively, given random processor communication, one would expect the effectiveness of intracluster cache-to-cache transfers to decline as the ratio of processors within the cluster to total processors decreases. However, in Tables 8-8 through 8-11, the percentage of remote references satisfied locally is relatively constant. While there are a number of factors that make sharing nonuniform, there are two that seem most important. First, neighbor-to-neighbor communication with a cluster structure implies that three of one's neighbors are usually within the same cluster. Second, even if the producer of data is not local, if the data is shared with a large number of consumers, then typically only one processor per cluster will have to fetch the data remotely. An example of this type of sharing is in the Water application. The molecule data produced at each time step is read by half of the processors in the next time step. Thus, the measured data indicates that the gains seen from the protocol optimizations will scale to larger systems.

8.3.2 Alternative Memory Operations

This section investigates the performance potential of the alternative memory operations such as prefetch, granting locks, Fetch&Op, and update writes. Although it would be desirable to present the effects of these operations on a variety of real benchmarks, such optimized benchmarks are not readily available. Furthermore, if only these results were given, it would be difficult to distinguish the performance potential of the operations from the particular application's ability to exploit them. Instead, this section quantifies the effectiveness of the alternative operations using small, atomic tests. These tests demonstrate how the operations would be commonly used and stress the individual operations heavily. In most cases, the results can be considered an upper bound on performance gain when using the operation in a real application. All of the atomic tests were run on the actual hardware, under a simple stand-alone multiprocessor monitor supplied with the SGI hardware.

8.3.2.1   Synchronization Operations

DASH provides four mechanisms for performing atomic read-modify-writes: uncached locks, invalidating locks, granting locks, and Fetch&Op. Uncached locks provide uncached test&set and clear operations, but spin waiting with uncached locks uses cluster and network resources. Invalidating locks are simple cached test&set locks. Unlocks, however, force waiting processors to rush for a contended lock when their cache copy is invalidated. Granting locks use the directory state to avoid needlessly invalidating all waiting processors when a lock is released. Instead, a *grant cluster* is chosen at random from one of the nodes caching (spinning on) the lock, and this cluster is allowed to acquire the lock with a local cluster operation. Thus, the granted lock reduces both traffic and latency when a contended lock is released. Fetch&Op operations perform noncombining Fetch&Increment or Fetch&Decrement on uncached memory locations. These operations can be very useful because they are serialized only by the access time of local memory. For all of these operations, the atomic synchronization update is done at memory because of limitations of the base SGI hardware. Although this precludes a processor from holding a lock in an exclusive state in its cache, which is ideal for locks with low contention and high processor affinity, memory updates are more efficient for the contended locks or locks with little processor affinity.

The test used to evaluate sychronization operations is the serialization time and network traffic when multiple processors update a simple counter variable. When using locks, the counter is kept in a cachable memory and protected by a spin lock. When Fetch&Inc is used, the Fetch&Inc location is updated in memory and no mutual exclusion is necessary. The test was run with the lock and counter variable in a cluster that was remote to all contending processors. Keeping these variables remote gives results that are more indicative of a large system.

To reduce latency for the counter in the lock case, the cache line with the count variable is brought into the cache in an exclusive state by writing to another variable in the same cache line, which eliminates the need to fetch the memory block twice (first to get a shared copy of the block to read the current value, and then to refetch to get an exclusive copy for the update). Likewise, the cache line with the counter is flushed back to memory after the mutual exclusion region is unlocked to avoid having the next incrementer fetch the data from a dirty-remote cache. These optimizations reduce the serialization by about 1 microsecond over simply leaving the counter variable uncached or in the updating processor's cache.

Figure 8-5(a) shows the time for one counter update when running the lock test with 1 to 44 processors spread across 1 to 11 clusters. The uniprocessor results show minimum time for the processor to execute one iteration of the loop, which includes at least one remote memory fetch. The uncached lock case spins over the network waiting on the lock. Thus, as processors are added, the serialization actually decreases because the lock is sampled without waiting for an indication that the lock is free. When going from eight to twelve processors (two to three clusters), however, the advantage from sampling is lost because the excess memory traffic interferes with the execution of the critical section. For invalidating locks, latency is relatively constant except for the first increase when going from one to four processors. This increase results from the processor immediately acquiring the lock in the unipro-

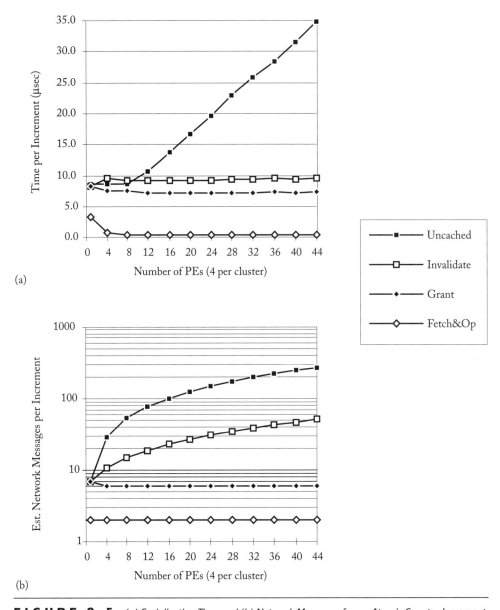

FIGURE 8-5 *(a) Serialization Time and (b) Network Messages for an Atomic Counter Increment.*

cessor case, while receiving a locked copy of the lock from a locally spinning processor and waiting for a cache invalidation in the multiprocessor case. In contrast, the serialization of a granted lock decreases when going between one to four processors because the lock grant takes place in parallel with the counter flush in the four-processor case, while in the uniprocessor case, the processor is not ready to fetch the lock immediately after the unlock. For the Fetch&Inc case, serialization is low and throughput constantly increases. For the uniprocessor case, throughput is limited by the latency to remote memory. When using a single cluster, the requesting cluster's bus limits throughput. Above the three clusters, throughput approaches the reply network outbound serialization limit in the home cluster.

Looking at Figure 8-5, Fetch&Inc is obviously the best when it is applicable. For the more general case, the granting lock offers approximately 33% less latency for an unlock/lock pair than the invalidating unlock. Furthermore, one important feature not revealed directly by this test is the decrease in traffic when using granting locks. As shown in Figure 8-5(b), the amount of traffic per counter increment grows with the number of processors when using uncached or invalidating locks,[13] but is constant for granting locks and Fetch&Ops. Whether these latency or traffic reduction gains are important depends upon the frequency of synchronization and the amount of lock contention, but most applications will be adversely affected by added synchronization overhead or increased memory traffic.

8.3.2.2 Update Write

Update write operations allow the producer of data to communicate data to consuming processors without forcing the consuming processors to fetch the data from the producing processor's cache. Update writes are best suited to communicating small data items that the consumers have already cached because each word written, as opposed to each cache line, generates a separate set of coherence messages. Likewise, update writes only deliver data to processors that are caching the block at the time of the write.

A useful application for update writes is in implementing the release from a barrier synchronization. Figure 8-6 summarizes the timing of a single barrier while varying both the number of clusters (1 to 11) and number of processors per cluster (1 or 4). As in other tests, we assume that the variables for the barrier reside in a remote cluster. The implementation of the barrier uses a Fetch&Op variable to count the incoming processors, and a flag to release the waiting processors. In the case that the processors are all in one cluster, an invalidating write is actually superior to an update because the release flag becomes dirty in the local cluster. Beyond this degenerate case, however, update write reduces the barrier time by approximately 6 μsec or about 20–40%.[14] Update writes also reduce serialization and traffic for release notification because the update is serialized only by the network send time. In the invalidation case, the refetch of the release flag is serialized by the first reader causing the dirty release flag to be written back to memory, and then by the other clusters serializing on the outbound reply network port in the home.

The barrier test is also useful in illustrating the power of the Fetch&Op variables. Shown in Figure 8-7 is the time for the same barrier test when the Fetch&Op operations are replaced by a simple memory counter protected by a test&set lock (using simple invalidating unlocks). As expected from the atomic counter test (see Figure 8-5), without the Fetch&Op variables, per processor serialization is greatly increased. The benefit of the update write becomes lost in the large increase in the time to count the arrival of the processors at the bar-

---

[13]Actual traffic growth for uncached locks can be unbounded since there is traffic generated during the entire time the critical region is held. Figure 8-5(b) assumes these retries are limited to 3 per processor per iteration since each lock attempt takes approximately 3 microseconds and the critical region is held for approximately 9 microseconds.

[14]The 6 μsec difference comes from the savings of reading the release flag from a processor's second-level cache instead of the dirty-remote cache of the cluster that issued the write.

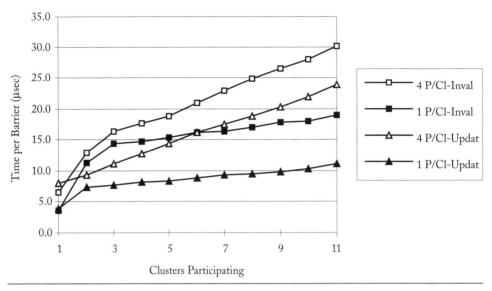

FIGURE 8-6 *Barrier Synchronization with Update Writes and Fetch&Op Variables.*

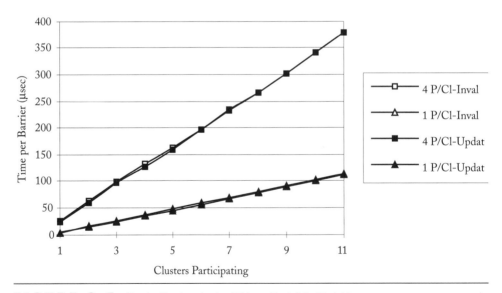

FIGURE 8-7 *Barrier Synchronization Without Fetch&Op Variables.*

rier. Comparing Figure 8-6 and Figure 8-7 makes clear that Fetch&Op variables are key to efficient barrier synchronization, and that without Fetch&Op, barriers with a large fan-in would require some form of software gather tree to count the synchronizing processors.

8.3.2.3   Prefetch Tests

DASH supports software-controlled nonbinding prefetch operations that can either bring data closer to the issuing processor or send data to a set of specified clusters. Consumer prefetch operations bring a shared or exclusive copy of the requested memory block closer to the issuing processor. Producer prefetch sends a shared copy of the given block to the set of remote clusters specified as an input operand to the operation. Prefetches are software-controlled since application software issues an explicit operation to prefetch a given memory block. They are nonbinding in the sense that they only move data between coherent caches (into the RAC on the prototype). Thus, prefetched blocks are always kept coherent, and the value of a location is only bound when an actual load operation is issued. Not binding the value of the prefetch is important because it allows the user or compiler to aggressively prefetch data without a conservative dependency analysis and without affecting the memory consistency model. Prefetch operations can increase the amount of computation-communication and communication-communication overlap substantially because they replace blocking cache load operations with nonblocking operations. This overlap is especially useful when accessing a large data set that does not fit into cache or when accessing data generated by another processor. In the prototype, the prefetch operations have the effect of converting the penalty of a remote cache miss to that of a local miss. Thus, throughput can theoretically be increased from one cache line every 101 processor clocks to one block every 29 clocks (an improvement of nearly 3.5 times).

The first atomic test used to stress prefetch operations uses a varying number of processors that read blocks (128 bytes or 8 cache lines) of data from remote memory. This test models a computation where at least one of the data structures is large and must always be fetched from memory. On each iteration, the processor picks a random remote cluster and reads a data block that is guaranteed to miss in the cache. When prefetching is enabled, the new block is prefetched while reading the previous block.

The results of the test are presented in Figure 8-8 when using 1 to 48 processors fetching data from any of the active clusters (i.e., ones with enabled processors). The results are given in terms of number of processor clocks per cache line read, and the total megabytes per second read by all the processors. The code to read a block includes approximately 20 instructions. This instruction count corresponds with the measured time for the loop,[15] which includes the 20 instructions plus one local (30 clock) or remote (100 clock) cache miss. Thus, prefetch results in a speedup of approximately 2.4 when the memory system is not saturated. As the number of processors increases beyond 12, the benefits of prefetching decrease because the memory system begins to saturate. In the prototype, the cluster buses saturate (as opposed to the mesh network bisection) because they are relatively slow (each cluster bus can sustain 20 MBytes/sec when doing remote references that require a total of three bus transactions per reference). Thus, on the prototype, bandwidth limits throughput to approximately one prefetch every 20 instructions/cluster.

---

[15]When using a small number of processors (1 to 12).

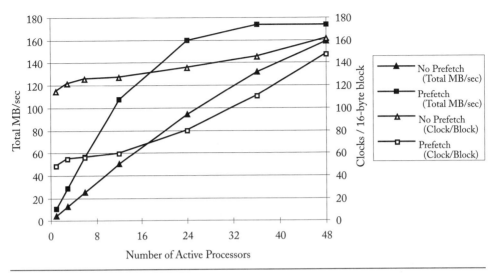

F I G U R E   8 - 8   *Effectiveness of Prefetch Operations When Doing Block Memory Reads.*

Another use of prefetch is in emulation of message-passing. To test the ability of prefetch to improve message-passing performance, a test was written to do simple one-way communications using a shared circular buffer. In the test, the sending processor checks for a free buffer in the message queue and, if available, writes a message into the buffer and increments the buffer full pointer. Similarly, the receiving processor polls the full pointer, reads each word of the message, and then increments the free buffer pointer. A large quantity of data is sent through the limited-size buffer, so throughput is determined by either the sender or receiver together with the latency to communicate that the message buffer has been filled or emptied.

Figure 8-9 shows the throughput (in MByte/sec) of running the message test with various optimizations and home clusters for the message queue. The test sends 64,000, 64-byte messages, using a queue capable of holding 32 messages. The first version of the test uses the normal invalidating protocol (with release consistency) and achieves a throughput of 2.2–2.6 MByte/sec. In this simple version, throughput is limited by the receiver who must fetch the data from the sending processor's cache. The first enhancement to the code uses writes with update coherence to store the incremented full and empty block pointers. This enhancement increases performance to 2.7–3.4 MByte/sec because the receiver can read the updated buffer pointer from its cache, not the remote processor's cache. The third version of the test uses consumer prefetch for both the sender and receiver. The receiver prefetches all four blocks of the message as soon as it is notified that they are available, and the producer prefetches buffers exclusively when they are freed. Prefetch improves performance by a factor of 1.8–2.1 to a rate of 4.6–4.8 MByte/sec. This improvement comes from converting the four remote misses to read the message to a single remote cache miss and three local misses (the miss time for these remote misses are pipelined with the miss time for the first block). In this test, using producer-prefetch instead of consumer prefetch would add little because

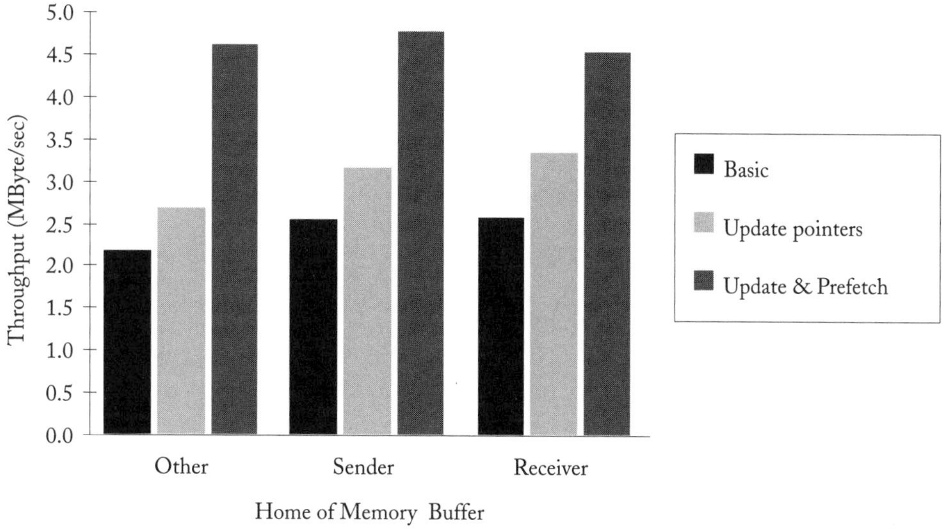

FIGURE 8-9 *Message-Passing Emulation Using Prefetch Operations.*

3/4 of the remote miss latency has already been hidden, and forcing the producer to send the data to the consumer, in addition to its other tasks, makes the sender the bottleneck.

As shown by these tests, prefetch can successfully overlap a significant amount of inter-processor communication delay. Furthermore, even when remote latency cannot be completely hidden, prefetch allows misses to be pipelined and greatly reduces the cost of communicating items that are larger than a single cache line. Overall, when memory bandwidth does not limit performance, we expect prefetch to be very useful in improving the performance of interprocessor communication.

8.4 Chapter Conclusions

In this chapter, the performance of the DASH architecture and prototype implementation have been characterized by the following:

1. The unloaded latencies and bandwidths for the individual memory system components and operations

2. The speedup of parallel applications and the corresponding reference characteristics that lead to these speedups

3. The effect of optimizations incorporated in the base coherence protocol

4. The performance of alternative memory operations as demonstrated by simple atomic tests

The most important latency metric given is the access time to various levels of the memory hierarchy. The access time ratios on the prototype are 1 : 15 : 29 : 101 : 132 for the first-level cache, second-level cache, local cluster memory, remote cluster memory, and dirty-remote cluster, respectively. These access time ratios are typical of what we expect for any large-scale system (e.g., see Section 9.3.1 in the next chapter). These ratios indicate the importance of cache locality (i.e., cache hit rates) and locality for memory in the same cluster as the processor. Because the access times beyond the caches are large, high processor utilization will only be achieved if cache hit rates are high, or nonblocking memory operations are used. Furthermore, since remote memory access times are large, it cannot be assumed that the shared-memory paradigm implies free interprocessor communication. Good application speedup on large-scale shared-memory systems still relies on managing the ratio of communication and computation.

Another important (and unfortunate) attribute of the prototype memory system is the relatively low bandwidth of the cluster bus, especially for remote accesses. In the prototype, cluster bandwidth limits total memory system bandwidth if uniform loading is assumed. This low throughput may limit the effectiveness of the latency hiding mechanisms if the memory bandwidth requirements of an application are high.

The performance of parallel applications on the DASH prototype is very encouraging. Without significant tuning for the prototype, over half the applications studied achieve over a 36-fold speedup on 48 processors. The harmonic mean of the speedup on 48 processors on nine of the applications (ignoring MP3D) was 34.4, and 23.9 when MP3D is included. As expected, the applications with high cache hit rates, or locality to the local cluster, achieve the best speedups. Since many applications in the scientific and engineering fields can either be blocked or exhibit natural locality in the problem domain, we expect many others of these types of applications to also perform well. In applications with substantial fine-grain sharing, however, speedup is limited by the costs of interprocessor communication. Latency hiding operations such as prefetch can be helpful in these situations, but the application must exhibit enough parallelism to hide the memory latency, and memory bandwidth must not be a limitation.

The reference behavior demonstrated by the parallel applications has many important implications. First, the performance improvement from caching shared data can be very significant. Second, although most parallel applications have a drop-off in performance when the first remote cluster is used, many exhibit a near-linear performance growth as more remote clusters are added. Since remote memory latency grows slowly as more clusters are added (50 ns per network hop, compared with 3,000 ns for any remote reference), these applications should continue to get good speedup as the system grows to 64 processors. Third, the reference statistics of the applications indicate that the protocol optimizations are quite effective. Forwarding requests to dirty clusters reduces remote latency an average of 6%, and forwarding invalidations for write requests reduced ownership latency by 8%. Likewise, cache-to-cache sharing within a cluster reduces the average latency for remote memory by 27%.

Finally, the atomic tests of the alternative memory operations indicate that some of these operations are well worth supporting. In particular, nonbinding prefetch can reduce effective memory latency by more than a factor of 2.5. The latency gains from granting locks are more modest, but the significant reduction in traffic may justify their inclusion. Likewise, the low serialization of noncombining Fetch&Op accesses can be very useful in implementing common operations such as distributed loops and barriers. Inclusion of similar operations (e.g., Compare&Swap), which can help coordinate processors without being serialized by the latency of memory, may also be warranted if they can be integrated well with the memory protocol.

PART 3

FUTURE TRENDS

CHAPTER

9

TeraDASH

The DASH prototype was developed to investigate the issues that arise in scalable single-address-space machines incorporating directory-based cache coherence. In general, the prototype is scalable and addresses the issues outlined in Chapter 4. Given the prototype's limited size and leverage of an existing cluster, however, some compromises were made in the design. This chapter describes a more ideal DASH system, TeraDASH, based on state-of-the-art technology and an optimized cluster design. It includes 2,048 processors and provides a peak execution rate exceeding one trillion operations per second. Although it exists only on paper, the TeraDASH design is realistic—its architecture and coherence protocol are extensions of the prototype, and its assumed technology is available today.

The first section of this chapter describes the TeraDASH system along with the assumed technology. The second section outlines the directory structure and protocol for TeraDASH and compares them with the DASH prototype. The third section develops a performance model of the system. The chapter concludes with a summary of the results and challenges raised by the preliminary design of TeraDASH.

9.1 TeraDASH System Organization

The system-level organization of TeraDASH is similar to the DASH prototype. The system includes 2,048 processors distributed in groups of four among 512 clusters. Each processor is assumed to be a superscalar microprocessor capable of simultaneously issuing one integer operation, one memory operation, one branch, and one floating point multiply-add per clock. The internal clock rate of the processors is 100 MHz. Thus, the 2,048 processors issuing 5 operations per clock at 100 MHz result in a peak operating rate of more than 1 Tera-OPS. Sustained operating rates would be significantly less than this figure, but should still be hundreds of GigaOPS. Memory and directories are distributed within the clusters, as in DASH. Each cluster contains 256 MByte of main memory, and the system as a whole contains 128 GByte of main memory. Clusters are connected in an $8 \times 8 \times 8$ torus grid that uses

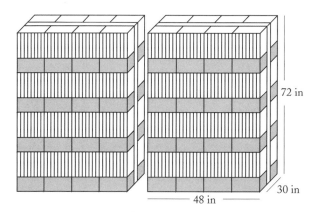

72 in

30 in

48 in

FIGURE 9-1 *TeraDASH System.*

virtual channels [Dal90a] to provide the function of the two independent mesh networks in the prototype.

Each cluster is implemented on a single printed circuit board measuring approximately $12'' \times 10''$. Eight such boards would contain one dimension of the mesh and could be conservatively packaged in a module measuring $16'' \times 12'' \times 12''$. The module size allows for a board-to-board spacing of $1.5''$ and a $6'' \times 12'' \times 12''$ section for cooling and power. Sixty-four such modules could be combined to form a full TeraDASH computation complex, possibly in the two-cabinet form shown in Figure 9-1. Each cluster also supports a high-speed I/O interface (e.g., Fiber Channel [Cum90]) that can provide a 100–1000 Mbit link to auxiliary cabinets containing disk arrays and high-speed network connections.

9.1.1 TeraDASH Cluster Structure

Key to the design of TeraDASH is the integration of a high-performance DASH cluster on a single printed circuit board. This board provides the modular building block from which a scalable system can be built with as few as 4 processors or as many as 2,048. The tight coupling within the cluster provides a controlled environment capable of supporting a high-speed cluster bus with a 10 ns cycle time and over 1 GByte/sec in bandwidth.

A block diagram of a cluster is shown in Figure 9-2. The cluster is based on eight VLSI chips together with a number of high-speed static and dynamic RAMs. Seven of the chips include a direct interface to the high-speed, split-transaction cluster bus. The cluster bus includes a 128-bit-wide multiplexed address and data bus. It also has separate control lines to allow pipelined bus arbitration. Every request transaction is tagged with a transaction identifier, allowing each processor to have 32 outstanding requests. The transaction ID also permits memory responses to return 32 bytes of data in two bus clocks without having a full-width address bus in parallel with the data bus. It is assumed that the processors operate synchronously with the 100 MHz bus clock (i.e., using phase-locked loops). The high-speed bus timing is achieved through small-swing signalling (e.g., GTL [GYN+92]), controlled bus loading (always seven loads and no connectors), and a relatively short length (less than 12 inches).

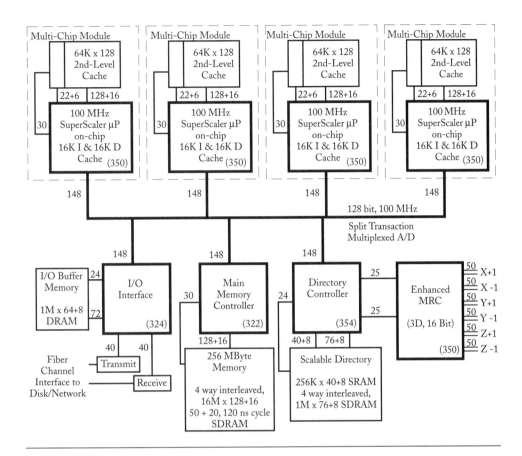

FIGURE 9-2 *TeraDASH Cluster Block Diagram.*

The processor chips are assumed to be superscalar processors capable of issuing four instructions per clock cycle to four different execution units (integer ALU, floating point ALU, memory port, and branch unit), which would be comparable to a 100 MHz PowerPC 601 [Moo93], or 200 MHz MIPS R4400 [Hei93] or Dec Alpha 21064 [Sit93]. The processors include first-level on-chip instruction and data caches, both 16 KByte. The processors directly control individual second-level, off-chip caches. The second-level cache is organized as $64K \times 16$ bytes, and is based on $64K \times 16$ pipelined SRAMs capable of accepting an address every 10 ns and supplying read data with a latency of 20 ns [Mot93]. Both caches use a 32-byte line size and a write-back protocol. The second-level caches are used to snoop on the bus as in the DASH prototype. The processor and the ten SRAMs are assumed to be packaged in a multichip module so that the second-level cache interface does not require external package pins. Alternatively, the SRAMs could be integrated on separate SIMMs. The second-level caches are protected by a SEC/DED error-correcting code.

The memory controller (MC) and directory controller (DC) chips are assumed to be built in semicustom technology since they require only moderate gate complexity and small RAM arrays. These two chips work together with the MC controlling the main memory array, and the DC controlling the directory array. The MC provides SEC/DED error correction on 256 MByte of dynamic memory. The MC communicates with four interleaved banks of SDRAM over separate address and data buses. Bank selection is based on low-order cache block address bits. Each bank interfaces to the 20 ns cycle address and data buses from the MC. Each interleave bank includes $4M \times 128$ of data plus $4M \times 16$ of ECC, and is built out of 2 SIMMs containing 18 SDRAM parts each. The SDRAMs are assumed to have an access time of 50 ns and a cycle time of 100 ns [Ng92, Vog94].

The DC controls a scalable directory structure and provides the cluster with an interface to the mesh intercluster network. The directory is based on a two-level SRAM and SDRAM structure that provides a four-way associative directory cache. The SRAM structure includes four tag and state entries that are accessed in parallel. The SRAM is organized as $256K \times 48$ and is built out of SIMMs containing two banks of three SRAMs of the same type as the second-level processor caches. The SRAM provides two low-order address bits for the SDRAM access. This structure permits the four-way associativity of the directory without the very wide interface needed to read four sets of pointers in parallel. The SDRAM portion of the directory is four-way interleaved in the same manner as main memory, but it is only 256K deep. Each directory bank is organized as $256K \times 84$ bits and is based on six $256K \times 16$ parts with the same timing specification as the main memory parts. Further details of the directory are provided in Section 9.1.4.

The DC chip also includes the network-to-bus and bus-to-network logic similar to the prototype's PCPU and RC logic. The number of RAM bits in the network FIFOs is reduced by decreasing the depth of the FIFOs from 1,024 words to 128 words. The RAM requirement for the RAC is greatly reduced because of the split-transaction bus and because the processor's second-level cache is assumed to take on most of the functions of the RAC, including support for prefetching and a dirty-sharing state. The processor caches are also responsible for maintaining the state of pending remote requests. RAC entries are only allocated when a reply is received that requires multiple (invalidation) acknowledgments, or in response to a lock grant. These functions could be implemented in a small, on-chip content-addressable memory (CAM) with approximately 64 entries.

9.1.2 Intracluster Operations

Cluster operations in TeraDASH are similar to those of the DASH prototype. The primary differences arise from the optimized processor bus interface and the split-transaction bus protocol.

The processor's second-level cache interface is assumed to be lockup-free [Kro81], allowing the processor to issue multiple, nonblocking operations and to maintain the state of these operations using transient cache states similar to the RAC states used in the prototype. For example, if a processor must acquire exclusive ownership of a cache block, the corresponding cache entry is updated with the new tag and a state indicating WRDX (waiting for read-exclusive). The write data is either kept in a write buffer or retired into the cache line. The processor is allowed to continue accessing the second-level cache as long as the entry with the pending miss does not need to be replaced. Accesses initiated by other processors to the same memory block can be merged with the outstanding access. Instead of occurring in

TABLE 9-1

TeraDASH Processor-Initiated Bus Operations

OPERATION	DESCRIPTION
Cache read	Normal and prefetch cache read
Cache read-exclusive	Normal and prefetch cache read-exclusive
Write-back	Send dirty copy of cache line to memory, purge cached copy
Sharing write-back	Send dirty copy of cache line to memory, retain shared copy
Uncached/DMA read	Coherent read with no caching
Update/DMA write	Write with update cache coherence
Producer prefetch	Flush dirty cache line and send shared copies to given clusters
Lock acquire	Attempt to acquire a cachable lock
Granting unlock	Grant lock to next waiting processor
Invalidating unlock	Same as cache read-exclusive
Fetch&Inc/Dec	Uncached Fetch&Increment and Fetch&Decrement

the RAC, the merging is done through the normal snoop operation which returns a *pending-dirty* status.

The TeraDASH design assumes that the processor, or its second-level cache, directly support alternative memory operations. These alternative operations could be supported by the processor's instruction set (e.g., a normal store and an update store operation), or through alternative physical address regions that are translated by the second-level cache interface. The instruction set mechanism is more efficient because it does not require redundant virtual address regions and extra TLB entries to specify the operations. In either case, all alternative operations are assumed to be issued directly by the processor's bus interface and do not require translation by the directory logic. The resulting set of operations initiated by the processor and the second-level cache to the bus is shown in Table 9-1.

Other differences between the prototype and TeraDASH operations result from the use of a split-transaction bus instead of the SGI MPBUS. The split-transaction bus naturally handles the variable response timing of local versus remote operations, and it removes the need for the bus retry and arbitration masking used in the prototype. The timing of a local cluster miss fill without any bus or bank queuing is shown in Table 9-2.

After detecting the miss in the processors first- and second-level caches, the processor issues the request on the bus. The bus operation initiates the main memory access, directory lookup, and snoops on the other processors' caches. The processor places the pending request into a small RAM (32 entries) that is indexed by the transaction ID used for this request. Main memory echoes the transaction ID with its response. The ID allows the processor to match the response with the multiple outstanding requests that it may have pending. A RAM lookup is needed because responses may return out of order (because of bank conflicts or local versus remote accesses). All cache snoops are done in order based on the

---

TABLE 9-2

TeraDASH Local Bus Timing

CLK	CPU MASTER & SNOOP	BUS	MEMORY	DIRECTORY
1	Detect 1st-level miss			
2	Miss addr. to cache pins			
3	Access 2nd-level cache			
4				
5	Detect 2nd-level miss			
6	Miss addr. to bus pins			
7		Addr. on bus		
8	Snoop addr. received		Addr. through MC	Addr. through DC
9	Addr. to 2nd-level pins		Addr. to SDRAM SIMM	Access SRAM dir.
10	Snoop 2nd-level cache		Addr. to SDRAM parts	
11			Access SDRAM	Detect SRAM dir. status
12	Determine snoop results			Update SRAM dir., Addr. to SDRAM dir. SIMM
13	Snoop results to bus			Addr. to SDRAM dir. parts
14				Access SDRAM dir.
15				if necessary
16			D0 to MC	
17				
18			D1 to MC, start precharge	
19			ECC on D0	SDRAM dir. data to DC
20		D0 on bus	ECC on D1	
21	D0 received in CPU	D1 on bus		Update SDRAM pointers
22	D0 to 1st/2nd-level cache, Restart CPU		End precharge	New pointers to SDRAM, end precharge if no update
23	D1 to 1st/2nd-level cache			
24				Write new pointers to SDRAM dir.
25				
26				Precharge SDRAM if SDRAM pointers updated
27				
28				
29				
30				

---

time the requests are placed on the bus. Each processor has dedicated snoop output lines that indicate when snoop results are valid. They allow the processors to have a variable snoop response time that is independent of the access time of main memory. Accesses in the home cluster also take the directory state into consideration through snoop lines from the directory controller that indicate the presence of shared-remote or dirty-remote copies of the given memory block.

Bus transactions to remote address locations are somewhat different than accesses for local addresses. The first difference is that, unlike the prototype, no memory or directory accesses are made for remote requests, reducing the bandwidth requirement on main memory and the directory. Second, while the DC contains all the necessary information about whether a local bus request generates any network requests, remote requests may have their corresponding network request canceled by a cache-to-cache transfer. In TeraDASH, timing of the cache snoop information is variable; in the DASH prototype, this timing is fixed, and no requests are sent out until the snoop information is known. In TeraDASH, this problem is resolved by having the DC wait a fixed amount of time for the snoop before sending any network requests. Processor caches snoop the remote access, and if they can satisfy or merge the request, then their snoop results indicate that the DC should cancel the outgoing network message. If the snoop results are not available before the DC sends the network message, the DC's snoop results indicate that the message has already been sent and cannot be canceled. The issuing processor can use the data transferred from the local cache, but it must track the outstanding request because a network reply will eventually be received and the transaction response made on the bus (which the requestor can then drop).

9.1.3 TeraDASH Mesh Network

The 3-D mesh network for TeraDASH provides the same basic functions as the pair of 2-D mesh networks in the prototype. Virtual channels [Dal87] are used so a single physical mesh can logically perform as two independent mesh networks. Virtual channels multiplex two channels onto the same physical link, but maintain independent queues within each routing chip. Additionally, the meshes in TeraDASH are assumed to have the following improvements over the mesh networks in the prototype:

1. The node fall-through times are reduced from 50 ns to 20 ns. This reduction results from the use of submicron CMOS, as opposed to 1.6μ CMOS in the prototype MRCs.

2. Cycle times are 4 ns instead of the 35 ns in the prototype. This reduction results from the use of pipelined acknowledge signals, which remove the dependence of cycle time on cable lengths, and the use of higher-speed CMOS.

3. The mesh topology is closed into a torus to make the network fully symmetric and reduce average routing distance. Note that this arrangement requires extra virtual channels, as explained in [Dal87], to avoid deadlock.

4. Three dimensions of routing information (5-bit, signed offsets) are stored in a single routing flit instead of being stored with one flit per dimension.

5. As in the prototype, the mesh links are 16 bits wide and full-duplex.

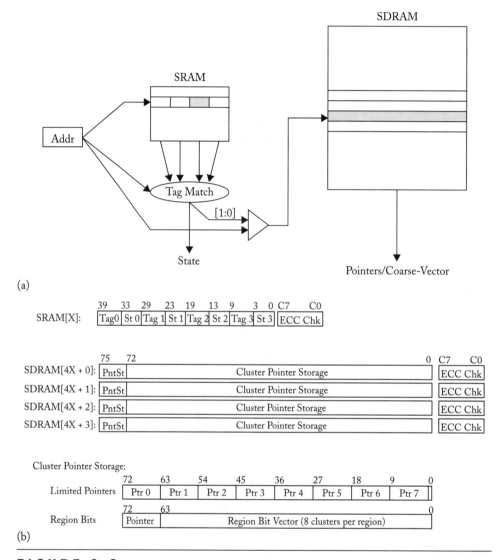

FIGURE 9-3 *(a) Access Mechanism and (b) Format of Sparse Directory Entries.*

Other useful enhancements that could be made to the TeraDASH mesh include support for multicast and adaptive routing within the network. Neither of these enhancements is assumed in the performance analysis in Section 9.3.

9.1.4 TeraDASH Directory Structure

As explained in Section 4.1.1, the bit-vector directory structure used in the DASH prototype does not scale well. With the 512 clusters and 32-byte cache lines used in TeraDASH, each directory entry would contain at least 512 bits, while each memory block would only include 256 bits of data. Such a large overhead is clearly intolerable. Instead, TeraDASH

TABLE 9-3

Memory and Directory Access Frequencies in TeraDASH

	CYCLES / ACCESS	WATER	BARNES-HUT	MP3D	PSIM4
SRAM dir. R-M-W	4	25	13	52	48
SDRAM dir read	10	23	10	52	15
SDRAM dir R-M-W	17	16	10	35	15
Main memory	12	25	13	52	48
SRAM dir util.		10%	5%	21%	19%
SDRAM dir bank util.		17%	8%	38%	13%
Main mem. bank util.		15%	8%	31%	29%

Note: Access frequencies estimated per 1,000 processor clocks. The SDRAM directory and main memory utilization numbers
assume that the four-way interleaving of these arrays weights the utilization of any one bank by a factor of two.

utilizes a sparse directory with region bits as outlined in Section 4.1.2. The   TeraDASH
directory structure is based on a serial lookup in separate static and dynamic memory arrays
(Figure 9-3). The sparse directory is four-way set-associative. Each SRAM entry stores four
sparse directory address tags and states. Each of the four tags has a corresponding location in
the SDRAM array. Each SDRAM entry holds a count field indicating the format of the
entry and the number of pointers in use, and the cluster pointers themselves. The additional
binary pointer available when in region bit mode allows for a priority field or queue pointer
whose use is explained in Section 9.2.2. Both directory arrays are protected by a SEC/DED
error-correcting code. Maintenance of the ECC code does not affect the timing of the directory because all directory writes are read-modify-write cycles.

The hybrid SRAM/SDRAM directory structure has three benefits. First, by doing the
accesses serially, the four-way associative directory memory does not need to be excessively
wide because only the pointers of the useful (hit) entry are accessed. Thus, the interface to
the directory is reduced from approximately 330 signals to 121. Second, the bandwidth to
the directory is increased because the SDRAM access can sometimes be avoided. The
importance of this bandwidth gain is explained in more detail in the next paragraph. Third,
the SRAM provides access to the directory state with the same timing as cache snooping,
while the SDRAM provides high-density storage for pointers. The disadvantages of the
scheme is the increased complexity to interface to the two arrays, and the added latency for
network messages whose destinations depend upon the actual pointer values read from the
SDRAM.

One of the major benefits of the hybrid directory structure is that it allows the directo-
ry's bandwidth to better match that of the main memory. A main memory access in Tera-
DASH occupies one of the four banks for 12 clocks including precharge. Likewise, when the
SDRAM directory is read, that directory bank is busy for 10 clocks. If the SDRAM direc-

tory is updated, the read-modify-write cycle occupies the bank for 17 clocks. The hybrid directory structure allows the SDRAM directory access to be bypassed when the directory pointers are not needed (e.g., for local accesses that are not dirty-remote). When only the SRAM directory is accessed, the directory is busy for just 4 clocks. Table 9-3 shows the access frequency for the main memory and the SRAM and SDRAM sections of the directory based on application data from the 48-processor DASH machine. The data in Table 9-3 assume that in moving from DASH to TeraDASH, the number of busy cycles is cut by one-fourth because of TeraDASH's superscalar processor, while the number of stall cycles stays constant.

As shown in Table 9-3, the hybrid directory structure reduces the number of SDRAM directory read-modify-write cycles significantly. The overall directory structure has a utilization very comparable (or much lower for PSIM4) than main memory, thus achieving the goal of matching the directory bandwidth to that of main memory.

In TeraDASH, the ratio of directory entries to cache lines (i.e., the directory size factor) is 8, and the directory has four-way associativity. The ratio of directory entries to main memory blocks (i.e., the memory size factor) is also 8. Thus, the total number of directory pointers is significantly more than the number of cache lines. As indicated by Figures 4-6 and 4-7 in Chapter 4, the rate of collisions should be less than 1 in 1,000 directory lookups. The overhead for the directory is limited because there is only one directory entry per eight memory blocks. The overhead of the directory SDRAM is 3.8% of main memory SDRAM, and 29% of processor cache SRAM. While the ratio of SRAM is high, the total amount of SDRAM to SRAM in the system is roughly 64:1 (256 MByte of main memory SDRAM per cluster compared with 4 MByte of SRAM cache). Historically, the cost ratio per bit of SRAM to SDRAM has varied from 8:1 to something less than 32:1 [Dat87]. Even assuming the pessimistic 32:1 ratio, the total overhead cost of the directory memory to total memory is 13.2%—less than the overhead in the DASH prototype, even though TeraDASH supports 32 times as many processors.

9.2 TeraDASH Coherence Protocol

The intercluster coherence protocol used by TeraDASH is very similar to that used in the prototype, especially for typical cases. Differences stem primarily from the loss of precise caching information in the directory. Additionally, enhancements could be made to the protocol to improve the prototype's performance and robustness. The following sections outline the necessary modifications and some of the more interesting optimizations.

9.2.1 Required Changes for the Scalable Directory Structure

The necessary changes in the protocol due to the sparse directory structure result because a memory access may need to replace a directory entry in use for another memory block. Since memory blocks without directory entries are assumed to be uncached, the replacement requires that the replaced block be flushed to memory. The flush is equivalent to forcing an exclusive copy of the block into the home cluster (i.e., a dirty copy must be written back to memory, or all shared copies invalidated).

(a) Request replaces a shared remote block.

- Request for new block sent to home cluster (1).
- Main memory supplies data for new request; home sends reply indicating replacement necessary (2a); invalidation requests (2b) are sent to the clusters sharing the block being replaced; directory entry set to new caching state with replacement pending.
- CPU request is satisfied; RAC entry allocated in local cluster to collect replacement invalidation acknowledgments.
- PCPUs issue invalidations on shared clusters; reply with invalidation ack replies (3).
- After all acknowledgments received, a replacement complete request (4) is sent to home to remove pending replacement tag on directory entry; RAC entry is deallocated.

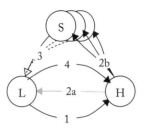

(b) Request replaces a dirty remote block.

- Request for new block sent to home cluster (1).
- Main memory supplies data for new request; home sends normal reply to local cluster (2a); replacement-flush request (2b) is sent to dirty cluster; directory entry set to new caching state with replacement pending.
- CPU request is satisfied by reply message.
- Dirty cache supplies data and goes to invalid state; dirty cluster sends replacement write-back (3) to home cluster.
- Home writes data back to memory and removes replacement tag on directory entry.

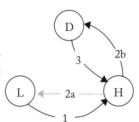

FIGURE 9-4 *Request Flows for a Replacement of a Sparse Directory Entry.*

The simplest extension to the prototype protocol to handle replacements is to have the requestor obtain exclusive ownership for the replaced block, and then write back the block to free up a directory entry. The requestor would then be able to repeat the original request and find a free directory entry. While simple, this scheme adds considerable latency to the common case of a sparse directory replacement (at least five serial network messages, compared with two when no replacement is necessary).

A better solution to this problem is to allow the replacement to take place in parallel with the response for the new block, as illustrated in Figure 9-4. In this scheme, the new request is serviced immediately in the home, and the corresponding associative directory set is marked as being in a *replacing* state. The replacing state indicates that the directory information is no longer complete for blocks that map to this set because the caching information for the old (replaced) block is currently inconsistent (i.e., there are cached copies, but there is not a directory entry). Once all copies of the replaced block have been flushed to memory the replacing status is cleared. Because the directory information is incomplete during the replacement, all requests that cause another replacement to the given associative set must be rejected while the replacing state exists for any entry in the set. Requests to the memory blocks in the set, including the newly added entry, can be satisfied, but another replacement cannot be initiated.

Imprecise information within a directory entry itself (i.e., when using region bits) also requires some modifications to the coherence protocol. In particular, there are modifications

Remote granting unlock in coarse-vector mode.

- CPU issues unlock on bus; allocate RAC entry; send granting unlock request to home (1).
- Granting unlock (while in coarse-vector mode) causes invalidations (2a) to be sent to one of the queued regions of clusters chosen at random from queued regions; grant is issued to the home itself (2b).
- Invalidated processors race to lock in the home (3).
- First processor to read the lock receives an unlocked lock reply (4a), which inhibits caching; an unlock ack reply (4b) is sent to local.
- Subsequent requests (if any) for the lock by other processors will requeue the grant region of clusters in the directory.
- Deallocate RAC entry when ack received.
- Other spinning clusters are not affected.

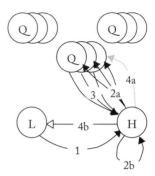

FIGURE 9-5 *Request Flow for a Remote Lock Grant When in Coarse-Vector Mode.*

needed for the queue-based locks and producer prefetch operations. When the directory entry stores a limited number of pointers, queue-based locks are handled as in the prototype with the possible enhancement of FIFO servicing of the lock requests. However, when region bits are in use, a unique cluster to grant the lock to cannot be determined. The easiest solution for this problem is to resort to invalidating all cached (spinning) regions, but this would eliminate the benefit of reduced traffic from the queue-based lock when it is needed most. A simpler solution is to grant the lock to the home cluster while simultaneously invalidating just one randomly selected region (see Figure 9-5). Whichever cluster re-requests first will get the lock, while any other clusters spinning in that region will requeue in the directory entry. If the invalidated region does not re-request the lock, then the normal granted lock time-out mechanism will cause another grant to the home and another region to be invalidated. The latency for the lock is no better than a simple invalidation in this case, but the traffic for each unlock/relock pair is greatly reduced.

The final protocol adjustment to handle the new directory format involves specifying the destination clusters for a producer prefetch. Assuming the processors support 64-bit store instructions, this is done by allowing a processor to either specify up to seven destinations with binary encoded cluster numbers, or to encode any number of destinations using the 64-bit region format. The format of the destination vector could be specified by different cache line offsets in a similar manner to how the prototype distinguishes between the different prefetch types.

9.2.2 Enhancements for Increased Protocol Robustness

Although the protocol used in the prototype is correct, there is room for improved robustness. These improvements come in three major areas: (1) the ability to gracefully handle pathological access patterns while avoiding livelock and request starvation; (2) support for a more general interconnection network that does not guarantee in-order delivery of messages between two nodes; and (3) an increased resilience to permanent and transient faults within the system. The following sections outline potential enhancements to the protocol that address these issues.

Strict request-reply protocol with dirty remote block.

- Read request for new block sent to home cluster (1).
- Home sends identity of dirty cluster as reply to local cluster (2).
- Local cluster sends read request directly to dirty cluster (3).
- Dirty cache supplies data and goes to shared state; dirty cluster sends read reply (4) to local cluster.
- Local cluster finishes transaction with a sharing write-back to the home cluster (5).

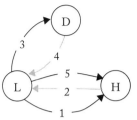

FIGURE 9-6 *Strict Request-Reply Protocol in the Face of Potential Deadlock.*

9.2.2.1 System Livelock and Request Starvation

The prototype coherence protocol is memoryless in the sense that each cluster reacts to requests based on its local state without a history of past events. When inconsistent actions result (e.g., forwarding two requests to the same dirty cluster), the problem is eventually resolved by retrying one of the requests. This approach simplifies the protocol and hardware, and it leads to good performance in most cases. It also eliminates the potential for deadlock because no globally shared resources are held while other resources are requested. In pathological cases, however, this protocol can degrade performance because of excessive retries. In the worst case, retries can lead to systemwide livelock or the starvation of an individual request.

The use of retries is much more likely to cause starvation than livelock because one of the contending accesses usually makes forward progress. It is this forward progress that causes other requests to be retried. For example, when more than one request is forwarded to a dirty cluster, the first request is usually satisfied, which causes the dirty cluster to lose ownership of the block, and the other requests to be retried. The one exception to this, where livelock could be possible, is the manner in which request-to-request network deadlocks are broken in the prototype. As explained in Section 6.1.3, whenever a node detects that its inbound and outbound request FIFOs are full, it assumes there is a request network deadlock and the node drains its inbound requests by sending NAK replies. In very pathological cases, once this condition is entered, all rejected requests might be retried immediately, and the deadlock-breaking mode might not terminate. In the prototype system, this does not happen because the FIFOs are large (1K words each), and there is a limited number of outstanding requests (64 processors with 32 requests per processor).

In TeraDASH, the much larger number of processors and reduced FIFO sizes imply that this guarantee does not hold. Fortunately, there is a simple way to avoid this livelock problem. Instead of rejecting inbound requests when a potential deadlock is detected, the protocol can resort to a strict request-reply protocol (see Section 4.2.1 and Figure 9-4). Thus, instead of forwarding requests from the home, memory can reply with the information necessary for the requestor to send the requests itself. For example, if a request needs to be forwarded to a dirty cluster, instead of sending the request from the home, memory can reply to the issuing cluster with the dirty cluster's node number. The local cluster would then take responsibility for sending the request to the dirty cluster. Thus, the dependency between inbound and outbound requests in the home can be removed, while forward progress is still made.

It is more difficult to guarantee that a single processor is not starved by a pathological access pattern of other processors. While the odds that the other processors repeatedly change ownership of a given block so that a request is never satisfied are very low, there is a finite possibility that a request could be retried an arbitrary number of times. Although many of the conditions that cause this unfairness in the prototype could be removed, most of them were not deemed likely enough to warrant inclusion in the original DASH system. In the prototype, if a request is retried too many times, it triggers a time-out mechanism for the operation itself or for some subsequent operation (e.g., fence) that relies on the processor not owning any RAC entries. This time-out varies from 25 to 50 millisec and allows approximately 7,600 retries before a bus error is triggered.

For TeraDASH, it would be desirable to remove all starvation cases and make the system more robust. There are some cases of potential starvation that can be easily removed. First, in the prototype, it is possible that local processors continually conflict for a particular RAC entry and that one processor never gets ownership of that entry. This problem is solved by providing dedicated RAC entries per processor, or enough associativity that each processor can always get a RAC entry. Dedicated RAC entries are easily incorporated in the Tera-DASH design where the processors' second-level caches take on most of the RAC functionality. Request starvation can also result when requests are merged in the prototype. In this case, all waiting processors are released simultaneously when the reply is received. The RC guarantees that at least one local request is satisfied, but it is possible that a remote operation from the PCPU invalidates the block or removes ownership before all local requests are satisfied. This case is solved by simply considering the block *busy* until all merged requests are satisfied. A similar starvation problem exists for cache read requests that are invalidated before the reply can be given to the requesting processor. In the prototype, if an invalidation is received while a RAC has a pending read for a given block, then the read reply is treated as a NAK regardless of the reply type (see Section 6.3.2.1). If the processor continually rereads and is reinvalidated, then the processor will eventually starve. A solution to this problem (first proposed by Wallach [Wal90]) is to allow the read reply to be given to the processor, but with an indication that it cannot be cached. The effect is that the individual request is satisfied, and the block is immediately invalidated. Allowing the processor to read the location does not affect memory consistency because the read operation logically occurred before the write that generated the invalidation.

The most difficult starvation cases arise when ownership of a given block is constantly changing (see Figure 9-7). For example, if there is a steady flow of read-exclusive requests, and corresponding dirty transfers and write-backs, a given request may never locate the current owner. Likewise, sparse directory replacements using the protocol outlined in the previous section can cause starvation if the sparse set has replacements continually ongoing. These starvation cases are not easily removed because they require that a global order on requests to each block be kept, but distributed in such a way that no local resource within a cluster needs to guarantee storage for all of the requests.

Ownership starvation example.

- Cluster D1 has the line dirty.
- Cluster D2 sends a read-ex request to home cluster (1).
- Read request for new block sent to home cluster (2).
- Home forwards read-ex request to dirty cluster D1 (3).
- Home forwards read request to dirty cluster D1 (4).
- Dirty cache supplies data and goes to invalid state; dirty cluster sends read-ex reply to cluster D2 (5a) and dirty transfer req to home (5b).
- Cluster D1 sends NAK reply to local cluster because it is no longer the owner (6).
- Home cluster sends ack to new dirty cluster D2 (7).
- Sequence repeats with roles of D1 and D2 reversed.

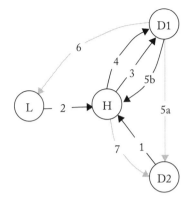

FIGURE 9-7 *Ownership Starvation.*

One solution to this problem is to rely on the variable delays in the system, or intentionally inserted random retry delays, to resolve the problem.[1] Although this solution does not guarantee fairness or predictable latencies, with a long enough time-out period, the odds of failure can be made arbitrarily low. Assuming that collision completion is random with respect to arrival time of requests, the probability of getting starved for a given amount of time can be calculated. For the worst case of all P processors colliding on a single directory SRAM line, the probability of a given processor getting NAKed during a round of requests is $(P-1)/P$. Given a directory service time for a single request t_s, and a time-out value t_{to}, a request has to fail $t_{to}/(P \cdot t_s)$ times in a row before the time-out is triggered. The probability of this happening is thus

$$\Pr(\text{time-out}) = \left(\frac{P-1}{p}\right)^{\frac{t_{to}}{P \cdot t_s}} \tag{9.1}$$

Figure 9-8 shows the probability that a request will not be satisfied in TeraDASH in less than a given time-out period (i.e., $P = 512$ because of merging within a cluster and $t_s = 11$ clocks = 110 nanoseconds). If the time-out is set to be half a second, then the probability of failure is less than 1 in 50 million. The probability of failure is, of course, much less if all processors are not pathologically trying to write a single block. Furthermore, it can be argued that if a program exhibits such behavior, system performance will be so poor that the user is better off receiving a bus error so that the problem can be identified.

A more conservative solution to the starvation problem is to use a *pending list*, as proposed in the IEEE Scalable Coherent Interface standard [JLG+90]. In this scheme, whenever memory cannot satisfy a request immediately, it puts the requestor on a distributed

---

[1] Generally, the solutions for the ownership starvation can be applied to replacement starvation, so only solutions to the former will be outlined in this section.

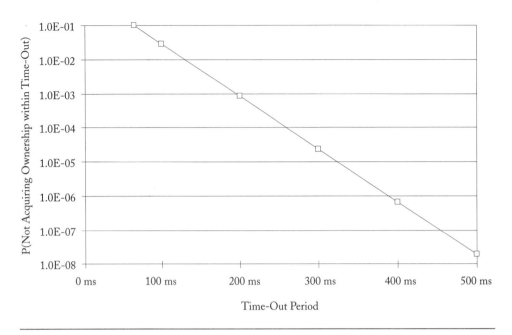

FIGURE 9-8 *Probability of Long Ownership Latency in Worst Case.*

pending list. The tail pointer of the list is maintained in the directory entry, and the set of requesting clusters form a singly linked list with the head being the current owner of the block.[2] Once a pending list is formed, new requests are added to the list by updating the tail pointer in the directory and forwarding the request to the old tail. The pending list persists until all requests are satisfied. The termination condition is detected by a directory update message (e.g., sharing write-back request) from a cluster that is still marked as the tail of the list. The advantage of this scheme is that FIFO servicing of requests can be guaranteed; however, latency can still be extremely long in pathological cases (e.g., queued behind all other processors). The disadvantage of this scheme is that when the series of pending requests are all read requests, they are still serviced serially by passing the block through the set of pending processors. Although various enhancements to the pending list concept are possible (especially with a memory-resident directory), they all add complexity to the protocol.

Another solution to the starvation problem is to use request priorities. The protocol is basically unchanged, but when a request is retried its priority is increased. Requests whose priority is higher than that stored in the directory are forwarded to the owning cluster, and their priority is stored in the directory. Lower-priority requests are immediately rejected by the home. If successful, a high-priority request resets the directory priority in a subsequent dirty transfer or sharing write-back request. The reset is only made in the directory if the

---

[2] The directory must have storage for both the pending queue tail pointer and a complete set of region bits so that cached copies can be tracked by the directory while there are pending requests.

priority of the directory update matches the current priority stored in the directory (i.e., an even higher-priority request has not been received). Given a suitable encoding of the priority count, this scheme requires the same amount of storage as the pending list scheme (i.e., approximately one pointer). It has the advantages of simplicity and the ability to reduce the serialization of pending read requests. Its disadvantage is that it does not guarantee FIFO servicing of requests.

9.2.2.2   Intercluster Network Independence

Another area where the protocol's robustness could be increased is the removal of the dependence on in-order delivery of messages between two clusters in the mesh. Such independence would allow for higher performance adaptive routing algorithms and for network retry in the event of transmission errors. The prototype protocol is insensitive to message delivery order in all cases except for two. The first is the ordering of DMA update messages (see Section 6.3.4.2) between the home and sharing clusters. If two update messages to the same location are received in different order in different clusters, then there will be a loss in cache coherence. Likewise, if a deliver (see Section 6.3.3.2) and subsequent DMA update or invalidation message are switched, then the deliver will leave a stale copy of the cache block in the destination cluster. These two problems can be solved by guaranteeing that these message types are not in transit between the home and sharing clusters simultaneously. In particular, when a DMA update or deliver message is sent from the home, they would force the directory entry into a busy state in which subsequent write operations to the block are rejected. Support of the busy state would require the producer prefetch to generate acknowledgment messages for each deliver, and for both DMA updates and producer prefetch requests to send a final acknowledgment to the directory to terminate the busy state.

9.2.2.3   Fault Tolerance

The final area in which the protocol's resilience can be improved is an increased level of fault tolerance within the system. In a maximum TeraDASH system, there are over 500 circuit boards and tens of thousands of ICs. With such large numbers, the mean time between failure (MTBF) of the system will be low. As discussed in Section 4.2.4, failures can be divided into three types based on the different fault tolerance techniques that are applicable to each type. The first category includes the memory ICs, which represent the majority of ICs in the system. Their reliability can be greatly increased through error-correcting codes. The second most important error class is likely to be network transmission errors resulting from transient noise on the interconnection cables or synchronizer failures within the network or at its interfaces. The easiest way to add fault tolerance to the network is to add a lower layer of the protocol that guarantees network delivery. Unfortunately, implementing such a protocol end-to-end across the network is expensive in terms of retransmission buffers and sequence number management because all nodes can directly talk to one another. A less costly approach used on Sun's S3.mp is to support retransmission over individual mesh router links.

The final level of fault tolerance is protection from failure of the logic ICs within the cluster and protection from failure of the power and cooling system of a module. Solving either of these problems requires some amount of duplication. For power and cooling, dual power supplies and fans could be used within a module with sufficient capacity to act as backups for one another. Handling faults in the logic ICs (processors, MC, DC, or MRCs) is more difficult. It requires added logic to supply backup resources and to add a high degree of data integrity so that failures do not corrupt the overall system state. Duplicate ICs with comparison circuitry at I/O pins, as in the Intel 432 [SiJ82] or MIPS R4000 [MIP91a], are the most straightforward way to add data integrity to the processors, memory controller, and directory controller. Mesh routing chip failures could be detected without duplication since all messages could include CRC checks.

Once a failure is detected, a cluster must either contain sufficient resources to mask the failure, or some form of redundancy between clusters must be implemented. If the redundancy is within the cluster (through TMR or Quadding [Elk82]), then the cluster also needs two independent access ports to the network in order to avoid a failure of its MRC from isolating it from the other clusters. Conversely, if the redundancy is between clusters, then MRC failures can be masked through adaptive routing and message retransmission. Backup of main memory and the caches becomes more difficult if implemented between clusters. The backup could be handled through a *hot spare* cluster for every active cluster, which operates in lockstep with the primary cluster. Or, a *logical spare* could be used that is not wholly redundant. At a minimum, the logical spare would include a duplicate copy of the writable main memory pages. This copy would represent the image of memory at some checkpoint and could be maintained by the hardware or a combination of the hardware and software. Similar to the fault tolerance scheme used by Sequoia [Ber88], at checkpoints all cached copies of a page would be flushed to memory, and the two memory images made identical. Upon failure of a memory or processor used by a given set of communicating tasks, the processes would be rolled back to the last checkpoint and restarted.

Overall, tolerance of faults in the logic ICs is likely to cost at least a factor of two in hardware resources and would not be applicable to many TeraDASH environments. As an alternative, the base system might support only fault tolerance for memories and network, with the option for lockstepping the processors for high data integrity. Thus, the system would tolerate the most common problems, and logic faults could be detected and quickly isolated. Quick isolation, together with distributed and robust kernel data structures, would allow the operating system to deallocate failing modules without disrupting overall system operation, but would require some user applications to be restarted.

9.2.3 Enhancements for Increased Performance

While the list of possible performance optimizations is limitless given unbounded increases in complexity, there are two enhancements that require only minor modifications to the protocol and are clearly worth implementing in TeraDASH.

The first enhancement is for processors to directly issue prefetch and update operations into the normal cache space. Performance would benefit in two ways from this enhancement. First, the processor's caches could be used to filter out requests that can be satisfied by the cache, which would reduce the load on the bus and the overhead on the issuing processor. Second, prefetch operations can bring data into the processor's first- or second-level cache, thus reducing the cost of the subsequent blocking load operations.

The second enhancement is to allow lock operations to complete in the processor's cache. This enhancement reduces the cost of lock acquisitions when a lock has affinity to a given processor. In the prototype, the processor is not capable of atomic read-modify-write operations on its cache, and the atomic update must occur at memory. This limitation implies that all successful lock operations access, at least, the local bus. For TeraDASH there is no reason why the processor's cache cannot support the atomic update of lock variables. Furthermore, if the processor's instruction set includes lock operations on memory, then all memory locations can be used for locks. The protocol for handling locks would be as follows:

1. Lock acquire operations are serviced in the processor's cache by an atomic update if the processor holds an exclusive copy of the block. Otherwise, the request is sent to the home. If the lock is unlocked, then the processor acquires an exclusive copy of the cache line and atomically updates the lock. Otherwise, a shared copy of the line is returned with the locked lock.

2. Invalidating unlock operations complete in the processor's cache if the processor holds the lock exclusively. Otherwise, the line is acquired exclusively by invalidating all cached copies, and then flushed to memory. Alternatively, if memory supports atomic updates, the lock can simply be flushed to memory and atomically updated there. In either case, the lock is returned to memory so that the waiting processors can acquire the lock without being forwarded to the releasing processor.

3. Granting unlock operations also complete within the processor's cache if held exclusively. If the lock is uncached, then it is acquired exclusively, unlocked, and flushed to memory. If the lock is in the sharing state, then the lock is granted to one of the waiting clusters. The lock grant proceeds as in the prototype (i.e., an unlocked value is returned to the grant processor that is viewable by the processor, but not cachable). One exception to this is if there is only one waiting cluster. This cluster could be granted an exclusive copy of the lock, allowing it to subsequently release the lock by an operation in its cache.

4. Another enhancement to the unlock operation is support for lock releases with and without flushes to memory. The optional flush allows both the case where the lock has a high level of processor affinity (i.e., the unlocked lock stays in the processor's cache) and the case that a lightly loaded lock has little affinity (i.e., flush the lock to memory so that requests do not need forwarding) to be optimized.

The actions to be taken at lock and unlock time are summarized in Table 9-4 for different coherence states.

Others [Goo89, GVW89] have proposed further optimizations for locks that support the acquisition of data protected by a lock in parallel with the lock itself. While the acquisition of the data would naturally happen in the protocol outlined above, complications occur before the lock is released when the waiting processors are spinning in their cache. Normal writes to the lock's protected data would cause invalidations and refetches by the spinning processors. Extensions to the coherence protocol can be made to handle these cases, but they

T A B L E 9 - 4

Enhanced Lock and Unlock Operations

OPERATION	LOCAL CACHING STATE	LOCK STATE	DIRECTORY STATE	ACTION
Lock	Exclusive[a]	Unlocked	Dirty local	Perform in cache
	Shared	Locked	Shared	Spin in cache
	Uncached[a]	Unlocked	Uncached	Get exclusive copy, perform lock in cache
	Uncached[a]	Unlocked	Dirty remote	Transfer exclusive copy, perform lock in cache
	Uncached	Locked	(Any)	Go to shared, spin in cache
Unlock	Exclusive[a]	Locked	Dirty local	Perform in cache
	Shared	Locked	Shared	Grant uncached if several waiters, grant exclusive if one waiter[a]
	Uncached	Locked	Uncached	Go to unlocked at home
	Uncached	Locked	Shared	Grant uncached if several waiters, grant exclusive if one waiter[a]
	Uncached	Locked	Dirty remote[a]	Transfer exclusive copy, perform unlock in cache

[a] These behaviors are different from the DASH prototype.

complicate the protocol and memory consistency model. Conversely, the primitives supported by DASH can achieve similar performance by using update writes of the protected data, or by splitting the data and the lock into separate cache lines and using producer prefetch operations to send the data in parallel with a granting unlock.

9.3 TeraDASH Performance

While not as detailed as the prototype description, the outline of the TeraDASH design in the previous sections contains enough detail to make a first-order approximation of its performance. The analysis in this section is broken into two parts. First, unloaded latencies for cache fills are calculated and then compared with the prototype system to show that latencies are similar when measured in processor clocks. Second, results from a stochastic, discrete event simulation of a 512-cluster TeraDASH are given. The reference characteristics of the simulator inputs are varied over the range of characteristics exhibited by the benchmarks studied in Chapter 2. The output of the simulations show the potential speedups for Tera-DASH and the effect of loading on memory system latencies.

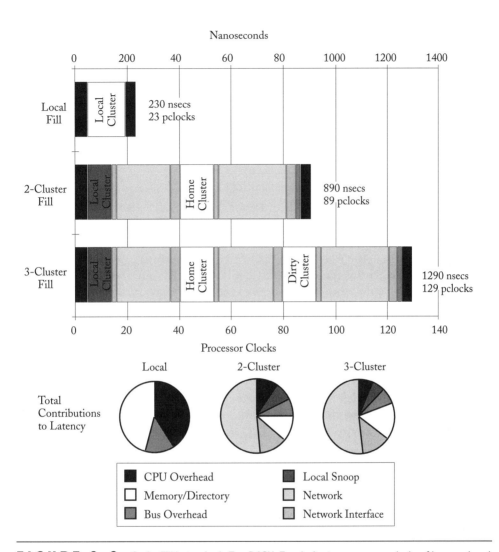

FIGURE 9-9 *Cache Fill Latencies in TeraDASH. For clarity, two processor clocks of bus overhead per bus transaction are not shown in the bar graphs, but are included in the total contribution breakdown.*

9.3.1 Access Latencies

Figure 9-9 shows a breakdown of the access latencies for a first-level cache miss satisfied by the local cluster, a remote cluster, and a dirty-remote cluster. These delays are derived directly from the bus timing given in Table 9-2 and the following assumptions about network timing:

1. Mesh routing chip fall-through delay (including cable delay) is 20 ns per network hop. On the $8 \times 8 \times 8$ bidirectional torus, the average message traverses three dimension changes and two node hops per dimension. Thus, the average network fall-through delay is 180 ns.

2. Network cycle time is 4 ns per flit, and an entire message must be received before being error checked and processed. Network requests are 7 flits; replies, including 32 bytes of data, are 20 flits. This adds 28 ns to each network request and 80 ns to each network reply.

3. The delay from receipt of a message to its issue on the bus is 35 ns (including synchronization), and the delay from the initiation of a network message to the first flit appearing at the input of the MRC is 20 ns.

The resulting ratio of access times in TeraDASH is 1:8:22:89:129 and is similar to the ratio in the prototype (1:14:29:101:133). Thus, although the delays have reduced by a factor of three in nanoseconds, when measured in processor clocks the latencies are very similar. The major difference is the lower penalty for misses serviced by the local cluster. The lower latencies in TeraDASH reflect the tighter coupling of the processor to the second-level cache and bus than in the SGI implementation. Of course, the TeraDASH numbers may be somewhat optimistic given the level of detail in the design, while the prototype numbers have been measured on the actual hardware. Note also that the ratio of the local miss penalty to the remote miss penalty is larger in TeraDASH (1.0:4.0:5.9) than in the prototype (1.0:3.5:4.6). This difference implies that TeraDASH is more sensitive to reference locality than the prototype.

It is also interesting to compare the breakdown of the delays in TeraDASH with the DASH prototype numbers given in Figure 8-2. For a local miss, the tighter coupling of the TeraDASH processors to their second-level cache and bus reduces the fraction of CPU overhead, and it results in a better balance between the memory access time and the CPU overhead than in the DASH prototype. For the remote accesses, however, TeraDASH exhibits a much higher ratio of network delay than intracluster delay because of the larger TeraDASH network (average of 9 hops versus 5.3) and the increased ratio of network latency to processor speed (20 ns fall-through and 10 ns processor clock versus 50 ns fall-through and a 30 ns cycle time). The other feature of note is the larger bus overhead in the prototype than in TeraDASH. This overhead is due to the need to emulate a split-transaction bus in the prototype by a retry in the local cluster, and the slow bus (relative to the processor) in the prototype.

9.3.2 Potential Application Speedup

A discrete event simulator was used to estimate the potential speedup of applications on TeraDASH. The simulation model was designed using SES/Workbench [JDB89] and models a single cluster. Remote references are simulated by routing remote requests back onto the cluster bus after a fixed network delay. Thus, the model only simulates uniform loading (i.e., the load that the local cluster puts on remote nodes is equal to the load that they put on this node) and does not model contention in the mesh network. Other simplifications in the model are as follows:

1. Only second-level misses are simulated. First-level misses satisfied by the second-level cache would affect processor utilization, but would only have a second-order

effect on the speedup of TeraDASH over a single cluster. Likewise, instruction cache and TLB misses are not simulated.

2. No contention between second-level cache snoops and processor accesses are modeled, nor is contention for posting invalidations to the first-level cache.

3. Because of the superscalar processors, it is assumed that each processor issues one memory reference per active clock. Writes are assumed to be perfectly buffered and never stall the processor. Processors issue only normal reads and writes. There are no synchronization or other special memory operations used.

4. All read and write misses fall into one of six categories: local uncached, local shared-remote, local dirty-remote, remote uncached, remote shared-remote, or remote dirty-remote. There are no exceptions (NAKs) or sparse directory replacements.

5. Misses occur at random (exponential distribution of time between misses), and accesses are uniformly distributed between memory and directory interleave banks.

These assumptions are purposely aggressive with respect to the processor's ability to generate memory references since this will put the most stress on the memory system. The memory timing is based on the numbers given in the previous section and models contention on the cluster bus, memory banks, and directory banks. Results of these simulations are given in Figure 9-10. Figure 9-10(a) shows processor utilization, while Figure 9-10(b) shows the increase in throughput of 512 clusters over the single cluster. The curves are plotted against the number of active processor clocks between shared read misses. This metric was chosen because shared variable misses tend to dominate private misses, and this metric incorporates both the shared variable reference rate and shared miss rate. Both graphs are parameterized by the ratio of shared misses that are local versus remote. As expected, locality can greatly effect processor utilization, especially when the shared miss rate is high.

The reference statistics not explicitly listed in Figure 9-10 are scaled to match the shared read miss rate observed on simulations of the applications studied in Chapter 2 on 64 processors. For example, the shared write miss rate is assumed to be one-third of the given shared read miss rate. Fifty percent of these write misses are assumed to be to shared blocks that generate one invalidation. While some writes should generate more invalidations, the actual ratio of writes to shared variables is lower than 50%. Ten percent of local read misses are assumed to be dirty-remote, while 60% of remote misses are dirty-remote (i.e., three-hop misses). Writes are assumed to never cause a fetch of a dirty-remote block. Such a fetch should be rare because it only results when there is false sharing or write races in an application. Finally, a background level of private misses is assumed to occur with a miss rate of 1–2%. These references generate a read miss every 225 clocks and a write miss every 450 clocks. Of these, it is assumed that 95% are local and the remaining misses are satisfied by a remote home.

An estimate of the potential speedups for the applications over a single cluster is also plotted in Figure 9-10. The simulator inputs for these runs were based on the characteristics of the benchmarks given in Chapter 2. Unfortunately, the data in Chapter 2 does not measure the memory locality of the applications. For the codes given in Chapter 2, there are

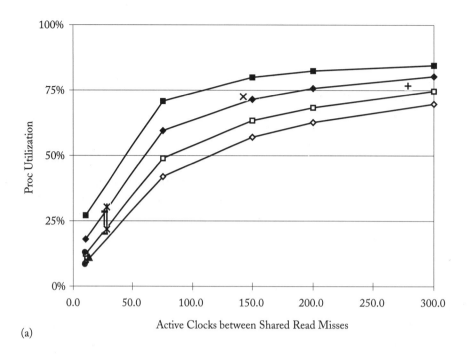

(a)

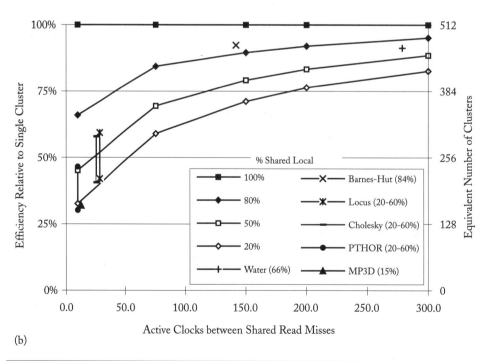

(b)

FIGURE 9-10 *(a) Processor Utilization and (b) Speedup in TeraDASH.*

many shared data items that have affinity to a given processor and could be allocated to that processor's cluster. Furthermore, as shown in Section 8.3.1, cache-to-cache and RAC-to-cache sharing within a cluster can add significantly to the fraction of references that are satisfied locally. For Water, Barnes-Hut, and MP3D, the fraction of shared references satisfied locally is assumed to be equal to the locality shown by these applications on the 48-processor DASH prototype. Note that these runs did not do any intelligent memory allocation for shared data that has affinity. For the other three applications studied in Chapter 2 (Locus-Route, Cholesky, and PTHOR), locality is simply varied between 20–60%.

Of course, the speedups shown in Figure 9-10 only represent the potential of the applications since the simulations do not account for speedup lost because of synchronization or limited parallelism. They more accurately represent scaled speedup (see Section 1.3.5) that can only be achieved by scaling the problem size with the number of processors. While this approach may not be practical for some of the applications shown, the figure does indicate that there is significant potential for good speedup, especially on applications with a low or moderate shared miss rate (i.e., greater than 50 clocks between shared read misses).

Although the simulations do not include network loading, the simulator does provide the arrival rate and occupancy time of network messages, so the effect of queuing can be estimated. Assuming there are enough virtual channels or FIFO stages so that each network link is independent, the network can be approximated as a series of queuing centers. The number of servers is equal to the average number of links that a message must traverse (which equals 2 per dimension, or 6 total for all three dimensions). The load on a given link is determined by the load on its particular one-dimensional path, and the fraction of the messages that travel in this path that must traverse the link. The effective load on the entire 1-D path is equal to 512/64 = 8 clusters. Furthermore, since each 1-D path is bidirectional, a particular link will only see traffic from its source node and its three upstream neighbors. Even from these nodes, each message may have one of eight destinations, and only some destinations require a message to traverse the given link (some messages will be routed in the opposite direction and some will change dimensions before reaching this link). The result is that each link sees 1/8 of the load on the 1-D path, equivalent to the load generated by a single cluster.[3] Figure 9-11 shows the resulting utilization of an individual link with varying load and the average delay for a complete network traversal through the six individual links. The individual link delays were calculated assuming an M/D/1 queue[4] with a service time equal to the average packet occupancy. The figures indicate that network queuing delays are small in all cases, with worst-case loads adding approximately 5% $(2 \cdot 2.5 / 100)$ queuing delay to a remote miss.

---

[3] The load from the upstream nodes is calculated as follows. If packets are routed in the direction that minimizes the number of network hops, then 3/8 of packets originating at the source of the link will be routed over the given link. Likewise, 2/8 and 1/8 of the messages from the two upstream neighbors will be routed over the link. Finally, for the cases that a message must traverse 4 links, the message could be routed in either direction. If it is assumed that 50% of these messages are routed in the direction that uses the given link, then the total load on the link is 3/8 + 2/8 + 1/8 + 4(1/2)(1/8) = 1 cluster.

[4] M/D/1: each link sees random packet arrivals (i.e., Markovian), provides a deterministic service time, and has one queue to hold inputs.

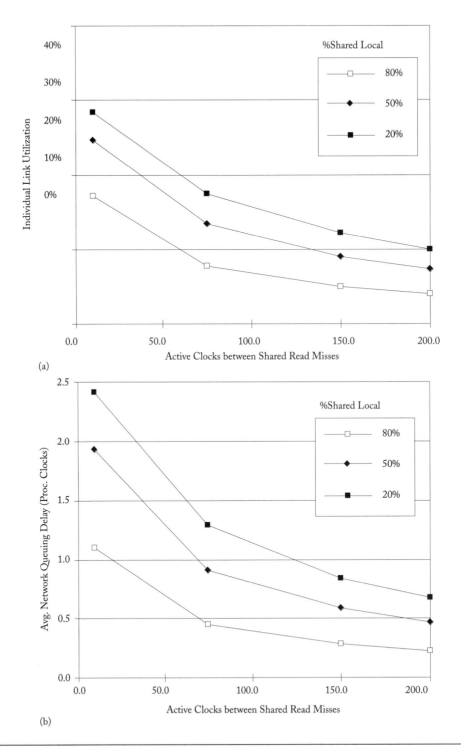

F I G U R E 9 - 1 1 *Queuing in the TeraDASH 3-D Mesh Network.*

Overall, the results of the simulations are very positive. They show that if applications contain enough parallelism to exploit 2,048 processors, they will run well on TeraDASH. Even applications with high sharing rates (e.g., MP3D), which have relatively poor processor utilization in a single cluster, get a speedup of over 150 on 512 clusters. Furthermore, the simulation shows that applications with reasonable miss rates do not cause excessive utilization of the cluster bus or the memory and directory banks. In particular, if each processor executes for 37 active clocks between each miss (corresponding to 75 active clocks between shared read miss stalls), then bus utilization is less than 27% and bus and memory/directory bank queuing adds less than 7% to the average miss penalty. Even under heavy loads, when each processor executes for only 6.4 active clocks between misses (corresponding to 10 active clocks between shared read miss stalls), bus loading is 51%, and bus and directory queuing add less than 17.5% to fill times.

9.4 Chapter Conclusions

The primary conclusion from the TeraDASH design experiment is that the DASH architecture is applicable to a large-scale implementation that can provide hundreds of GigaOPS performance. More specifically, with relatively minor modifications the architecture can be made to support the following:

- A fully integrated implementation based on state-of-the-art components
- Very high performance (100 MHz) superscalar processors with good utilization
- A scalable memory system that supports thousands of processors with a logic and memory overhead of less than 20%

Of course, a realization of the TeraDASH design still entails many challenges. At the circuit level, the aggressive bus and I/O timing assumed in the VLSI circuits would be difficult to achieve. Similar comments hold for the interconnection network. Another practical problem is the "shape" of the sparse directory SDRAM. The directory requires bandwidth comparable to main memory, but only needs 1/16 the depth. Since all of main memory SDRAMs are used to increase bandwidth, it is difficult to effectively use the same density of parts for the directory. This shape problem will continue to be an issue unless the bandwidth of individual SDRAMs increases (i.e., the parts have wider or faster data interfaces).

At the architectural level, there are also many detailed problems to be worked out. Particularly challenging are the details of the split-transaction bus protocol, snooping, and transient cache states. Likewise, any modifications made to support network or logic IC fault tolerance in hardware or software are difficult to achieve, but may be required for such a large machine. Overall, the biggest challenge of all is likely to be the creation of a software environment (OS, languages, debug tools, and applications) that can effectively use the power of a TeraDASH-like system to solve a wide variety of problems.

10

Conclusions and Future Directions

It is becoming increasingly difficult to obtain higher performance from uniprocessor systems, even with a combination of technology and architecture advances. In contrast, parallel processing has the potential to provide order-of-magnitude increases in compute power. The problem with parallel machines is that programming them is difficult. Parallel programming has all the problems of sequential programming, and adds the complexities of coordinating multiple threads of control, distributing data, and load-balancing. A shared-memory paradigm helps reduce these complexities. For example, coordinating threads is made easier by shared-memory because global synchronization can be achieved through direct accesses to shared variables. Furthermore, a shared address space simplifies data distribution and load-balancing because all processors can access all locations directly. Thus, it is possible to bring up a parallel application without much regard to data and process placement. After obtaining correct behavior, the programmer can improve performance if necessary by applying locality optimizations. This incremental tuning capability is a major advantage of the shared-memory programming paradigm compared with message-passing or SIMD machines. Shared-memory machines have the additional advantage of being able to support today's standard software environments, including operating systems, compilers, debuggers, etc.

Small-scale shared-memory multiprocessors are in common use today. They are most often bus-based systems that utilize snoopy cache coherence. The problem with these machines is that neither the bus bandwidth nor the cache coherence scheme scale to a larger number of processors. Scalable shared-memory multiprocessors (SSMPs) are shared-memory multiprocessors that overcome this scaling problem. SSMPs are just now moving out of the research labs and into the commercial world. In this book, we have discussed the most important design issues of SSMPs and illustrated these issues with the discussion of the design and performance of the DASH multiprocessor.

10.1 SSMP Design Conclusions

The key design challenge of a large-scale multiprocessor with a shared address space is the memory system. Both sufficient bandwidth and low latency must be provided for memory accesses from any processor to any location in the system. Achieving high bandwidth is relatively easy. Most often, it is just a cost issue—providing enough wires between nodes in the system. Reducing latency, however, is much more challenging. It is difficult to provide low-latency access by all processors to all memory in a physically large system. Memory latency has to be fought at all levels of the design.

The most important latency reduction technique used in shared-memory multiprocessors is the provision of per-processor caches. However, the introduction of caches raises the cache coherence problem. Directory-based cache coherence solves the coherence problem without compromising the scalable bandwidth of an SSMP system. Our studies of a set of scientific/engineering applications have shown that directory-based cache coherence using an invalidating cache coherence protocol is well matched to the sharing patterns of these applications. Directories have their own scalability problems in terms of storage overhead, but these can be solved without sacrificing significant performance using techniques such as limited pointers, region bits, and sparse directories.

Once caches are used, we still need to worry about the latency incurred by cache misses. Several techniques have been used successfully to reduce or hide the latency of cache misses. One of the most important is coupling memory with the processing nodes in a nonuniform memory architecture (NUMA), in which some memory is very close to each processing node, while other memory is further away. Locality optimizations in data placement take advantage of the reduced latency to local memory. Placing private data and code in local memory is relatively easy. The problem of locality optimization for shared data is very application-dependent and generally much more difficult. For requests that cannot be locally satisfied, the coherence protocol can be optimized to reduce latency by limiting the number of network traversals (hops) to the minimum required to complete a given transaction.

Additional techniques for latency reduction and hiding are weaker memory consistency models, multiple-context processors, producer-initiated communication, and prefetch. These techniques generally take advantage of additional parallelism available within a single thread or between threads to overlap communication latency with computation or other communication. Weaker consistency models allow for the buffering and pipelining of memory references, especially writes. Multiple-context processors switch to a new thread when the current thread encounters a long-latency operation. Producer-initiated communication reduces the latency inherent in the demand-driven communication paradigm offered by invalidation-based coherence protocols—especially important for synchronization operations. Prefetch issues long-latency operations early to reduce or hide their latency.

Many of the techniques mentioned above have been embodied in the DASH multiprocessor. The prototype system, built at the Computer Systems Laboratory of Stanford University, is the first operational multiprocessor with a cache coherence mechanism that scales beyond the confines of a single bus. This machine is proof that SSMPs can be built and work well. In addition, the completion of the DASH prototype enables us to place a price tag on the hardware required to turn a scalable multiprocessor into a scalable shared-memory multiprocessor. The cost of the additional mechanisms is less than 10% of system cost.

Many conclusions can also be drawn from the performance of DASH. Most importantly, a variety of real applications achieved good performance and speedups on DASH. Second, we see that in both DASH and TeraDASH the ratio of remote-to-local memory latency is approximately 3 to 1, and the absolute delay to remote memory is over 100 processor clocks. Thus, good performance relies first on optimizing cache performance and second on maximizing the ratio of local misses. Furthermore, when misses cannot be avoided, mechanisms such as prefetch can substantially improve performance. The TeraDASH design also illustrates that in future designs, memory latency will be very dependent on interconnection latencies. Thus, the system design should minimize network latency as much as possible. Finally, the performance of synchronization, especially global synchronization, is very dependent on the serialization of memory operations to the same location. While software trees using different locations can reduce this dependence, providing low serialization operations such as at-memory Fetch&Inc can be very beneficial.

Overall, the experience with DASH indicates that the performance gain (a factor of 2–3) from adding shared-memory and coherent caches to a scalable multiprocessor clearly outweighs its costs.

10.2 Current Trends

Today, parallel processing seems inevitable. Multiprocessor features are showing up in most microprocessor architectures. New processors support such features as prefetch, invalidation and flushing of on-chip caches, support for weak memory consistency models, and other latency tolerating techniques.

SSMPs are an active area of architecture and system software research. One of the trends in computer architecture is the closing gap between shared-memory and message passing machines. After all, most SSMPs build their memory system and cache coherence protocol on an underlying infrastructure of simple node-to-node messages. The MIT Alewife machine has added support for fast message-passing that leverages its cache coherency logic. Likewise, the FLASH multiprocessor system, a follow-on to DASH work at Stanford, integrates a communications processor onto each node. The communications processor can launch and process messages without interrupting the main processor. This flexible hardware is optimized to support the small messages used to maintain cache coherence, but it also supports explicit messaging-passing.

Another interesting topic is the ongoing debate between COMA and NUMA architectures. COMA claims all the advantages of a NUMA shared-memory multiprocessor with the addition of providing automatic data locality by migrating memory towards the processor using it. Opinions are divided about the utility of this feature and about the performance cost incurred from additional directory lookups in the COMA architecture. A compromise may be some form of combined hardware/software solution that relies on a software migration algorithm but uses hardware to gather processor miss statistics.

10.3 Future Trends

The future will no doubt bring the commercialization of SSMPs. The machines from Kendall Square Research, Convex, and Cray are the first commercial offerings of this class of machine, but certainly not the last. Other SSMPs are under development at several companies, including HaL and Silicon Graphics. Even traditional message-passing vendors such as Intel and Meiko are rumored to be adding shared-memory support to their latest designs.

Economic arguments also heavily favor SSMP systems over traditional message-passing MPP systems. In particular, providing scalable shared memory allows shared-memory multiprocessors to span the range from very small-scale, low-cost systems to very large-scale systems. Since smaller-scale systems have a significantly higher sales volume, this range provides SSMP systems with much greater leverage of hardware, system software, and application software development. Because of the complexity of programming message-passing machines, they have only been popular in large-scale configurations where they offered more processors than traditional shared-memory machines. SSMP systems with hundreds or thousands of processors will satisfy virtually all large-scale applications. The handful of remaining users who can afford systems with multiple thousands of processors and who have embarrassingly parallel jobs that could use even more processors do not provide enough revenue to support the necessary development efforts. The demise of Thinking Machines Corporation is evidence of this phenomenon.

Of course, one could make the same economic argument about SSMP systems versus clusters or networks of workstations (NOW [Pat94b]). Total annual workstations volumes are measured in the hundreds of thousands, while SSMP volumes are 20–40 times less. Thus, there is an economic advantage to building a large-scale multiprocessor out of a set of workstations connected via a standard or proprietary network, especially if idle workstations on desktops can be exploited.

There are a number of reasons why a collection of workstations does not replace an SSMP machine. First, the standard network interfaces on a workstation (even ATM or FDDI links) provide much lower bandwidth than found in an SSMP. More importantly, standard network interfaces have even larger latencies than the proprietary networks found in message-passing machines. These constraints imply that a NOW can only exploit very coarse-grain parallelism. Second, the individual nodes of a NOW lack the memory and I/O resources to support many large-scale workloads. While the aggregate I/O of a NOW may be similar to an SSMP, the throughput of high-performance I/O devices (e.g., a large RAID disk array or 100 MByte/sec HIPPI network connection) is limited by the I/O bandwidth of an individual workstation's I/O bus or network interface. Furthermore, even when one can distribute the I/O devices throughout the network, the higher communication cost in a NOW make it hard to aggregate these into a single high-performance stream. Third, a NOW provides a message-passing interface, and as discussed before, such a model is much more difficult to program, especially when communication patterns are irregular. Finally, SSMPs exploit much of the same technology as workstations and have enough volume to support the development of SSMP hardware and software solutions. Thus, while ganging-up workstations as a physical or virtual central resource is a trend that will become increasingly popular, the differences between SSMPs and NOWs are likely to make them complementary rather than competing technologies. Over time, these technologies may eventually merge so that every workstation could become a node within a larger SSMP system (as in Sun's S3.mp project).

With the proliferation of commercial SSMP machines will come the much needed experience in both software and hardware for this class of machine, further driving the evolution of SSMPs. Most likely, the wide range of architectural features provided in the early SSMPs will be pared down to a useful standard set, much like the convergence in RISC instruction set architectures in recent years. New applications of these machines will also drive their evolution. The redundant resources of an SSMP already provide the basis for fault tolerance and high availability. Commercial use of these machines is likely to motivate the improvements in system architecture and coherence protocols to fully support such features. Likewise, multimedia services and support of high-speed networking are likely to change the requirements for I/O interfacing.

With technology trends driving up processor clock rates at a seemingly unrelenting pace while memory speeds increase much more slowly, many of the latency hiding and tolerating techniques developed for large-scale shared-memory multiprocessors will become applicable to smaller multiprocessors and even uniprocessors. For example, even with just a handful of processors, today's bus-based multiprocessors can run out of memory bandwidth. The natural evolution of these small-scale multiprocessors is onto higher-bandwidth interconnects such as distributed networks, which will in turn cause directory-based cache coherence schemes to replace the snoopy coherence schemes used in today's small-scale machines.

Even high-performance uniprocessors can benefit from SSMP latency-hiding techniques such as prefetching. Future uniprocessor compilers will automatically place prefetch instructions to bring operands from memory before they are actually needed, thus hiding the memory access latency. Automatic placement of prefetch instructions in uniprocessor code is much simpler than in multiprocessor applications, and we might see this feature appear relatively soon—maybe even in the next couple of years.

The future of general-purpose, high-performance multiprocessing belongs to SSMPs. These systems are just now making the transition from research to development, and their obvious advantages in ease of use, performance, and cost-performance will make them the clear winner over other alternatives. The design and widespread use of production SSMP systems will drive their evolution and keep this an exciting area of computer architecture and design for some time to come.

APPENDIX

Multiprocessor Systems

T able A briefly describes the multiprocessor systems referred to in this book and supplies references for more details.

TABLE A

Multiprocessor Systems Mentioned in this Text

SYSTEM	DESCRIPTION	REFERENCES
*T and *T-NG	Hybrid dataflow and von Neumann multiprocessor developed at MIT. Includes a dedicated message processor and in *T-NG global cache coherence. Work on *T has been discontinued; *T-NG in the design stage during 1994.	5.6.3, [Bec92, NPA92, AAC94]
Alewife	Directory-based multiprocessor developed at MIT. Includes multithreaded processor that context switches on remote cache misses and synchronization failures. Project began in 1988; first prototype functional in 1994.	5.1.2, [ALK+90, ALK+91]
BBN Butterfly and TC2000	Two generations of multiprocessors supporting a NUMA shared-memory architecture and up to 256 and 512 processors, respectively. No support for hardware cache coherence though. Butterfly introduced in early 1980s, the TC2000, in 1989.	5.4.2, [BBN86, BBN89]
Burroughs Scientific Processor (BSP)	Follow-on to the Illiac IV machine utilizing 16 vectoring SIMD processing elements. Project began in 1973; initial prototype functional in 1978.	[KuS82]
Cedar	A shared-memory multiprocessor developed at the University of Illinois. The system supports 32 processors distributed into four clusters each with local memory (based on Alliant FX/8). The clusters are connected to a central non–cache-coherent, global memory. Work began in the early 1980s, and the initial prototype was operational in 1988.	[GKL+83]

Continued on next page

TABLE A

Multiprocessor Systems Mentioned in this Text (Continued)

SYSTEM	DESCRIPTION	REFERENCES
C.mmp	Early shared-memory multiprocessor developed at CMU that connected 16 minicomputers to 16 memory modules via a crossbar switch. Work began in 1971, and the machine was operational in 1975.	[Mas82]
Convex C4/XA	GaAs-based vector supercomputer with up to four 1.6 GFLOPS peak processors. Introduced in 1994.	[Gar94]
Convex Exemplar	Directory-based multiprocessor utilizing 128 processors in 16 clusters interconnected by four parallel IEEE SCI compliant rings. Introduced in 1994.	5.1.5, [Con94]
Cray SuperServer 6400	Bus-based UMA multiprocessor supporting up to 64 60MHz SuperSparc processors on four interleaved buses capable of a total of 1.76 GB/sec. Introduced in 1993.	[Cra93b, Boz93]
Cray T3D	MPP NUMA system supporting up to 2,048 DEC Alpha 21064 processors. No global cache coherence. Introduced in 1993.	5.4.3, [Cra93a, KeS93]
Cray X-MP	First multiprocessor Cray vector supercomputer supporting up to four processors running at 8.5 ns with a peak of 235 MFLOPS each. Introduced in 1983.	[Hwa93]
Cray Y-MP	Second-generation Cray vector multiprocessor capable of supporting eight processors running at 6 ns with a peak of 333 MFLOPS each. Introduced in 1989.	[SHH90]
Cray Y-MP C90	Third-generation Cray vector multiprocessor capable of supporting 16 processors running at 4.2 ns with a peak of 1 GFLOPS each. Introduced in 1991.	5.5.1, [Rob92]
DASH	Directory-based multiprocessor developed at Stanford. Features up to 16 clusters each with four processors sharing a snoopy bus. First operational in 1991.	Chapters 6–8, [LLG+90, Len91, LLG+92]
Data Diffusion Machine	Hierarchical system supporting cache-coherent COMA architecture developed at the Swedish Institute for Computer Science (SICS). In bring-up stage during 1994.	5.2.3, [HHW90, HLH92]
Denelcor HEP	Early MIMD shared-memory multiprocessor supporting multiple-context processor; contexts are swapped on a cycle-by-cycle basis. First introduced in the early 1980s.	[Smi81]
Encore GigaMax	Hierarchical snoopy bus-based system supporting up to 64 processors in four clusters of 16. Design began during 1987, but was discontinued in 1991.	5.2.1, [Wil87, WWS+89]
FLASH	Follow-on to the DASH project at Stanford. Features programmable directory controller capable of different coherence protocols. In design stage during 1994.	[KOH+94]

TABLE A

Multiprocessor Systems Mentioned in this Text (Continued)

SYSTEM	DESCRIPTION	REFERENCES
Gould SCI-Clone/32	Commercial system aimed at real-time applications utilizing reflective memory. First introduced in 1984.	[Gou84]
HP 735CL	Clustered HP 735 workstations interconnected by either Ethernet or FDDI. Introduced in 1993.	[HP94]
IBM ES/9000	Mainframe multiprocessor supporting up to 10 processors with a shared UMA memory. Introduced in 1991.	[NoL91]
IBM RP3	Research machine that grew out of work on NYU Ultracomputer. Featured combining Fetch&Op memory operations. Operational in the mid-1980s.	5.4.2, [PBG+85]
IBM SP1	Clustered IBM Power1 workstations connected by dedicated MIN interconnection network. Supports up to 64 processors with a peak of 125 MFLOPS per processor. Introduced in 1993.	[SSG+94]
IBM SP2	Clustered IBM Power2 workstations connected by dedicated MIN interconnection network. Supports up to 512 processors with a peak of 266 MFLOPS per processor. Introduced in 1994.	[IBM94, StH94]
IEEE 1596-1992 SCI	IEEE standard interface that supports distributed link-list directories. Base standard ratified in 1992. First system based on the standard is the Convex Exemplar.	5.1.4, [JLG+90, IEE92]
Illiac IV	Early SIMD multiprocessor developed by the U. of Illinois in the 1960s. 64-processing-element unit built by Burroughs in 1972.	[HwB84]
Intel Delta	Message-passing MIMD machine based on 570 Intel i860 processors connected by Caltech Mesh Routing Chips. First operational at Caltech in 1991.	[Mye91]
Intel iPSC	First commercial hypercube MIMD message-passing machine. Introduced in 1985.	[AtS88]
Intel Paragon	Follow-on message-passing MIMD machine to the Intel Delta. Systems with as many as 1,800 nodes have been built. The latest systems support up to three 75 MFLOPS peak Intel i860 processors per node. First version introduced in 1991.	[Int93, Hwa93]
IVY	The first virtual shared-memory system. Developed at Yale University, this software system supports shared-memory semantics on top of set of networked or message-passing nodes. First implementation on Apollo workstations in the mid-1980s.	5.6.1, [LiH86, Li88, LiH89]

Continued on next page

TABLE A

Multiprocessor Systems Mentioned in this Text (Continued)

SYSTEM	DESCRIPTION	REFERENCES
J-Machine	Flexible multiprocessor based on a collection of message-driven processors (MDPs) connected in a 3-D torus. Supports shared-memory, message-passing, and data flow architectures. Developed at MIT and first operational in 1991.	5.6.2, [DCF+89, Wal90]
KSR-1 and KSR-2	First commercial COMA machine based on a hierarchy of rings. KSR-1 supports up to 1,088, 40 MFLOPS processors while the KSR-2 supports over 5,000, 80 MFLOPS processors. The KSR-1 was first introduced in 1991, the KSR-2 in 1993.	5.2.4, [Bur91, FRB93, KSR93a, KSR93b]
MasPar MP-1 and MP-2	First- and second-generation SIMD machines supporting up to 16K processing elements. The MasPar MP-1 was introduced in 1989, and the MP-2 in 1993.	[Bla90, KiT93]
Meiko CS-2	A message-passing MIMD machine supporting up to 256 processors connected by a fat tree interconnect. First introduced in 1993.	[HoM93, BCM94]
Merlin	A paper design for a reflective memory system devised by Sandia National Labs and SUNY–Stony Brook. System consists of a set of workstations connected through a reflective memory interface by fiber optic links. First described in 1990.	[MaW90]
MPP	An SIMD machine designed by Goodyear Aerospace employing 16K processors in a 128×128 array specialized for image processing. The machine was operational in the early 1980s.	[HwB84]
Munin and Treadmarks	A virtual shared-memory system developed at Rice University. Munin increases performance through a set of coherence protocols that depend upon the class of data. Performance also increased by the use of lazy release consistency (LRC). Munin first described in 1990; LRC in 1992.	5.6.1, [BCZ90a, KCZ92, CDK+94]
nCUBE 1 and 2	Two generations of highly integrated, message-passing MIMD hypercube multicomputers. The nCUBE 1 supports up to 1,024 processors and was introduced in 1985. The nCUBE 2 supports up to 8K processors and was introduced in 1992.	[Pal88, NCu92]
ParaDiGM	Research machine developed at Stanford that combines a hierarchy of directory-based nodes and networked systems. This system was in development in 1994.	5.2.2, [CGB91]
Plus	A reflective memory system developed at CMU. First described in 1990.	5.3.1, [BiR90]

TABLE A

Multiprocessor Systems Mentioned in this Text (Continued)

SYSTEM	DESCRIPTION	REFERENCES
S-1	An early multiprocessor supercomputer that was to support directory-based coherence. This system was first described in 1980, but the multiprocessor version was not completed.	[WiC80, HwB84]
Sun S3.mp	A directory-based multiprocessor consisting of clusters of MBUS-based nodes. System interconnected by a set of point-to-point gigabit serial links. The serial links were operational in 1993, and the overall system is in design during 1994.	5.1.3, [NMP+93, NoP93]
Sequent Symmetry	Second-generation bus-based UMA multiprocessor supporting up to 30 processors. Introduced in 1988.	[LoT88]
Sequoia	Dynamic fault-tolerant shared-memory multiprocessor featuring roll-back and recovery using cache state. First introduced in the mid-1980s.	[Ber88]
Sesame	A paper design follow-on to the Merlin system with reflective memory developed at SUNY–Stony Brook. First described in 1990.	5.3.2, [WHL90]
SGI 4D/340	Snoopy bus-based multiprocessor used as the basis of the clusters in the Stanford DASH machine. The first version of these systems was introduced in 1988.	[BJS88]
Stratus	Static fault-tolerant shared-memory multiprocessor featuring a "quadded" processor arrangement with pairs of processors functioning as self-checked modules that can back each other up in the event of a failure. The first system was introduced in 1981.	[WeB91]
Sun SparcCenter 2000	Snoopy bus-based multiprocessor featuring up to 20 processors and dual buses with an aggregate transfer rate of 880 MBytes/sec. Introduced in 1992.	[CYS+93]
Sun SparcServer 1000	Scaled down desktop version of the SparcCenter 2000 that supports eight processors and a single 440 MByte/sec bus. Introduced in 1992.	[Sun94a]
Sun SparcStation 10	Desktop multiprocessor workstation supporting up to four processors based on the snoopy MBUS. First introduced in 1992.	[Sun94b]
Systran Scramnet	Reflective memory subsystem that can be added to various standard I/O buses. Used primarily in real-time applications. First introduced in 1989.	[Boh94, Sys94]
Tera Computer MTA	GaAs supercomputer supporting up to 256 multi-threaded processors in a 3-D torus configuration. In design during 1994.	5.5.2, [ACC+90]

Continued on next page

TABLE A

Multiprocessor Systems Mentioned in this Text (Continued)

SYSTEM	DESCRIPTION	REFERENCES
TeraDASH	A paper design, described in this text, that outlines an integrated version of the DASH design supporting up to 2,048 processors and one trillion operations per second.	Chapter 9, [Len91]
TMC CM-1 and CM-2	SIMD machines supporting up to 16K and 64K, respectively, 1-bit processing elements. The CM-1 was introduced in 1985 and the CM-2 in 1987.	[Hil85, Hil87b, Thi87]
TMC CM-5	Message-passing MIMD follow-on to the TMC SIMD line featuring up to 16K SuperSparc processors with attached vector units. Interconnect network is a fat tree. Introduced in 1993.	[Thi93]
Ultracomputer	A paper design done at NYU that introduced the notion of combining Fetch&Op operations. First described in 1983. In 1994 there is ongoing work on Ultra III, a follow-on actual design incorporating a combining network.	5.4.1, [GGK+83, FrG91, DiK92, GBD+93, FRB93]

References

AdH90   S. Adve and M. Hill. Weak Ordering—A New Definition. In *Proc. 17th Int. Symp. on Computer Architecture*, pages 2–14, May 1990.

ALK+90   A. Agarwal, B.-H. Lim, D. Kranz, and J. Kubiatowicz. April: A Processor Architecture for Multiprocessing. In *Proc. 17th Int. Symp. on Computer Architecture*, pages 104–114, May 1990.

ALK+91   A. Agarwal, B.-H. Lim, D. Kranz, and J. Kubiatowicz. LimitLESS Directories: A Scalable Cache Coherence Scheme. In *Proc. Fourth Int. Conf. on Architectural Support for Programming Languages and Operating Systems,* pages 224–234, April 1991.

ASH+88   A. Agarwal, R. Simoni, J. Hennessy, and M. Horowitz. An Evaluation of Directory Schemes for Cache Coherence. In *Proc. 15th Int. Symp. on Computer Architecture*, pages 280–289, June 1988.

ACG86   S. Ahuja, N. Carriero, and D. Gelernter. Linda and Friends. *IEEE Computer* **19**(8):26–34, August 1986.

AlB93   M. Allen and M. Becker. Multiprocessing Aspects of the PowerPC 601. In *Proc. Compcon Spring 93*, pages 117–126, February 1993.

Als90   M. Alsup. Motorola's 88000 Family Architecture. *IEEE Micro* **10**(3):48–66, June 1990.

ACC+90   R. Alverson, D. Callahan, D. Cummings, B. Koblenz, A. Porterfield, and B. Smith. The Tera Computer System. In *1990 Int. Conf. on Supercomputing*, pages 1–6, September 1990.

Amd67   G. Amdahl. Validity of the Single Processor Approach to Achieving Large Scale Computing Capabilities. In *AFIPS Spring Joint Computer Conf. Proc.*, pages 483–485, April 1967.

AAC94   B. Ang, Arvind, and D. Chiou. *StarT the Next Generation: Integrating Global Caches and Dataflow Architecture.* MIT Laboratory of Computer Science Technical Report—CSG Memo 354, February 1994.

ArB86a   J. Archibald and J.-L. Baer. Cache Coherence Protocols: Evaluation Using a Multiprocessor Simulation Model. *ACM Transactions on Computer Systems* **4**(4):273–298, November 1986.

ArB86b   J. Archibald and J.-L. Baer. An Economical Solution to the Cache Coherence Problem. In *Proc. 12th Int. Symp. on Computer Architecture*, pages 355–362, June 1986.

AtS88   W. Athas and C. Seitz. Multicomputers: Message-Passing Concurrent Computers. *IEEE Computer* **21**(8):9–24, August 1988.

BBC+92   J. Bartlett, W. Bartlett, R. Carr, D. Garcia, J. Gray, et al. Fault Tolerance in Tandem Computer Systems. In *Reliable Computer Systems: Design and Evaluation*, ed. D. Siewiorek and R. Swarz. Digital Press, Maynard, MA, 1992.

BCM94   E. Barton, J. Cownie, and M. McLaren. Message Passing on the Meiko CS-2. *Parallel Computing* **20**(4):497–507, April 1994.

BJS88   F. Baskett, T. Jermoluk, and D. Solomon. The 4D-MP Graphics Superworkstation: Computing + Graphics = 40 MIPS + 40 MFLOPS and 100,000 Lighted Polygons per Second. In *Proc. Compcon Spring 88*, pages 468–471, February 1988.

BBN86   BBN Laboratories, Inc. *Butterfly Parallel Processor Overview*, March 1986.

BBN89   BBN Advanced Computers, Inc. *TC2000 Technical Product Summary*, November 1989.

Bec92   M. Beckerle. *An Overview of the START(*T) Computer System*. Motorola Technical Report MCRC-TR-28, July 1992.

BCZ90a   J. Bennett, J. Carter, and W. Zwaenepoel. Munin: Distracted Shared-Memory Based on Type-Specific Memory Coherence. In *Proc. of 1990 Conf. on Principle and Practice of Parallel Programming*, pages 168–179, March 1990.

BCZ90b   J. Bennett, J. Carter, and W. Zwaenepoel. Adaptive Software Cache Management for Distributed Shared Memory Architectures. In *Proc. 17th Int. Symp. on Computer Architecture*, pages 125–134, May 1990.

Ber88   P. Bernstein. Sequoia: A Fault-Tolerant Tightly Coupled Multiprocessor for Transaction Processing. *IEEE Computer* **21**(2):37–45, February 1988.

Ber89   M. Berry et al. *The Perfect Club Benchmarks: Effective Performance Evaluation of Supercomputers*. Technical Report CSRD No. 827, Center for Supercomputing Research and Development, Urbana, IL, May 1989.

BiR90   R. Bisiani and M. Ravishankar. PLUS: A Distributed Shared-Memory System. In *Proc. 17th Int. Symp. on Computer Architecture*, pages 115–124, May 1990.

BlK92   G. Blanck and S. Krueger. The SuperSPARC Microprocessor. In *Proc. Compcon Spring 92*, pages 136–141, February 1992.

Bla90   T. Blank. The MasPar MP-1 Architecture. In *Proc. Compcon Spring 90*, pages 20–24, March 1990.

Boh94   T. Bohman. *Shared-Memory Computing Architectures for Real-Time Simulation—Simplicity and Elegance*. Systran Corporation, 1994.

Bou94   A. Boughton. Arctic Routing Chip. In *IEEE Hot Interconnects II*, pages 164–172, August 1994.

Boz93   J. Bozman. Cray Research Gets Commercial SPARC. *Computerworld* **27**(44):10, November 1993.

Bur91   H. Burkhart III et al. *Overview of the KSR1 Computer System*. Technical Report KSR-TR-9202001, Kendall Square Research, Boston, February 1992.

CYS+93   M. Cekleov et al. SPARCcenter 2000: Multiprocessing for the 90's! In *Proc. Compcon Spring 93*, pages 345–353, February 1993.

CeF78   L. Censier and P. Feautrier. A New Solution to Coherence Problems in Multi-cache Systems. *IEEE Transactions on Computers* **C-27**(12):1112–1118, December 1978.

CFK+90   D. Chaiken, C. Fields, K. Kurihara, and A. Agarwal. Directory-Based Cache Coherence in Large-Scale Multiprocessors. *IEEE Computer* **23**(6):49–58, June 1990.

ChM81   K. Chandy and J. Misra. Asynchronous Distributed Simulation via a Sequence of Parallel Computations. In *Communications of the ACM*, pages 198–206, April 1981.

CLG+94   P. Chen, E. Lee, G. Gibson, R. Katz, and D. Patterson. RAID: High-Performance, Reliable Secondary Storage. *ACM Computing Surveys* **26**(2):145–186, June 1994.

CGB91   D. Cheriton, H. Goosen, and P. Boyle. ParaDiGM: A Highly Scalable Shared-Memory Multi-Computer Architecture. *IEEE Computer* **24**(2):33–46, February 1991.

Com94   Compaq Computer Corporation. *Compaq ProLiant 4000 Product Bulletin*, Document Number 020A/1194, December 1994.

Con94   Convex Computer Corporation. *Convex Exemplar Architecture*, 1994.

CDK+94   A. Cox, S. Dwarkadas, P. Keleher, B. Lu, R. Rajamony, and W. Zwaenepoel. Software versus Hardware Shared-Memory Implementation: A Case Study. In *Proc. 21st Int. Symp. on Computer Architecture*, pages 106–117, April 1994.

CoF93   A. Cox and R. Fowler. Adaptive Cache Coherency for Detecting Migratory Shared Data. In *Proc. 20th Int. Symp. on Computer Architecture*, pages 98–108, May 1993.

Cra93a   Cray Research. *Cray T3D Technical Summary*, October 1993.

Cra93b   Cray Research. *Cray Superserver CS6400 Product*. Brochure, 1993.

Cro90   J. Croll. VAX 6000 Model 400 System Overview. In *Proc. Compcon Spring 90*, pages 110–114, February 1990.

Cum90   R. Cummings. New Era Dawns for Peripheral Channels. In *Laser Focus World*, pages 165–174, September 1990.

Dal87   W. Dally. Wire-Efficient VLSI Multiprocessor Communication Networks. In *Proc. Stanford Conf. on Advanced Research in VLSI*, pages 391–415, March 1987.

Dal90a   W. Dally. Virtual-Channel Flow Control. In *Proc. 17th Int. Symp. on Computer Architecture*, pages 60–68, May 1990.

Dal90b   W. Dally. Performance Analysis of k-ary n-cube Interconnection Networks. *IEEE Transactions on Computers* **39**(6):775–785, June 1990.

DCF+89   W. Dally, A. Chien, S. Fiske, W. Horwat, J. Keen, M. Larivee, R. Lethin, P. Nuth, and S. Wills. The J-Machine: A Fine-Grain Concurrent Computer. In *Proc. of the IFIP Congress*, pages 1147–1153, August 1989.

DaS87   W. Dally and C. Seitz. Deadlock Free Message Routing in Multiprocessor Interconnection Networks. *IEEE Transactions on Computers* **C-36**(5):547–553, May 1987.

Dat87   Dataquest. MOS Memory Market Forecast. *Semiconductor Industry Service: Products, Markets and Technology* **II**:11, April 1987.

DiK92   S. Dickey and R. Kenner. Hardware Combining and Scalability. In *Proc. of the 4th ACM Symp. on Parallel Algorithms and Architectures (SPAA)*, pages 296–305, June 1992.

DEC92   Digital Equipment Corporation. Alpha AXP Architecture and Systems. *Digital Technical Journal* **4**(4), Special Issue, 1992.

Don94   J. Dongarra. *Performance of Various Computers Using Standard Linear Equations Software*. Technical Report CS-89-85, University of Tennessee—CS Dept., July 1994.

DSB86   M. Dubois, C. Scheurich, and F. Briggs. Memory Access Buffering in Multiprocessors. In *Proc. of the 13th Int. Symp. on Computer Architecture*, pages 434–442, June 1986.

DSB88   M. Dubois, C. Scheurich, and F. Briggs. Synchronization, Coherence, and Event Ordering in Multiprocessors. *IEEE Computer* **21**(2):9–21, February 1988.

DBW+91   M. Dubois, L. Barroso, J. Wang, and Y. Chen. Delayed Consistency and Its Effects on the Miss Rate of Parallel Programs. In *Supercomputing '91*, pages 197–206, November 1991.

EgK88   S. Eggers and R. Katz. A Characterization of Sharing in Parallel Programs and Its Application to Coherency Protocol Evaluation. In *Proc. 15th Int. Symp. on Computer Architecture*, pages 373–383, May 1988.

EgK89a   S. Eggers and R. Katz. The Effect of Sharing on the Cache and Bus Performance of Parallel Programs. In *Proc. 3rd Int. Conf. on Architectural Support for Programming Languages and Operating Systems*, pages 257–270, April 1989.

EgK89b   S. Eggers and R. Katz. Evaluating the Performance of Four Snooping Cache Coherency Protocols. In *Proc. 16th Int. Symp. on Computer Architecture*, pages 2–15, May 1989.

Elk82   S. Elkind, Reliability and Availability Techniques. In *The Theory and Practice of Reliable System Design*, ed. D. Siewiorek and R. Swarz, pages 63–182. Digital Press, Maynard, MA, 1982.

Fen81   T. Feng. A Survey of Interconnection Networks. *IEEE Computer* **14**(12):12–27, December 1981.

Fla87   C. Flaig. *VLSI Mesh Routing Systems*. Technical Report 5241:TR:87, California Institute of Technology, May 1987.

Fly72   M. Flynn. Some Computer Organizations and Their Effectiveness. *IEEE Trans. on Computers* **21**(9):948–960, September 1972.

FoW78   S. Fortune and J. Wyllie. Parallelism in Random Access Machines. In *Proc. 10th Symp. on the Theory of Computing*, pages 114–118, May 1978.

FRB93   S. Frank, J. Rothnie, and H. Burkhardt III. The KSR1: Bridging the Gap Between Shared Memory and MPPs. In *Proc. Compcon Spring 93*, pages 285–294, March 1993.

FrG91   E. Freudenthal and A. Gottlieb. Process Coordination with Fetch-and-Increment. In *Proc. Fourth Int. Conf. on Architectural Support for Programming Languages and Operating Systems*, pages 260–268, April 1991.

Gar94   G. Garry. Convex Counting on Gallium Arsenide in Its C Series Line. *Digital News & Review* **11**(13):3, July 1994.

GGP+89   P. Gelsinger, P. Gargini, G. Parker, and A. Yu. Microprocessors Circa 2000. *IEEE Spectrum* **26**(10):43–47, October 1989.

GLN80   A. George, J. Liu, and E. Ng. *User's Guide for SPARSPAK: Waterloo Sparse Linear Equations Package*. Research Report CS-78-30, Department of Computer Science, University of Waterloo, 1980.

GGH91   K. Gharachorloo, A. Gupta, and J. Hennessy. Performance Evaluation of Memory Consistency Models for Shared-Memory Multiprocessors. In *Proc. Fourth Int. Conf. on Architectural Support for Programming Languages and Operating Systems*, pages 245–257, April 1991.

GLL+90   K. Gharachorloo, D. Lenoski, J. Laudon, P. Gibbons, A. Gupta, and J. Hennessy. Memory Consistency and Event Ordering in Scalable Shared-Memory Multiprocessors. In *Proc. 17th Int. Symp. on Computer Architecture*, pages 15–26, May 1990.

GMG91   P. Gibbons, M. Merritt, and K. Gharachorloo. *Proving Sequential Consistency of High-Performance Shared Memories*. Technical Report 11211-910509-09TM, AT&T Bell Laboratories, May 9, 1991.

GKL+83   D. Gajski, D. Kuck, D. Lawrie, and A. Sameh. Cedar: A Large-Scale Multiprocessor. In *Proc. 1983 Int. Conf. on Parallel Processing*, pages 524–529, August 1983.

GjM91   S. Gjessing and E. Munthe-Kaas. *Formal Specification of Cache Coherence in a Shared Memory Multiprocessor*. Technical Report in Informatics, No. 158, University of Oslo, October 1991.

GDF94   D. Glasco, B. Delagi, and M. Flynn. Update-Based Cache Coherence Protocols for Scalable Shared-Memory Multiprocessors. In *Proc. 27th Hawaii Int. Conf. on System Sciences*, Vol. I: Architecture, pages 534–545, 1994.

Gol93   S. Goldschmidt. *Simulation of Multiprocessors: Accuracy and Performance*. Ph.D. Thesis, Stanford University, June 1993.

Goo89   J. Goodman. *Cache Consistency and Sequential Consistency*. Technical Report 61, SCI Working Committee, March 1989.

GVW89   J. Goodman, M. Vernon, and P. Woest. Efficient Synchronization Primitives for Large-Scale Cache-Coherent Multiprocessors. In *Proc. Third Int. Conf. Architectural Support for Programming Languages and Operating Systems*, pages 64–73, April 1989.

GGV90 E. Gornish, E. Granston, and A. Veidenbaum. Compiler-Directed Data Prefetching in Multiprocessors with Memory Hierarchies. In *Proc. Int. Conf. on Supercomputing*, pages 354–368, 1990.

GGK+83 A. Gottlieb, R. Grishman, C. Kruskal, K. McAuliffe, L. Rudolph, and M. Snir. The NYU Ultracomputer—Designing an MIMD Shared Memory Parallel Computer. *IEEE Transactions on Computers* **C-32**(2):175–189, February 1983.

GBD+93 A. Gottlieb, R. Bianchini, S. Dickey, J. Edler, G. Goodman, R. Kenner, and J. Wang. The Ultra III Prototype. In *Proc. 7th Int. Parallel Processing Symp. and Parallel Systems Fair*, pages 2–9, April 1993.

Gou84 Gould Computer Systems. *SCI-Clone/32 Distributed Processing System*. Brochure, 1984.

Gra90 J. Gray. A Census of Tandem System Availability Between 1985 and 1990. *IEEE Trans. on Reliability* **39**(4):409–418, October 1990.

GYN+92 B. Gunning, L. Yuan, T. Nguyen, and T. Wong. A CMOS Low-Voltage-Swing Transmission-Line Transceiver. In *Proc. 1992 IEEE Int. Solid State Circuits Conf.*, February 1992.

GHG+91 A. Gupta, J. Hennessy, K. Gharachorloo, T. Mowry, and W.-D. Weber. Comparative Evaluaton of Latency Reducing and Tolerating Techniques. In *Proc. 18th Int. Symp. on Computer Architecture*, pages 254–263, June 1991.

GWM90 A. Gupta, W.-D. Weber, and T. Mowry. Reducing Memory and Traffic Requirements for Scalable Directory-Based Cache Coherence Schemes. In *Proc. 1990 Int. Conf. on Parallel Processing*, pages I:312–321, August 1990.

Gus88 J. Gustafson. Reevaluating Amdahl's Law. *Communications of the ACM* **31**(5):532–533, May 1988.

GMB88 J. Gustafson, G. Montry, and R. Brenner. Development of Parallel Methods for a 1024-Processor Hypercube. *SIAM Journal Scientific and Statistical Computing* **9**(4):532–533, July 1988.

HHW90 E. Hagersten, S. Haridi, and D. Warren. The Cache Coherence Protocol of the Data Diffusion Machine. In *Cache and Interconnect Architectures in Multiprocessors*, ed. M. Dubois and S. Thakkar, pages 165–188. Kluwer Academic Publishers, Norwell, MA, 1990.

HLH92 E. Hagersten, A. Landin, and S. Haridi. DDM—A Cache-Only Memory Architecture. *IEEE Computer* **25**(9):44–54, September 1992.

HSL94 E. Hagersten, A. Saulsbury, and A. Landin. Simple COMA Node Implementation. In *Proc. Hawaii Int. Conf. on System Science*, pages 522–533, January 1994.

HaF88 R. Halstead and T. Fujita. MASA: A Multithreaded Processor Architecture for Parallel Symbolic Computing. In *Proc. 15th Int. Symp. on Computer Architecture*, pages 443–451, June 1988.

Hei93 J. Heinrich. *MIPS R4000 User's Manual*. PTR Prentice Hall, Englewood Cliffs, NJ, 1993.

HeP90   J. Hennessy and D. Patterson. *Computer Architecture: A Quantitative Approach.* Morgan Kaufmann Publishers, San Francisco, CA, 1990.

HeJ91   J. Hennessy and N. Jouppi. Computer Technology and Architecture: An Evolving Interaction. *IEEE Computer* **24**(9):18–29, September 1991.

Her91   M. Herlihy. Wait-Free Synchronization. In *ACM Trans. Programming Languages and Systems*, Vol. 13, pages 124–149, January 1991.

HP94   Hewlett-Packard Co. *HP 9000 Series 700 Model 735CL Computational Cluster.* Brochure, 1994.

Hil87a   M. Hill. *Aspects of Cache Memory and Instruction Buffer Performance.* Ph.D. Thesis, Univ. of Calif. at Berkeley, Computer Science Div., Technical Report UCB/CSD 87/381, November 1987.

Hil90   M. Hill. What is Scalability? *Computer Architecture News* **18**(4):18–21, December 1990.

Hil85   W. Hillis. *The Connection Machine.* MIT Press, Cambridge, MA, 1985.

Hil87b   W. Hillis. The Connection Machine. *Scientific American* **256**(6):108–115, June 1987.

HoM93   M. Homewood and M. McLaren. Meiko CS-2 Interconnect Elan—Elite Design. In *Hot Interconnects '93*, pages 2.1.1–2.1.4, August 1993.

Hsu94   P. Hsu. Designing the TFP Microprocessor. *IEEE Micro* **14**(2):23–33, April 1994.

HwB84   K. Hwang and F. Briggs. *Computer Architecture and Parallel Processing.* McGraw-Hill, New York, NY, 1984.

Hwa93   K. Hwang. *Advanced Computer Architecture: Parallelism, Scalability, Programmability.* McGraw-Hill, New York, NY, 1993.

Ian88   R. Iannucci. Toward a Dataflow/von Neumann Hybrid Architecture. In *Proc. 15th Int. Symp. on Computer Architecture*, pages 131–140, June 1988.

IBM   IBM. *System/370 Principles of Operation.* Order Number GA22-7000.

IBM94   IBM. *IBM Announces New Family of POWERparallel Systems.* IBM press release, April 1994.

IEE91   IEEE. *IEEE Standard for Futurebus+ Logical Protocol Specification.* IEEE Std. 896.1-1991, 1991.

IEE92   IEEE. *ANSI/IEEE Std. 1596-1992, Scalable Coherent Interface (SCI)*, 1992.

Int93   Intel Corporation, Supercomputer Systems Division. *Intel Paragon Supercomputers.* Brochure, 1993.

JDB89   P. Jain, S. Dhingra, and J. Browne. Bringing Top-Down Synthesis into the Real World. *High Performance Systems*, pages 86–94, July 1989.

JWB94   R. Jain, J. Werth, and J. Browne. Special Issue on Input/Output in Parallel Computer Systems: Introduction. *Computer Architecture News* **22**(4):3–4, September 1994.

JLG+90   D. James, A. Laundrie, S. Gjessing, and G. Sohi. Distributed-Directory Scheme: Scalable Coherent Interface. *IEEE Computer* **23**(6):74–77, June 1990.

Joh93 R. Johnson. *Extending the Scalable Coherent Interface for Large-Scale Shared-Memory Multiprocessors.* Ph.D. Thesis, University of Wisconsin-Madison, 1993.

Joh89 W. Johnson. *Super-Scalar Processor Design.* Technical Report CSL-TR-89-383, Stanford University, June 1989.

Jou90 N. Jouppi. Improving Direct-Mapped Cache Performance by the Addition of a Small Fully-Associative Cache and Prefetch Buffers. In *Proc. 17th Int. Symp. on Computer Architecture*, pages 364–373, May 1990.

KMR+86 A. Karlin, M. Manasse, L. Rudolph, and D. Sleator. Competitive Snoopy Caching. In *Proc. 27th Ann. Symp. on Foundations of Computer Science*, pages 244–254, October 1986.

KCZ92 P. Keleher, A. Cox, and W. Zwaenepoel. Lazy Release Consistency for Software Distributed Shared Memory. In *Proc. 19th Int. Symp. on Computer Architecture*, pages 13–21, May 1992.

KSR93a Kendall Square Research. *KSR Technical Summary*, 1993.

KSR93b Kendall Square Research. *KSR2 Product.* Brochure, 1993.

KeK79 P. Kermani and L. Kleinrock. Virtual Cut-Through: A New Computer Communication Switching Technique. *Computer Networks* 3:267–286, March 1979.

KeS93 R. Kessler and J. Schwarzmeier. Cray T3D: A New Dimension for Cray Research. In *Proc. Compcon Spring 93*, pages 176–182, February 1993.

KiT93 W. Kim and R. Tuck. Maspar MP-2 PE Chip: A Totally Cool Hot Chip. In *Hot Chips V*, August 1993.

Kle89 B. Kleinman. *DASH Protocol Verification.* Technical Report, EE 391 Class Project, Stanford University, April 1989.

KuS82 D. Kuck and R. Stokes. The Burroughs Scientific Processor (BSP). *IEEE Transactions on Computers* **C-31**(5):363–376, May 1982.

Kni87 T. Knight. Talk at Stanford Computer Systems Laboratory, March 1987.

Kro81 D. Kroft. Lockup-Free Instruction Fetch/Prefetch Cache Organization. In *Proc. 8th Int. Symp. on Computer Architecture*, pages 81–86, May 1981.

KOH+94 J. Kuskin, D. Ofelt, M. Heinrich, J. Heinlein, R. Simoni, K. Gharachorloo, J. Chapin, D. Nakahira, J. Baxter, M. Horowitz, A. Gupta, M. Rosenblum, and J. Hennessy. The Stanford FLASH Multiprocessor. In *Proc. 21st Int. Symp. on Computer Architecture*, pages 302–313, April 1994.

LRW91 M. Lam, E. Rothberg, and M. Wolf. The Cache Performance and Optimizations of Blocked Algorithms. In *Proc. Fourth Int. Conf. on Architectural Support for Programming Languages and Operating Systems*, pages 63–74, April 1991.

Lam79 L. Lamport. How to Make a Multiprocessor Computer That Correctly Executes Multiprocess Programs. *IEEE Transactions on Computers* **C-28**(9):241–248, September 1979.

LGH92 J. Laudon, A. Gupta, and M. Horowitz. *Architectural and Implementation Trade-offs in the Design of Multiple-Context Processors.* Stanford University Technical Report CSL-TR-92-523, May 1992.

Lee87 R. Lee. *The Effectiveness of Caches and Data Prefetch Buffers in Large-Scale Shared Memory Multiprocessors*. Ph.D. Thesis, University of Illinois at Urbana-Champaign, May 1987.

LYL87 R. Lee, P.-C. Yew, and D. Lawrie. Data Prefetching in Shared Memory Multiprocessors. In *Proc. Int. Conf. on Parallel Processing*, pages 28–31, August 1987.

Lei85 C. Leierson. Fat-Trees: Universal Networks for Hardware-Efficient Supercomputing. *IEEE Transactions on Computers* **C-34**(10):892–901, October 1985.

Len91 D. Lenoski. *The Design and Analysis of DASH: A Scalable Directory-Based Multiprocessor*. Ph.D. Thesis, Stanford University, December 1991. Also available as Stanford University Technical Report CSL-TR-92-507.

LLG+90 D. Lenoski, J. Laudon, K. Gharachorloo, A. Gupta, and J. Hennessy. The Directory-Based Cache Coherence Protocol for the DASH Multiprocessor. *Proc. 17th Int. Symp. on Computer Architecture*, pages 148–159, May 1990.

LLG+92 D. Lenoski, J. Laudon, K. Gharachorloo, W.-D. Weber, A. Gupta, J. Hennessy, M. Horowitz, and M. Lam. The Stanford DASH Multiprocessor. *IEEE Computer* **25**(3):63–79, March 1992.

LiH86 K. Li and P. Hudak. Memory Coherence in Shared Virtual Memory Systems. In *Proc. 5th ACM Sym. on Prin. of Distributed Computing*, pages 229–239, August 1986.

Li88 K. Li. IVY: A Shared Virtual Memory System for Parallel Computing. In *Proc. 1988 Int. Conf. on Parallel Processing*, pages 94–101, August 1988.

LiH89 K. Li and P. Hudak. Memory Coherence in Shared Virtual Memory Systems. *ACM Trans. on Computer Systems*, **7**(4):321–359, November 1989.

LiA94 D. Lilja and S. Ambalavanan. A Superassociative Tagged Cache Coherence Directory. In *Proc. IEEE Conf. on Computer Design: VLSI in Computers and Processors*, pages 42–45, October 1994.

LoT88 T. Lovett and S. Thakkar. The Symmetry Multiprocessor System. In *Proc. 1988 Int. Conf. on Parallel Processing*, pages 303–310, August 1988.

LOB+87 E. Lusk, R. Overbeek, J. Boyle, R. Butler, T. Disz, B. Glickfeld, J. Patterson, and R. Stevens, *Portable Programs for Parallel Processors*. Holt, Rinehart and Winston, Orlando, FL, 1987.

MaW79 T. May and M. Wood. Alpha-Particle-Induced Soft Errors in Dynamic Memories. *IEEE Transactions on Electron Devices* **ED-26**(1):2–16, January 1979.

MaW90 C. Maples and L. Wittie. Merlin: A Superglue for Multicomputer Systems. In *Proc. Compcon Spring 90*, pages 73–81, February 1990.

Mas82 H. Mashburn. The C.mmp/Hydra Project: An Architectural Overview. In *Computer Structures: Principles and Examples*, ed. D. Siewiorek, C. Bell, and A. Newell, pages 350–370. McGraw-Hill, New York, NY, 1982.

McB88 J. McDonald and D. Baganoff. Vectorization of a Particle Simulation Method for Hypersonic Rarified Flow. In *Proc. AIAA Thermodynamics, Plasmadynamics and Lasers Conf.*, June 1988.

McD91   J. McDonald. Particle Simulation in a Multiprocessor Environment. AIAA Paper No. 91-1366. In *26th Thermophysics Conf.*, June 1991.

McS91   K. McMillan and J. Schwalbe. Formal Verification of the GigaMax Cache Consistency Protocol. In *Proc. Int. Symp. on Shared Memory Multiprocessing*, pages 242–251, April 1991.

MIP91a   MIPS Computer Systems. *Introduction to the R4000 Microprocessor*, 1991.

MIP91b   MIPS Computer Systems. *R4000 Microprocessor Users Manual*, 1991.

Moo93   C. Moore. The PowerPC 601 Microprocessor. In *Proc. Compcon Spring 93*, pages 109–116, February 1993.

Mot93   Motorola, Inc., *Fast Static RAM Data Book*, 1993.

MoG91   T. Mowry and A. Gupta. Tolerating Latency Through Software-Controlled Prefetching in Shared-Memory Multiprocessors. *Journal of Parallel and Distributed Computing* **2**(4):87–106, June 1991.

Mow94   T. Mowry. *Tolerating Latency Through Software-Controlled Data Prefetching*. Ph.D. Thesis, Stanford University, April 1994.

Mye91   W. Myers. Caltech Dedicates World's Most Powerful Supercomputer. *IEEE Computer* **24**(7): 96–97, July 1991.

NaO94   B. Nayfeh and K. Olukotun. Exploring the Design Space for a Shared-Cache Multiprocessor. In *Proc. 21st Int. Symp. on Computer Architecture*, pages 166–175, April 1994.

NCu92   nCUBE Corporation. *nCUBE 2 Systems – Technical Overview*, 1992.

Ng92   R. Ng. Memory Catches Up. *IEEE Spectrum* **29**(10):34–39, October 1992.

NPA92   R. Nikhil, G. Papadopoulos, and Arvind. *T A Multithreaded Massively Parallel Architecture. In *Proc. 19th Int. Symp. on Computer Architecture*, pages 156–167, 1992.

NHN+92   O. Nishii, M. Hanawa, T. Nishimukai, et al. A 1,000 MIPS BiCMOS Microprocessor with Superscalar Architecture. In *Proc. 1992 IEEE Int. Solid State Circuits Conf.*, pages 114–115. February 1992.

NoL91   W. Nohilly and V. Lund. IBM ES/9000 System Architecture and Hardware. In *Proc. IEEE Conf. on Computer Design: VLSI in Computers and Processors*, pages 540–543, October 1991.

NMP+93   A. Nowatzyk, M. Monger, M. Parkin, E. Kelly, M. Browne, and G. Aybay. S3.mp: A Multiprocessor in a Matchbox. *3rd PASA Workshop*, April 1993, proceedings in PARS #11, ISSN 0177-0454, June 1993.

NoP93   A. Nowatzyk and M. Parkin. The S3.mp Interconnect System and TIC Chip. In *IEEE Hot Interconnects '93*, pages 2.3.1–2.3.4, August 1993.

NuA91   D. Nussbaum and A. Agarwal. Scalability of Parallel Machines. *Communications of the ACM* **34**(3):56–61, March 1991.

OKN90   B. O'Krafka and A. Newton. An Empirical Evaluation of Two Memory-Efficient Directory Methods. In *Proc. 17th Int. Symp. on Computer Architecture*, pages 138–147, May 1990.

Ora94   Oracle Corporation. *Oracle Parallel Server in the Digital Environment*, Oracle Corporation White Paper. Part A19242, June 1994.

Pal88   J. Palmer. The nCUBE Family of High-Performance Parallel Computer Systems. In *Proc. 3rd Conf. on Hypercube Concurrent Computers and Applications*, pages 847–851, January 1988.

PaP84   M. Papamarcos and J. Patel. A Low Overhead Coherence Solution for Multiprocessors with Private Cache Memories. In *Proc. 11th Int. Symp. on Computer Architecture*, pages 348–354, May 1984.

Pat94a   Y. Patt. The I/O Subsystem: A Candidate for Improvement. *IEEE Computer* **27**(3): 15–16, March 1994.

Pat94b   D. Patterson. The Case for NOW (Networks-of-Workstations). In *IEEE Hot Interconnects II*, pages 24–39, August 1994.

PGK88   D. Patterson, G. Gibson, and R. Katz. A Case for Redundant Arrays of Inexpensive Disks (RAID). In *Proc. ACM SIGMOD*, pages 109–116, June 1988.

Pea77   M. Pease III. The Indirect Binary n-Cube Microprocessor Array. *IEEE Transactions on Computers* **C-26**(5):458–473, May 1977.

PBG+85   G. Pfister, W. Brantley, D. George, S. Harvey, W. Kleinfelder, K. McAuliffe, E. Melton, V. Norton, and J. Weiss. The IBM Research Parallel Processor Prototype (RP3): Introduction and Architecture. In *Proc. 1985 Int. Conf. on Parallel Processing*, pages 764–771, 1985.

Por89   A. Porterfield. *Software Methods for Improvement of Cache Performance on Supercomputer Applications*. Ph.D. Thesis, Rice University, May 1989.

Prz90   S. Przybylski. *Cache and Memory Hierarchy Design*. Morgan Kaufmann Publishers, San Francisco, CA, 1990.

Ree87   D. Reed. *Multicomputer Networks: Message-Based Parallel Processing*. MIT Press, Cambridge, MA, 1987.

Rob92   W. Robb. The CRAY Y-MP C90 Supercomputer System. In *Proc 4th Int. Exhibition and Conf. on High-Performance Computing*, February 1992.

Ros88   J. Rose. LocusRoute: A Parallel Global Router for Standard Cells. In *Proc. 25th Design Automation Conf.*, pages 189–195, June 1988.

RoG90   E. Rothberg and A. Gupta. Techniques for Improving the Performance of Sparse Factorization on Multiprocessor Workstations. In *Proc. Supercomputing*, pages 232–241, November 1990.

RSG93   E. Rothberg, J. Singh, and A. Gupta. Working Sets, Cache Sizes, and Node Granularity Issues in Large-Scale Multiprocessors. In *Proc. 20th Int. Symp. on Computer Architecture*, pages 14–25, May 1993.

SCE90   R. Saavedra-Barrera, D. Culler, and T. von Eicken. Analysis of Multithreaded Architectures for Parallel Computing. In *ACM Symposium on Parallel Algorithms and Architectures*, pages 169–178, July 1990.

Sch94   S. Schaefer. DRAM Soft Error Rate Calculations. *Micron Design Line* **3**(1):1–3, January 1994.

Sco91   S. Scott. A Cache Coherence Mechanism for Scalable, Shared-Memory Multiprocessors. In *Proc. Int. Symposium on Shared Memory Multiprocessing*, pages 49–59, April 1991.

Shi93   D. Shippy. The Second Generation RIOS Chip Set. In *Proc. of Microprocessor Forum 1993*, pages 29-1–29-13, October 1993.

SiJ82   D. Siewiorek and D. Johnson. A Design Methodology for High Reliability Systems: The Intel 432. In *The Theory and Practice of Reliable System Design*, ed. D. Siewiorek and R. Swarz, pages 621–636. Digital Press, Maynard, MA, 1982.

Sil94   Silicon Graphics, Inc. *Power Challenge Technical Report*, 1994.

Sim90   R. Simoni. *Implementing a Directory-Based Cache Consistency Protocol*. Technical Report CSL-TR-90-423, Stanford University, March 1990.

SiH91   R. Simoni and M. Horowitz. Dynamic Pointer Allocation for Scalable Cache Coherence Directories. In *Proc. Int. Symp. on Shared Memory Multiprocessing*, pages 72–81, April 1991.

Sim92   R. Simoni. *Cache Coherence Directories for Scalable Multiprocessors*. Ph.D. Thesis, Stanford University, July 1992.

SHT+92   J. Singh, C. Holt, T. Totsuka, A. Gupta, and J. Hennessy. *Load Balancing and Data Locality in Parallel N-Body Techniques*. Technical Report CSL-TR-92-505, Stanford University, 1992.

SWG92   J. Singh, W.-D. Weber, and A. Gupta. SPLASH: Stanford Parallel Applications for Shared Memory. *Computer Architecture News* **20**(1):5–44, March 1992.

SHG93   J. P. Singh, J. L. Hennessy, and A. Gupta. Scaling Parallel Programs for Multiprocessors: Methodology and Examples. *IEEE Computer* **26**(7):42–50, July 1993.

SJG+93   J. Singh, T. Joe, A. Gupta, and J. Hennessy. An Empirical Study of the Kendall Square Research KSR-1 and Stanford DASH Multiprocessors. In *Proc. of Supercomputing '93*, pages 214–225, November 1993.

Sit93   R. Sites. Alpha AXP Architecture. In *Communications of the ACM* **36**(2):33–44, February 1993.

Smi78   A. Smith. Sequential Program Prefetching in Memory Hierarchies. *IEEE Computer* **11**(12):7–21, December 1978.

Smi81   B. Smith. Architecture and Applications of the HEP Multiprocessor Computer System. *SPIE* **298**:241–248, 1981.

SHH90   J. Smith, W.-C. Hsu, and C. Hsiung. Future General Purpose Supercomputer Architectures. In *Proc. Supercomputing '90*, pages 796–804, November 1990.

SJH89   M. Smith, M. Johnson, and M. Horowitz. Limits on Multiple Instruction Issue. In *Proc. Third Int. Conf. Architectural Support for Programming Languages and Operating Systems*, pages 290–302, April 1989.

SoG91   L. Soule and A. Gupta. An Evaluation of the Chandy-Misra-Bryant Algorithm for Digital Logic Simulation. *ACM Transactions on Modeling and Computer Simulation* **1**(4):308–347, October 1991.

Spa94   Sparc International. The SPARC Architecture Manual, Version 9. Prentice Hall, Englewood Cliffs, NJ, 1994.

Spe94a   Standard Performance Evaluation Corporation. *SPEC Newsletter* **6**(2):33, June 1994.

Spe94b   Standard Performance Evaluation Corporation. *SPEC Newsletter* **6**(3):38, September 1994.

Ste94   P. Steenkiste. A Systematic Approach to Host Interface Design for High-Speed Networks. *IEEE Computer* **27**(3):47–57, March 1994.

Ste90   P. Stenstrom. A Survey of Cache Coherence Schemes for Multiprocessors. *IEEE Computer* **23**(6):12–24, June 1990.

SJG92   P. Stenstrom, T. Joe, and A. Gupta. Comparative Performance Evaluation of Cache-Coherent NUMA and COMA Architectures. In *Proc. 19th Int. Symp. on Computer Architecture*, pages 80–91, May 1992.

SBS93   P. Stenstrom, M. Brorsson, and L. Sandberg. An Adaptive Cache Coherence Protocol Optimized for Migratory Sharing. In *Proc. 20th Int. Symp. on Computer Architecture*, pages 109–118, May 1993.

SSG+94   C. Stunkel, D. Shea, D. Grice, P. Hochschild, and M. Tsao. The SP1 High-Performance Switch. In *Proc. Scalable High Performance Computing Conf.*, pages 150–157, May 1994.

StH94   C. Stunkel and P. Hochschild. SP2 High-Performance Switch Architecture. In *IEEE Hot Interconnects II*, pages 115–120, August 1994.

SuN90   X.-H. Sun and L. Ni. Another View of Parallel Speedup. In *Proc. Supercomputing '90*, pages 324–333, November 1990.

Sun94a   Sun Microsystems, Inc. *Sparcserver 1000 Product Overview*, 1994.

Sun94b   Sun Microsystems, Inc. *Sparcstation 10 Product Overview*, 1994.

Sun90   V. S. Sunderam. PVM: A Framework for Parallel Distributed Computing. *Concurrency: Practice and Experience* **2**(4):315–339, December 1990.

SwS86   P. Sweazy and A. Smith. A Class of Compatible Cache Consistency Protocols and Their Support by the IEEE Futurebus. In *Proc. 13th Int. Symp. on Computer Architecture*, pages 414–423, June 1986.

Sys94   Systran Corporation. *SCRAMNet-LX Network Short Form Catalog*, 1994.

Tan81   A. Tanenbaum. *Computer Networks*. Prentice-Hall, Englewood Cliffs, NJ, 1981.

Tan76   C. Tang. Cache Design in a Tightly Coupled Multiprocessor System. In *AFIPS Conf. Proc., pages* 749–753, June 1976.

ThD90   M. Thapar and B. Delagi. Stanford Distributed-Directory Protocol. *IEEE Computer* **23**(6):78–80, June 1990.

Thi87   Thinking Machines Corporation. *Connection Machine CM-2 Technical Summary*. Technical Report HA87-4, April 1987.

Thi93   Thinking Machines Corporation. *Connection Machine CM-5 Technical Summary*, November 1993.

TLH90   J. Torrellas, M. Lam, and J. Hennessy. *Measurement, Analysis, and Improvement of the Cache Behavior of Shared Data in Cache-Coherent Multiprocessors*. Technical Report CSL-TR-90-412, Stanford University, February 1990.

Tuc86   S. Tucker. The IBM 3090 System: An Overview. *IBM System Journal* **25**(1):4–19, January 1986.

VaR94   A. Varma and C. Raghavendra. *Interconnection Networks for Multiprocessors and Multicomputers: Theory and Practice.* IEEE Computer Society Press, Los Alamitos, CA, 1994

Vog94   B. Vogley. 800 Megabyte per Second Systems via Use of Synchronous DRAM. In *Proc. Compcon Spring 94*, pages 255–260, February 1994.

VCG+92   T. von Eicken, D. Culler, S. Goldstein, and K. Schauser. Active Messages: A Mechanism for Integrated Communication and Computation. In *Proc. 19th Int. Symp. on Computer Architecture*, pages 256–266, May 1992.

Wal91   D. Wall. Limits of Instruction-Level Parallelism. In *Proc. Fourth Int. Conf. Architectural Support for Programming Languages and Operating Systems*, pages 176–188, April 1991.

Wal90   D. Wallach. *A Scalable Hierarchical Cache Coherence Protocol.* SB Thesis, MIT, May 1990.

WeB91   S. Webber and J. Beirne. The Stratus Architecture. In *Proc. 21st Int. Symp. on Fault-Tolerant Computing*, pages 79–85, June 1991.

WeG89a   W.-D. Weber and A. Gupta. Analysis of Cache Invalidation Patterns in Multiprocessors. In *Proc. Third Int. Conf. Architectural Support for Programming Languages and Operating Systems*, pages 243–256, April 1989.

WeG89b   W.-D. Weber and A. Gupta. Exploring the Benefits of Multiple Hardware Contexts in a Multiprocessor Architecture: Preliminary Results. In *Proc. 16th Int. Symp. on Computer Architecture*, pages 273–280, June 1989.

Web93   W.-D. Weber. *Scalable Directories for Cache-Coherent Shared-Memory Multiprocessors.* Ph.D. Thesis, Stanford University, January 1993. Also available as Stanford University Technical Report CSL-TR-93-557.

WiC80   L. Widdoes, Jr., and S. Correll. The S-1 Project: Developing High-Performance Digital Computers. In *Proc. Compcon Spring 80*, pages 282–291, February 1980.

Wil88   J. Willis. *Cache Coherence in Systems with Parallel Communication Channels & Many Processors.* Technical Report TR-88-013, Phillips Laboratories–Briarcliff, March 1988.

Wil87   A. Wilson, Jr. Hierarchical Cache/Bus Architecture for Shared Memory Multiprocessors. In *Proc. 14th Int. Symp. on Computer Architecture*, pages 244–252, June 1987.

WHL90   L. Wittie, G. Hermannsson, and A. Li. *Scalable Eagerly Shared Distributed Memory.* SUNY-Stony Brook, Computer Science Technical Report TR# 90/48, November 1990.

WWS+89   P. Woodbury, A. Wilson, B. Shein, L. Gertner, P. Chen, J. Barttlet, and Z. Aral. Shared Memory Multiprocessors: The Right Approach to Parallel Processing. In *Proc. Compcon Spring 89*, pages 72–80, February 1989.

WFP90   K.-L. Wu, W. Fuchs, and J. Patel. Error Recovery in Shared Memory Multi-processors Using Private Caches. *IEEE Trans. on Parallel and Dist. Systems* **1**(2):231–240, April 1990.

Xil91   Xilinx. *The Programmable Gate Array Data Book*, 1991.

YYF85   W. Yen, D. Yen, and K.-S. Fu. Data Coherence Problem in a Multicache System. *IEEE Transactions on Computers* **C-34**(1):56–65, January 1985.

Zos93   M. Zosel. High Performance FORTRAN: An Overview. In *Proc. Compcon Spring 93*, pages 132–136, February 1993.

ZuB92   R. Zucker and J.-L. Baer. A Performance Study of Memory Consistency Models. In *Proc. 19th Int. Symp. on Computer Architecture*, pages 2–12, May 1992.

Index

A

Alewife   27, 30, 93, 104,
        115, 124, 134, 144,
        145, 151, 161, 170,
        307, 311
ALLCACHE   156
alternative memory
        operations   170,
        183, 184, 203, 260,
        264, 271, 272, 281
Amdahl's Law   35, 36
ANL macros   5, 41, 43, 47
    BARRIER   44, 48, 109,
        112, 116, 162, 200,
        267, 268
    CREATE   5, 16, 43,
        129, 142, 143, 147,
        200
    G_MALLOC   41, 42,
        43, 51
    GET_PID   43, 44
    LOCK   45, 46, 48, 52,
        53, 64, 65, 69, 71, 73,
        98, 99, 108, 109, 113,
        114, 115, 167, 187,
        189, 198, 199, 212,
        215, 218, 219, 221,
        224, 244, 251, 252,
        254, 256, 258, 262,
        265, 266, 267, 280,
        281, 288, 295, 296
    UNLOCK   45, 46, 65,
        67, 71, 99, 114, 198,
        199, 200, 219, 243,

244, 245, 251, 254,
256, 258, 266, 267,
281, 288, 295, 296
ARCTIC router   169
attraction memory   91, 92,
        154

B

bandwidth, memory   237, 238
Barnes-Hut   47, 50, 51, 52,
        53, 54, 55, 57, 60, 62,
        64, 65, 73, 75, 79, 81,
        82, 83, 124, 247, 248,
        249, 250, 253, 254,
        259, 260, 261, 262,
        263, 285, 301
barrier   44, 48, 109, 112,
        116, 162, 200, 267,
        268
bisection bandwidth   24, 25,
        27, 28, 29, 30, 147,
        159, 165, 238, 239
block-copy   109
Bolt Beranek and Newman
        (BBN)
    Butterfly   6, 25, 87, 90,
        159, 311
    TC 2000   159, 160, 161,
        236, 311
Burroughs Scientific Processor
        (BSP)   311
bus utilization   231, 250,
        251, 253, 254, 255,

256, 258, 303
busy RAC state   189, 201,
        219

C

Cache-Aided Rollback   141
cache line size   51, 56, 76,
        80, 81, 84, 89, 128,
        133, 234
cache miss
    capacity   15, 79, 91, 170,
        293
    coherence   xvii, xviii, 5,
        13, 15, 16, 17, 18, 19,
        20, 21, 23, 30, 31, 32,
        34, 39, 50, 56, 59, 60,
        61, 62, 64, 65, 76, 79,
        85, 88, 89, 90, 94, 95,
        96, 100, 101, 108,
        109, 110, 111, 113,
        115, 117, 118, 119,
        120, 121, 126, 129,
        132, 136, 139, 141,
        143, 144, 145, 146,
        147, 148, 149, 150,
        151, 152, 153, 157,
        158, 159, 160, 161,
        162, 166, 167, 168,
        170, 173, 175, 176,
        177, 184, 185, 186,
        187, 192, 195, 202,
        205, 206, 211, 224,
        232, 234, 236, 237,

coherence *(continued)* 259, 267, 270, 271, 277, 281, 286, 287, 289, 293, 295, 305, 306, 307, 309, 311, 312, 314, 315
compulsory 15
conflict 15, 79, 155, 179, 201, 219, 221, 223, 224, 263, 290
penalty 8, 15, 55, 59, 88, 89, 90, 124, 164, 177, 241, 261, 263, 269, 298, 303
cache-to-cache sharing 187, 195, 260, 262, 264, 272
Caltech Cosmic Cube 25
Caltech Mesh Routing Chip 27, 226
CC-NUMA 143, 154, 157, 182
Cedar 25, 93, 311
Cholesky 47, 49, 50, 51, 52, 53, 54, 57, 59, 60, 62, 64, 73, 74, 76, 77, 81, 247, 248, 249, 301
circuit-switched 24
circular buffer 270
cluster cache 151, 152, 153, 170, 175, 180, 262, 263
C.mmp 25, 312
COMA 91, 92, 93, 154, 155, 156, 170, 307, 312, 314
combining 34, 106, 107, 109, 112, 115, 116, 154, 160, 167, 170, 313, 316
communication-to-computa-tion ratio 59, 76, 92
Compare&Swap 115, 273
consumer-initiated communication 96, 108

consumer prefetch 192, 269, 270
context switch overhead 103, 104, 106, 110
Convex
C4/XA 4, 312
Exemplar xvii, 149, 150, 170, 183, 312, 313
correctness proofs 141
Cray Research
SuperServer 6400 28, 312
T3D 27, 30, 90, 93, 118, 161, 162, 170, 183, 234, 312
X-MP 4, 6, 87, 163, 312
Y-MP 6, 25, 163, 164, 312
Y-MP C90 4, 6, 25, 36, 162, 163, 164, 312
critical region 45, 46, 97, 98, 113, 267

D

DASH xvii, xviii, 27, 30, 50, 90, 93, 94, 96, 101, 109, 114, 118, 120, 128, 136, 138, 139, 140, 142, 144, 146, 147, 148, 150, 151, 161, 170, 173, 174, 175, 176, 177, 181, 182, 183, 184, 185, 192, 198, 200, 202, 203, 205, 206, 207, 209, 210, 211, 217, 225, 232, 233, 234, 235, 236, 237, 238, 241, 242, 243, 244, 245, 246, 248, 249, 250, 255, 257, 260, 262, 265, 269, 271, 272, 277, 278, 279, 280, 283, 284, 286, 290, 296, 298, 301, 303, 305, 306,

307, 312, 315, 316
directory controller (DC) 177, 179, 181, 211, 215, 236, 279
logic overhead 232, 234
memory controller 18, 111, 136, 169, 279, 294
network interface 10, 11, 13, 135, 170, 205, 215, 226, 228, 230, 240, 308
pseudo-CPU (PCPU) 179, 181, 186, 193, 224, 226, 227, 228, 236
RCPU 180, 186, 193, 194, 195, 199, 211, 219, 223, 224, 226, 227, 243
remote access cache (RAC) 179, 187, 189, 192, 193, 198, 200, 202, 211, 219, 221, 223, 234, 236
reply controller (RC) 177, 179, 218, 219, 223, 228, 236
Data Diffusion Machine (DDM) 29, 154, 156, 170, 312
data object classification 62
frequently read/written objects 63
migratory objects 63, 67, 69, 71, 95, 157
mostly-read objects 63, 67, 69, 71, 73, 82
read-only data objects 63
data sharing 62, 88, 93, 166
deadlock 49, 69, 71, 134, 135, 136, 138, 142, 145, 176, 177, 180, 181, 201, 224, 227, 228, 260, 261, 283, 289

demand-driven
communication 95, 306
Denelcor HEP 89, 312
design verification 134, 141
Digital Equipment Corporation (DEC)
Alpha 21064 162, 183, 279, 312
direct-mapped cache 15
directory-based cache coherence 30, 143, 170
directory size factor 127, 129, 130, 131, 286
directory storage 119, 125, 127, 132
cache-based linked list 126, 127
coarse-vector (DiriCV$_r$) 122, 123, 127
dynamic pointer 125, 127
extended pointer schemes 124, 126, 133
full-bit vector directory (DirP) 120, 133
hierarchical 28, 29, 47, 50, 93, 94, 95, 111, 113, 120, 132, 133, 134, 143, 150, 151, 152, 154, 155, 156, 167, 170, 249, 253, 312
limited pointer 120, 121, 123, 203
with broadcast (Dir$_{iB}$) 121, 123
without broadcast (Dir$_{iNB}$) 121, 123
distributed shared-memory (DSM) 12
DMA 10, 11, 16, 33, 175, 176, 180, 184, 193,

195, 196, 197, 203, 206, 210, 211, 212, 221, 224, 228, 236, 239, 281, 293

E

Encore GigaMax 29, 151, 312
execution-driven simulation 50

F

false sharing 19, 81, 82, 83, 89, 90, 120, 138, 142, 158, 166, 167, 168, 261, 299
fault tolerance 24, 119, 134, 139, 140, 141, 146, 147, 293, 294, 309
fence operation 98, 196, 200
full-fence 196, 200
stall-fence 200
Fetch&Op 115, 116, 150, 160, 198, 200, 203, 212, 213, 215, 218, 219, 264, 265, 267, 268, 273, 313, 316
FLASH 115, 307, 312
flit 181, 283, 298
FMM 247, 248, 249, 259
FuturebusPlus 28

G

GigaMax 29, 94, 151, 152, 153, 154, 168, 170, 312
Gould NP1 157, 313
granting locks 109, 198, 199, 203, 237, 264, 265, 267, 272
Gustafson 35

H

Hewlett-Packard
735CL 13, 313
Precision Architecture (HP-PA) 183
hierarchical systems 150, 170
bus xvii, 5, 8, 11, 17, 18, 19, 20, 24, 28, 29, 30, 31, 32, 39, 136, 147, 151, 152, 153, 157, 170, 175, 176, 177, 178, 179, 180, 185, 186, 187, 189, 191, 192, 193, 194, 195, 196, 197, 198, 199, 200, 201, 202, 205, 206, 207, 209, 210, 211, 212, 215, 216, 218, 219, 222, 223, 224, 227, 230, 231, 232, 234, 236, 238, 239, 240, 241, 242, 243, 245, 247, 250, 251, 252, 253, 254, 255, 256, 258, 259, 267, 269, 272, 278, 279, 280, 281, 282, 283, 288, 290, 291, 294, 295, 297, 298, 299, 303, 305, 306, 308, 309, 312, 315
coherence schemes 64, 93
ring 28, 29, 30, 147, 148, 149, 156, 157
high-availability 119
high-latency operation 96
home cluster 185, 186, 187, 188, 191, 195, 199, 211, 216, 253, 260, 262, 267, 286, 287, 288, 289, 291
hot spot 112, 113, 116, 132
hypercube 25, 26, 27, 29, 87, 313, 314

I

IBM
3090   232, 313
Power2   36, 313
RP3   xvii, 6, 25, 93, 98, 112, 159, 160, 161, 236, 313
SP-1   13, 25, 313
SP-2   13, 25, 313
IC Equivalents   210, 218, 232
Idle time   52, 53, 55, 57, 59, 84, 85, 99, 104, 106
IEEE 1596-1992 - Scalable Coherent Interface (SCI)   28, 126, 138, 147, 149, 170, 313
Illiac IV   6, 8, 311, 313
Illinois (MESI) protocol   175
incremental tuning   305
Intel
Delta   27, 313
iPSC   4, 6, 25, 30, 313
Paragon   6, 13, 30, 93, 162, 313
Pentium   36
interconnection networks   5, 12, 23, 25, 26, 29, 87, 116, 118, 135, 226, 236
adaptive routing   24, 137, 284, 293, 294
Banyan   25, 87
Baseline   25
Benes   25
bus   xvii, 5, 8, 11, 17, 18, 19, 20, 24, 28, 29, 30, 31, 32, 39, 136, 147, 151, 152, 153, 157, 170, 175, 176, 177, 178, 179, 180, 185, 186, 187, 189, 191, 192, 193, 194, 195, 196, 197, 198, 199, 200, 201, 202, 205, 206, 207, 209, 210,

211, 212, 215, 216, 218, 219, 222, 223, 224, 227, 230, 231, 232, 234, 236, 238, 239, 240, 241, 242, 243, 245, 247, 250, 251, 252, 253, 254, 255, 256, 258, 259, 267, 269, 272, 278, 279, 280, 281, 282, 283, 288, 290, 291, 294, 295, 297, 298, 299, 303, 305, 306, 308, 309, 312, 315
Butterfly   6, 25, 87, 90, 159, 311
crossbar   24, 25, 29, 87, 135, 149, 312
direct   4, 5, 15, 24, 29, 55, 93, 95, 96, 111, 116, 135, 147, 150, 167, 175, 178, 179, 234, 241, 245, 262, 278, 305
fat-tree   27, 156, 169
indirect   9, 24, 29, 93, 173
in-order delivery   193, 198, 288, 293
k-ary n-cube   181
mesh   26, 27, 32, 34, 87, 93, 118, 142, 144, 145, 147, 157, 167, 174, 179, 181, 187, 193, 198, 202, 205, 226, 230, 236, 237, 238, 253, 269, 278, 280, 283, 284, 293, 294, 297, 298, 302, 313
multi-stage interconnection networks (MIN)   25, 87
packet switched   24
ring   28, 29, 30, 147, 148, 149, 156, 157
static routing   24

torus   26, 27, 29, 34, 161, 165, 168, 277, 283, 297, 314, 315
utilization   xvii, 6, 8, 13, 85, 88, 89, 103, 104, 116, 152, 156, 158, 162, 164, 165, 231, 238, 240, 245, 246, 250, 251, 253, 254, 255, 256, 258, 259, 272, 285, 286, 298, 299, 300, 301, 303
invalidating locks   199, 265, 267
invalidating write   64, 65, 71, 76, 77, 78, 79, 83, 84, 85
invalidation   16, 19, 20, 30, 31, 56, 59, 60, 61, 62, 64, 65, 66, 67, 68, 69, 70, 71, 72, 74, 75, 76, 77, 78, 79, 80, 81, 82, 83, 84, 85, 90, 108, 109, 110, 111, 113, 114, 115, 121, 122, 123, 126, 132, 134, 144, 150, 157, 158, 167, 173, 179, 181, 187, 188, 189, 190, 191, 192, 193, 195, 198, 199, 200, 201, 218, 220, 221, 234, 241, 244, 245, 247, 252, 261, 262, 264, 266, 267, 280, 287, 288, 290, 293, 299, 306, 307
cache line size   51, 56, 76, 80, 81, 84, 89, 128, 133, 234
distribution graph   65
finite caches   51, 78, 79, 84
frequent   10, 13, 53, 64, 65, 89, 124, 131, 140, 154, 158, 170, 253

large   xvii, xviii, xix, 3, 4,
     5, 8, 10, 12, 20, 23,
     25, 30, 32, 33, 34, 37,
     39, 42, 46, 47, 48, 49,
     51, 53, 56, 60, 61, 63,
     64, 65, 67, 69, 71, 73,
     76, 77, 79, 81, 83, 85,
     87, 88, 89, 90, 92, 93,
     94, 95, 98, 99, 100,
     101, 103, 109, 110,
     111, 113, 115, 116,
     117, 118, 120, 121,
     123, 124, 129, 130,
     132, 134, 139, 140,
     142, 144, 147, 148,
     149, 151, 152, 153,
     154, 156, 158, 159,
     163, 165, 166, 167,
     168, 169, 170, 181,
     183, 184, 195, 202,
     203, 246, 248, 249,
     255, 257, 259, 261,
     264, 265, 267, 268,
     269, 270, 272, 284,
     289, 293, 303, 306,
     308, 309
  number of processors   xvii,
     4, 12, 20, 23, 24, 28,
     29, 30, 34, 35, 37, 44,
     46, 63, 64, 67, 69, 71,
     76, 77, 79, 82, 84,
     111, 115, 116, 119,
     120, 121, 123, 124,
     126, 129, 130, 132,
     133, 142, 159, 163,
     168, 181, 238, 246,
     247, 249, 252, 253,
     267, 269, 289, 301,
     305
  problem size   36, 63, 76,
     249, 250, 301
  replacement hints   78, 79,
     80, 84, 129, 130, 132
invalidations per invalidating
     write   64, 65, 77, 79,
     83, 84
I/O   6, 16, 29, 33, 140, 141,

     147, 149, 156, 163,
     169, 174, 175, 176,
     180, 181, 184, 193,
     195, 196, 203, 206,
     207, 210, 211, 212,
     215, 221, 233, 234,
     235, 236, 243, 278,
     294, 303, 308, 309,
     315
issue rate   237, 243
IVY   166, 167, 313

J

J-Machine   27, 94, 167, 168,
     170, 314

K

Kendall Square Research   xvii,
     155, 156, 170, 308
  KSR-1   xvii, 29, 94, 155,
     156, 314
  KSR-2   29, 155, 156,
     157, 314

L

latency   xvii, 11, 13, 14, 16,
     22, 23, 24, 25, 26, 27,
     28, 29, 30, 33, 34, 35,
     41, 46, 52, 53, 55, 56,
     57, 59, 85, 87, 88, 89,
     90, 91, 92, 93, 94, 95,
     96, 98, 99, 100, 101,
     103, 104, 106, 107,
     108, 109, 110, 111,
     113, 114, 115, 116,
     124, 132, 134, 135,
     138, 139, 144, 145,
     146, 147, 148, 150,
     151, 152, 153, 155,
     156, 157, 158, 159,
     160, 161, 162, 163,
     164, 165, 166, 167,
     170, 175, 180, 181,
     182, 187, 192, 198,

     199, 200, 202, 203,
     207, 216, 228, 231,
     236, 237, 238, 240,
     241, 242, 243, 244,
     245, 250, 252, 253,
     255, 259, 260, 262,
     263, 264, 265, 266,
     267, 270, 271, 272,
     273, 279, 285, 287,
     288, 292, 298, 306,
     307, 309
  interprocessor   6, 9, 19,
     36, 52, 53, 93, 113,
     145, 162, 176, 195,
     198, 203, 237, 244,
     245, 246, 271, 272
  local   7, 8, 11, 12, 18, 24,
     25, 51, 55, 91, 93, 94,
     95, 111, 115, 124,
     131, 144, 146, 147,
     149, 150, 151, 152,
     153, 154, 155, 156,
     157, 160, 161, 162,
     164, 168, 174, 175,
     176, 177, 178, 179,
     180, 185, 186, 187,
     188, 189, 190, 191,
     192, 193, 194, 195,
     196, 197, 198, 199,
     200, 202, 211, 218,
     219, 223, 224, 227,
     231, 236, 238, 239,
     240, 241, 242, 243,
     244, 245, 247, 251,
     252, 253, 254, 255,
     256, 257, 258, 259,
     262, 263, 264, 265,
     267, 269, 270, 272,
     281, 282, 283, 286,
     287, 288, 289, 290,
     291, 295, 296, 297,
     298, 299, 306, 307,
     311
  remote   11, 12, 90, 91,
     93, 94, 99, 103, 109,
     111, 113, 115, 116,
     136, 144, 146, 148,

remote *(continued)* 149,
150, 151, 152, 153,
154, 155, 157, 158,
159, 161, 162, 167,
169, 170, 175, 176,
177, 178, 179, 180,
181, 182, 185, 186,
187, 188, 189, 190,
191, 192, 193, 194,
195, 196, 197, 198,
199, 200, 201, 202,
212, 216, 218, 219,
220, 224, 231, 236,
238, 239, 240, 241,
242, 243, 244, 245,
247, 251, 252, 253,
254, 255, 256, 257,
258, 259, 260, 261,
262, 263, 264, 265,
266, 267, 269, 270,
271, 272, 280, 281,
283, 286, 287, 288,
289, 290, 296, 297,
298, 299, 301, 307,
311
tolerance   24, 103, 119,
134, 139, 140, 141,
146, 147, 293, 294,
303, 309
lazy release consistency
(LRC)   167
LimitLESS   124, 125, 126,
127, 145, 294
Linda   5
LINPACK   36, 175
livelock   134, 142, 288, 289
load balancing   45
locality   14, 15, 48, 49, 60,
71, 81, 82, 93, 111,
116, 128, 153, 156,
161, 162, 185, 231,
245, 246, 250, 252,
253, 255, 257, 258,
259, 272, 298, 299,
301, 305, 306, 307
lock waiter distribution   65
locks   42, 45, 47, 50, 63, 64,

65, 67, 69, 71, 73, 98,
109, 110, 113, 114,
115, 198, 200, 203,
206, 210, 213, 215,
219, 234, 237, 241,
243, 252, 264, 265,
267, 272, 288, 295
LocusRoute   47, 48, 49, 51,
52, 53, 54, 57, 59, 60,
62, 63, 64, 71, 72, 76,
77, 78, 81, 84, 124,
247, 248, 250, 301
LU-factorization   96

M

MasPar
MP-1   6, 314
MP-2   6, 314
Matrix Multiply   36, 247,
248
Meiko CS-2   6, 28, 30, 314
memory consistency
models   96, 182,
306, 307
memory latency   xvii, 14, 16,
34, 41, 52, 53, 55, 57,
59, 85, 88, 89, 90, 91,
93, 95, 100, 106, 110,
113, 116, 144, 146,
150, 156, 160, 164,
165, 192, 238, 240,
241, 244, 250, 252,
262, 272, 306, 307
hiding   89, 95, 96, 99,
103, 106, 110, 116,
145, 161, 162, 164,
245, 255, 259, 272,
306, 309
reduction   57, 61, 83, 87,
89, 93, 94, 95, 100,
103, 106, 127, 134,
147, 162, 166, 252,
257, 261, 262, 263,
267, 272, 283, 306
memory size factor   127, 128,
129, 130, 286

memory system   5, 8, 9, 10,
11, 13, 19, 41, 50, 53,
55, 56, 58, 59, 61, 62,
85, 87, 88, 90, 95, 97,
104, 111, 112, 116,
118, 123, 124, 134,
140, 142, 156, 162,
163, 164, 182, 193,
200, 202, 232, 234,
236, 237, 238, 239,
242, 244, 253, 255,
259, 260, 269, 271,
272, 296, 299, 303,
306, 307, 313, 314
bandwidth   xvii, 13, 14,
16, 19, 23, 24, 25, 27,
28, 29, 30, 31, 32, 33,
34, 39, 61, 62, 85, 87,
88, 90, 93, 94, 95,
100, 101, 109, 111,
112, 113, 116, 118,
119, 121, 126, 129,
132, 142, 144, 147,
152, 153, 156, 157,
159, 161, 163, 165,
166, 175, 176, 180,
181, 192, 202, 207,
211, 237, 238, 239,
240, 241, 244, 245,
253, 255, 259, 269,
271, 272, 278, 283,
285, 286, 303, 305,
306, 308, 309
traffic   18, 19, 23, 24, 27,
30, 32, 33, 56, 59, 60,
61, 62, 64, 65, 79, 80,
85, 95, 109, 111, 113,
114, 115, 120, 121,
123, 124, 126, 129,
132, 133, 134, 158,
159, 160, 165, 167,
198, 199, 203, 236,
238, 239, 253, 263,
265, 267, 272, 288,
301
memory system models
PRAM   53, 54, 55, 59,

60, 61, 62, 85, 87
shared data cached   56, 58
shared data uncached   55,
    56, 59
Merlin   158, 314, 315
MESI   175, 179, 186
Message Driven Processor
    (MDP)   167
message-passing   xvii, 6, 8, 9,
    10, 11, 12, 13, 109,
    143, 145, 146, 150,
    159, 162, 166, 167,
    170, 193, 270, 271,
    305, 307, 308, 313,
    314, 316
microprocessors   xvii, 3, 4, 5,
    8, 13, 36, 37, 104,
    110, 162, 163, 169
MIMD   6, 7, 8, 11, 20, 39,
    143, 312, 313, 314,
    316
MIPS R3000   50, 175, 202,
    207, 209, 232, 236
MOESI   179
Motorola 88110   169
MP3D   47, 48, 51, 52, 53,
    54, 57, 59, 60, 61, 62,
    63, 64, 66, 67, 81, 96,
    99, 100, 101, 102,
    104, 105, 106, 107,
    110, 124, 130, 131,
    132, 247, 248, 250,
    253, 255, 256, 257,
    259, 260, 261, 262,
    263, 272, 285, 301,
    303
MPP   8, 148, 163, 308, 312,
    314
MRC   27, 226, 228, 229,
    230, 294, 298
multiple context
    processors   89, 103,
    104, 144, 164, 170,
    306
Munin systems   167, 314
mutual exclusion   42, 45, 47,

97, 98, 113, 115, 198,
    200, 265

N

nCube
    nCube-1   13, 25, 30, 314
    nCube-2   6, 25, 30, 314
networks of workstations
    (NOW)   308
non-waited operations   227,
    243
NUMA   12, 13, 22, 33, 46,
    90, 91, 92, 93, 95,
    111, 133, 143, 144,
    154, 155, 157, 161,
    182, 306, 307, 311,
    312
NYU Ultracomputer   xvii,
    112, 159, 160

O

Omega network   25, 28, 159
owning cluster   185, 187, 292

P

packaging   4, 118, 142, 162,
    210
ParaDiGM   xvii, 13, 23, 39,
    87, 94, 152, 153, 154,
    167, 170, 272, 305,
    306, 314
parallel programming   41, 42,
    44, 46, 305
pending list   138, 139, 291,
    292, 293
performance monitor   178,
    229, 231, 236
Plus   27, 157, 158, 159, 269,
    280, 314
prefetching   89, 96, 100,
    101, 102, 103, 104,
    106, 108, 110, 111,
    116, 162, 170, 192,
    255, 269, 280, 294,

306, 309
binding   100, 162, 269
buffer   10, 11, 24, 96, 98,
    99, 101, 102, 106,
    134, 136, 138, 139,
    166, 175, 179, 181,
    182, 187, 189, 192,
    193, 201, 205, 207,
    212, 215, 227, 241,
    242, 243, 247, 248,
    252, 260, 261, 262,
    270, 280
compiler   6, 98, 100, 101,
    108, 109, 110, 159,
    169, 269
coverage   101, 103
exclusive   16, 18, 19, 30,
    31, 50, 90, 94, 101,
    103, 120, 131, 137,
    138, 140, 153, 175,
    182, 187, 188, 189,
    190, 191, 192, 198,
    201, 219, 221, 242,
    243, 244, 251, 254,
    256, 258, 261, 262,
    265, 269, 280, 281,
    286, 287, 290, 295,
    296
hardware-issued   100
latency reduction   100,
    162
non-binding   100
overhead   xvii, xviii, 8, 9,
    10, 13, 19, 20, 21, 22,
    24, 30, 32, 35, 42, 43,
    56, 59, 60, 61, 67, 85,
    91, 92, 101, 102, 103,
    104, 106, 108, 110,
    116, 117, 118, 119,
    120, 121, 124, 125,
    127, 128, 132, 133,
    134, 138, 141, 142,
    144, 145, 147, 152,
    157, 159, 162, 166,
    167, 168, 178, 205,
    209, 232, 234, 236,

overhead *(continued)* 238, 241, 242, 243, 247, 248, 250, 252, 255, 267, 284, 286, 294, 297, 298, 303, 306
read-only 63, 91, 94, 96, 121, 186, 187, 192, 253
software-issued 100, 101, 103
presence bits 30, 31, 32, 118, 120, 122
processor consistency 182, 189, 247, 261, 262
processor utilization xvii, 13, 85, 88, 89, 104, 116, 152, 158, 162, 165, 245, 246, 250, 253, 255, 258, 259, 272, 298, 299, 300, 303
producer prefetch 109, 192, 193, 194, 195, 203, 243, 245, 269, 281, 288, 293
producer-consumer access 95
producer-initiated communication 96, 108, 109, 110, 306
protocol robustness 288
pruning cache 133
PSIM4 48, 247, 248, 250, 255, 257, 258, 260, 261, 262, 263, 285, 286
PTHOR 47, 48, 49, 51, 52, 53, 54, 57, 59, 60, 61, 62, 64, 65, 69, 70, 79, 80, 81, 96, 99, 100, 101, 102, 103, 105, 106, 107, 110, 247, 301
PVM 5

Q

QOLB 114

queue-based locks 288

R

Radiosity 247, 248, 249
RAID 33, 141, 308
read request 137, 177, 187, 188, 189, 191, 192, 196, 202, 289, 291
read/write ratio 51
read-after-write (RAW) 136
read-exclusive request 188, 189, 191, 192
reflective memory 143, 157, 158, 159, 162, 170, 313, 314, 315
release consistency 98, 99, 100, 102, 103, 106, 108, 144, 145, 146, 167, 182, 183, 189, 200, 219, 236, 242, 261, 262, 270, 314
remote cluster 185, 272, 297
replacement-before-invalidation probability 79
replacement hints 78, 79, 80, 84, 129, 130, 132
request forwarding 136, 181, 203, 237, 243, 260
request-reply protocol 136, 289
request starvation 134, 139, 140, 142, 288, 289, 290
run-length 103

S

S-1 32, 315
Scalability xviii, 3, 5, 20, 21, 22, 23, 24, 28, 29, 30, 32, 34, 35, 36, 39, 110, 112, 116, 117, 118, 119, 126, 134, 142, 145, 147, 159, 162, 163, 202, 203, 234, 306

costs 9, 10, 13, 20, 21, 22, 23, 28, 33, 34, 36, 55, 87, 103, 116, 117, 118, 141, 142, 165, 173, 215, 216, 224, 232, 234, 245, 260, 272, 307
directory 5, 30, 31, 32, 33, 34, 39, 50, 65, 76, 79, 80, 85, 111, 114, 117, 118, 119, 120, 121, 122, 123, 124, 125, 126, 127, 128, 129, 130, 131, 132, 133, 134, 136, 137, 138, 139, 140, 141, 142, 143, 144, 145, 146, 147, 148, 149, 150, 152, 153, 155, 156, 157, 167, 168, 170, 173, 175, 176, 177, 178, 179, 183, 184, 185, 186, 188, 189, 190, 191, 193, 194, 195, 196, 197, 198, 199, 200, 201, 202, 205, 206, 207, 209, 210, 211, 212, 213, 214, 215, 216, 217, 218, 219, 221, 226, 229, 230, 231, 232, 233, 234, 235, 236, 237, 240, 260, 265, 277, 279, 280, 281, 282, 283, 284, 285, 286, 287, 288, 290, 291, 292, 293, 294, 296, 299, 303, 306, 307, 309, 311, 312, 314, 315
I/O 6, 16, 29, 33, 140, 141, 147, 149, 156, 163, 169, 174, 175, 176, 180, 181, 184, 193, 195, 196, 203, 206, 207, 210, 211, 212, 215, 221, 233,

234, 235, 236, 243, 278, 294, 303, 308, 309, 315

memory bandwidth 16, 19, 30, 31, 32, 87, 111, 112, 116, 144, 161, 175, 176, 192, 238, 240, 241, 271, 272, 309

performance xvii, xviii, 3, 4, 5, 6, 8, 9, 10, 11, 12, 13, 16, 19, 20, 21, 22, 23, 24, 27, 28, 30, 33, 34, 36, 37, 39, 41, 42, 46, 55, 57, 59, 61, 79, 85, 87, 88, 89, 92, 93, 94, 95, 96, 98, 99, 103, 104, 106, 107, 108, 109, 110, 111, 113, 116, 117, 118, 121, 123, 124, 126, 127, 128, 129, 131, 132, 133, 134, 141, 142, 143, 144, 146, 148, 151, 154, 155, 158, 159, 160, 162, 163, 164, 165, 166, 167, 168, 169, 170, 173, 175, 176, 178, 179, 180, 182, 191, 192, 198, 202, 203, 216, 229, 230, 231, 232, 233, 234, 236, 237, 238, 243, 244, 245, 246, 247, 250, 253, 255, 257, 259, 260, 261, 262, 263, 264, 270, 271, 272, 277, 278, 284, 286, 289, 291, 293, 294, 296, 303, 305, 306, 307, 308, 309, 314

range 5, 14, 20, 21, 23, 36, 37, 39, 53, 85, 103, 109, 117, 118, 142, 149, 183, 198,

218, 234, 250, 296, 308, 309

scaled caches 56, 57, 58, 60, 79, 130, 259

self-invalidation 191, 193

sequential consistency 97, 100, 102, 104, 105, 106, 110

Sequent Symmetry 6, 315

Sequoia 141, 294, 315

Sesame 158, 159, 315

set-associative 15, 128, 129, 285

shared-memory xvii, 5, 6, 8, 9, 10, 11, 12, 13, 14, 20, 33, 37, 39, 41, 46, 51, 56, 59, 87, 88, 90, 95, 109, 110, 111, 117, 118, 140, 142, 143, 146, 147, 149, 159, 163, 166, 167, 170, 173, 181, 193, 202, 203, 259, 272, 305, 306, 307, 308, 309, 311, 312, 313, 314, 315

sharing patterns 49, 62, 78, 95, 198, 306

Silicon Graphics
  MPBUS 176, 181, 185, 191, 195, 200, 206, 207, 208, 211, 212, 215, 218, 224, 227, 281
  POWER Station 4D/340 175, 205, 236, 315
  R8000 4, 36
  SYNCBUS 206, 209, 211, 212, 215

SIMD 6, 7, 8, 20, 168, 305, 311, 313, 314, 316

snoopy cache coherence 17, 18, 30, 151, 175, 206, 305

software scalability 5, 34

SPARCLE 104, 144

sparse directories 127, 128, 132, 133, 134, 285, 306
  collisions 48, 67, 128, 129, 131, 132, 286
  replacement 56, 78, 79, 80, 84, 91, 125, 126, 129, 130, 131, 132, 210, 286, 287, 291

spatial locality 14, 82

speedup 20, 22, 34, 35, 36, 39, 53, 54, 55, 100, 103, 106, 234, 237, 246, 247, 248, 249, 250, 251, 252, 253, 254, 255, 256, 257, 258, 259, 269, 271, 272, 298, 299, 300, 301, 303
  algorithmic 41, 55, 259
  fixed-execution time 36
  scaled 23, 28, 32, 33, 35, 36, 37, 56, 57, 58, 60, 64, 79, 128, 130, 249, 259, 299, 301, 315

spin locks 113, 114, 198, 200, 203, 206

spin waiting 113, 198, 265

SPLASH 47

split-transaction
  protocol 176, 278

Store-and-forward 24, 135

Stratus 141, 315

Sun Microsystems
  S3.mp 146, 147, 150, 159, 170, 293, 309, 315
  SparcCenter 2000 28, 315
  SparcServer 1000 28, 315
  SparcStation 10 315
  SuperSparc 36, 312, 316

superscalar processor 156, 279, 286

synchronization   41, 44, 45, 47, 48, 50, 51, 52, 53, 55, 59, 63, 64, 65, 66, 67, 68, 69, 70, 71, 72, 73, 74, 75, 76, 85, 97, 98, 99, 109, 110, 112, 113, 115, 116, 144, 145, 153, 159, 162, 163, 167, 169, 173, 183, 184, 189, 198, 203, 243, 246, 247, 252, 255, 265, 267, 268, 298, 299, 301, 305, 306, 307, 311

  barrier   44, 48, 109, 112, 116, 162, 200, 267, 268

  lock   45, 46, 48, 52, 53, 64, 65, 69, 71, 73, 98, 99, 108, 109, 113, 114, 115, 167, 187, 189, 198, 199, 212, 215, 218, 219, 221, 224, 244, 251, 252, 254, 256, 258, 262, 265, 266, 267, 280, 281, 288, 295, 296

Systran Scramnet   157, 315

T

*T   169, 170, 311

Tango-Lite   50

task scheduling   44, 47

  dynamic   24, 41, 44, 46, 47, 67, 113, 115, 125, 127, 134, 141, 142, 146, 147, 154, 156, 205, 278, 280, 285, 315

  static   24, 41, 44, 47, 134, 141, 155, 163, 205, 236, 278, 285, 315

temporal locality   14

Tera Computer MTA   30, 164, 165, 166, 170, 315

TeraDASH   118, 148, 277, 278, 279, 280, 281, 282, 283, 284, 285, 286, 289, 290, 291, 293, 294, 295, 296, 297, 298, 299, 300, 302, 303, 307, 316

test&set   113, 114, 198, 265, 267

test-and-test&set   113, 114

Thinking Machines Corporation (TMC)

  CM-1   6, 8, 316

  CM-2   6, 8, 20, 25, 316

  CM-5   6, 8, 20, 28, 30, 93, 117, 316

*T-NG   170, 311

traffic

  coherence   xvii, xviii, 5, 13, 15, 16, 17, 18, 19, 20, 21, 23, 30, 31, 32, 34, 39, 50, 56, 59, 60, 61, 62, 64, 65, 76, 79, 85, 88, 89, 90, 94, 95, 96, 100, 101, 108, 109, 110, 111, 113, 115, 117, 118, 119, 120, 121, 126, 129, 132, 136, 139, 141, 143, 144, 145, 146, 147, 148, 149, 150, 151, 152, 153, 157, 158, 159, 160, 161, 162, 166, 167, 168, 170, 173, 175, 176, 177, 184, 185, 186, 187, 192, 195, 202, 205, 206, 211, 224, 232, 234, 236, 237, 259, 267, 270, 271, 277, 281, 286, 287, 289, 293, 295, 305, 306, 307, 309, 311, 312, 314, 315

  data   5, 6, 7, 8, 9, 10, 13, 14, 15, 16, 18, 19, 23, 24, 31, 34, 35, 36, 39, 41, 42, 43, 44, 45, 46, 47, 48, 49, 50, 51, 52, 55, 56, 57, 58, 59, 60, 61, 62, 63, 64, 65, 67, 69, 71, 73, 76, 77, 78, 79, 80, 81, 82, 83, 84, 85, 88, 89, 91, 92, 93, 94, 95, 96, 98, 100, 101, 103, 108, 109, 110, 111, 112, 113, 115, 120, 121, 124, 126, 130, 131, 134, 136, 137, 139, 140, 141, 144, 147, 150, 151, 152, 153, 154, 155, 156, 157, 158, 159, 160, 161, 162, 163, 165, 166, 167, 169, 170, 175, 176, 179, 180, 182, 187, 188, 189, 190, 191, 192, 193, 194, 195, 196, 200, 202, 206, 207, 209, 210, 214, 215, 216, 218, 219, 221, 222, 223, 224, 228, 231, 238, 239, 240, 243, 245, 246, 247, 248, 249, 250, 252, 253, 255, 257, 259, 261, 262, 264, 265, 267, 269, 270, 271, 272, 278, 279, 280, 282, 283, 284, 286, 287, 289, 291, 294, 295, 296, 298, 299, 301, 303, 305, 306, 307, 312, 314

  ideal   23, 30, 34, 39, 53, 59, 60, 61, 85, 87, 118, 119, 123, 124, 173, 202, 265, 277

Transputer   6

Treadmarks   166, 167, 314

tree saturation   240

U

Ultracomputer   xvii, 112, 159, 160, 170, 313, 316
UMA   12, 22, 25, 33, 312, 313, 315
uncached locks   265, 267
uncached read   195, 196, 243
unwaited accesses   221
update write   16, 19, 109, 173, 183, 196, 197, 198, 221, 243, 244, 267

V

vector supercomputers   162, 163, 166

virtual channels   135, 278, 283, 301
Virtual cut-through   24
Virtual shared-memory systems   143, 166
VME   157, 211, 212, 234, 236
VolRend   247, 248, 259

W

Water   47, 48, 51, 52, 53, 54, 55, 57, 60, 61, 62, 64, 67, 68, 69, 79, 80, 81, 82, 247, 248, 250, 251, 252, 253, 259, 260, 261, 262, 263, 264, 285, 301
weak consistency   96, 98, 264

working set   46, 92, 93
wormhole   24, 181, 202, 236
write-after read (WAR) hazard   136
write-after-write (WAW) hazard   136
writeback   16, 188, 191
write buffer   96, 98, 99, 101, 106, 175, 182, 187, 189, 192, 193, 241, 242, 243, 247, 252, 280
write-fence   200
write-through   16, 19, 96, 109, 157, 158, 159, 175, 189, 236